SUBTERRANEAN FANON

Subterranean Fanon

AN UNDERGROUND THEORY OF RADICAL CHANGE

Gavin Arnall

Columbia University Press
New York

Columbia University Press
Publishers Since 1893
New York   Chichester, West Sussex
cup.columbia.edu
Copyright © 2020 Columbia University Press

Library of Congress Cataloging-in-Publication Data
Names: Arnall, Gavin, 1986– author.
Title: Subterranean Fanon : an underground theory of radical change / Gavin Arnall.
Description: New York : Columbia University Press, 2020. | Includes bibliographical references and index.
Identifiers: LCCN 2020000300 | ISBN 9780231193641 (hardback) |
ISBN 9780231193658 (trade paperback) | ISBN 9780231550437 (ebook)
Subjects: LCSH: Fanon, Frantz, 1925–1961—Political and social views. | Change. | Social movements.
Classification: LCC B1029.F354 A86 2020 | DDC 199/.729—dc23
LC record available at https://lccn.loc.gov/2020000300

Columbia University Press books are printed on permanent and durable acid-free paper.
Printed in the United States of America

Cover design: Milenda Nan Ok Lee

Cover art: Guillermo Kuitca (b. 1961), *Untitled, 2003–2015.*
Oil on canvas. 196.5 × 196.3 cm / 77 3/8 × 77 1/4 inches.
Copyright Guillermo Kuitca. Private collection.
Courtesy the artist and Hauser & Wirth.

Photo credit: Alex Delfanne

CONTENTS

ACKNOWLEDGMENTS

This book is the result of a collective effort. My writing has sought to work through and expand upon ideas that have emerged from countless conversations and collaborations with others.

For their impact on my thinking and for their support during the prehistory, formation, and completion of this book, I wish to acknowledge: Bachir Adjil, Anthony Alessandrini, Ben Baer, Étienne Balibar, Banu Bargu, Ericka Beckman, Karen Benezra, Sandra Bermann, Ritwik Bhattacharyya, Anthony Bogues, Bruno Bosteels, Eduardo Cadava, Sarika Chandra, Zahid Chaudhary, Katie Chenoweth, Eric Cheyfitz, Youngkyun Choi, Souleymane Bachir Diagne, Arcadio Díaz-Quiñones, Luiza Duarte Caetano, Brent Edwards, Frieda Ekotto, Sara Farris, Yanie Fecu, Silvia Federici, Anna Fisher, Alessandro Fornazzari, Moira Fradinger, Marvin Geller, Clifton Granby, Erin Graff Zivin, Marta Hernández Salván, Emilio de Ípola, Jill Jarvis, Adriana Johnson, R. A. Judy, David Kazanjian, Robin D. G. Kelley, Ethan Kleinberg, Jeff Lawrence, Horacio Legrás, Jacques Lezra, Peter Linebaugh, Barry Maxwell, Natalie Melas, Ronald Mendoza-De Jesús, Sandro Mezzadra, Fred Moten, Gabriela Nouzeilles, Jaime Ortega Reyna, Pablo Pérez Wilson, Rachel Price, Eileen Reeves, Cate Reilly, Effie Rentzou, Antonio de Ridder-Vignone, Camille Robcis, Freya Schiwy, Marcelo Starcenbaum, Alejo Stark, Jill Stockwell, Peter Thomas, Kira Thurman, Massimiliano Tomba, Alberto

Toscano, Antoine Traisnel, Geoff Waite, Gavin Walker, Audrey Wasser, Ron Wilson, Michael Wood, and Robert J. C. Young.

Susana Draper and Nick Nesbitt deserve special recognition for their invaluable mentorship and infinite generosity throughout the years. Gary Wilder deserves special recognition as well for his encouragement, guidance, and solidarity at the most important stages of this project.

I would like to thank all of the members of the Department of Romance Languages and Literatures at the University of Michigan for their contributions to making our intellectual community so vibrant and stimulating. For their thoughtful questions and insights in support of my research, I especially want to thank Paulina Alberto, Vincenzo Binetti, David Caron, Nilo Couret, Enrique García Santo-Tomás, Nick Henriksen, Alejandro Herrero-Olaizola, Juli Highfill, George Hoffmann, Kate Jenckes, Anette Joseph-Gabriel, Victoria Langland, Cristina Moreiras, Dan Nemser, Bill Paulson, Javier Sanjinés, Teresa Satterfield, Ryan Szpiech, Gustavo Verdesio, Sergio Villalobos-Ruminott, and Gareth Williams.

At Columbia University Press, Wendy Lochner has been a constant source of support and encouragement. I am greatly indebted to Wendy, to Lowell Frye, to my anonymous readers, and to the entire editorial team at the press for their enthusiasm and careful work on the project throughout the review and publication process. Isis Sadek also played an important role in helping me prepare the manuscript for submission.

Completing this book would not have been possible without the generous financial support of the Woodrow Wilson / Andrew Mellon Career Enhancement Fellowship for Junior Faculty. At the fellowship retreat, I greatly benefited from the atmosphere of camaraderie and the helpful suggestions that I received. My gratitude to Magdalena Barrera, Mary Bucholtz, Roosbelinda Cardenas, Katerina Gonzalez Seligmann, Toussaint Losier, Andrea Pitts, Julie Skurski, and Jamie Thomas for the meaningful discussions that we have had together.

I was very fortunate to gain access to the Frantz Fanon Archive of L'Institut Mémoires de l'édition contemporaine (IMEC) near Caen, France before many of the papers held there were anthologized in a recently published volume. I want to acknowledge the archivists and librarians of the archive for their help during my time at the institute.

Early versions of sections from this book were presented at the 2019 Modern Languages Association Convention, the 2016 Congress of the Latin

ACKNOWLEDGMENTS

American Studies Association, the 2014 Congress of the Latin American Studies Association, and the 2011 Caribbean Philosophical Association Conference. To the organizers and participants of these events, I extend my thanks for the generous reception and conversation.

On a personal note, I would like to recognize that nothing that I do would be possible without the love of my friends and family spread out across the United States, Mexico, and beyond. Special shout-outs to Brynn, Joanne, and Michael Arnall, Matthew Cohen, Susan and Ted Dushane, Yolanda Espinosa, Alejandra, Dorian, and James Foerg, Shuja Haider, Ted Hamilton, John Hockenberry, Ajay Kurian, Mithra Lehn, Ross Lerner, Cory Mills, Andrew, Lisa, Rich, and Sara Moreau, Karla Peña, Conor Tomás Reed, Hernán and Mila Sabau, Bécquer Seguín, Jeremy Siegman, and Daniel, Emilio, Maya, Lucía, and Pedro Sordo.

Above all, I want to thank my partner, Ana Sabau. We did it!

TWO FANONS

I explode. Here are the fragments put together by another me.

—FRANTZ FANON, *BLACK SKIN, WHITE MASKS*

FANON NOW

I begin this book with a sense of urgency. Now is the time to return to Fanon, to theorize and practice alongside him, to read his work with fresh eyes and recover the unapologetic radicalism of his vision. The urgency of this task stems in part from recent events in what has come to be known as "Fanon studies"[1]—namely, the emergence, over fifty years after Fanon's death, of a new volume of writings containing an array of hitherto unpublished texts as well as previously published works that could only be consulted in specialized archives and private collections. Released in 2015 with the title, *Écrits sur l'aliénation et la liberté* (and three years later in English translation as *Alienation and Freedom*), the volume includes Fanon's single-authored and coauthored psychiatric papers, drafts of two theatrical plays, a series of political essays, Fanon's correspondence with his publishers, and an annotated inventory of Fanon's library.[2] The circulation of so much new material, which has received little—if any—attention in a veritable sea of secondary literature, impels us to read Fanon anew, to read the new texts but also to reread the more well-known works.[3] How might these previously unknown or inaccessible writings inspire a new understanding and appreciation of Fanon's thought as a whole?

I found myself grappling with this question while studying much of the new material before its publication at the archives of the Institut Mémoires de l'édition contemporaine (IMEC) in a small village near Caen, France, where Fanon's papers are held. It was at that time that I developed the main focus and argument of this book, for I became increasingly aware of something that I had only vaguely noticed before: that Fanon was internally split throughout his life and that, in the frequent tensions, inconsistencies, and silences of his writings, in the paradoxical, unexpected, and conflicting formulations permeating his books and essays, an explosive underground current of thought struggles to gain expression. In my reading, consequently, the new texts are new in a specific sense. They do not represent a fundamental departure from Fanon's major philosophical and political concerns but rather shed new light on an often latent yet persistent division in his thinking, inviting us to reconsider the more familiar works in this same light.

Accordingly, in this introduction, I will present the book's central hypotheses concerning the existence of two Fanons, which is to say, two distinct modes of thought at stake in Fanon's oeuvre. Chapter 1 will elaborate upon these hypotheses by drawing from the new material to highlight some concrete examples of the internal division traversing Fanon's writings. It will focus on the subtle conceptual friction of the psychiatric papers, which span Fanon's career as a doctor, before turning to the more overt clash of theoretical frameworks that can be observed in one of Fanon's earliest pieces of writing, the difficult and provocative play *Parallel Hands*. Subsequent chapters will build upon this analysis by examining how Fanon's dividedness manifests itself in each of his major works, from *Black Skin, White Masks* (chapter 2) to *A Dying Colonialism* and the essays anthologized in *Toward the African Revolution* (chapter 3) to *The Wretched of the Earth* (chapters 4 and 5). Although events in Fanon's life will occasionally be mentioned when context is necessary, it should be stated at the outset that this book is not another intellectual biography; many of those—some very good—already exist. Rather, it is a sustained critical engagement with Fanon's ideas and the ideas that engaged him.[4] It should also be emphasized that in order to access Fanon's more subterranean propositions, this book will pursue a close and symptomatic reading of his texts, one that is as cognizant of how Fanon uses language, rhetoric, and extended metaphors as it is of the larger philosophical and political debates informing his interventions.

But the urgency of Fanon also far exceeds Fanon studies. It has to do with the existing order of things, the unfreedom of today's world, which is admittedly not Fanon's world—yes, many things are different now—"and yet!" In the words of Achille Mbembe:

Neo- and para-colonial wars are, after all, flourishing once again. The forms of occupation have changed with torture, internment camps, and secret prisons, and with today's mix of militarism, counterinsurgency, and the pillage of resources from a distance. The question of the people's self-determination may have moved to a new location, but it remains as fundamental as it was in Fanon's time. In a world that is rebalkanizing itself within increasingly militarized fences, walls, and borders, where the fury to unveil women remains vehement and the right to mobility is more and more constrained for those in a number of racialized categories, Fanon's great call for an opening up of the world will inevitably find many echoes. We can, in fact, see this in the organization of new forms of struggle—cellular, horizontal, lateral—appropriate for the digital age, which are emerging in the four corners of the world.[5]

By acknowledging that the location of the struggle has shifted, Mbembe joins Homi Bhabha, David Scott, and other critics who have argued that reading Fanon today entails attending to the historical disjuncture between the anticolonial movements of his time, which were typically (though not exclusively) organized around a demand for national sovereignty, and recent developments associated with globalization, which have contributed to the waning of the nation-state as a privileged site of struggle and potential site of freedom.[6] Yet Mbembe argues that certain contradictory aspects of globalization, such as the proliferation of walls and borders, the enhanced policing of cultural practices and movement, the renewed fabrication of racialized subjects and patriarchal norms, and the intensification of neo- and paracolonial wars, actually signal the continued relevance and contemporaneity of Fanon's writings. In this way, Mbembe ultimately places emphasis on a different point, a point that I would like to emphasize as well: what is truly at stake in Fanon's understanding of decolonization, which is collective freedom, self-determination, and a radical opening up of the world, is just as urgent today as it was in Fanon's time. It is, as Grant Farred puts it, an "ongoing matter," an "imperative of the now."[7]

Along these lines, Mbembe is right to observe an elective affinity between Fanon and the new forms of struggle, even if they may differ in certain ways when it comes to the issue of political organization. Fanon's emphasis in *The Wretched of the Earth* on the importance of intellectual leadership and the formation of a mass party at specific moments in the decolonization process complicates (which is not to say that it forecloses) the comparison of his work with today's more cellular and horizontal experiments, since these typically harbor significant skepticism toward the party form and the place of leadership in political organizing.[8] That being said, a number of critics have convincingly made a case for putting Fanon in direct conversation with the social movements that have experimented with these new forms of struggle, from the Arab Spring and Occupy Wall Street to Idle No More, Rhodes Must Fall, and Black Lives Matter.[9] What's more, if you have participated in the general assemblies or committee meetings of these movements, if you have marched in the streets, gathered in the plazas, attended the teach-ins, or followed the discussions on social media, then you have likely encountered—as I have on many occasions—Fanon's name, his words, and his urgency.

One of the most striking examples of such an encounter occurred shortly after the killing of Eric Garner, who was strangled to death by New York City police officers on July 17, 2014. In video footage of the event, Garner can be heard repeatedly gasping the words, "I can't breathe," which became a rallying cry at Black Lives Matter demonstrations and protests.[10] Just moments earlier in that same video, Garner mentions that he has been subjected to police harassment on a number of previous occasions and summons the courage to state: "I'm tired of it! This stops today!" A few months later, activists extended and combined both of these statements—"I can't breathe" but also "this stops today"—by widely circulating the following words, which were attributed to Fanon: "When we revolt it is not for a particular culture. We revolt simply because, for many reasons, we can no longer breathe."[11] These two sentences, often accompanied by a portrait of Fanon, went viral on popular social media platforms in the autumn of 2014 and were displayed on banners and signs at demonstrations across the United States.[12] Although these exact words cannot be found in Fanon's writings, he did say the following in *Black Skin, White Masks*: "It's not because the Indo-Chinese discovered a culture of their own that they revolted. Quite simply this was because it became impossible for them to breathe, in more than one sense of the word."[13] Some important things occur in the move from Garner's words and Fanon's passage to what could be described as their *translation* by Black Lives Matter activists. Garner's "I" and Fanon's "they" become a "we," and a singular scene of suffocation is connected to a broader condition of multiple forms of breathlessness. In this way, Fanon is invoked to remember Garner not as an isolated victim but rather as one of the vanquished in an ongoing revolt against an asphyxiating society.[14]

Although it may seem counterintuitive, what makes this intervention in political memory truly Fanonian is less the citation of Fanon than the creative miscitation of him, the way his words are translated so that they can speak to a new context. This is not to say that Fanon is used as "merely a background device" for the articulation of ideas that did not and could not have concerned him, which is something that happens to all major thinkers but seems to be especially prevalent among some of Fanon's readers.[15] No, in this case there is a compelling and meaningful connection between what Fanon said and the way that his words are repurposed to address a different situation. And this is precisely what Fanon does in his own writing when he translates concepts and categories inherited from various traditions of thought (including but not limited to Marxism, psychoanalysis, continental philosophy, and the *négritude* movement) for the theorization of racism, colonialism, and their overcoming. At times, such as in the following passage from *The Wretched of the Earth*, he even alludes to this translational method of theorization while simultaneously practicing it: "Looking at the immediacies of the colonial context, it is clear that what divides this world is first and foremost what species, what race one belongs to. In the colonies the economic infrastructure is also a superstructure. The cause is effect: You are rich because you are white, you are white because you are rich. *This is why Marxist analyses should always be slightly stretched when it comes to addressing the colonial problem.*"[16] I will return to this complicated passage and elaborate upon its precise significance for Fanon's thinking, but for now I want to reiterate the following point: If Fanon stretches Marxism to analyze colonial reality, Black Lives Matter activists follow in his footsteps by stretching Fanon to analyze today's conjuncture.

The urgent task of returning to Fanon and recovering his radicalism is thus already underway. The social movements that have contributed to this task necessarily interrupted my writing on various occasions but also inspired me to continue writing and profoundly shaped what I ended up writing about. Reading Fanon with(in) recent struggles brought into greater relief the stakes of his work; it allowed me to better appreciate the extent to which he was, perhaps above all else, a student, thinker, and instigator of change. Over the course of his life, Fanon's attention shifted from Martinique to Algeria, from the Caribbean to Africa, and from psychical and material disalienation to economic, political, and cultural decolonization. The constant throughout this trajectory, however, was Fanon's commitment to exploring the question of change in all of its facets.[17] He sought to understand what constitutes an instance of change, what role the past and the present play in effecting or obstructing change, how something new comes into existence, and how the new relates to what precedes it. He explored these issues in theory and in practice as a philosopher, a psychiatrist, and a revolutionary. This is why Mbembe characterizes Fanon's project as one of "metamorphic thought," because Fanon approached the question of change not as a mere intellectual exercise but rather as a form of critical engagement with the world that "had to be deployed like an artillery shell aimed at smashing, puncturing, and transforming the mineral and rocky wall and interosseous membrane of colonialism."[18] Change was therefore not only the object of Fanon's thinking but also its primary objective.

DIALECTICS AND THE SUBTERRANEAN ALTERNATIVE

This book combines the lessons gleaned from encountering Fanon in the archives and in the streets to argue that the question of change is at the heart of Fanon's internal division, such that his metamorphic thought is ultimately split in two. There is, on the one hand, the more prevalent and explicitly developed mode of thought, the thought of the dominant Fanon, which conceives of change as a dialectical process. Before introducing the subterranean alternative to this kind of thinking, it will be helpful to take a slight detour and reflect upon what it means to characterize a process of change as dialectical, not only because the meaning of this term is not immediately self-evident but also, relatedly, because that which is called dialectics has been a major source of philosophical and political debate since at least the ancient Greeks and especially after Marx's critique of its Hegelian "mystification."[19] This is where things get complicated, however, given that, in a scholarly work such as this one, the rule is to define the key terms yet dialectics—by definition—resists definition. To rigidly define dialectics as though it were a stable and timeless concept is to misunderstand it from the start, for, as Fredric Jameson has argued, one of its fundamental contributions to philosophy has been the introduction of time into concepts and thus the overturning of conceptual stability.[20]

But perhaps, in dialectical fashion, the problem can become its own solution.[21] This is because the apparent paradox of dialectics, that it definitionally resists definition, that it stably overturns stability, reveals its sine qua non: contradiction.[22] As Jameson asserts in his discussion of the great dialectician Bertolt Brecht: "Wherever you find [contradictions], you can be said to be thinking dialectically; whenever you fail to see them, you can be sure that you have stopped doing so."[23] To think dialectically thus entails observing a given phenomenon as a unity of opposites, as containing opposing yet interpenetrating sides.[24] But dialectical thinking also entails recognizing that this oppositional relation is the very source of change, that the unity is unstable, and that a given phenomenon becomes new through the internal movement of its contradictory aspects. In Hegel's words, "Contradiction is the root of all movement and vitality; it is only in so far as something has a contradiction within it that it moves, has an urge and activity."[25] For Fanon, as well as a number of other dialecticians, including Brecht, C. L. R. James, and Mao Tse-Tung, this understanding of contradiction is at the core of dialectics as such.[26] It is what Marx called, showcasing his own attention to contradiction, "the rational kernel within the mystical shell" of Hegel's idealism.[27]

When I refer to the dominant Fanon's thought, I have this specific view of change in mind: that change entails a dialectical process set in motion through contradiction. This is not to say that dialectical change is a uniform and unchanging process. On the contrary, as Fanon knew, the nature of dialectics is such that the contradictions involved, the moments of becoming, and the rhythms of movement vary depending on the phenomenon in question. It is with this caveat in mind that I will highlight two further tendencies of Fanon's dialectical thinking. Addressing these tendencies now will facilitate the subsequent discussion of a subterranean alternative to dialectics.

The first tendency involves Fanon's frequent construal of processes of change as moving toward the dialectical overcoming of a given phenomenon, such that said phenomenon is not completely destroyed but rather simultaneously abolished and maintained, canceled and preserved in a new, elevated form. Hegel's technical term for this kind of operation is *"Aufheben,"* a notoriously difficult word to translate, which is typically rendered as *"supprimer," "dépasser,"* or *"relever"* in French and as "to sublate," "to overcome," or "to supersede" in English.[28] If the precise meaning of this term for Hegel remains subject to debate, this study draws from Alexandre Kojève's interpretation of it, given the decisive role that he played in shaping the intellectual trajectory of Fanon and an entire generation of francophone Hegelians.[29] Hence, for Kojève: "'To overcome dialectically' ['*Supprimer dialectiquement*'] means to overcome while preserving what is overcome; it is sublimated [*sublimé*] in and by that overcoming which preserves or that preservation which overcomes."[30] Kojève offers this précis of dialectical overcoming in his commentary for the French translation of the lordship and bondage section in Hegel's *Phenomenology of Spirit*. It immediately follows the paragraph in which Hegel distinguishes between two forms of negation that can occur during the life-and-death struggle of opposing self-consciousnesses. On the one hand, the struggle can result in "abstract negation" or the death of one side of the opposition.[31] This kind of negation eliminates contradiction by reducing the negated aspect to nothing, by completely destroying it, which consequently terminates dialectical movement instead of setting it in motion. On the other hand, the struggle can result in a "negation [carried out] by consciousness, which overcomes in such a way that it *keeps* and *preserves* the overcome-entity and, for that very reason, survives the fact of being overcome."[32] Instead of death, in other words, one self-consciousness can submit to the other, become the other's slave, which negates the former's autonomy while preserving their life. This negation constitutes a fundamental transformation but not a total annihilation, and a new contradictory relationship is formed—the opposition of master and slave. This kind of negation also propels the master-slave dialectic forward, initiating the process whereby the slave, through their own labor, overcomes the condition of slavery, thereby negating themselves qua slave or negating the negation of their autonomy. However, this double negation does not mark, as in formal logic, a return to the starting point, a restitution of the original autonomy, but rather the emergence of a new kind of autonomy forged out of (and therefore to some extent containing) the preceding process.[33] While these moments of negation are not equivalent, Kojève argues that a dialectical overcoming occurs in both instances; the new develops out of the old in such a way that some given thing persists in a qualitatively different, sublimated form.

While Fanon does not strictly adhere to this notion of dialectical overcoming, as if it were a kind of formula that could be applied to each and every situation, he identifies a similar movement of canceling and preserving the old to make the new in his analysis of different historical situations throughout his oeuvre. Fanon's preferred term for this kind of process is *mutation*; however, this book will demonstrate that he deploys a number of other concepts and metaphors to conceive of change in the same light.[34] We have, in fact, already encountered one example: Fanon's assertion that Marxist analyses should always be "slightly stretched [*légèrement distendues*]" to account for the specificity of the colonial context.[35] Fanon characterizes this stretching as light, gentle, or subtle (*léger*) to underscore that he is not breaking with Marxism as such but rather necessarily extending it, making it swell from within (*distendre*). This does not mean that Fanon's intervention is slight or insignificant. On the contrary, to say that the economic infrastructure is also a superstructure, that the primary contradiction of colonial society is not class but race, is to effectively negate the standard meaning of some fundamental Marxist notions while nevertheless keeping them and imbuing them with new meaning. Fanon's Marxism, in other words, propels Marxist analysis beyond the limits of its own categories. And it is only as a result of this internal movement of overcoming that Marxism—in its new, stretched form—can adequately address the colonial problem.

Earlier, I referred to this process of change as a kind of translation. Now I can clarify how I am attempting to recast this word. When Fanon deploys the metaphor of stretching Marxist analyses, he implies that Marxism cannot simply be applied within a colonial context as if its analytic reach automatically encompassed the latter's specificity. He recognizes that certain Marxist categories are in contradictory tension with the material reality of the colony and that this tension confronts Marxism with the boundaries of its own analysis. But he does not suggest that such a situation is impossible to overcome and that Marxism should always be rejected when grappling with the colonial problem. Instead of application or rejection, which ultimately construe Marxism in the same way, as a static, unchanging doctrine, Fanon gestures toward a third option, that of translation, such that Marxism is "carried across" (*translatio*) the analytic boundaries of its current instantiation. For this to occur, its categories must be rewritten on the basis of the colony's material conditions, inaugurating the continued life or afterlife of the "original."[36]

While translation may not be one of Fanon's keywords, I am introducing this concept in part because of how other dialectical thinkers have developed it when reflecting on structurally similar situations. Antonio Gramsci's theorization of translation in his *Prison Notebooks* stands out in this regard. In one brief but important note, Gramsci recalls how Lenin, "in dealing with organizational questions, wrote and said (more or less) this: we have not been able to 'translate' our language into those of Europe."[37] Gramsci is alluding to and paraphrasing Lenin's speech, "Five Years of the Russian Revolution and the Prospects of the World Revolution."[38] During this speech, Lenin engages in a self-critique of the Communist International's resolution on "political structures" because "everything in it is based on Russian conditions." This leads Lenin to conclude: "We have not learnt to present our Russian experience to foreigners."[39] For Gramsci, Lenin is underscoring the importance of translation for a truly internationalist politics, a politics that does not impose the Russian experience on other countries, irrespective of their specific material conditions, but likewise does not construe the revolution of 1917 as an isolated incident that only affects the future of one country. Instead, Lenin calls for the Russian experience to be "translated" so that it can contribute to raising the prospects of world revolution. This entails insisting on the thorough adaptation of Russia's organizational structures when they travel abroad based on the needs of their new, non-Russian sites. José Carlos Mariátegui, who studied in the same milieu as Gramsci before returning to his native Peru, summarizes this point nicely when he writes: "We certainly do not want socialism in Latin America to be a copy or imitation. . . . We have to give life to Indo-American socialism with our own reality, in our own language."[40]

Fanon's reflections on Marxism situate him within this same tradition of thinking, even if he was not familiar with the writings of Gramsci and Mariátegui and may not have read Lenin's speech on world revolution. Indeed, he likely joined this school of thought via a different route, through his lifelong intellectual conversation and exchange with Aimé Césaire, who wrote these powerful sentences in his letter of resignation from the French Communist Party:

I believe I have said enough to make it clear that it is neither Marxism nor communism that I am renouncing, and that it is the usage some have made of Marxism and communism that I condemn. That what I want is that Marxism and communism be placed in the service of black peoples, and not black peoples in the service of Marxism and communism. That the doctrine and the movement would be made to fit men, not men to fit the doctrine or the movement. And, to be clear, this is valid not only for communists. If I were Christian or Muslim, I would say the same thing. I would say that no doctrine is worthwhile unless rethought by us, rethought for us, converted to us.[41]

According to Césaire, the Stalinized Third International and its followers in the French Communist Party exchanged Lenin's internationalism for "fraternalism" when they assumed the position of the "advanced" big brother and forcibly told their younger, "backward" siblings (e.g., the colonies, semicolonies, and dependent countries) what path of development they needed to take in order to catch up.[42] This ultimately colonialist dynamic led Césaire to conclude that there was no room within the party for black peoples to pursue, on their own terms, a fundamental rethinking and conversion of Marxism and communism. Such a "labor of translation," as Sandro Mezzadra and Brett Neilson might put it, would need to be pursued elsewhere.[43] Fanon, who never joined an official communist party, contributed to such a pursuit through his writings and through other forms of political engagement. But his labor of translation was not restricted to Marxism. It extended to all worthwhile doctrines that played a role in his thinking, such that his simultaneous cancellation and preservation of Marxist ideas and categories should be understood as exemplary of a general approach to theoretical analysis. Indeed, for the dominant Fanon, *to theorize is to translate*, to dialectically convert any inherited doctrine into a new version of itself so as to place it in the service of the struggle for liberation.

If Fanon's works perform a labor of translation, they also tend to be meditations on translation. This is because Fanon regularly confronts the question of how to respond to the legacy of colonialism without falling into the trap of either assimilationism or traditionalism, accepting colonial domination or calling for an impossible return to precolonial times. Frequently, his answer to this question is to point, once again, to a third option and argue that the struggle for liberation should approach—and sometimes succeeds in approaching—past and present beliefs, institutions, cultural practices, political forms, and subject positions as translatable material to be abolished and maintained in the production of the new. In these moments, Fanon is once again very close to Césaire, whose *Discourse on Colonialism* includes the following key passage:

For us, the problem is not to make a utopian and sterile attempt to repeat the past, but to go beyond it [*Pour nous, le problème n'est pas d'une utopique et stérile tentative de réduplication, mais d'un dépassement*]. It is not a dead society that we want to revive. . . . Nor is it the present colonial society that we wish to prolong. . . . It is a new society that we must create, with the help of all our brother slaves, a society rich with all the productive power of modern times, warm with all the fraternity of olden days.[44]

Instead of repeating the past or capitulating to the present, Césaire calls for a going beyond or an overcoming (*un dépassement*) of both.[45] This would create a new society out of elements translated from modern times as well as olden days. The dominant Fanon shares this vision of change with Césaire, even if—as I will discuss at other moments in this book—he does not always agree with Césaire on how to realize such a vision. To describe and critically reflect on the struggle for this kind of change, Fanon experiments with a series of concepts and metaphors, including *dépassement*, mutation, stretching, and many others. If one of my objectives moving forward is to consider each of these terms in their specificity, I also want to underscore their interconnectedness. I hope to accomplish this through the concept of translation, which will help reveal a major tendency in the dominant Fanon's thought, a pattern of thinking that permeates his varied imagery and terminology. In this way, I seek to develop and extend Robert J. C. Young's perceptive observation that translation, broadly construed, is a "guiding thread" in Fanon's oeuvre.[46] This means, in my view, accounting for how translation occurs in Fanon's writings at two different levels: his theoretical practice *as* translation (of certain inherited doctrines) and his theoretical practice *about* translation (of society and its many components).

Another major tendency of the dominant Fanon's thought is the articulation of a dynamic universalism, which construes universality not as the invariable quality of something that can be posited in advance, like in the case of axiomatic truths or first principles, but rather as a condition that takes shape over time, that has movement, and that rises from the abstract to the concrete. Fanon repeatedly explores how processes of change follow this kind of movement, yet, as with translation, it can also be observed at the level of Fanon's own theoretical practice. Indeed, to some extent I have been describing this movement all along via the running example of Fanon stretching Marxist analysis. To appreciate the example from this angle, it will be helpful to turn to the work of Slavoj Žižek, who is one of today's most dedicated theorists of "this 'inner life' of universality itself, this process of passage in the course of which . . . [universality is] submitted to transformations."[47] His account of the passage in Marxism from Marx to Lenin to Mao is especially germane. Beginning with the passage from Marx to Lenin, Žižek maintains that a kind of "betrayal" occurs, for the first Marxist revolution takes place, despite Marx's expectations, in a country without a long history of capitalist development.[48] The Russian Revolution is therefore not only a revolution against capital but also a revolution against (Marx's) *Capital*.[49] Yet this betrayal of Marx is paradoxically the birth of Marxism's universality. As Žižek maintains, "It is an inner necessity of the 'original' teaching to submit to and survive this 'betrayal,' to survive this violent act of being torn out of one's original context and thrown into a foreign landscape where it has to reinvent itself—*only in this way, universality is born*."[50] The Russian Revolution is not a mere exemplification of Marx's ideas, a confirmation of the preestablished universality of their scope. What Lenin shows, on the contrary, is that universality is "the result of hard theoretical work and struggle," that Marxism can only "emerge as effectively universal" if Marx's ideas are fundamentally transformed, reinvented in such a way that they survive being torn out of their original context and thrown into a new one.[51] Is not the same movement of universality at stake in Fanon's stretching of Marxist analysis? Does he not also "betray" Marx by reinventing the latter's ideas and categories when they travel to the colony?[52]

Žižek's discussion of the passage from Lenin to Mao clarifies how this movement is one that rises from the abstract to the concrete. The betrayal, in Mao's case, is to insist that the agents of Marxist revolution in China, those who have nothing to lose but their chains, are the peasants. Žižek contends that "the theoretical and political consequences of this shift [in Marxism] are properly shattering: they imply no less than a thorough reworking of Marx's Hegelian notion of the proletarian position as the position of 'substanceless subjectivity,' of those who are reduced to the abyss of their subjectivity. *This* is the movement of 'concrete universality,' this radical 'transubstantiation' through which the original theory has to reinvent itself in a new context."[53] Whereas, for Marx, the abstractly universal notion of substanceless subjectivity names the position of the proletariat, the lesson of Mao is that this notion can only become concrete in China if it is reinvented as the position of the peasantry. Mao's intervention in Marxism is not a "logical continuation" or "application" of the original theory, a simple verification of its universality, nor is it a repudiation of theory's universality from the standpoint of Chinese particularity.[54] Instead, the dialectical tension between universality and particularity, between an abstract notion and a concrete situation, propels Mao to reinvent Marxism from within, to transform its very substance. This also occurs when Fanon stretches the abstractly universal categories of infrastructure, superstructure, and class on the basis of the colony's particular conditions. They too become concrete, "the concentration of many determinations," through their reinvention.[55]

If Žižek does not refer directly to the concept of translation when describing this movement, it is certainly implied in his discussion of an original teaching, a kind of "text," that is betrayed but survives its own betrayal.[56] As the famous adage goes, "*traduttore, traditore*," "to translate is to betray." Yet in this case, there is a certain fidelity intrinsic to infidelity, insofar as Marxism is faithfully unfaithful to itself. The true Marxist tradition, in other words, is nothing but a series of translations that betray its previous iterations in accordance with changing historical circumstances. Whether in the case of Lenin, Mao, or Fanon, Marxism's abstractly universal categories and notions are canceled and preserved at the same time, negated in such a way that they persist in the afterlife of their original form, taking on a new, concrete one. The two tendencies that I have been describing are therefore intertwined, for the movement of concrete universality entails a process of translation that results in the dialectical overcoming of a preexisting phenomenon.[57] But I want to reemphasize that, for Fanon, this movement is not restricted to Marxism but extends to all the worthwhile doctrines that inform his thinking. We can equally see it at work, for example, in Fanon's approach to psychoanalytic and existentialist categories, which likewise need to be translated and made concrete if they are to remain relevant in the colony.

Although much more could and will be said about the constellation of ideas and concepts that make up the dominant Fanon's thought, I have traced its core elements: contradiction as the source of dialectical change, translation as the process of dialectical overcoming, and universality as the movement of rising dialectically from the abstract to the concrete. I can now telegraphically introduce the main features of another mode of thought corresponding to the subterranean Fanon. As the reader will have anticipated, the latter mode of thought is ultimately nondialectical and sometimes even antidialectical. If contradiction is the sine qua non of dialectical thinking, the subterranean Fanon thinks about other kinds of opposition: oppositions without interpenetration or unity, oppositions that do not follow a both-and logic, oppositions between incommensurable or radically heterogeneous phenomena. Oppositional relationships of this kind appear throughout Fanon's oeuvre; however, the example that has garnered the most attention among critics can be found in *The Wretched of the Earth*. There Fanon asserts: "The zone inhabited by the colonized is not complementary to the zone inhabited by the colonizers. The two zones confront each other [*s'opposent*], but not in the service of a higher unity. Governed by a purely Aristotelian logic, they follow the principle of mutual exclusion: There is no conciliation possible, one of the terms is superfluous."[58] If the colonizer-colonized relationship is theorized elsewhere as a dialectical opposition, the subterranean Fanon emerges in this passage to posit that the two zones of the colonial world relate as opposites in the Aristotelian rather than Hegelian or Marxian sense, opposites that, in Aristotle's words, "are not in any way interdependent, but are contrary one to the other. The good is not spoken of as the good *of the bad*, but *the contrary of the bad*, nor is the white spoken of as the white *of the black*, but as *the contrary of the black*."[59] Insofar as this nondialectical logic governs the colonizer-colonized relationship, the opposition is characterized as a "Manichaean" one of mutual exclusion rather than a contradictory one of interpenetrating opposites.[60]

For the subterranean Fanon, such nondialectical oppositions are not static but rather generate a different, nondialectical kind of change. Instead of canceling and preserving the old to make the new, the old is to be cleared away, completely destroyed, irreversibly annihilated so that something new can emerge as the result of sheer invention, autonomous movement, ex nihilo creation. Decolonization, from this viewpoint, is at once a "tabula rasa,"[61] an event of all-encompassing erasure, and an "authentic birth," the dawning of an absolutely new species to replace the colonizers *and* the colonized.[62] In conversation with Nietzsche and others tied to his thought, Fanon often associates this kind of change with affirmation over negation, the cosmic, Dionysian joy of the "yes" over the weak, stubborn resentment of the "no," the "actional" over the "reactional."[63]

Does this alternative understanding of change gesture toward an alternative conceptualization of translation, one uncoupled from dialectical overcoming?[64] My sense is that it actually entails far more devastating consequences for translation insofar as it renders the very concept inadequate. This is because it conceives of the new as detached from all previous conditions, without an original or earlier version that lives on through it. When confronting the legacy of colonialism, in other words, the subterranean Fanon searches for a *fourth* option that rejects assimilation, tradition, and translation—capitulating to the present, returning to the past, and reinventing both—in the name of starting from scratch, of a new beginning, of a life after afterlife. Such a view holds significant consequences for Fanon's own theoretical practice as well. It undercuts, if not outright precludes, the practice of stretching Marxism and other inherited doctrines so as to convert them into new versions of themselves. Instead, for the subterranean Fanon, *to theorize is to invent*, to bring into existence an entirely new way of thinking corresponding to an entirely new society.

For the sake of symmetry, it would be tempting to construe the subterranean Fanon as striving to think beyond universality just as he strives to think beyond contradiction and beyond translation. My argument, however, is that both Fanons are universalists, so their divergence on this particular issue concerns how they theorize the universal. In lieu of a dynamic universalism that passes through the movement whereby universality becomes concrete, the subterranean Fanon ascribes to what I will call a *universalism of the void*.[65] In my usage, this terminology refers to a theoretical and political project of breaking with everything that exists and that has ever existed, as well as evacuating and emptying out—actively making void—all universalist systems, in order to clear the ground for what Fanon describes as "the discovery and advancement of universalizing values," values that pertain to a totally different world in the making.[66]

This preliminary discussion of two Fanons and their distinguishing features begs the question of their relationship. What kind of relationality is implied in the distinction between a dominant Fanon and a subterranean

Fanon, a dialectical mode of thought and an alternative to it? To begin to answer this question, I should note that my use of the term "subterranean" alludes to Althusser's discussion of the underground or subterranean current of materialism (*le courant souterrain du matérialisme*) that "runs through the whole history of philosophy, and was contested and repressed there" by a form of idealism that disguised itself as another form of materialism. According to Althusser, this latter "materialism" of essence, teleology, and necessity forced underground "a wholly different mode of thought" that he interchangeably refers to as aleatory materialism or the materialism of the encounter.[67] Emilio de Ípola, in his remarkable book, *Althusser, The Infinite Farewell*, demonstrates that this underground current of materialism also runs through the whole of Althusser's writings, that late in life Althusser directly engages with the materialist tradition of the encounter but that it is there, in a latent and often repressed form, from the beginning, alongside a divergent philosophical and political project that Althusser more explicitly recognizes as his own and for which he is more commonly remembered—namely, the renewal of Marxism in opposition to various ideological deviations (e.g., economism, historicism, humanism).[68]

While Althusser draws a stark line of demarcation between the aforementioned materialisms, de Ípola offers a more complicated discussion of the relationship between Althusser's "*declared* project" and an "*other thought*" that is "*not so much different from the thought that Althusser develops in explicit terms as incommensurable with it.*"[69] If "a kind of tension, even a kind of enmity" forms between these modes of thought, de Ípola nevertheless observes that sometimes they are "juxtaposed without hostility" and are therefore "not necessarily always contradictory." He even suggests that they "intersect and coincide at certain points, blurring the borders that separate the one from the other."[70] In sum, for de Ípola, Althusser's other thought gradually emerges from its underground location over the course of his life, and, as this occurs, its relationship with the declared project vacillates between at least three different modalities: outright antagonism and incommensurability; relatively peaceful coexistence and mutual development; and latent and unresolved tension.

The way I approach Fanon's internal division draws upon how de Ípola approaches Althusser's. The analogy is not a strict one since I am not arguing that both thinkers participate in the same underground current of materialism or that they both contribute to renewing Marxism in the same way.

My claim, rather, is that Fanon likewise has a mode of thought running sub-terraneously through the whole of his writings that is distinct from his more overtly declared and explicitly developed project of dialectical analy-sis. With few exceptions, dialectical thinking is dominant in Fanon's oeu-vre, typically occupying center stage; it is not gradually overtaken in the later works by the subterranean alternative. However, as in the case of Althusser, this dominant-subterranean relationship vacillates between three modalities. On certain occasions, an idea or a concept is articulated that is blatantly antagonistic toward dialectics, or, inversely, a kind of self-critique or revision of previous claims is pursued on the basis of their divergence from dialectical thinking. When this occurs, Fanon reveals the extent to which he is deeply divided and internally split, "a battlefield in himself," a site of warring positions.[71] On other occasions, the dominant and the sub-terranean Fanon appear juxtaposed without hostility. They coexist by describing different aspects of the same phenomenon or even by advanc-ing strange and unexpected formulations that blur the conceptual bound-aries between them. Frequently, however, the underground current of thought in Fanon's oeuvre manifests itself in a more ambiguous manner. Symptomatic slips introduce terms, notions, or images that subtly diverge from the argument being developed, producing a general sense of latent and unresolved tension. In this book, I explore each of these modalities of rela-tion in an attempt to illuminate what—borrowing from Stuart Hall—I would describe as "the multivocality of the dialogue going on in [Fanon's] head."[72] By approaching Fanon in this way, this book enters into a dialogue of its own, a critical dialogue with Fanon studies that draws upon but also challenges some of the most influential interpretations of Fanon's work.

ON FANON STUDIES: POSTCOLONIAL, DECOLONIAL, AFRO-PESSIMIST

Fanon's internal division divides Fanon studies. Many of the contentious disagreements in the field can be traced back to how the reader approaches Fanon's contentious disagreements with himself.[73] Or, as Anthony Alessan-drini has observed, the debates among Fanon's readers are so polarized, the claims and counterclaims to his legacy are so divergent, in large part because of "the very real splits, discontinuities, and occasional outright contradictions that can be found in Fanon's body of work."[74] Yet to say this about Fanon is already to take a position within Fanon studies, to align one-self with those who acknowledge Fanon's dividedness over those who attempt to disavow this quality of his work or explain it away. The present book aims to develop and expand upon the former approach to reading Fanon, joining Alessandrini and other critics who have resisted the urge to resolve what remains unresolved in Fanon's writings and have instead opted to sit with and reflect upon the perplexing tensions and incongruencies that traverse his oeuvre. This way of reading Fanon is difficult, even frustrating, but it is also the only way to access the subterranean dimension of think-ing about change, the latent, enigmatic, and unsettling mode of thought that often flows just beneath the dialectical surface.

What follows is not a complete map of Fanon studies but rather a par-tial mapping of the divisions that have formed in the field around Fanon's dividedness, as well as a discussion of how this book positions itself among said divisions. I begin with the scholarship of critics who work within or against what could be characterized as the "postcolonial" wing of Fanon studies, insofar as their different readings of Fanon implicitly or explicitly attempt to intervene in and shape contemporary debates in postcolonial theory.[75] I dedicate the most attention to this wing of the field because it is particularly divided on the issue of Fanon's dividedness and because its understanding of his internal division—as tied to a vacillating stance on dialectics—resonates most directly with my own. While this book is in con-versation with the broader discussions of postcolonial theory, which have created, in the words of Jini Kim Watson and Gary Wilder, "a scene of debate over domination, emancipation, and knowledge production with regard to colonial pasts and the present," my main concern at this point is with the readings of Fanon that have emerged from the aforementioned scene of debate and especially with how these readings grapple with or fail to grapple with the inconsistencies, conflicting arguments, and paradoxi-cal assertions that permeate Fanon's writings.[76]

The obvious starting point in this regard is Homi Bhabha's canonical essay, "Remembering Fanon," which is perhaps the most widely discussed (and criticized) text in the field. Appearing as the foreword to the 1986 English translation of *Black Skin, White Masks* and later republished with some modifications in *The Location of Culture*, Bhabha's essay opens with the following observation: "To read Fanon is to experience the sense of division that prefigures—and fissures—the emergence of a truly radical thought that never dawns without casting an uncertain dark. His voice is most clearly heard in the subversive turn of a familiar term, in the silence of a sudden rupture."[77] Bhabha will go on to offer a telling example of Fanon subverting himself: "Fanon's Hegelian dream for a human reality *in-itself-for-itself* is ironized, even mocked, by his view of the Manichaean structure of colonial consciousness and its non-dialectical division."[78] Bhabha thus enjoins Fanon's readers—much in the way that this book does—to remember Fanon as a divided thinker whose internal division is tied to a wavering position on dialectics.

For Stuart Hall, this is the main lesson to be gleaned from Bhabha's take on Fanon. In an effort to restate and elaborate upon Bhabha's argument, Hall writes, "Fanon constantly and implicitly poses issues and raises questions in ways which cannot be adequately addressed within the conceptual framework into which he seeks often to resolve them; . . . a more satisfactory and complex 'logic' is often implicitly threaded through the interstices of his text, which he does not always follow through but which we can discover by reading him 'against the grain.'"[79] This assessment of Fanon, as someone torn between an explicit conceptual framework and another, more implicit logic, accurately describes Bhabha's argument and deeply resonates with my own. However, unlike Bhabha, I do not view this other logic as "more satisfactory and complex" than the prevailing conceptual framework, as presenting an opportunity to pit a "truly radical" Fanon against another, less satisfactory, less complex, and less radical one. This is where Bhabha begins to lead his readers astray, as his commendable recognition of Fanon's dividedness collapses into a one-sided focus on the nondialectical moments of his oeuvre, which align more directly with Bhabha's own theoretical commitments. On the few occasions when Bhabha does discuss the other side of Fanon's division—what he refers to as Fanon's "desperate, doomed search for a dialectic of deliverance"—it is treated in a cursory and demeaning way.[80] As a result, Bhabha reduces the complicated and multifaceted relationship between two Fanons into a facile either-or choice. He remembers Fanon's dividedness to save Fanon from himself, to rescue a nondialectical Fanon from a more familiar, dialectical one. This book offers a different approach. Its underlying question is not "Which Fanon should we choose?" but rather "What might we learn if we take both Fanons seriously, if we consider the different modalities of relation that can occur between dialectical and nondialectical thought?"

Another point of difference between Bhabha's work and my own concerns the scope of Fanon's splits and discontinuities. While we both agree that to read Fanon is to experience a sense of division, I find Bhabha's understanding of this division to be too narrow and limiting. Consider, along these lines, the following passage: "No, there can be no reconciliation, no Hegelian recognition, no simple, sentimental promise of a humanistic 'world of the You.' Can there be life without transcendence? Politics without the dream of perfectibility? Unlike Fanon, I think the *non-dialectical* moment of Manichaeanism suggests an answer. By following the trajectory of colonial desire . . . it becomes possible to cross, even to shift the Manichaean boundaries."[81] This passage clarifies what is at stake in the aforementioned example of Fanon subverting himself. For Bhabha, Fanon is divided between a Hegelian dream and a Manichaean reality, a dialectical vision for the future and a nondialectical analysis of the present. Bhabha then situates his argument as departing from Fanon's insofar as Bhabha develops an alternative vision for the future, a nondialectical answer to a nondialectical condition. This is misleading, however, given that Fanon's vision for the future is also a site of internal division and that Fanon vacillates between a dialectical and a nondialectical dream of what is to come, just as he vacillates between a dialectical and a nondialectical analysis of colonial reality. In short, Fanon's dividedness cuts across Bhabha's analysis of it, dividing each side of the dream/reality division in two.

Yet it is true that Bhabha diverges from Fanon regarding the *kind* of nondialectical answer being proposed. There is little textual evidence in Fanon's writings that would support Bhabha's call to cross and shift (rather than dialectically overcome or nondialectically destroy) the Manichaean boundaries separating colonizer and colonized. Many of Bhabha's critics focus on this aspect of his work, admonishing him for using Fanon—in the words of Cedric Robinson—as "merely a background device" to explore ideas that did not and could not have concerned him.[82] Critics who take this line of argument maintain that Bhabha's re-membering of Fanon results in an egregious distortion of his thought, that Bhabha converts the committed revolutionary into a "poststructuralist *avant la lettre*," a "premature poststructuralist," a "precocious postmodernist,"[83] or, as one particularly disgruntled commentator puts it, "some trendy postmodern bullshitter."[84] While there may be some truth to these charges, I tend to agree with Hall that Bhabha's critics, "in their haste, do not always acknowledge how clearly

Bhabha marks out the points in his text at which his interpretation departs from and goes beyond his Fanonian brief."[85] This is certainly the case in the previously cited passage from Bhabha's essay, although a careful reader will find a number of other examples as well. But I would go further and push Hall's point to its logical conclusion: Bhabha's analyses of race and (post)colonialism, which are often provocative and stimulating in their own right, are only tenuously related to Fanon's thinking—in both its dialectical and nondialectical variations—and consciously so. For this reason, they will not play an important role in the present study.

Bhabha's essay has elicited an array of responses, many of which can be grouped into two major tendencies that split the field of Fanon studies. The first tendency is to coincide with Bhabha's diagnosis of Fanon as a divided thinker while taking issue with other aspects of his argument, whereas the second tendency is to put pressure on the claim surrounding Fanon's dividedness in an effort to showcase the unity and total coherence of Fanon's thought. Anne McClintock's reading of Fanon is exemplary of the first tendency. In *Imperial Leather: Race, Gender, and Sexuality in the Colonial Contest*, McClintock takes Fanon and Bhabha to task for their problematic assertions and silences concerning gender in general and the agency of women in particular, while maintaining, in dialogue with Bhabha, that Fanon's "anticolonial project is split between a Hegelian vision of colonizer and colonized locked in a life-and-death conflict and an altogether more complex and unsteady view of agency." She continues: "These paradigms slide discrepantly against each other throughout his work, giving rise to a number of internal fissures. These fissures appear most visibly in his analysis of gender as a category of social power."[86] By implying, and at other moments more directly stating, that the dialectical paradigm is less complex than the nondialectical one, McClintock's reading of Fanon opens itself up to the same problems as Bhabha's. The avowed preference for ideas that "radically disrupt the binary dialectic" ironically turns a multifaceted relationship between two paradigms into a decidedly undialectical binary, a quasi-Manichaean dichotomy between a bad Fanon (tied to "the inexorable machinery of Hegelian dialectics") and a more promising, if not quite good, Fanon (whose views are "bereft of dialectical guarantees").[87]

Instead of joining McClintock in this adjudication between competing Fanons, I want to retain her insightful image of two paradigms sliding against each other, which implies contact as much as divergence, an encounter as much as a missed encounter. This contact is sometimes discrepant, as McClintock suggests, leading to incompatible statements clashing against each other in the same text and sometimes even in the same paragraph. But often the quality of the contact is more ambiguous. The dialectical mode of thought and the subterranean alternative rub together to generate a vague but unmistakable feeling of conceptual friction, unresolved tension, and enduring pressure. On occasion, these paradigms even seem to move with each other rather than against each other and suggest ways to blend their discordant logics. This is especially the case, as I will argue in the third chapter of this book, for Fanon's discussion of women revolutionaries and their fundamental contributions to the Algerian Revolution. For now, however, I want to emphasize a different point, which is that it is impossible to appreciate the profound entanglement between these paradigms, and the shifting nature of their relationship, if said relationship is reduced to a simple and fixed antagonism.

From a very different angle, Benita Parry's *Postcolonial Studies: A Materialist Critique* participates in the same tendency as McClintock's *Imperial Leather*. Parry is far more critical of Bhabha's overall approach to reading Fanon, yet, like Bhabha, she cautions against "smooth[ing] over the persistent instabilities in Fanon's writings," adding that "Fanon may well have perceived his mode of thought as dialectical; however, the language of his flamboyant writings . . . is witness to the conflicting predications remaining disjunct."[88] Despite this promising observation, Parry's book says very little about Fanon's conflicting predications and how they diverge from dialectics. It could even be said that Parry goes against her own cautionary advice and smooths over one of Fanon's core instabilities when she presents his thought as a dialectical salvo against the undialectical proclivities of "colonial discourse theorists" like Bhabha.[89] The unintended consequence is that her reading mirrors Bhabha's in inverted form, one-sidedly emphasizing the dialectical thought at work in Fanon's writings while underplaying the nondialectical moments of his oeuvre. And yet, despite our different appreciations of Fanon, Parry raises a very important point for this book, one that I will return to again and again in the pages that follow. To fully grapple with Fanon's internal division, it is not enough to examine his contrasting views; it is also necessary to examine *how* these views gain expression, how Fanon's exuberant style, the powerful and moving way in which he uses language, introduces strange and startling formulations that destabilize the argument and upset the reader's expectations.

The second tendency that has emerged in the wake of Bhabha's essay is to some extent an intensification of Parry's position. It not only favors Fanon's dialectical thinking but attempts to dialectize the nondialectical moments in his oeuvre, to weave every inconsistent statement and jarring image into an overarching dialectical narrative, in order to make a case for the unity and coherence of his thought. Ato Sekyi-Otu's trailblazing book, *Fanon's Dialectic of Experience*, is the best example of this approach to reading Fanon. Drawing from Hegel's *Phenomenology of Spirit*, Sekyi-Otu's reading hinges on a distinction between the apprehension of an object in its immediacy and that object's true comprehension.[90] The movement from apprehension to comprehension is dialectical in nature and mediated by experiences that reveal new aspects of the object. Through a series of close readings, Sekyi-Otu argues that *The Wretched of the Earth* alludes to and performs this dialectic of experience in its analysis of colonial reality and the process of decolonization. From this perspective, the nondialectical claims that open the book should not be read as "propositional statements and doctrines" but rather as a "dramaturgical" staging of the opposition between the colonizer and the colonized in its simplistic immediacy.[91] What follows is "the reflexive and revisionary commentary of Fanon's text upon its own inaugural claims." As readers advance through *The Wretched of the Earth*, they advance along the road of knowledge toward "richer and more complex configurations of social being and consciousness," which is to say, toward a true comprehension of colonial reality and the process of decolonization.[92] The conflicting depictions of these phenomena thus serve a specific purpose in the narration of Fanon's overall argument, and the tension that they generate is dialectically resolved over time. In this way, *The Wretched of the Earth* replicates the dialectic of experience of the colonized, a dialectic that passes from a simplistic view of Manichaean mutual exclusion to a more complex outlook of contradictory interpenetration and from a spontaneous thirst for destruction and invention to a conscious political project of dialectical overcoming.[93]

The strength of Sekyi-Otu's reading is that it ingeniously accounts for the passages from "On Violence" and "Grandeur and Weakness of Spontaneity," the first two chapters of *The Wretched of the Earth*, that call into question and critique the book's initial experimentation with a nondialectical form of analysis. When Fanon observes that "consciousness stumbles upon partial, finite, and shifting truths" in the development of the decolonization process, there is no denying that a dialectical revision of the book's inaugural claims is taking place.[94] What Sekyi-Otu's reading obscures, however, is the extent to which an underground current of nondialectical thought continually resurfaces throughout *The Wretched of the Earth* to interrupt the book's dialectical narrative and to unsettle its reflexive and revisionary commentary. As I will demonstrate in my own discussion of Fanon's final work, the nondialectical logic of "On Violence" is not progressively abandoned in the later chapters. It returns over and over again and even becomes more prevalent and more explicit in the book's concluding pages. The movement of the text is therefore not one of unified progression but rather one of incessant discontinuity; the text does not steadily dialectize the nondialectical moments but rather jaggedly shuffles back and forth between dialectical and nondialectical reason. Instead of gradually resolving the tension between two divergent modes of thought, *The Wretched of the Earth* is marked by the persistence of this tension, by its recurrence rather than its resolution.[95]

If Sekyi-Otu focuses primarily on *The Wretched of the Earth*, he does not restrict his argument to that text. In the prologue to *Fanon's Dialectic of Experience*, he proposes that we read all of Fanon's texts together, "as though they formed one dramatic dialectical narrative."[96] To read Fanon in this way, according to Sekyi-Otu, is to appreciate the dialectical movement that occurs across his texts, much in the way that it occurs within *The Wretched of the Earth*. From this standpoint, Fanon's oeuvre consists of two moments. The first moment pairs *Black Skin, White Masks* with the opening claims of "On Violence," since a nondialectical, Manichaean discourse of "absolute difference and total opposition" is "manifestly predominant" in both.[97] The second moment pairs *A Dying Colonialism* with the remainder of *The Wretched of the Earth*, for these "more dialectical texts of the 'later' Fanon" dramatize relationships that are "infinitely more complex" than the earlier Fanon's Manichaean oppositions.[98] When these moments are read together, Fanon's oeuvre narrates a now familiar process of internal overcoming, of reflexively correcting and revising its own claims, of passing from the simple immediacy of nondialectical oppositions to more complex and properly dialectical configurations.

While I appreciate the ambitiousness of Sekyi-Otu's argument—his attempt, not unlike my own, to say something about the whole—I find the overarching dialectical narrative that he ascribes to Fanon's oeuvre to be unconvincing for a number of reasons. First of all, it presents *Black Skin, White Masks* as a predominantly nondialectical text without sufficiently substantiating such a claim. While it is true that Fanon's first book contains a number of nondialectical interludes, dialectical thinking is ubiquitous in the text and even informs its overall organization, what Fanon calls the "progressive infrastructure" of its chapters.[99] Sekyi-Otu's narrative swings too far in the other direction when it comes to Fanon's later works, obscuring the extent to which nondialectical thought permeates them. I have already discussed this point with respect to *The Wretched of the Earth*, but it applies equally to *A Dying Colonialism*. When Sekyi-Otu encounters evidence of nondialectical thought in the latter text, which threatens to undermine the cogency of his argument, he dismisses it as mere "poetic excess" and "Nietzschean hyperbole."[100] It is peculiar that a critic who is so commendably sensitive to the richness of Fanon's language and to the complexity of his thought would be so dismissive toward some of the very elements that make Fanon's writings the rich and complex texts that they are. This book argues for a more thoughtful reading of Fanon's experimentation with poetic language and Nietzschean themes, one that approaches these aspects of his writing as signs of a complex (rather than simplistic) mode of nondialectical thought straining to express itself. But this difference in approach leads to the heart of my disagreement with Sekyi-Otu. He depicts Fanon's internal division as something that resolves itself over time, so that the transition from *Black Skin, White Masks* to *The Wretched of the Earth* entails a dialectical progression from an earlier, nondialectical Fanon to a later, dialectical Fanon. In contrast, this book sustains that Fanon's internal division is a constant feature of his oeuvre, that dialectical thinking tends to be dominant from beginning to end, and that a nondialectical current of thought runs subterraneously through the whole of this body of work. To say this is not to deny that many important changes occur between Fanon's earlier texts and his later ones. I will leave plenty of room in what follows to discuss these changes as they arise. But the real wager of this book is that a certain dividedness traverses these changes, that two Fanons can be heard throughout.

Nigel Gibson is another major voice within the "dialectizing" tendency of Fanon studies. In explicit dialogue with Sekyi-Out and Lewis Gordon,

Gibson puts forward the following argument in his most systematic commentary, *Fanon: The Postcolonial Imagination*: "What makes Fanon's work of a piece is Fanon's dialectic. That is not to say that the dialectic is worked out theoretically in *Black Skin* and simply applied to his later work. Fanon's dialectic itself undergoes development, takes on concretion, in terms of the Algerian revolution."[101] Much like Sekyi-Otu, Gibson's aim is to illuminate the dialectical movement that occurs across Fanon's oeuvre. For Gibson, however, it is not a matter of Fanon's nondialectical claims becoming more dialectical but rather of Fanon's dialectic becoming more concrete, taking on new determinations in response to new historical conditions.[102] This is the great strength and the great weakness of Gibson's argument. He astutely recognizes that, for Fanon, dialectics is not a stable doctrine but rather a living method of analysis that changes over time. As a result, Gibson's treatment of Fanon's dialectical thinking is more nuanced than that of the majority of his peers. Yet Gibson's exclusively dialectical depiction of Fanon's thought is far too restrictive. He goes on to write that "the thesis of this book is a fairly simple one. Though often remembered for his powerful descriptions of, and prescriptions for, a violent engagement with colonialism and its logic, [Fanon's] project and goal is to get beyond Manicheanism both in its colonial form and as an anticolonial reaction."[103] He adds: "This move, I hope to show, is dialectical and historical."[104] To put forward such a sweeping generalization of Fanon's project is to gloss over a generalized problem, to resolve what remains unresolved in Fanon. There is no recognition on Gibson's part, in other words, that what also makes Fanon's work of a piece is the persistent expression of another kind of thinking that is distinct from and often in tension with Fanon's dialectical project. This is because Gibson wants to take Fanon "seriously as a consistent theorist," as someone consistently working within dialectical reason to theorize and advocate for the overcoming of Manichaean oppositions.[105] But, as I will demonstrate throughout this book, Fanon is ultimately inconsistent on this point, often gesturing toward a nondialectical destruction of Manichaean oppositions that is not reducible to "anticolonial reaction" or to the mere inversion of colonial Manichaeanism. To take Fanon seriously is therefore to acknowledge his inconsistencies rather than disavow them and, indeed, to explore the extent to which he is consistently inconsistent.

At this point, it is worth turning to another major wing of Fanon studies, the "decolonial" wing, as the readings of Fanon that have emerged from this sector of the field converge with and diverge from the dialectizing tendency in revealing ways. Playing an influential role in shaping how Fanon is read not only in the United States but across the Americas and beyond, this wing of Fanon studies likes to invoke Fanon as a founding figure and practitioner of "decolonial thought," which, as Nelson Maldonado-Torres explains, begins with two basic premises: colonialism is "a fundamental problem" throughout modern history rather than a secondary concern and decolonization is an "unfinished project" rather than a completed historical process.[106] Like Sekyi-Otu and Gibson, the critics associated with this approach typically treat Fanon as a consistent and unified thinker rather than a conflicted and divided one. At the same time, decolonial readings of Fanon are far more insistent upon how his thought critiques and distinguishes itself from that of his European interlocutors. While there are many examples of this approach in recent decolonial scholarship,[107] I will stay with Maldonado-Torres because of how he construes Fanon's relationship with Hegel in *Against War: Views from the Underside of Modernity*. In this book, Maldonado-Torres repeatedly asserts that "Fanon's thought can hardly be integrated into the premises of neo-Hegelianism" and that, for Fanon, there are "forms of bondage with existential dimensions that cannot be spelled out in relation to the Hegelian dialectic of master and slave."[108] As Maldonado-Torres develops his argument in favor of these propositions, it becomes increasingly unclear if Fanon's decolonial thought challenges dialectics as such and points toward a nondialectical logic governing the relationship between master and slave,[109] or, alternatively, if Fanon's decolonial thought is its own form of dialectical thinking that more narrowly "challenges basic methodological premises of *Hegelian* dialectics."[110] This ambiguity in the argument could easily be construed as a flaw; however, I find it illuminating if read symptomatically as a reflection of Fanon's own ambiguity, for he too is not always clear on where he stands in relation to this issue.

But I am less sympathetic toward Maldonado-Torres's exclusive focus on an external division, on what separates Fanon from other thinkers, since we cannot truly appreciate such distinctions unless we first clarify which Fanon we are talking about, unless we come to terms with the internal division that splits Fanon in two. If, on the one hand, the dominant Fanon never simply applies Hegel to analyze the colonial context, this is because he is *deeply* and *thoroughly* Hegelian, which is to say, someone who, in rigorous conversation with Hegel, holds that any inherited school of thought—including Hegelian dialectics itself—must be submitted to a form of translation that would dialectically concretize its abstract universals.[111] For the subterranean Fanon, on the other hand, Hegel cannot simply be applied to the colonial context for a different reason, because, from this standpoint, colonial reality exceeds any dialectical analysis of it and requires a kind of transformation that likewise cannot be thought from within dialectical reason. So yes, Fanon is not reducible to Hegel or to any of his other European interlocutors, but what kind of relationship he maintains with their thought depends on a more fundamental relationship that he maintains with himself.

That said, it is not always the case that decolonial readings of Fanon avoid explicitly grappling with his internal dividedness. George Ciccariello-Maher's *Decolonizing Dialectics* is an exception to the rule. At various points in his book, Ciccariello-Maher alludes to Fanon's "misgivings" and his "skepticism" toward dialectics; he notes when Fanon is "hesitant to embrace a dialectical framework," and he even describes Fanon as someone who occupies a "liminal position that straddles the very border of dialectical thought."[112] But these suggestive remarks do not lead to a sustained discussion of Fanon's nondialectical thinking. This is because, for Ciccariello-Maher, the liminality of Fanon's position leaves him "neither rejecting nor uncritically embracing the dialectical tradition" but instead pursuing "the total decolonization and reconstruction of Hegel's approach from the ground up," which entails "[subjecting] the dialectical tradition to its own decolonizing *Aufhebung*, transcending its limitations by preserving what is useful and shedding what is not."[113] Fanon's critique of Hegel, from this perspective, dialectically decolonizes dialectics and therefore does not completely break with dialectics as such. Ciccariello-Maher thus takes a less ambiguous stance than Maldonado-Torres on the issue of Fanon and dialectics, but, as a result, it becomes harder to appreciate this issue's persistent ambiguity in Fanon's own writings. Like Sekyi-Otu and Gibson before him, Ciccariello-Maher ultimately dialectizes Fanon's dividedness and resolves what remains unresolved in his work. The nuances of the argument are different, but the effect is the same: to contribute to making the subterranean Fanon illegible.

Something very different occurs among theorists who participate in yet another wing of Fanon studies that looks to Fanon for help in exploring the "ensemble of questions" that is Afro-Pessimism.[114] Attracting ardent followers and critics alike, Afro-Pessimism has generated a prolific, thought-provoking, and often controversial body of scholarship. Fanon is a key referent in this scholarship; however, not unlike Bhabha's approach to reading Fanon, the theorists who work within Afro-Pessimism or who are in critical conversation with its questions typically depart from and go beyond Fanon's texts to reflect on political and philosophical problems that he did not consider during his lifetime. David Marriott makes a similar point in his review of the intellectual exchange between Fred Moten and Jared Sexton: "Although Moten and Sexton are ostensibly writing about Fanon, the matter of their dispute is informed by another debate that both constantly refer to, which turns on what it means to read blackness optimistically or pessimistically, and the onto-political consequences that follow." As a result, Marriott goes on to observe, "the strategically justified claim to offer a reading of Fanon involves further questions of interpretation and history for which Fanon is the substitute or stand-in."[115] The debate to which Marriott is referring, one that circles around the similarities and differences between Afro-Pessimism and what Moten calls "black optimism," is beyond the scope of the present study.[116] But, in line with what has been said up to this point, I do want to reserve some space to address how these theorists treat Fanon's dividedness.

With few exceptions, Afro-Pessimist readings of Fanon join the tendency in Fanon studies to acknowledge him as a divided thinker while highlighting one side of this division over and against the other.[117] The division is framed in various ways and is sometimes—though not always—linked to Fanon's vacillating stance on dialectics.[118] So as to not go too far afield, I will limit myself to one particularly relevant example.[119] I have in mind Sexton's discussion of Fanon and Fanon studies in an extended interview with Daniel Coluccielo Barber. Here is the key passage:

There is an unreconstructed humanist reading of Fanon's notion of disalienation that sees it as the return of the human being, and so of humanity, to its proper form and function, freed of the artificiality and abnormality imposed upon them by the slavery and colonialism and capitalism of western modernity. And Fanon is, of course, steeped in the mid-century debates over humanism, especially as they unfold in the francophone context, so it's easy to be led astray and miss his more profound suggestions.[120]

Among other possible references, Sexton is likely alluding to Sekyi-Otu's reading of Fanon, which affirms that the "crowning goal of Fanon's dialectic of experience" is a "new humanism" that corresponds with "the rebirth of the colonized as an autonomous modern subject."[121] This rebirth is not a simple "return to primal origins."[122] It is, rather, a dialectical return, a process of humanity returning to itself from alienation in such a way that its very substance is transformed and reborn, so that, in Hegel's words, it is "revealed for the first time in its actuality and truth."[123] Sexton's point is not to refute this reading of Fanon but rather to suggest an alternative reading based on Fanon's "more profound suggestions," suggestions that challenge "our common purview on change across spatiotemporal scales."[124] He thus implies that Fanon's divergent perspectives on change authorize divergent readings of his oeuvre. Unfortunately, this insightful hypothesis does not propel Sexton to reflect upon the dynamic relationship between these perspectives. Instead, he focuses exclusively on the nondialectical moments in Fanon's writings, as if to extract Fanon from his commitment to a political project of dialectical humanism.[125] In this way, his approach is not that different from Bhabha's and perpetuates many of the same limitations.[126]

Yet Sexton and his interlocutors demonstrate a greater appreciation for what is at stake subterraneously in Fanon and develop certain formulations that can contribute to a better understanding of Fanon's underground thinking about change. This is especially the case for how Sexton treats Fanon's theorization of ex nihilo creation, which, as Sexton understands it, "does not mean [the creation of] something from a preexisting nothing, but instead something from a nothing or nothingness that is achieved, however fleetingly. It is creation from a particular type of destruction or deconstruction, a type of annihilation—an affirmative reduction to nothing."[127] Sexton also invites comparison between ex nihilo creation and what Marriott labels "the pursuit of *tabula rasa* as aspiration, not as assumption."[128] As Marriott argues in his own work on Fanon, aspiring for a blank slate, actively pursuing such a condition, is what renders possible "this creating out of a void," which occurs "quite independently of any dialectics of emergence."[129] These formulations are worth highlighting because they powerfully capture some key features of the mode of thought proper to the subterranean Fanon. But they also risk falling into a common trap of reducing the relationship between dialectical and nondialectical thinking to one of incommensurability, whereas, in Fanon, the relationship is often blurrier and takes on different forms throughout his oeuvre, such that, for example, ex nihilo creation does *not* always occur quite independently of dialectics.[130] Accordingly, in this book, I will expand upon these formulations while striving to offer a more intricate and thorough account of the subterranean Fanon's conflicted entanglement with dialectical reason.

Turning finally to Moten, his search for a kind of optimism in Fanon that would unsettle Afro-Pessimist readings of his work stands out for its unique attunement to Fanon's dividedness.[131] Moten writes extensively on the "profound ambivalence" and "viciously constrained movement" that Fanon's texts perform, even going so far as to state that "what is important about Fanon is his own minor internal conflict."[132] Although Moten tends to construe this conflict differently than I do, his reading practice, which insists on thinking from Fanon's internal division rather than from one side of it, serves as a model for my own. At times our respective appreciations of Fanon's dividedness resonate in more direct ways as well. This is the case, for example, when Moten addresses "what Fanon is after" in a conversation with Stefano Harney and Stevphen Shukaitis.[133] According to Moten, Fanon's aim is "to critique but also to destroy and disintegrate the ground on which the settler stands, the standpoint from which the violence of coloniality and racism emanates."[134] Note that Moten's "but also" is not a "both . . . and," nor is it an "either . . . or." He is effectively naming a relationship of disjuncture at the core of what Fanon is after. If Fanon participates in the dialectical tradition of critique, which identifies the limits of an object of analysis so that said limits may be transcended, Moten reminds his readers of another Fanon who participates in a different yet related tradition, one that strives for a "complete lysis of this morbid universe," its absolute disintegration rather than its dialectical sublation.[135] In this way, Moten taps into the subterranean dimension of thinking about change without losing sight of the more familiar dimension or the strange, seemingly impossible travel that occurs between them. The present study aims to flesh out what this interdimensional travel looks like in Fanon's oeuvre and reflect upon its implications for thinking about—and bringing about—radical change.

While much more could be said about the vast field of Fanon studies, I have decided to highlight only some of the most relevant tendencies, critics, and texts for my argument. It is now time to move on to the new material collected in *Alienation and Freedom* so as to begin the work of substantiating the many claims made in this introduction. Doing so will then allow me to turn to the more well-known works and offer a new assessment of the internal division that traverses Fanon's oeuvre.

Chapter One

THE PSYCHIATRIC PAPERS
AND *PARALLEL HANDS*

ANNIHILATION THERAPY AND DIVERGENT
FORMS OF OVERCOMING

I begin my discussion of Fanon's work with the psychiatric papers collected in the recently published anthology *Alienation and Freedom*. These texts were all written between 1951 and 1960, which is to say, from around the time that Fanon drafted his first book (*Black Skin, White Masks*) up until just before he completed his final work (*The Wretched of the Earth*). It follows that, when read together, the psychiatric papers can help reveal patterns of thinking that correspond to the entirety of Fanon's career as a published writer. Indeed, in my view, they reveal the extent to which an underground mode of thought persists throughout the many changes of Fanon's life, often flowing just beneath the surface of an equally persistent but far more dominant form of analysis.

A subtle tension between two distinct theoretical frameworks is already palpable in some of Fanon's earliest papers, which stem from his residency at the Saint-Alban clinic in France, where he worked as an intern under the supervision of Maurice Despinoy and François Tosquelles. The latter mentor played a particularly important role in shaping how Fanon would come to think about and practice medicine. Tosquelles was a founding member of the Partido Obrero de Unificación Marxista (Workers' Party of Marxist

Unification), and his antifascist activism during the Spanish Civil War informed his subsequent experimentation in exile with a method of treatment known interchangeably as social therapy or institutional psychotherapy.[1] The method's aim was to treat mental illness within an institutional setting while simultaneously combatting the oppressive and alienating conditions of institutionalization (e.g., isolation, punitive treatment, rigid hierarchies), which, far from creating an environment conducive to therapy, often contributed to exacerbating the patient's ailments. Tosquelles and his colleagues sought to achieve this dual aim by transforming the hospital into a "neo-society" in which patients could engage in group and cultural activities alongside doctors and medical staff to work through psychical conflicts and build communal bonds.[2] Fanon helped organize and participated in numerous activities of this kind, such as theater and choral performances, sporting events, the celebration of major holidays, craft making, movie viewings, open forums to discuss hospital life, and the production of an interior journal.[3] The journal's title, *Trait d'Union* (*Hyphen*), emphasized the intersubjective and social dimension of institutional psychotherapy, its commitment to "disalienating" patients, by facilitating the formation of connections between individuals and uniting the entire hospital around collective practices and a common organ.[4]

When faced with particularly serious cases of mental illness, the doctors of Saint-Alban also experimented with different forms of shock therapy, such as the Bini method (electroconvulsive therapy) and Sakel's therapy (insulin comas), which were not understood as cures in themselves—an idea that Fanon and Tosquelles describe as "complete nonsense" in one of their coauthored papers—but rather as potentially integral aspects of a broader plan of treatment.[5] In their own words, this work involved "some concrete cases of psychiatric therapy in which organotherapy and psychotherapy, with everything that is most antithetical and most complementary about them, together combine in a coherent and effective ensemble. The point here is to situate annihilation therapy through repeated shocks within an institutional therapeutic performance."[6] To a degree, this work built off of Fanon's previous research as a medical student in Lyon, where he wrote a dissertation on a "single problem": "the relations between neurological disorders and psychiatric disorders," or, put differently, the extent to which mental illness accompanies certain diseases of the central nervous system yet cannot be reduced to these diseases in a mechanistically causal way.[7]

At Saint-Alban, Fanon similarly explored the relations between two different kinds of phenomena, in this case between organic and psychotherapeutic
forms of treatment. But there is a noticeable shift in emphasis between
the dissertation and the coauthored papers on shock therapy. If the former
text emphasizes the "respective limits of neurology and of psychiatry" so
as to combat "anatomo-clinical" reductionism, the latter works strive to
overcome the limits that separate the organic and the psychotherapeutic by
grasping the dialectical union, the relation of antithetical complementarity,
that these realms of medicine can form as combined aspects of psychiatric
practice.[8]

Fanon and Tosquelles detail one case that they take as exemplary of this
approach. A forty-five-year-old nun presenting delusions of persecution,
severe behavioral problems, and psychomotor agitation passed through
three "broad stages" of treatment while in their care.[9] The first stage entailed
sedation through narcosis sessions combined with "active intervention psychotherapy, which aimed at unveiling to the patient . . . the psychological
interpretation of her behavior as a whole."[10] Once this stage was complete,
the second stage began, which consisted of electroconvulsive shock sessions
occurring over the course of five days. This was the moment of full annihilation, of the "dissolution" of the patient's personality,[11] of her entrance
into an "amnesiac confusional" state.[12] The third stage, the moment of
the "reconstruction" of the personality and the "rediscovery of the ego and
the world," involved forty days of insulin shock therapy paired with institutional psychotherapy.[13] This stage included a number of "complexual
'nodes'"[14] or "fantasmatic stages"[15] within it, corresponding to important
events in the patient's psychical life from birth to the present day. Fanon
and Tosquelles relate that the patient "'went beyond [*a dépassé*]'" each of
these complexual nodes in collaboration with the psychotherapist.[16] For this
to occur, the doctors, the medical staff, and the social life of the institution
as a whole adapted to and evolved with the patient's fantasmatic investments
and conflicts so as to "facilitate their overcoming [*dépassement*]."[17] Once
this process of overcoming was complete, Fanon and Tosquelles assert, the
patient's "behavior became entirely normal and no signs of deterioration
remained. She returned to her community and quickly adapted to it."[18]

In the discussion section of one text from this collaboration, Tosquelles
confirms the dialectical nature of the final stage of treatment, which
he describes as "the dialectic of identifications and mythical transfers

established by the patient with the milieu."[19] By passing through this dialectic, the patient's personality, her ego, and her relationship with the world are canceled and preserved in such a way that she can return to her community as a qualitatively different person. It would appear that this dialectical process also occurs within the broader, previously discussed dialectic of three stages, which, borrowing from Tosquelles, we could call "the dialectic of the cure."[20] It follows that the transition from the second stage to the third stage of treatment is a movement of dialectical inversion, of the patient's personality passing from dissolution into its opposite, that of reconstruction.

Such an interpretation of these coauthored papers is very much in line with the dominant Fanon's mode of thinking about change; however, the careful reader will detect a subtle and latent discontinuity between how Fanon and Tosquelles theorize the method of annihilation and the dialectical process of identifications and mythical transfers that ensues. As Jean Khalfa and Robert J. C. Young both note in their essays for *Alienation and Freedom*, annihilation therapy wipes the slate clean, erasing from the patient her memories and even her sense of self, and thus converts the patient into a kind of tabula rasa.[21] This is why Fanon and Tosquelles describe the nun awaking from insulin coma and seeing the nurse's face at the initiation of the third stage of treatment as "objectively set on the same plane of maternal confusion in which 'one comes into the world.'"[22] After annihilation, the lived experience of the patient is that of a new beginning, a starting from scratch, an authentic birth.[23] Yet we are told that the patient gradually recovers her memories and works through her past conflicts so as to dialectically reconstruct her personality rather than create an entirely new one. Much of what has been wiped clean returns in a radically modified form. This is where the underlying tension of the text resides, in its discrepant approaches to theorizing the method of annihilation. If it is sometimes presented as a therapeutic practice that exceeds dialectical reason, at other times it is construed as the moment of negativity within a broader dialectic of the cure.

To attend to this tension is to catch a glimmer of the subterranean Fanon. Doing so also opens up another possible interpretation of electroconvulsive shock therapy's contribution to treatment. Fanon and Tosquelles resort to this extreme and risky method only when the patient's illness is so severe that it halts the normal dialectical movement of institutional psychotherapy.[24] In such cases, these texts sometimes imply, a nondialectical procedure is necessary, one that does not replace psychotherapy but rather *jolts* it into motion. When read in this way, Fanon's coauthored papers with Tosquelles hint at how dialectical and nondialectical thinking might work in tandem, insofar as they describe different aspects or moments of the same process of change.

Other writings from this period in Fanon's life suggest a slightly more conflictual relationship between dialectical and nondialectical modes of thought. This is the case for an editorial that Fanon wrote for *Trait d'Union* titled, "Yesterday, Today, and Tomorrow."[25] Its main argument is that it is important to remain cognizant simultaneously of the past, the present, and the future to avoid ignoring the consequences of yesterday, living today without hope, or circumscribing tomorrow to the repetition of the same. Yet partway through the essay there is another moment of tension, the vague surfacing of a discordant idea within the doctor's general prescription. After emphasizing how memory combines all three modes of time, how truly remembering past actions means recognizing their continued effect on the present and the future, Fanon writes: "However, memory ought not to get the upper hand with man. Memory is often the mother of tradition. But if it is good to have a tradition, it is also enjoyable to go beyond [*dépasser*] that tradition in order to invent the new mode of life."[26] How this passage is interpreted depends entirely on the reader's understanding of the French verb "*dépasser*," which has been mobilized historically by different philosophical schools to conceptualize change. In the introduction, I emphasized this term's centrality for a dialectical mode of thinking not only in Fanon's work but also in a broader francophone Hegelian milieu. Along these lines, it is worth recalling that the word appears prominently in the epigraph at the beginning of Alexandre Kojève's *Introduction to the Reading of Hegel*, where he cites the 1806 Jena lecture during which Hegel explains how the contemporary moment of Spirit "has gone beyond its previous concrete form [*a dépassé sa forme concrète antérieure*] and acquired a new one."[27] As I have just discussed, Fanon and Tosquelles deploy the related noun, "*dépassement*," to name the dialectical overcoming of the patient's psychical conflicts and her obtainment of a new, reconstructed personality. If the notion of *dépasser* is understood in this way, Fanon's call to go beyond tradition is not a call to abandon it entirely but rather to translate it, to dialectically refashion one's memory of the past so that the new mode of life, paraphrasing Walter Benjamin, may issue from the afterlife of the original.[28]

Yet the idea of going beyond tradition, as it is expressed in Fanon's editorial, also suggests a divergent form of overcoming, one that is more closely tied to a Nietzschean school of thought. Recall when Zarathustra invokes the "new nobility," those who are noble not because of where they come from but because of where they are going.[29] To this group, Zarathustra counsels: "Your will and your foot, which wants to go over and beyond yourself [*der über euch selber hinaus will*]—let that constitute your new honor!"[30] Henri Albert's French translation of *Thus Spoke Zarathustra*, which Fanon cites in the marginalia of his copy of Nietzsche's *Untimely Meditations*, renders this passage accordingly: "*Votre volonté et votre pas en avant qui veut vous dépasser vous-mêmes—que ceci soit votre nouvel honneur!*"[31] What Nietzsche is describing by way of Zarathustra is the teaching of the overman, of the noble will to "overcome" man ("*überwinden*" in the original German, "*surmonter*" in French translation), to go over and beyond oneself as man.[32] Gilles Deleuze, in his canonical study of Nietzsche, insists on the difference between this kind of overcoming and dialectical overcoming. He writes: "Overcoming is opposed to preserving but also to appropriating and reappropriating. Transvaluing is opposed to current values but also to dialectical pseudo-transformations."[33] This is why Zarathustra's speech on self-overcoming invokes "a creator" who is also "an annihilator," someone who will "break values" and "write new values."[34] Overcoming, for Nietzsche, is the name for this dual process of clearing away the old and inventing the new, which is to be distinguished from dialectical transformations that preserve, cancel, and elevate what already exists. Overcoming in this sense does not appropriate current values so that they can be translated but rather transvaluates them, which is to say, voids their value in the advancement of a "*new way of evaluating.*"[35]

When Fanon's appeal to joyfully go beyond tradition is read in this light, the accompanying call to invent a new mode of life stands out in greater relief. It is as though Fanon is inviting the reader—his patients and colleagues—to withdraw from translation so that something completely new can be created, a life after afterlife. Fanon the psychiatrist seems to be making an untimely observation, that active forgetting is sometimes healthy, that the weighty history of the past is sometimes disadvantageous for life.[36] His discussion of tradition and going beyond it, of memory and the new, thus evokes Nietzsche as much as Hegel, creation and annihilation as much as translation and dialectical becoming. In this way, it is symptomatic of the internal division traversing Fanon's oeuvre, of the fundamental conflict that splits him in two.

THE TRANSLATION AND TRANSMUTATION
OF SOCIAL THERAPY

This same division would mark the next phase of Fanon's career as a psychiatrist, which began shortly after he passed a series of exams in the summer of 1953 that qualified him to hold the position of head doctor (*médecin-chef de service*) in a psychiatric hospital setting. He applied for a job in Guadeloupe but ultimately accepted an offer to work at the Blida-Joinville Psychiatric Hospital in Algeria.[37] Because of the hospital's policy of segregating its patients, Fanon was assigned to a ward of 168 European women and a ward of 225 Muslim men.[38] Immediately upon his arrival, he set out to revolutionize the hospital's approach to treating mental illness by implementing the method of social therapy practiced at Saint-Alban. The challenges were numerous and required structural changes to replace the stifling, prison-like conditions of the hospital with a dynamic and collective therapeutic environment. Although Fanon was able to institute a number of important reforms, he quickly realized that his efforts had partly failed. While the European women responded well to the new method of treatment, it did not have an equally positive effect on the Muslim men. In a paper titled "Social Therapy in a Ward of Muslim Men: Methodological Difficulties," Fanon and his intern Jacques Azoulay report that these latter patients often refused to participate in the organized group and cultural activities. They showed disinterest in gatherings and celebrations that did not have a religious or familial basis; they felt uncomfortable acting and singing in front of others; they found the films to be boring; and the few patients who could read the journal chose not to do so.[39]

Distancing themselves from the infamous Algiers School of psychiatry, Fanon and Azoulay maintain that passive or active resistance toward social therapy is not evidence of neurological "primitivism" among Muslim patients.[40] Instead of relying on this racist, pseudoscientific explanation for the failed experiment, Fanon and Azoulay argue that the doctors—they themselves—were responsible for the missed encounter between social therapy and this group of individuals since they had not modified their method of treatment to account for the specificity of the method's new site of implementation:

We had wanted to create institutions and we had forgotten that all such development must be preceded with a tenacious, concrete, and real interrogation of the organic basis of the autochthonous society. By virtue of what impairment of judgment had we believed it possible to undertake Western-inspired social therapy in a ward of mentally ill Muslim men? How was a structural analysis possible if geographic, cultural, and social frameworks were put in parentheses?[41]

Fanon and Azoulay offer two self-critical explanations for their miscalculation. The first mistake was to approach North Africa as French territory, which led to the adoption of a "politics of assimilation" such that North African peoples were expected to conform to the Western method rather than, inversely, the Western method conforming to the needs of North African peoples.[42] This ultimately colonialist dynamic informed how Fanon and Azoulay grafted a historically determined method of treatment onto a society that could not fit its contours insofar as that society did not share the same historical conditions.[43]

It is important to note, however, that Fanon and Azoulay do not stop at what could be called the *provincialization* of social therapy, at the recognition of its determinate limits, at the critique of the Western method's application in Algeria.[44] Instead, they maintain that it is indeed possible to "escape the impasse" between the method and its new site once the site's geographic, cultural, and social frameworks are taken out of parentheses.[45] For this to occur, the psychiatrist must adopt "a revolutionary attitude" by "pass[ing] from a position in which the supremacy of Western culture [is] evident to one of cultural relativism."[46] Fanon and Azoulay thus describe a dialectical process—set in motion through the failed experiment—that moves from self-evident cultural hierarchies to their dissolution. As a result of passing through this process, Fanon and Azoulay come to the conclusion that they must translate social therapy so as to attend to North Africa's particular circumstances,[47] thereby contributing to the method's *deprovincialization*, its further development and realization beyond the limits of Western society.[48] This sets in motion another dialectical process, what I have referred to as the movement of concrete universality, whereby an abstractly universal method becomes concrete through its reinvention in a new context.

Fanon and Azoulay go on to offer a second self-critical explanation for their experiment with social therapy in Algeria, one that stems from the shortcomings of their predecessors, the Algiers School of psychiatry. When confronting mental illness in North Africa, the tendency was to focus on the biological at the expense of the psychological and the sociological, even though psychiatry ought to take all three realms into consideration during treatment. Fanon and Azoulay report that they perpetuated this misguided approach when they attempted to practice psychiatry in Algeria without having done the necessary research to understand the psychological and sociological particularities of their Muslim patients. The failed experiment helped them realize their mistake and once again pushed them to adopt a revolutionary attitude, one that went against the prevailing outlook toward treating mental illness at the time. As Fanon and Azoulay write:

It was necessary to change perspectives or at least supplement [*compléter*] the initial ones. It was necessary to try to grasp the North African social fact. It was necessary to demand that "totality" in which [Marcel] Mauss saw the guarantee of an authentic sociological study. A leap had to be performed, a transmutation of values had to be achieved. Let's say it: it was essential to pass from the biological to the institutional, from natural existence to cultural existence.[49]

Overcoming the limitations of the Algiers School of psychiatry by grasping the North African social fact in its totality is presented as a precondition for the possibility of effectively practicing social therapy in Algeria.[50] Fanon and Azoulay return to the unmistakably dialectical language of passing from one stage to another to theorize this process of overcoming. Yet they also introduce a different kind of language when they describe the necessary change of perspectives as a *leap*. This is not to say, of course, that there is no place for leaps in the conceptualization of dialectical change. Hegel famously wrote about the "qualitative leap" that bursts from the quantitative "gradualness" of Spirit's movement, a theme that Lenin and C. L. R. James, among others, would develop in their own work on dialectics.[51] But to describe the leap as a transmutation of values is to momentarily leap out of dialectical thinking; it is to suggest that the new perspective does not complete the previous one but rather develops from a completely different basis, from a new way of evaluating values that annihilates the racist values underpinning the pseudoscience of the Algiers School of psychiatry.[52] As with the *Trait d'Union* editorial, this is an example of a subterranean, Nietzschean form of thinking unsettling the text's predominantly dialectical mode of analysis. But in this case, not unlike the case of Fanon's articles with Tosquelles, dialectical and nondialectical change appear to be aspects of the same process, so there is an implicit suggestion that these distinct schools of thought can coexist even as their coexistence generates significant conceptual friction.

Another important feature of the paper is that, midway through its call to translate the method of social therapy, it advances a strong critique of translation in the strict, linguistic sense of the term. Fanon and Azoulay reflect on how using an interpreter during interactions with patients "fundamentally vitiates doctor-patient relations," even as this was a necessary aspect of Fanon's own psychiatric practice in Algeria because he could speak neither Arabic nor any of the Berber languages. Relying on translation has this negative effect, in part, because it "spontaneously triggers a distrust" in patients who associate the interpreter with those administrative figures of colonial authority working within the judicial system and alongside the police.[53] Under such conditions, the patient is not able to truly communicate with the doctor, to "commune *with* this person."[54] Using an interpreter also has a negative impact on the doctor's experience insofar as such a practice obstructs them from understanding the patient, even as it promises to do the opposite. Fanon and Azoulay explain:

The doctor, and especially the psychiatrist, makes his diagnostic through language. But here gestural and verbal components of language are not perceived in a synchronous fashion. While the face is expressive, the gestures abundant, it is necessary to wait until the end of the speech to grasp the meaning. At that moment, the interpreter sums up in two words what the patient had related in detail for ten minutes: "He says they took his land, or that his wife cheated on him." Often, the interpreter, in his own way, "interprets" the thought of the patient according to some stereotypical formulas, depriving it of all of its richness.[55]

Since so much is lost in translation, particularly when the interpreter has recourse to stereotypes, Fanon and Azoulay suggest that diagnosis via translation is necessarily limited and perhaps even impossible. They gesture toward a certain untranslatability of the patient's speech, which represents a potentially insurmountable difficulty for effective psychiatric treatment across languages. As Diana Fuss puts it, "Strictly speaking, the speech Fanon analyzes in the sessions with his Muslim patients is the translator's, not the patient's, a situation that impossibly confuses the analytic process."[56] To redress this situation, the doctor and the patient must—at a minimum— speak the same language, and, if a politics of assimilation is to be rejected, this implies that it is the responsibility of the doctor to learn the language(s) of his method's new site of implementation. "Going through an interpreter is perhaps acceptable when it comes to explaining something simple or trans-mitting an order," Fanon and Azoulay write, "but it is no longer [acceptable] when it is necessary to begin a dialogue, a dialectical exchange of questions and answers alone capable of conquering reluctances and bringing to light abnormal or pathological behavior."[57] To translate social therapy in Algeria, in other words, is not to translate the patient's speech but to do the language work necessary to understand the patient's speech without an interpreter. A "three-way dialogue" inhibits "the phenomenon of the encounter," which is to say, the formation of a dialectical relationship between doctor and patient based on mutual understanding and trust.[58]

THE BREAK OF DAY HOSPITALIZATION

For roughly three years, Fanon would attempt to overcome the methodolog-ical difficulties of practicing social therapy in a non-Western context. This experiment coincided with the early days of the Algerian Revolution, an insurrectionary process that completely altered the course of Fanon's life. The struggle for decolonization intensified dramatically in this period, as did the French military's violent repression of the Algerian people by means of torture, aerial bombings, and murderous raids. Fanon became increas-ingly skeptical of practicing psychiatry under conditions of "systematized de-humanization" and resigned from his post in Blida-Joinville.[59] This led to his rapid expulsion from Algeria in January 1957, which forced him to seek refuge in neighboring Tunisia. Far from putting an end to his career as a psychiatrist, however, Fanon's resignation and exile initiated a new phase of experimentation, this time at the Neuropsychiatric Day Centre of Tunis, where he would shift his focus from social therapy to day hospital-ization. Under this method of treatment, instead of remaining confined and isolated within a hospital or mental asylum for days, weeks, months, or years, patients would travel every morning to the clinic, engage in various psychotherapeutic activities throughout the day, and return to their homes and communities in the evening.[60] After many months of experimentation with this approach to treatment, Fanon produced two papers on its value and limits, one detailing the conditions of the experiment with various graphs and tables and another, coauthored with his colleague Charles Geronimi, offering a more theoretical account of day hospitalization's implications for the doctrine of psychiatry.[61] While these papers exhibit a significant transformation in Fanon's thinking about his own psychiatric practice, they also showcase a certain continuity in terms of the latent and unresolved tension that permeates his work.

As with social therapy, Fanon's experiment with day hospitalization raises the question of its translatability. Citing successful experiments in England, Denmark, and Canada, Fanon's first paper acknowledges that it is important "to ask whether the day hospital is possible in a country with low-levels of industrialization."[62] In the second paper, Fanon and Geronimi optimistically answer in the affirmative, maintaining that the success of their experiment not only signals that day hospitalization is translatable in Tunisia but also "proves that this technique, which first emerged in countries with high economic development, could be transplanted in a so-called underdeveloped country and lose nothing of its value."[63] Fanon and Geronimi are enthusiastic about day hospitalization's translatability because they view it as the preferred method of treatment for disorders that do not require constant monitoring or emergency attention. They argue that the psychiatrist's capacity to diagnose and treat mental illness is generally enhanced when patients retain their freedom to leave the clinic and when they maintain their relationship with the outside world, thus challenging conventional wisdom surrounding the purportedly therapeutic practice of internment in asylums and hospitals.

Both papers offer brief histories of psychiatric practice to argue this point. Starting with the traditional asylum, the papers maintain that interned patients typically experience a momentary reprieve from their symptoms because they are removed from the conflictual situations that give rise to them. As a result, the psychiatrist's attention shifts from treating mental illness to managing the patient's behavioral problems, which are often not a product of some underlying disorder but rather of the asylum's horrific living conditions. The core pathology thus remains untreated, and the symptoms return once the patient regains contact with the outside world. Social therapy is presented as a method of treatment that attempts to rectify this situation by placing patients in controlled scenarios that simulate the outside world so that they can actively work through their psychical conflicts with the aid of the institution's doctors and medical staff. While Fanon and Geronimi describe social therapy as "indispensable" in an asylum setting, insofar as it contributes to socializing patients and staving off the negative psychological effects of isolation, they signal their divergence from Fanon's former mentor, Tosquelles, when they express serious doubts about social therapy's curative value because of its "inert character," the lack of real movement and crisis inside the institution, and the patient's "lived experience of internment-imprisonment."[64]

Day hospitalization, on the other hand, gives "total freedom to the patient, breaking resoundingly [*brisant de façon éclatante*] with the relative and sometimes absolute coercion that internment comes to have."[65] Instead of working with patients cut off from their social milieu, moreover, "the psychiatrist is confronted with an illness as lived by a patient, a personality in crisis within an environment that is still present."[66] By observing the patient's lived experience of mental illness, by studying the "syncopated dialogue" between the patient's personality and the surrounding environment, the psychiatrist can come to appreciate how "the conflictual situation is the conclusion of the uninterrupted dialectic of the subject and the world" and can intervene in that dialectic's further movement, in the "overcoming [*dépassement*]" of the psychical conflict.[67] This is why Fanon and Geronimi write that "symptomatology presents itself dialectically and the psychiatrist acts and thinks only dialectically," because in most cases the patient's illness can be truly understood and cured only if the method of treatment does not disarticulate the dynamic relationship between patient and environment.[68]

Both papers deploy a series of terms and images to depict this disarticulation. In the first paper, Fanon describes how "the patient is subtracted [*on soustrayait*] from his conflictual milieu" and how the effect of internment is "to remove patients from the circuitry of social life [*hors-circuiter le malade de la vie sociale*]."[69] In the second paper, Fanon and Geronimi address how family unity is "broken [*brisée*]" as a result of internment, whereas, under day hospitalization, the patient "has not broken [*n'a pas rompu*] with his milieu," so no such "cut [*coupure*]" occurs.[70] Each of these passages contributes to describing the thoroughly undialectical nature of traditional psychiatric treatment, its one-sided approach to the dialectic of subject and world, which results in the "genuine thingification" of patients, their abstraction from a "multi-relational reality."[71] When read together, these passages name a nondialectical or even antidialectical procedure: internment as subtraction, as removal, as an act of interrupting the dialectic, of severing a dynamic, contradictory relationship. As good dialecticians, this is precisely what Fanon and Geronimi aim to combat with the method of day hospitalization. But it is intriguing that they use one of the same terms, "*briser*" ("to break" or "to shatter"), when describing the (non)relation between their approach to treatment and the relative or absolute coercion of internment. It is as if Fanon and Geronimi are suggesting that the history of psychiatry moves nondialectically, that the transition from the tradition of internment to day hospitalization is better understood as a total cut or absolute rupture than as a process of dialectical overcoming.

Elsewhere in the paper, Fanon and Geronimi turn to the phenomenon of the encounter between patient and doctor, which varies under day hospitalization and therapeutic internment, and deploy the same term to theorize the transition from one encounter to the other: "The *a minima* dialectic of master and slave, prisoner and prison guard created by internment or the threat of internment is radically broken [*est radicalement brisée*]. In the setting of the day hospital, the doctor-patient encounter forever remains an encounter of two freedoms."[72] In this passage, Fanon and Geronimi translate Hegel to theorize two different encounters of psychiatric treatment. They turn to Hegel's master-slave dialectic to conceptualize the unequal, carceral encounter between the doctor and the confined patient, whereas they draw from Hegel's discussion of the dialectically reciprocal recognition of freedom between two self-consciousnesses to conceptualize the encounter between the doctor and the patient participating in day hospitalization.[73] While it is clear that both encounters are dialectical in nature, the nature of the transition from one encounter to the other is far less clear. To fully grasp what is at stake here, it is worth recalling that, for Hegel, the master-slave dialectic and the historical unfolding of freedom are necessarily intertwined. As Kojève puts it, "Man achieves his true autonomy, his authentic freedom, only after passing through Slavery."[74] If day hospitalization is the result of a dialectical progression that overcomes the slavery of internment, that negates internment's negation of autonomy, then it could be said that the Patient—which is not to say any given individual patient—passes through this same historical movement to arrive at the encounter of two freedoms.

But the terminology Fanon and Geronimi use suggests that freedom is not the culmination of the master-slave dialectic but rather what comes after said dialectic has been radically broken, resoundingly shattered into pieces. The text performatively breaks with dialectical reason by theorizing the transition from one encounter to another as a nondialectical break. As in other psychiatric papers, nondialectical thinking interrupts the text's dialectical narrative, but the interruption is only momentary since the complete break results in the formation of a new dialectical encounter. The reader is yet again left with a strange coexistence between divergent and seemingly conflictual theoretical frameworks. In the context of the paper as a whole, the image of breaking the dialectic rather than passing through it reads like a relatively inconsequential imprecision or perhaps exaggeration within an otherwise thoroughly dialectical argument. The wager of this book, however, is that the previously cited passage constitutes a symptomatic slip of a much broader pattern of thinking that runs subterraneously through the whole of Fanon's oeuvre. So that the passage can be appreciated in this light, a systematic approach to Fanon's writings is necessary, one that patiently identifies and reflects upon similar moments of parapraxis. This has been my approach to reading the psychiatric papers, and it will continue to inform my interpretation of Fanon's other works.

Before turning to those other works, it is worth pausing to appreciate how the psychiatric papers, when read together, reveal the shifting nature of an enduring relationship between a dominant mode of thought and a subterranean alternative. The relationship between these paradigms is generally one of latent and unresolved tension, marked by sudden and unexpected turns in the argument that introduce discordant terms and images and divergent conceptualizations of change and the new. But, on occasion, the psychiatric papers signal the possibility of a more cooperative relationship between these paradigms, even as their underlying tension remains unresolved. Less frequently but no less importantly, these texts offer a glimpse of yet another modality of relation, that of blatant antagonism, of the subterranean Fanon advancing an antidialectical rather than simply a nondialectical form of thinking. There are only subtle hints of this overtly conflictual relationship in the psychiatric papers, whereas in other writings it is far more pronounced. In terms of the recently published material, it is most clearly staged in *Parallel Hands*, a theatrical play that predates all of Fanon's psychiatric papers as well as his first book, *Black Skin, White Masks*. To truly appreciate the extent to which Fanon can be a site of warring positions, in other words, we must begin again at the beginning.

THE ACT AS AFFIRMATION AND NEGATION

Fanon wrote three plays while studying medicine in Lyon, two of which have survived and are now available to the public: *The Drowning Eye* and *Parallel Hands*. Both drafted in 1949, these plays are dense and cerebral texts that combine free verse and prose, wordplay and neologisms, surreal images and pervasive philosophical references. Their language, style, and content invite comparisons with some of Césaire's great literary works and pose significant interpretive challenges for the reader, challenges that are only compounded by the fact that whole scenes are missing from both pieces.[75] Robert J. C. Young's extensive essay introducing these texts helpfully prepares the reader for the intellectually demanding journey ahead. He parses out the subtle Hegelian and Nietzschean themes in *Drowning Eye* and argues that the "more overtly Nietzschean" *Parallel Hands* contains a "dialectical structure" that performs an immanent critique of its Dionysian (anti)hero.[76] While both plays are remarkable, I will focus exclusively on *Parallel Hands* in this book because its rich meditations on the question of change are more directly relevant to my overall argument. While my interpretation of the play differs from Young's in various respects, I want to extend and build upon his implicit suggestion that *Parallel Hands* is a text at odds with itself and that this clash stems from the copresence of traditionally opposing schools of thought.

Written as a Greek tragedy, *Parallel Hands* is set in the mythical island of Lébos and takes place on the day that Épithalos, son of King Polyxos and Queen Dràhna, is to marry Audaline, the daughter of Ménasha. The wedding never occurs, however, as Épithalos commits parricide and regicide by slitting Polyxos's throat, sparking an insurrection that leads to the death of many others, including Audaline, who commits suicide after witnessing the rampant bloodshed and carnage. The play is thus principally about a violent "Act" that is elevated to the status of an "EVENT," since it marks "a beginning," a "metamorphosis," and a "transmutation" that puts an end to two thousand years of "eternal calm," "absolute silence," and "total darkness" on the island.[77] At the center of this event is a struggle between two opposing forces, darkness (*obscurité*) and light (*lumière*), which Polyxos and Épithalos respectively embody and which gain expression through vivid imagery and extended metaphors that revolve around a series of further oppositions, including night and day, the moon and the sun, the old and the new, death and life, serenity and adventure, inertia and movement, reason and unreason. Anticipating Fanon's future psychiatric papers, *Parallel Hands* exhibits persistent instability concerning the dialectical or nondialectical character of this core oppositional relationship and of the change that it generates. But, to reiterate, the tension between these different modes of thought is significantly more pronounced in the play. In a way that we have not yet seen in this book, the subterranean Fanon gains expression in long, developed passages rather than in brief, symptomatic slips, and his Nietzschean tendencies lead to a far more openly combative stance toward dialectics.

The play's philosophical influences can already be appreciated in act 1, when Polyxos takes credit for engineering the fixity of Lébos and its people and describes himself as "the architect of Fate," "the artisan of human rest," and the one who "discovered the point of equilibrium where consciousness [*conscience*] is immobilized."[78] The reader is immediately reminded of what Nietzsche characterizes in *The Birth of Tragedy* as the Apollonian tendency in Greek art, "that measured restraint, that freedom from the wilder emotions, that calm of the sculptor god."[79] Yet various premonitions from the dream world, nature, the gods, and other voices of the play warn Polyxos that a radical change is on the horizon, that "anarchical effusions [will] wound the uniformity of [the king's] permanence."[80] These effusions are likewise reminiscent of certain images from *The Birth of Tragedy*, especially what Nietzsche describes as "the high tide of the Dionysian," an outpour of force that destroys "all those little circles in which the one-sidedly Apollonian 'will' had sought to confine the Hellenic spirit."[81]

When Épithalos shares his plan with Audaline in act 2, it becomes clear that what he intends to unleash will reduce to rubble everything that Polyxos has sought to preserve in stone. The following lines play a particularly important role in the text insofar as they announce the explosive act to come and offer a highly suggestive account of its significance and consequences:

ÉPITHALOS: Audaline, speech reaching volcanic extremes makes itself act!

. . .

A rhythm of rupture bathes my thoughts
Abruptly I compose incendiary scales
On a single theme I want to develop
The streaming chords of my ascent.
I demand thunderbolts to stick into my hands

. . .

An act and man opens the circle where consciousness rests

. . .

I climb flaying my sonorous hands
And I burst onto the stage.
EVENT! Absolute precipice in which dissociation is forged.
World coldly erased consciousness
Which believes in History
World awaiting which postulates Fate
I force open the ribs of my tranquil
Depth and I explode
Such final certainty.[82]

At no point in this passage or in any other passage from the play does Épithalos describe the specifics of his act. He does not concretely detail what he intends to do (kill Polyxos), nor how he intends to do it (slit his throat). Instead, he depicts the act in much broader terms, emphasizing its promise to change absolutely everything. This is because it is the act itself, the act as such, that has been missing in Lébos for two thousand years. There will be an act, and, as a result, the little circle that is the island will be split open, its consciousness will come alive again, and its Hellenic spirit will once more flourish. The act will thus put an end to the seemingly eternal calm, interrupt human rest and tranquility, and unbalance the island's immobilizing equilibrium. But this violent destruction of the island's current state of existence is also an act of creation. As Épithalos proclaims, "the ACT's assailant force *invents* sublime metamorphoses."[83]

It follows that Épithalos's act is not circumscribed to overthrowing the reign of Polyxos. On the contrary, the reign of Polyxos is overthrown *as a consequence* of the act. The act is accordingly not a reaction to the way things are, a negative force of revenge that rebels against that which exists, but rather a positive force of attack that invents with "exhilarating intoxica-tion."[84] It is, moreover, an absolute bursting onto the stage that dissociates what was from what will be. The act is therefore not so much an event in History as an event that ruptures History itself, an event strong enough, in Nietzsche's words, "to break up the history of mankind in two."[85] While Lébos is its site, the act—as event—transforms the entire World. By crack-ing History in two, it erases the World's belief in what Épithalos elsewhere describes as the "Eucharistic beauty of the Past / Ancestral virtues."[86] Along with destroying such reverence for what has been, the act targets what will be. It is not the fulfillment of Fate but rather Fate's explosion, an expres-sion of freedom that lethally wounds permanence and "distorts the deter-mined."[87] If the Fate of Lébos is to be a "city oblivious to *living*," Épithalos exclaims, "I see my *life* vertiginously grasped / Attached to the ACT!"[88]

Those familiar with Nietzsche's writings will recognize many parallels in the previously cited passages that extend beyond *The Birth of Tragedy*. One obvious reference is Nietzsche's positive valuation of the noble type, of those who say "Yes" to life and act affirmatively instead of reacting out of weakness and resentment.[89] As I will demonstrate in later chapters, this is an impor-tant theme that will reappear frequently in Fanon's writings. But Épitha-los also evokes Zarathustra's creator, the one "who wants to create over and beyond himself and thus perishes," insofar as his creative act of invention is also an explosion of the self, a self-overcoming.[90] As a result, the act sets off a brilliant flash of light in the darkness of Lébos, which signals the coming of Zarathustra's overman, "the lightning from the dark cloud 'human being.'"[91]

Whereas the play's experimentation with these Nietzschean motifs is often subtle and implicit, they are explicitly deployed in the following exchange:

ÉPITHALOS: Audaline, astonished root of my being, discover the brilliant super-humanity [*surhumanité*] in my gaze!
AUDALINE: O formidable Cults! Temperatures too unequal! Finished intellectual ecstasies standing at the temples of life, will you ever know how to proclaim the unverifiable affirmation? May imprudently solicited negations sink and crumble![92]

While the prefix "*über-*" (over, above, across, beyond) in Nietzsche's *Über-mensch* is rendered alternatively in English as "overman" and "superman,"

the concept standardly appears as *"surhomme"* in French.[93] When Audaline looks into Épithalos's eyes, she sees over and beyond him to the
surhumanité that will be borne by the lightning strike of the creative-
explosive act. Inspired by what she has just seen in Épithalos's vision,
the noble Audaline chides intellectual ecstasies that are already finished
(*achevées*), dead before the temples of life, and therefore incapable of
affirming the affirmation that is unpredictable and life-willing. In a
decidedly antidialectical moment, Audaline does not call for the negation of imprudently solicited negations but rather for their annihilation,
as though soliciting a negation in any context would be imprudent, even
slavish.

Unlike her daughter, Ménasha takes a highly critical stance toward
Épithalos's act. She asks, "What fatal separations drive him?" and immediately calls out, "Peace to men of good will! / Peace to beings of reason!"[94]
When she returns to the question of what animates Épithalos, her answer
once again renders legible an antidialectical dimension of the play. According to Ménasha, what drives Épithalos and the "fierce multitude" that joins
him are "Inner excitations devoid of reciprocity . . . Separated spaces beam
with aborted syntheses. / Infinite destructions unintelligible rotations ado-
lescent discoveries."[95] As this passage implies by inversion, the equilibrium
of Lébos and its people is one of "accepted syntheses," dialectical reciprocity,
reconciliation, and reason.[96] Épithalos's act, on the other hand, is an abor-
tion of once accepted syntheses, an irrational force beyond good and evil
that joyously destroys the equilibrium of reciprocity through youthful discovery. Instead of signaling the formation of a higher unity, it signals the
separation necessary to affirm absolute difference. The implication here is
that the play's central opposition of light against darkness, Épithalos against
Polyxos, ought to be compared to Zarathustra's opposition against Christ,
which is "not a dialectical opposition, but opposition to the dialectic itself:
differential affirmation against dialectical negation."[97]

Yet at other moments in the play these same oppositions do appear to
form contradictory relationships that generate dialectical movement. We
have already glimpsed an example of this in the way that Épithalos describes
speech, at the point of volcanic extremes, becoming its opposite (within the
logic of the play) and transforming into action. However, it is ironically the
Chorus, which for Nietzsche voices the Dionysian wisdom of tragedy, that
most often exercises dialectical reason in *Parallel Hands*.[98] Consider the

following passage from the very beginning of the play, when the Chorus foreshadows the spectacular act to come: "Yet the spectacle is born from darkness! Human thought reaching maximal heights cannot not transmute [*ne peut qu'elle ne se transmue*]."[99] The spectacle of light that is yet to occur is presented here as something that already exists latently in the darkness of Lébos and that will emerge from this darkness instead of effecting an absolute rupture with it. The act, formerly breaking History in two, is thus placed back into the flow of History. The Chorus similarly presents human thought as undergoing a historical process of becoming, climbing to the heights of volcanic extremes, at which point its transmutation cannot not take place. A hint of dialectical necessity is to be detected in this double negative that complicates any account of the act as an expression of freedom absolutely unencumbered by—and ultimately undoing—the determined.[100] It is tempting, along these lines, to read the double negative as conveying something deeper about the change that it describes, as though the grammatical structure of the phrase is alluding to a conceptual structure of double negation, to a Hegelian movement that dialectically passes from the moment of negation to the moment of negating the negation. In other words, the reign of Polyxos, as the negation of thought, as the immobilization of consciousness, is to be negated in turn by the explosive act of Épithalos, thereby transmuting thought and remobilizing consciousness.[101] It is then very telling that, when this line is repeated, the Chorus prefaces it with an image of dialectical inversion: "On the other side of the emaciated Word [*Verbe*], / The initial ACT is established / Human thought reaching maximal heights cannot not transmute."[102] The play thus offers conflicting accounts of the same phenomenon, construing Épithalos's act as antidialectical and dialectical, as exemplary of Nietzschean affirmation and Hegelian negation. Indeed, if *Parallel Hands* is about a battle between two opposing forces, it is also, in itself, the staging of a battle between opposing schools of thought.

TRAGIC REPETITION, ETERNAL RETURN

It is important to note that the central act of *Parallel Hands* is also construed as tragic in the more properly Hellenic sense of the term. This occurs when different characters refer to Épithalos's "fundamental mistake [*l'erreur fondamentale]*" or what Aristotle termed *hamartia*.[103] To make sense of this third account of the act, recall that, throughout the play, Épithalos promises a volcanic eruption of life and of the new as an expression of his freedom. To those "who speak of my existence as impotent causality," he responds with images of willful virility: "An act! I want to spatter this pregnant sky with a vertiginous act! / Parallel hands make the stiff world reverberate with a new act!"[104] But, as Ménasha enigmatically puts it toward the end of the play, "Creation twists the hands [*La création se tord les mains*]."[105] Épithalos's act of creation is his own downfall; at some point he makes a grave miscalculation, his parallel hands cross, and he impotently fails to spawn what has been promised. For both Ménasha and Dràhna, the tragic hero's supposedly virile act of creation is nothing more than a fated repetition of the old that brings with it only death and destruction. Although it is never explicitly discussed how Polyxos came to power, Dràhna's haunting memories of the past suggest that his reign was founded on a violent act not unlike that of his son. In fact, she condemns "vainglorious males" for generations of masculinist violence, which she opposes to feminine peace and order.[106] For her, the masculine and the feminine form a cyclical relationship, the one necessarily passing into the other as day passes into night and light into darkness. From this perspective, the core event of the play is not really an instantiation of radical change. Whether it disrupts the calm of Lébos affirmatively or dialectically, Épithalos's act is merely a repetition of the same, for he follows in the wake of his father and the men that came before him.

This idea of tragic repetition resulting from error is itself repeated throughout the play in passages that often repeat Épithalos's words while twisting their meaning. Consider these three examples:

DRÀHNA: I shall speak the fundamental mistake
I shall speak the *returned* twilight . . .
Glories of men *eternally* vanquished
I shall speak the opulence of your defeats.[107]

MÉNASHA: Thus Polyxos is dead!
Épithalos in the Palace
LOOK at the volcanic illusions![108]

DRÀHNA: DEATH once again
Frightful speeds once again
(*she staggers.*)
Definitive ruptures once again
The illusory ABSOLUTE once again[109]

The repetition of passages likes these produces a sense of eternal return, another Nietzschean theme that is all but explicitly named in the first of these three excerpts.[110] However, instead of supporting Épithalos's account of his act, the notion of eternal return is paired with Aristotelian *hamartia* to offer a conflicting account of it. Épithalos, at the very moment when he thinks that he is rupturing with endless repetition, is actually contributing to the completion of a cycle that is eternally recurring.[111] In this way, Fanon stages a dilemma within Nietzsche's thought that has troubled many of his readers. As one commentator puts it, "Whereas the teaching of the overman is designed to inspire us to create something new and original, the doctrine of eternal return contains the crushing thought that the same will return eternally, and, therefore, all creation is in vain."[112]

Audaline's realization in act 3 of such "circular fatalities" precipitates her suicide.[113] She wakes up from an intoxicated, dream-like state during a dialogue with Dràhna and realizes that all the death and suffering was for nothing. By depicting how "rebel efforts broke juvenile hopes," *Parallel Hands* introduces the well-worn trope of a revolutionary event resulting in nothing but defeat and disillusionment.[114] Dràhna most clearly gives voice to this trope when she exclaims: "With blood will we wash our eyes!"[115] The blood of the event allows Audaline to retrospectively see its true nature. As though this frightful vision of endless destruction becomes unbearable, she closes her eyes forever by adding her own blood to that which has already been shed. It would seem that Audaline's blood then washes the eyes of Épithalos in act 4. When Dràhna informs her son of Audaline's passing, the play includes the following stage direction: "he staggers [*il vacille*] for the first time."[116] This staggering or wavering movement conveys the vacillation of Épithalos's previously steadfast conviction, the sudden internal conflict regarding the ultimate significance of his act. What follows is a dialogue that appropriately vacillates between three nearly homophonic words: "*jour* [day]," "*amour* [love]," and "*mort* [death]."[117] Épithalos's act sought to usher in a new day for Audaline and was therefore an act of love ("*Un jour et c'est l'Amour*"), but, as Dràhna insists, the new day only brought Audaline death, including ultimately her own ("*Un jour et c'est la mort!*").[118] Épithalos at least partially comes to recognize this as true when he repentantly begs forgiveness for what has occurred from both Dràhna and the recently deceased Audaline. Facing the same vision of death and destruction that plagued his fiancée, Épithalos reacts in a structurally similar way. Whereas he once sought to expand his mind and seize the light, he now wavers: "Severely broadened light / Measure the hydra of destruction. . . . Disappear you inventions of my new consciousness!"[119] He even goes on to state: "Night, I beseech you / Come back / To see no more / To see the VOID no more."[120] Like Nietzsche's spectator contemplating the tragic myth, Épithalos "sees more extensively and profoundly than ever, and yet wishes he were blind."[121] Once Épithalos begs the night to return, the stage lighting goes out and the house lighting is turned on. Shrouded in darkness at this point, Ménasha assures Épithalos that Lébos is "once again" returning to order.[122] In response, "like flesh torn by a hail of bullets," Épithalos pronounces his final words just before the curtain falls: "I SEE."[123]

Such a melancholic and arguably counterrevolutionary ending will likely surprise readers familiar with Fanon's oeuvre. The final scene depicts a defeated Épithalos who accepts the inevitable return of order and the equally inevitable failure of his act. Instead of exemplifying Zarathustra's creator, it would seem that Épithalos was actually a "firehound," someone who volcanically bellowed about "freedom" and "great events" on various occasions, but, "when [the] noise and smoke cleared, it was always very little that had happened."[124] The play accordingly leaves its reader wondering if radical change is even possible or if the only kind of revolution is that of cyclical rotation. Along these lines, it is worth recalling that Fanon never sought to publish this play during his lifetime and that, shortly before dying, he asked his brother to destroy the manuscript because it "did not correspond to his intellectual evolution and [was] far removed from his political choices at that time."[125] These details suggest that Fanon was well aware of the potentially defeatist overtones of the text and wished to distance himself from what could be called its "Thermidorian" message.[126] That being said, there are at least two alternative interpretations of the play that go beyond repentant defeatism and melancholic leftism and return us to the two Fanons of this book.[127]

SELF-SACRIFICE AND COURAGE BEFORE THE ABYSS

The first alternative, as the reader will have guessed, is to interpret the play's ending as the culmination of a dialectical process. If Épithalos were merely the repetition of his father and the men who came before him, he would assume power and rule Lébos until he fathered a son of his own who would then violently replace him and complete another iteration of the same circular movement from order to spectacle to order again. At certain moments, however, the play suggests that this will not happen by alluding to a *second* act, one that will finally break the endless cycle of repetition. If the fierce multitude of Lébos sacrificed many lives to overcome the oppressive conditions of the island, their leader Épithalos comes to realize that this process of overcoming remains incomplete if he does not sacrifice himself, if he does not step into the hail of bullets that mangle his words at the end of the play. To voice this realization, he exclaims:

I rise up
Sacrificial ACT I rise.
. . .
My dreadful finitude
my flesh
Ah! The path that leads to man is barren
Tough is the path that leads me to myself.[128]

Épithalos's initial, creative-explosive act is therefore not—as previously presented—a true instantiation of the Hegelian negation of negation, since it occurs within the logic of the old order and merely sets up the replacement of one king with another. But when Épithalos announces the sacrificial negation of himself, he performatively negates the very logic of the old order by negating his own reign and the reign of those who would follow him.[129] The Chorus once again succinctly articulates this movement of double negation: "Fire devours the nascent fire!"[130] Such an arduous dialectical trajectory leads Épithalos back to himself on a higher plane, for he rises up at the same time that he is abolished. In this way, he endures a movement of becoming not unlike that of Hegel's Spirit. Recall that after alienating itself by taking itself as an object, Spirit "returns to itself from this alienation, and is only then revealed for the first time in its actuality and truth."[131]

If Épithalos's sacrificial act is read in a similar vein, the tragic circle of repetition is replaced with a rising helix that leads to the truth and actuality of man. Revolution, from this vantage point, is not diametrically opposed to tragedy but rather must pass through tragedy, including the tragic suffering of revolution itself.[132] It follows that the play does not force its audience to view all attempts at change under the sign of defeat. Rather, as it draws to a violent close and the lights of the auditorium are turned on, the illuminated audience is invited to imagine a new world, a world not just without King Polyxos but, more radically, without any kings. As I will demonstrate in the chapters ahead, Fanon's future writings likewise invite the reader to conceive of change dialectically so as to imagine an equally radical new world without colonizers, capitalists, masters, and other kings in disguise.

A very different interpretation of the play's ending hinges on Épithalos's tendency to vacillate. Throughout act 4, he wavers between obstinately affirming the act and recognizing ultimate defeat, opening his eyes to the light and wishing he were blind. At times this back-and-forth movement is so abrupt and severe that it can seem as though two different characters are speaking. This kind of wavering can helpfully be read alongside Zarathustra's account of courage during his exchange with the Dwarf: "Courage . . . slays dizziness at the abyss. . . . Is seeing itself not—seeing the abyss? . . . As deeply as human beings look into life, so deeply too they look into suffering. But courage is the best slayer, courage that attacks."[133] The wavering movement of Épithalos after hearing the news of Audaline's death is an embodied example of dizziness before the abyss. Although Épithalos shows courage while attacking the reign of Polyxos, his courage wavers when he wishes to no longer look into the void of suffering. This explains why the act is repeatedly described as "vertiginous," because it causes a feeling of dizzy vertigo before the deep chasm that it reveals. Yet Épithalos also wavers in the other direction, regaining his courage late in the final scene of the play so as to continue his solitary journey: "Alone I want to go to the bold abyss into which consciousness sinks. / Day, enchanting light enveloping my reality."[134] The juxtaposed imagery of these lines evokes what Zarathustra calls the "abyss of light," the open sky just before the dawn of a new day.[135] "To hurl myself into your height," Zarathustra claims, "that is *my* depth."[136] Instead of closing his eyes to the abyss, even as he is tempted to do so, Épithalos seeks it out so that his consciousness can similarly be heightened by sinking down, by deepening and becoming more profound. If he loses his courage yet again when begging the night to return, he regains it once more when he affirmatively pronounces his final words—"I SEE"— and faces the suffering that accompanies life by continuing to peer into the abyss of light. Perhaps the house lighting is to be turned on just before Épithalos's final statement to create such an abyss out of the auditorium itself. If the scene is read in this way, Épithalos's act represents the fulfill- ment of his vision of explosive self-overcoming; it clears the way for the emergence of an entirely new species, a *surhumanité*.

To put it another way, even as he is generally wracked with doubt by the end of the play, it is possible to glimpse another Épithalos in those brief moments when he expresses courage before the abyss. The texts that I have analyzed in this chapter, as well as the books and essays that will be dis- cussed in subsequent chapters, likewise allow one to glimpse another, sub- terranean Fanon bubbling volcanically beneath the dominant form of analysis and occasionally exploding to the surface. While never lapsing into defeatism, Fanon's future works vacillate much like Épithalos's act between affirmative creation and dialectical negation, absolute rupture and the overcoming of contradictions. While this vacillation often occurs without Fanon explicitly addressing it, which contributes to the general sense of unresolved tension in his writings, there are some instances in which he seems to obliquely allude to it, even as his focus is on a different matter. This is the case in *Black Skin, White Masks* when Fanon returns to a memorable line spoken by Épithalos to describe *le Noir*, or "the Black," as internally divided, as split in two. Referring to a scenario vaguely reminiscent of the rigidity of Lébos, in which *le Noir* is fixed and thingified by the gaze, atti- tude, and gestures of the Other, Fanon writes: "I lose my temper, demand an explanation. . . . Nothing doing. *I explode.* Here are the fragments put together by *another me.*"[137]

In his phenomenological analysis of the "lived experience" of *le Noir*, Fanon often utilizes first-person narratives like this one to convey what Maurice Merleau-Ponty, whose lectures Fanon attended, describes as the subject's "internal communication with the world, the body and other."[138] It would therefore be a mistake to read the previously cited passage as a purely autobiographical statement, but it is still possible to see in it an implicit or secondary reflection by Fanon on his own dividedness. Indeed, this passage nicely captures certain basic characteristics of the two Fanons of this book: a subterranean Fanon who conceptualizes change as a sudden bursting into action that voids everything in a whirlwind of explosive energy and a dominant Fanon who conceptualizes change as a dialectical overcoming of the current state of things that translationally reorganizes existing fragments into a qualitatively new configuration. The passage also nicely captures the relationality between these two versions of a single self, how the explosive *Je* faces not only *un Autre* but also *un autre moi*.[139] This is what I hope to express with the idea of two Fanons: that the two modes of thought to which they refer are not completely separate and static but rather intimately entangled in a dynamic and shifting relationship. On occasion, like in *Parallel Hands*, the relationship between these two Fanons takes on an overtly antagonistic form. At other moments, as we saw in some of the psychiatric papers, their distinct voices are juxtaposed without hostility and work together in strange and unexpected ways. But most of the time, as the previously cited passage from *Black Skin, White Masks* suggests, the relationship is a more ambiguous one of latent and unresolved tension.

Of course, it is possible to interpret the explosion of the "I" and the subsequent gathering together of the fragments as two moments of the same dialectical process, as a moment of dissolution passing into a moment of reconstruction. But it is also possible to conceive of the act of the *autre moi* as a more categorical departure from the initial, explosive act, as though the *autre moi* undoes the explosion by putting the exploded pieces back together again according to a different logic. A very similar dynamic can be observed between the two Fanons of this study. When the subterranean Fanon subtly but undeniably interrupts an overt and explicit project of dialectical analysis to introduce incongruent terms and images that conceptualize change in a nondialectical way, another Fanon often interjects to reconceptualize change under dialectical reason, only to later have that reason unsettled once again by the subterranean Fanon. This is how the internal division traversing Fanon's oeuvre most frequently gains expression. If the new material in *Alienation and Freedom* allows us to appreciate this division, it can only be fully grasped with a new assessment of Fanon's work as a whole. Such is the aim of this book's remaining chapters.

Chapter Two

BLACK SKIN, WHITE MASKS

TRANSLATING CÉSAIRE, DESCARTES, FREUD, MARX . . . AND NIETZSCHE?

Fanon's introduction to his first book, *Black Skin, White Masks*, is one of his most complicated and lyrical pieces of writing. Its form moves between prose and poetry, such that its manifesto-like argumentation is often accompanied by erratic line breaks, vivid imagery, and rapid shifts in focus and content. It reads much like the most powerful sections of Aimé Césaire's *Discourse on Colonialism*, from which Fanon extracts a passage to use as his opening epigraph.[1] *Black Skin, White Masks* thus begins with citation; it refers to, while at the same time participating in, a specific tradition of thought. Even Fanon's very gesture of citation is citational, since it nods to Césaire's own nod to René Descartes's *Discourse on Method*. If the title of Césaire's essay implicitly alludes to Descartes's "charter of universalism," this allusion becomes explicit when Césaire discusses how European intellectuals act as "watchdogs of colonialism"[2] by repudiating Descartes's axiom that reason "is found whole and entire in each man" and that, "where individuals of the same species are concerned, there may be degrees in respect of their accidental qualities, but not in respect of their forms, or natures."[3] Fanon's epigraph accordingly situates his work as contributing to a tradition of universalist thinking that runs from Descartes to Césaire and beyond.[4]

The passage Fanon cites from *Discourse on Colonialism* describes the colonial process of inferiorization, an anti-universalist process of systematically fracturing and differentiating the human species: "I am talking about millions of men whom they have knowingly instilled with fear and a complex of inferiority, whom they have infused with despair and trained to tremble, to kneel and behave like flunkeys."[5] What draws Fanon to this passage is its focus on the psychoaffective impact of colonialism, on the way colonization transforms the psyche of millions of people so that they feel and act in ways that are amenable to colonial rule. Fanon will go on to reframe this issue through the lens of desire: "What does man want? What does the black man want? . . . The black man [*Le Noir*] wants to be white. The white man [*Le Blanc*] is desperately trying to achieve the rank of man."[6] While *le Blanc* strives for self-realization, *le Noir* strives to be other. This incongruous situation is the symptomatic expression of a complex of inferiority. Like Césaire, Fanon understands such complexes to be products of colonialism and calls for their overcoming.

Along with the colonial imposition of inferiority complexes, Fanon is concerned with the "double narcissism" that characterizes "the Black-White relationship," how "the white man is locked in his whiteness. The black in his blackness."[7] Fanon sees this relationship as a form of alienation and maintains that psychoanalysis can play an important role in the process of "disalienation."[8]

We have just used the word "narcissism." We believe, in fact, that only a psychoanalytic interpretation of the black problem can reveal the affective disorders responsible for this network of complexes. We are aiming for a complete lysis [*une lyse totale*] of this morbid universe. We believe that an individual must endeavor to assume the universalism inherent in the human condition. And in this regard, we are thinking equally of men like [Arthur de] Gobineau or women like Mayotte Capécia. But in order to apprehend this we urgently need to rid ourselves of a series of defects inherited from childhood [*il est urgent de se débarrasser d'une série de tares, séquelles de la période enfantine*].[9]

Psychoanalysis, by aiding in the diagnosis of certain psychoaffective disorders, contributes to the liberation of individuals from complexes of inferiority (Capécia) and superiority (Gobineau), as well as from narcissistic attachments to the particularity of separate "camps" or racialized groups.[10]

It helps set in motion the transformational process of disalienation, which results in the individual, whether black or white, man or woman, assuming a universal condition as human.

Yet Fanon's discussion of disalienation implies a translation of the traditional Enlightenment universalism of thinkers like Descartes and, in his own way, Césaire.[11] This is because Fanon introduces time into his understanding of the human condition, whereas the human is standardly defined in Enlightenment discourse through axiomatic principles that are held to be timeless truths. If Descartes considers reason to be a universal presupposition of the human species, for example, Fanon suggests that the universalism inherent in the human condition has not yet been realized because the human does not yet fully exist, because the morbid universe of colonialism is *inhuman*.[12] Fanon describes the situation accordingly: "Uprooted, dispersed, dazed, and doomed to watch as the truths he has elaborated vanish one by one, [Man] must stop projecting his antinomy into the world."[13] The truth of humanity's universal condition, though already articulated by thinkers like Descartes, is doomed to vanish or dissolve (*"se dissoudre"*) as a result of its impossible coexistence with its antinomy.[14] Psychoanalysis, Fanon suggests, can contribute to a total rupture—like the lysis of a cell membrane—with this inhuman, antinomical condition. As he states just a few paragraphs later, "We believe that the juxtaposition of the black and white races has resulted in a massive psycho-existential complex. By analyzing it we aim to destroy it."[15]

One of the most cited passages of Fanon's introduction elaborates on this condition of inhumanity as it pertains to *le Noir*: "Running the risk of angering my black brothers, I shall say that the Black is not a man. There is a zone of nonbeing, an extraordinarily sterile and arid region, an incline stripped bare of every essential, from which a genuine new departure can emerge [*d'où un authentique surgissement peut prendre naissance*]. In most cases, the black man cannot take advantage of this descent into a veritable hell."[16] Richard Philcox's English translation of this passage takes some interpretive liberties, but it does accurately convey the idea that something can come from nothing. While the original French more explicitly evokes existentialist themes of authenticity and individual freedom, themes that are explored at other moments in the book as well, it is worth reflecting on the structural similarity between the condition of *le Noir* in this passage and the Marxian paradox of the proletariat, whose negative universality, the condition of having nothing to lose, makes possible the positive universality of a communist society without classes.[17] It could be argued, in fact, that this passage translates the aforementioned paradox by theorizing the slim—but not entirely foreclosed—possibility of *le Noir* dialectically transforming the veritable hell of nonbeing into its opposite.

The introduction invites such a reading of this passage through its more direct conversation with Marx and Marxism, which occurs when Fanon draws upon basic premises of dialectical materialism to analyze the antithetical processes of inferiorization and disalienation:

The analysis we are undertaking is psychological. It remains, nevertheless, evident that for us the true disalienation of the black man implies a brutal awareness of the social and economic realities. The inferiority complex can be ascribed to a double process: First, economic. Then, internalization or rather epidermalization of this inferiority. . . . The black man must wage the struggle on two levels: whereas historically these levels are mutually dependent, any unilateral liberation is flawed, and the worst mistake would be to believe their mutual dependence automatic. . . . For once, reality requires total comprehension. An answer must be found on the objective as well as the subjective level. . . . Genuine disalienation will have been achieved only when things, in the most materialist sense, have resumed their rightful place.[18]

Fanon's initial description of *le Noir*'s inferiority complex could be confused with a kind of economism, an example of mechanical—instead of dialectical—materialism. But he goes on to clarify the relationship between the objective and the subjective by stating that historically these contradictory levels are mutually dependent, that a change at one level tends to reciprocally affect the other, although their reciprocity is neither automatic nor guaranteed. This leads Fanon to maintain that disalienation demands a struggle on two fronts, for a change in material conditions will not necessarily entail a change in psychical conditions or vice versa. Total comprehension of reality requires *both* Marxism *and* psychoanalysis, and genuine disalienation requires a transformation in *both* material *and* psychical conditions. Only this dual process of transformation can dialectically negate and transcend the dual process of inferiorization.

This passage and others like it demonstrate why the popular periodization of Fanon's thought as starkly divided between a pre-political psychoanalytic stage and a later overtly political stage is deeply deceiving.[19] For

Fanon, the psyche is a region of the political battlefield, and *Black Skin, White Masks* represents a politically charged intervention in that very region. It should nonetheless be emphasized that Fanon's aim with psychoanalysis, as with Enlightenment universalism and Marxism, is not to merely apply the method to what he refers to as the "black problem." Anticipating the conclusion of his self-critical reflection on social therapy in Algeria,[20] Fanon explains the need to translate the psychoanalytic method so that it can attend to the specificity of *le Noir*'s condition: "Reacting against the constitutionalizing trend at the end of the nineteenth century, Freud demanded that the individual factor be taken into account in psychoanalysis. He replaced the phylogenetic theory by an ontogenetic approach. We shall see that the alienation of the black man is not an individual question. Alongside phylogeny and ontogeny, there is also sociogeny."[21] Instead of unthinkingly applying Freudian ideas to a distinct set of circumstances, Fanon is responsible for a more radical project of *repeating* Freud, of performing the same critical gesture of revolutionizing the method of psychoanalysis to account for a different—social—factor of psychical life.[22] In this way, Fanon engages in a dialectical practice of translation, which simultaneously cancels and preserves a method inherited from the past, reinventing it so that it can take on a new, concrete form.

The introduction of *Black Skin, White Masks* thus allows us to see dialectics at work both in how Fanon approaches different schools of thought and in how he conceptualizes the transformation of the world's material and psychical conditions. Yet even at this early stage in the text there are already numerous examples of latent and unresolved tension in the argument that subtly but no less importantly complicate the straightforward reading of Fanon as a dialectician who translates Césaire, Descartes, Freud, and Marx to theorize the negation of objective and subjective alienation. Consider, along these lines, the language that is used in the introduction to describe disalienation. For the most part, Fanon develops images and terminology that construe disalienation as a dialectical process of overcoming colonial contradictions, such that the disalienated future is "a construction supported by man in the present. This future edifice is linked to the present insofar as I consider the present something to be overtaken [*comme chose à dépasser*]."[23] Such a view of disalienation is nonetheless complicated when the concept of "antinomy" is deployed to describe what appears to be a nondialectical opposition of strict incompatibility between the inhuman condition of colonialism and the truth of humanity.[24] To overcome this opposition, the introduction calls for a "complete lysis of this morbid universe," a ruptural event that would disintegrate an entire network of alienating complexes and relations, allowing in turn for the construction of a future completely severed from the period of time in which such a morbid universe existed. The language used to describe disalienation also suggests a divergence from the standard Freudian position that analysis is a lengthy, if not interminable, practice of working through the past, for it is presented instead as a practice that "destroys" present traces of the past, as a kind of annihilation therapy that aims to "rid" or "clear" (*"se débarrasser"*) the subject of that which has been internalized since childhood.[25] Fanon's particular vocabulary in these instances suggests that perhaps the new is not dialectically latent in what already exists, that it is not an analytical resignification of what has already happened. Perhaps, on the contrary, the new is entirely new, something that only emerges from the total clearing away of the old, a clearing that opens a path for ex nihilo creation and authentic birth.

This alternative conceptualization of the new invites an alternative interpretation of that memorable passage on the zone of nonbeing. There Fanon observes that *le Noir* is rarely able to take advantage of the descent into veritable hell. This claim begs the question: What would it mean to take advantage of such a descent? What advantage could it possibly hold? In light of what has just been said, it could be that the very absence of content, the void that is nonbeing, remains open, in its emptiness, to something beyond the future overcoming of the past and the present, to a genuine beginning of authentic upsurging (*"un authentique surgissement"*).[26] This would explain why the introduction turns to another line of thinking just after describing such an upsurging, one that is traditionally antithetical to Hegelian-Marxian dialectics. The reader is told that "Man is not only the potential for self-consciousness or negation. . . . Man is a 'yes' resonating from cosmic harmonies."[27] In this intriguing passage, Fanon blurs the conceptual boundaries between competing schools of thought by positing that man is not only Hegelian-Marxian negation but also Nietzschean affirmation. Yet the relationship between these distinct views toward man is still fraught with tension, since the effect of the passage is to associate the "yes" with a fundamentally different approach to the morbid universe of colonial inhumanity, what could be called a "disjunctive synthesis" or "non-dialectical couple" that consists of total destruction and affirmative creation instead of dialectical overcoming.[28] Put another way, the introduction's treatment of disalienation at times sounds less like the negation of the negation of man and more like what Nietzsche describes as the cosmic event of rupture that will "break the history of the world in two."[29]

Would it therefore be accurate to characterize Fanon as a translator of Nietzsche as well? While Nietzsche should certainly be included in the list of thinkers with whom Fanon is in conversation, the Nietzschean ideas that he translates are in tension with his very practice of translation. This is because to translate is to contribute to the continued life or afterlife of present or past phenomena, but Fanon is translating ideas that are opposed to such a continuation insofar as they call for a more fundamental break with the past and the present. This tension invites the reader to consider a series of urgent and complex questions: Should Enlightenment universalism or psychoanalysis or Marxism or Nietzscheanism be considered elements of the morbid universe that must be destroyed? What about Césairean *négritude*? Can these traditions be translated in an effort to achieve total rupture? Or would such a practice undermine the project of complete lysis? There are no easy answers to these questions, and Fanon does not ultimately provide answers to them in *Black Skin, White Masks*. Instead, as I will demonstrate in what follows, the latent and unresolved tension of the introduction intermittently but persistently resurfaces throughout the remainder of the text. These instances of tension should be read as signs of a subterranean Fanon struggling to gain expression; they point to a nondialectical mode of thought experimenting with an alternative theorization of disalienation, one that diverges from and unsettles the more developed account of disalienation as a dialectical process. And yet, at very specific points in the text, dialectical and nondialectical thinking appear to contribute to theorizing different paths of disalienation rather than competing accounts of disalienation as such. These brief moments of relatively peaceful coexistence between distinct modes of thought displace the latent tension of the text but never fully resolve it. On the contrary, as the text draws to a close, the tension intensifies and becomes more antagonistic with the proliferation of nondialectical and even antidialectical formulations. *Black Skin, White Masks* thus concludes much as it began, with a subterranean Fanon destabilizing its predominantly dialectical argument concerning the question of change.

LANGUAGE AND SPECTERS

The first chapter of *Black Skin, White Masks*, which addresses *le Noir*'s relationship to language, is far more consistent than the introduction in its contribution to theorizing disalienation as a dialectical process. This is already evident at the beginning of the chapter, when Fanon's brief analysis of how language affects *le Noir*'s being-for-others is interrupted by Marx's specter, whose ghostly voice speaks to Fanon's present:

But once we have taken note of the situation, once we have understood it, we consider the job done. How can we not hear that voice again tumbling down the steps of History: "It's no longer a matter of knowing the world, but of transforming it." This question is terribly present in our lives. To speak means being able to use a certain syntax and possessing the morphology of such and such a language, but it means above all assuming a culture and bearing the weight of a civilization.[30]

After deploying this striking image of a voice from the dead tumbling down the stairs of history into the living present, Fanon suggests that this is effectively how all speaking functions, for to speak in a language is to be haunted by its past and to participate in the reanimation of a culture and a civilization that precedes the speaker. It follows that language is always citational and to speak a language is already a kind of translation practice, one that moves across time rather than across languages.

But the passage also implies, by paraphrasing Marx's eleventh thesis on Feuerbach, that historical change occurs translationally, that the old contributes to the construction of the new in the process of its overcoming.[31] The voice that haunts Fanon is not just any voice but one that calls for and elicits a revolutionary transformation of the world. The past is therefore not only a burdensome weight that one assumes when speaking, for it also provides the present with a language through which the very question of transformation can be formulated. The future, in other words, is bound up in the past and the present such that their relationship cannot be reduced to that of nondialectical rupture. Fanon attempts to convey this lesson when he enigmatically states that "it is important . . . to tell the black man that an attitude of rupture [*l'attitude de rupture*] has never saved anybody; and although it is true that I must free myself from my strangler because I cannot breathe, nevertheless it is unhealthy to graft a psychological element (the impossibility of expanding) onto a physiological base (the physical difficulty of breathing)."[32] Drawing from his medical research on the distinction between psychiatric and neurological disorders, between a psychological and a physiological pathology, Fanon suggests that breaking free from the stranglehold of an inferiority complex is not the same as breaking free from a strangler.[33] The strangler wants to make breathing impossible, so ultimately the only option is a complete separation from the assailant. The language, culture, and civilization of the colonizer similarly produce the effect of psychological asphyxiation, but these violently inherited symbolic systems can also contribute to reopening the psyche's airways. Although they remain enduring traces of the history of colonialism, Fanon's work itself presupposes that French language and European culture can function in a contradictory way as tools of disalienation.

To develop this point, much of the first chapter is dedicated to exploring the opposite of an attitude of rupture—namely, the desire to assimilate—that sets in motion a transformative process that only *appears* to liberate *le Noir* from an alienated condition. Fanon is particularly interested in the case of the black Antillean student who travels to France to acquire a proper French accent and adopt French cultural traditions. This journey across land and sea makes possible a psychical and social transformation of the student's personality and being-for-others. The first signs of this change become apparent at the very beginning of the journey: "On departure, the amputation of his being vanishes as the ocean liner comes into view. He can read the authority and mutation he has acquired in the eyes of those accompanying him to the ship: '*Adieu madras, adieu foulard.*'"[34] As the student sets sail for Europe, his amputation of being, his being as the absence of being, is itself amputated and replaced with the authoritative prosthesis of French language and culture. Fanon explains the logic of this mutation accordingly: "The more the black Antillean assimilates the French language, the whiter he gets—i.e., the closer he comes to becoming a true human being. We are fully aware that this is one of man's attitudes faced with Being."[35] Assimilating the fullness of French language and culture appears to be a possible escape route from the emptiness of nonbeing; however, it is actually an expression of the black Antillean student's desire to be white and therefore of the persistence of his inferiority complex. Instead of having a disalienating effect, the student's mutation is nothing but the growth of a white mask that disguises black skin and covers up an amputated condition.

This is a particularly salient example of Fanon diagnosing a "misfire [*raté*]," a behavior that, like "an engine misfiring," fails to properly initiate the combustion process of disalienation.[36]

For Fanon, black Antillean students seem destined to misfire, for they are left with the dead-end choice between assimilation or rupture: "Either support the white world—i.e., the real world—and with the help of French be able to address certain issues and aim at a certain degree of universalism in their conclusions. Or reject Europe . . . and come together thanks to Creole by settling comfortably in what we'll call the Martinican *Umwelt*."[37] The choice is between French or Creole, the abstract universalism of the white world or the isolated particularism of the black island. Yet Fanon hints at a third option beyond these two choices through the inclusion of a lengthy passage from Michel Leiris's essay, "Martinique-Guadeloupe-Haïti":

If in the Antillean writer there is a desire to break [*volonté de rupture*] with the literary forms associated with official education, such a desire, striving toward a freer future, would not assume the appearance of folklore. Seeking above all in literature to formulate a message that is their very own and, in the case of some of them at least, to be the spokesmen of a real race with unrecognized potential, they scorn the artifice which for them, whose intellectual education has been almost exclusively French, would represent recourse to a language they could only use as a second language they have learned.[38]

According to Leiris, Antillean writers use French, the primary language of their education, to realize their desire of rupturing with canonical French literary forms and to formulate their own messages. Their desire for rupture does not gain expression in the form of a complete break that would have them subsequently retreating into a folkloric, precolonial past. It leads, on the contrary, to a kind of splintering, the formation of an internal contradiction from within French language and culture that sets in motion a process of self-expression. This movement is one of translation rather than assimilation, a movement that dialectically repurposes French language and culture for new ends. If speaking a language entails assuming the spectral weight of a culture and civilization, a particular use of language can ease the burden of that weight and open up new airways not beholden to the asphyxiating dead-ends of either blanketly assimilating white colonial culture or rupturing with it in the name of an artificial return to tradition.

Although not fully developed here, Fanon also suggests through Leiris that the third term of translation offers an alternative to the dichotomy between abstract universalism and isolated particularism, an alternative that could be called—in anticipation of my argument—the movement of concrete universality.

EXPELLING THE FLAW, RESTRUCTURING THE WORLD, AND MAKING CONSCIOUS THE UNCONSCIOUS

Fanon opens the next chapter of *Black Skin, White Masks* by examining the deep psychosocial rift that constitutes the Black-White relationship. In his critical discussion of the semiautobiographical novel, *Je suis Martiniquaise*, he describes how this rift is lived by its author, Mayotte Capécia:

Apparently for her, Black and White represent the two poles of a world, poles in perpetual conflict: a genuinely *Manichaean* notion of the world. There, we've said it—Black or White, that is the question. I am white; in other words, I embody beauty and virtue, which have never been black. I am the color of day. I am black; I am in total fusion with the world, in sympathetic affinity with the earth. . . . I am black, not because of a curse, but because my skin has been able to capture all the cosmic effluvia. I am truly a drop of sun under the earth. And there we are in a hand-to-hand struggle with our blackness or our whiteness, in a drama of narcissistic proportions, locked in our own particularity.[39]

In this passage, Fanon describes a conception of the world as divided into two opposing poles, "Black or White," a Manichaean opposition that sounds less like a union of contradictory opposites than a nondialectical antinomy, a (non)relation of heterogeneity. Each pole is depicted as its own separate prison, walled off from the other by narcissistic particularism. But Fanon also suggests that each pole contains a "Weltanschauung" or a "metaphysics" that consists of "customs and the agencies to which they refer."[40] As perhaps with all particularisms, intrinsic to each pole of this Manichaean world is a certain worldview, a belief structure that competes with the Weltanschauung of the other. This comes through most vividly when Fanon contrasts *le Blanc*'s particular embodiment of the universals of Beauty and Virtue with the naturalistic or pantheistic description of (the black) Man's relationship with the earth. The psychosocial rift that Fanon is exploring accordingly demarcates both narcissistic particularisms and competing universalisms.[41]

At this point in the book, Fanon is primarily concerned with cases in which *le Noir*, driven by an inferiority complex and an emotional state of hypersensitivity termed "affective erethism," aims to leap over the deep chasm that divides the Manichaean world to join the other side, to mutate into *le Blanc*.[42] If, in the first chapter, Fanon reflects upon how the black Antillean student attempts this leap through French language and culture, he shifts focus in the second and third chapters to how black men and women endeavor to perform the same leap via romantic relationships with their white partners. More specifically, he examines the desire of black men and women to undergo a process of "lactification," of "whitening the race," a kind of mutation that can only occur when these men and women feel recognized by their significant others as *equally white*.[43] This is how Fanon imagines the mutation of Nini, a mulatto woman in Abdoulaye Sadji's fictional text of the same name, after a white man asks to marry her: "The day the white man confessed his love for the mulatto girl, something extraordinary must have happened. There was recognition and acceptance into a community that seemed impenetrable. . . . Overnight the mulatto girl had gone from the rank of slave to that of master. . . . She was no longer the girl wanting to be white; she was white. She was entering the white world."[44] Nini's mutation into the other as a result of being recognized by the other as the same constitutes a modified resolution of the Hegelian master-slave dialectic that pairs reciprocal recognition with romantic love.[45] Yet the resolution is not dialectical, even as Nini seemingly transcends the rank of slave.[46] Overcoming the Manichaean opposition of black or white entails, in this instance, an operation of substitution rather than sublation, which eliminates one of the antinomical poles so that Nini can gain admittance and assimilate into a homogeneously white world. As the reader will have anticipated, this is not a true instance of overcoming for Fanon. Instead of freeing *le Noir* from their inferiority complex, attempting to become white through the love of a white partner is a pathological expression of that very complex. *Le Noir*'s actions result in yet another misfire that further entrenches alienation.

Fanon concludes the second and third chapters by hinting at a possible beyond to this situation, an alternative approach that would effectively set the process of disalienation in motion. In the final lines of the second chapter, he responds to those who might ask: "Are there no other possibilities" for *le Noir* than a series of pathological behaviors?[47] To such "pseudo questions," which cynically entertain the idea that perhaps nothing can change, Fanon tersely replies: "What we can say is that the flaw must be expelled once and for all [*la tare doit être expulsée une fois pour toutes*]."[48] Of course there are possibilities other than pathological behavior, Fanon tells us, but they only become real possibilities after finally expelling "the flaw." There is an apparent similarity in this regard between how Capécia and Nini react to their inferiority complexes and how Fanon proposes to treat them, since both approaches involve a project of forcefully abandoning what was for what could be. Yet, for Fanon, the flaw to be abandoned is not black skin but the psychoaffective and socially conditioned belief and feeling that black skin is a flaw. To get beyond *le Noir*'s alienation *une fois pour toutes*, Fanon calls for an expulsion of inferiority complexes from the psyche, their full eradication. The conclusion of the second chapter accordingly returns the reader to certain formulations from the introduction that depict disalienation as a kind of annihilation therapy, which nondialectically rids the subject of a series of defects or flaws ("*une série de tares*") inherited from childhood.[49] In this way, the second chapter also diverges from the main thrust of the first. Assimilationism is rejected in both instances, and the kind of rupture that results in an artificial return to folkloric traditions is implicitly rejected as well, but the alternative to these positions is conceptualized in very different ways, as translation but also as expulsion, as dialectically repurposing the old but also as totally rupturing with the old. The latent tension that can be felt *within* the introduction of *Black Skin, White Masks*, in other words, can also be felt *between* the book's first two chapters.

The final lines of the third chapter keep this tension alive in yet another brief and evocative allusion to the kind of change that disalienation requires. Citing Claude Nordey's *L'Homme de couleur*, Fanon writes:

In no way must my color be felt as a stain [*comme une tare*]. From the moment the black man accepts the split imposed by the Europeans, there is no longer any respite; "and from that moment on, isn't it understandable that he will try to elevate himself to the white man's level? To elevate himself into the range of colors to which he has attributed a kind of hierarchy?" We shall see that another solution is possible. It implies a restructuration of the world [*une restructuration du monde*].[50]

Accepting the split or cleavage of European colonialism, which divides the world into a Manichaean opposition of black or white, leads to an internalization of the European valuation of black as inferior and of white as superior. Once this occurs, *le Noir* becomes trapped in a closed and delusional cycle of hallucinatory whitening. To break out of this cycle, Fanon implies that *le Noir* must refuse the terms of Manichaeanism by rejecting both poles of the opposition. For such a transformation in psychical life to occur, a restructuration of the world is required. With this claim, the conclusion of the third chapter returns the reader once again to certain formulations from the introduction; however, in this instance, the chapter's final lines evoke the dialectical theorization of disalienation as a dual process of transformation occurring at both the subjective and the objective level. The choice of words is noteworthy as well, since the future disalienated world is not depicted as an entirely new creation but rather as a restructuration of the current, alienated world. Restructuration thus names a dialectical process of overcoming that would translate the old world into a new version of itself. But this kind of process is potentially irreconcilable with the project of annihilatory expulsion and complete lysis, since this latter case implies that nothing would remain to be restructured. Far from resolving matters, the previously cited passage revives and extends the latent tension surrounding the text's treatment of disalienation.

These ideas continue to be explored in the fourth chapter, which largely consists of a critical dialogue with French psychoanalyst Octave Mannoni. In opposition to Mannoni's *Psychologie de la colonisation*, Fanon maintains that pathological psychoaffective complexes are products of—rather than preconditions for—colonial rule. If these complexes successfully take over the psyche, it is because a world exists that actively produces them and reciprocally "draws its strength by maintaining [them]."[51] Fanon thus elaborates upon his analysis of the dialectical relationship between the social structure and the psyche to explain the historical correlation between processes of colonization and mental disorders. This leads him to conclude that proper treatment entails "combined action on the individual and the group. As a psychoanalyst, I must help my patient to *'consciousnessize'* his unconscious, to no longer be tempted by hallucinatory lactification, but also to act along the lines of a change in social structure."[52] By making pathological complexes and impulses conscious, therapeutic treatment helps free individuals and groups to choose a form of collective action that would

negate the material conditions producing and maintaining such patholo-
gies. This is how psychoanalysis can prepare the individual and the group
to realize a change in social structure, to accomplish a restructuration of
the world, so that color would no longer be felt as a flaw and the European-
imposed opposition of black or white would no longer be accepted and
internalized. As in the introduction, Fanon is describing a dialectical relationship of mutual dependence in which a transformation at the subjective
level reciprocally conditions a transformation at the objective level that in
turn conditions a further transformation at the subjective level. If this process of transformation sounds rather smooth and straightforward, the
reader will soon discover that it is not without further misfires that obstruct
the properly dialectical movement of disalienation. Fanon turns his attention to these misfires and their overcoming in the next section of the book.
He momentarily departs from the nondialectical formulations of previous
chapters to engage in some of the most rigorous dialectical analysis of
his entire body of work. But a subterranean alternative to this kind of
analysis will return before the text draws to a close, which will have the effect
of generating further conceptual friction and of destabilizing the argument
yet again.

RATIONALISM AND IRRATIONALISM

The fifth chapter of *Black Skin, White Masks*, perhaps the most discussed
section of the book, gives a phenomenological account of the *"expérience
vécue"* or "lived experience" of *le Noir*.[53] As David Macey has rightly argued,
Fanon's use of the phrase *"expérience vécue"* puts his work in direct conversation with that of Maurice Merleau-Ponty, who popularized the French
phrase as a translation of the technical German term (used by both Hus-
serl and Heidegger), *"Erlebnis."*[54] If, for Merleau-Ponty, to experience is "to
be in internal communication with the world, the body and other, to be with
them rather than alongside them," Fanon considers this kind of experience
as it is lived by *le Noir*.[55] But the generic quality of the category—*Noir*—is
deceiving, since, as Fanon informs the reader in the introduction, "there is
nothing in common between the black man in this chapter and the black
man who wants to sleep with the white woman. The latter wants to be
white. . . . In this chapter, on the contrary, we are witness to the desperate
efforts of a black man striving desperately to discover the meaning of black

identity. . . . We shall demonstrate furthermore that what is called the black soul is a construction by white folk."[56] True to what Fanon describes as the "progressive infrastructure" that organizes the chapters of *Black Skin, White Masks*, le *Noir* of the fifth chapter is not beholden in the same way to the inferiority complex that afflicts le *Noir* in the previous chapters.[57] The new *Noir* has become conscious of unconscious desires for whitening and experiences the world, the body, and the other differently as a result.

Although the new *Noir* desperately searches for the meaning of black identity, Fanon assures the reader that such a search will not lead to the discovery of an identitarian essence, since the black soul is a construction, something historically produced by white folk. While many scholars have turned to the fifth chapter of *Black Skin, White Masks* to develop important work on Fanon's treatment of identity and identification—not to mention his ruminations on existential phenomenology and ontology— this work often loses sight of how the chapter contributes to the broader movement of the book, which traces the process of disalienation from its initial misfires to its ultimate realization.[58] My discussion, in contrast, will redirect attention toward this aspect of the chapter so as to further elaborate upon how the book approaches the question of change. To do this, the following two sections will focus on Fanon's discussion of various responses to racial prejudice and alienation that are not circumscribed by the desire for whiteness.

The first response that Fanon considers is that of rationalism, a response that aims to "rationalize the world and show the white man he was mistaken."[59] Fanon turns to Jean-Paul Sartre's *Anti-Semite and Jew* [*Réflexions sur la question juive*] to elucidate this point because, despite the many differences between anti-Semitism and anti-Black racism, reason is often considered a tool in the critique of both forms of discrimination. Fanon isolates a particularly suggestive passage from the aforementioned book, in which Sartre claims that inside the Jew resides "a sort of impassioned imperialism of reason: for he wishes not only to convince others that he is right; his goal is to persuade them that there is an absolute and unconditioned value to rationalism. He feels himself to be a missionary of the universal; against the universality of the Catholic religion, from which he is excluded, he asserts the 'catholicity' of the rational, an instrument by which to attain to the truth and establish a spiritual bond among men."[60] What is remarkable about this passage and Fanon's choice to cite it is that it constitutes a rather precise translation of Hegel's conceptualization of the historical progression from the alienated universality of the Church to the absolutely rational universality of the State.[61] Like the State in its actuality, reason assumes an absolute quality as an end in itself, and, as in Hegel's dialectic of history, the individual, while appearing to be the rational wielder of instruments, is in fact the instrument of reason's cunningly imperial universalization.[62] For Fanon, there is a similar compulsion within *le Noir* to become rationalism's missionary, a servant to the latter's actualization, someone who opposes the racist universals of (white) Beauty and (white) Virtue with the universality of reason. Yet this transposition of Sartre's Hegelian portrayal of the Jew onto Fanon's theorization of *le Noir* is not without some conceptual dissonance. In earlier chapters of *Black Skin, White Masks*, Fanon presents these competing universals as forming an antinomical, Manichaean opposition, whereas in the Hegelian process from which Sartre is drawing, the opposition between Church and State, including their corresponding universals, is ultimately sublated in the form of a higher unity.[63]

Fanon nevertheless veers away from both Manichaean antinomies and Hegelian dialectics to present a different theorization of the rationalist mission that underscores its incapacity to contribute to disalienation. Although the goal of construing reason as universal is to reveal the irrationality of racial prejudice, Fanon notes that such efforts are easily undermined by the uncompromising persistence and rationalization of racist myths:

Everyone was in agreement with the notion: the Negro [*le nègre*] is a human being—i.e., his heart's on his left side, added those who were not too convinced. But on certain questions the white man remained uncompromising. Under no condition did he want any intimacy between the races, for we know [in the words of Jon Alfred Mjøen] that "crossings between widely different races can lower the physical and mental level. . . . Until we have a more definite knowledge of the effect of race-crossings we shall certainly avoid crossings between widely different races."[64]

This passage demonstrates how the pseudoscience of eugenics rationalizes the belief that romantic life should be segregated based on the racist myth that failing to do so would contribute to mental and physical devolution. Even when reasoned arguments force *le Blanc* to accept that *le nègre* is a human being, the white world preserves, on the basis of its own rationalizations, the same alienating racial hierarchy of inferiority and superiority that rationalism had sought to abolish. If the rationalist strategy religiously defends reason's capacity to overcome myth, Fanon points to an alternative, circular dialectic of Enlightenment in which reason turns on itself and becomes myth's instrument.[65]

Fanon subtly develops his account of this circular dialectic by revealing how even the forefather of European rationalism can become mythical: "It's in the name of tradition, the long, historical past and the blood ties with Pascal and Descartes, that the Jews are told: you will never belong here. Recently, one of these good French folks declared on a train where I was sitting: 'May the truly French values live on and the race will be safeguarded! . . . A united front against the foreigners (and turning to me) whoever they may be.'"[66] In this passage, Fanon shows how the author of that famed charter of universalism—which holds that all men, irrespective of their accidental properties, equally share the same faculty of reason— can become a symbol of white French particularity, a tradition that can be preserved and protected only by excluding (Jewish and Black) others. It follows that the reasoned defense of the universal equality of man on the basis of a shared attribute, be it of the mind (reason) or of the body (the position of the heart), is inadequate in the struggle against racism, for it will be met with mythic counterrationalizations that undermine the realization of a disalienated universal condition.[67] Gary Wilder helpfully describes this misfire as "the rationalist impasse . . . : to speak reason to race oftentimes confirms rather than challenges racial hierarchies."[68]

Once rationalism's limitations are exposed, *le Noir* turns to its logical opposite: "I had rationalized the world, and the world had rejected me in the name of color prejudice. Since there was no way we could agree on the basis of reason, I resorted to irrationality."[69] Throughout this section of the chapter, Fanon cites foundational texts of the *négritude* movement written by Césaire and Léopold Sédar Senghor, which contrast black rhythm, emotion, and poetry with white reason, intellect, and science. Whereas rationalism starts with a premise of commonality, of the universality of human reason, irrationalism begins with alterity, an oppositional assertion of black particularity and difference. "I finally made up my mind to shout my blackness," Fanon writes.[70] Upon making this decision, *le Noir* unapologetically affirms *négritude* and reclaims the disparaging title of *nègre*. The irrationalist position also advances a competing universalism, which I described previously as a quasi-pantheistic worldview. To convey what is at stake in the advancement of this worldview, Fanon borrows from the expressive language and poetic style of Césaire and Senghor:

Yes, we are (the *nègres*) backward, naïve, and free. For us the body is not in opposition to what you call the soul. We are in the world. And long live the bond between Man and the Earth! . . . I embrace the world! I am the world! The white man has never understood this magical substitution. The white man wants the world; he wants it for himself. He enslaves it. His relationship with the world is one of appropriation. . . . Between the world and me there was a relation of coexistence. I had rediscovered the primordial One.[71]

According to this passage, the irrationalist worldview opposes the Enlightenment tradition of construing man's relationship with nature as one of domination with an alternative and indeed prior, more fundamental relationship of mystical unity, to which *le nègre* retains privileged access.[72]

Irrationalism is predictably shown to be just as incapable of effectively challenging racial prejudice and alienation as rationalism. The introduction foreshadowed this conclusion when it claimed that the black soul, often celebrated as an alternative to white civilization, is itself a construction of white civilization, upon which that civilization posits its superiority. Fanon accordingly describes the sensation of being persecuted by something that he cannot not embrace: "Black magic, primitive mentality, animism and animal eroticism—all this surges toward me. All this typifies people who have not kept pace with the evolution of humanity. . . . I was long reluctant to commit myself. Then even the stars became aggressive. I had to choose. What am I saying? I had no choice."[73] A few pages later, Fanon echoes this same sentiment of being forcefully tied to blackness by white civilization: "I was haunted by a series of corrosive stereotypes: the Negro's sui generis smell . . . the Negro's sui generis good nature . . . the Negro's sui generis naiveté. I tried to escape without being seen, but the Whites fell on me and hamstrung me on the left leg."[74] Both of these passages show how irrationalism misfires in its response to racial prejudice and alienation insofar as it "accepts the split imposed by the Europeans," which is to say the Manichaean antinomy that renders "black" as equivalent to "inferior."[75] What appears to be an escape is actually a trap.

NÉGRITUDE: TARRYING WITH THE NEGATIVE

Fanon considers a third response to racial prejudice and alienation that draws from both the rationalist and the irrationalist position. It begins by "excavat[ing] black antiquity" in order to bring to light the historical existence of a black civilization and "learned black men."[76] The unearthing of an alternative history, buried by official history, refutes the myth that only white civilization is rational and therefore fully human: "The white man was wrong, I was not a primitive or a subhuman; I belonged to a race that had already been working silver and gold 2,000 years ago."[77] Unearthing this alternative history also refutes *négritude*'s account of its own "mystical past," which ultimately reproduces the myth that white civilization enjoys exclusive sovereignty over the realm of the rational.[78] As Fanon notes, it was Senghor who wrote that "emotion is Negro as reason is Greek."[79] Accordingly, the third response that Fanon explores entails not only challenging white narratives of history that dehumanize and inferiorize *le Noir* but also translating *négritude* out of its irrationalism so as to "claim . . . negritude intellectually as a concept."[80]

If Fanon ultimately offers a highly critical appraisal of those who dedicate themselves to excavating black antiquity, this occurs only after his spirited defense of the concept of *négritude*, that "last illusion," which Sartre "shattered" in his essay, *Black Orpheus*.[81] In Fanon's words: "I take this negritude and with tears in my eyes piece together the mechanism."[82] Before considering why Fanon would want to piece back together an illusory concept or mechanism, it is important to examine how exactly Sartre shattered it. According to Fanon, Sartre smashed *négritude* to pieces when he "proved to me that my reasoning was nothing but a phase in the dialectic."[83] Fanon then cites an extended passage from *Black Orpheus* that I include in abbreviated form below:

The Negro, as we have said, creates an anti-racist racism. He does not at all wish to dominate the world; he wishes the abolition of racial privileges wherever they are found; he affirms his solidarity with the oppressed of all colors. At a blow the subjective, existential, ethnic notion of *Negritude* "passes," as Hegel would say, into the objective, positive, exact notion of the *proletariat*. "For Césaire," says Senghor, "the 'White' symbolizes capital and the Negro, labor. . . . Among the black men of his race, it is the struggle of the world proletariat which he sings." This is easier to say than work out [*C'est facile à dire, moins facile à penser*]. And without doubt it is not by chance that the most ardent of apostles of Negritude are at the same time militant Marxists. But nevertheless the notion of race does not intersect [*ne se recoupe pas*] with the notion of class: the one is concrete and particular, the other is universal and abstract. . . . Negritude appears as the weak stage of a dialectical progression: the theoretical and practical affirmation of white supremacy is the thesis; the position of Negritude as antithetical value is the moment of negativity. But this negative moment is not sufficient in itself and the Blacks who employ it well know it; they know that it serves to pave the way for the synthesis or the realization of the human society without race. Thus Negritude is dedicated to its own destruction, it is transition and not result, a means and not the ultimate goal.[84]

For Sartre, *négritude* is a necessary but insufficient moment in the dialectical overcoming of racism. While the negativity of *négritude* sets in motion the process of disalienation, this negativity must ultimately negate itself and clear the way for the emergence of the positivity of a human society without race. Sartre's application of the Hegelian triad of affirmation / negation / negation-of-negation construes *négritude* as incomplete and transitory. Sartre also gives a Marxian twist to the Hegelian story by maintaining that *négritude* will pass into the notion of the proletariat and that this passage will constitute a dialectical progression from the subjectively particular and negative to the objectively universal and positive. This assertion is strange because it inverts the classic theorization of the proletariat as a *negatively* universal notion, and Sartre appears skeptical of the intelligibility of such a passage from race to class anyway. His assertion nonetheless has the effect of further weakening the role of *négritude* in the dialectical movement of history, for even its ultimate goal of a society without race appears to be merely a stage in the truly ultimate goal of a classless society.[85]

Many commentators have misread Fanon as criticizing Sartre's interpretation of *négritude* for its Hegelianism.[86] The truth is that Fanon faults Sartre not for being too Hegelian but for being *not Hegelian enough*. His response is to counter Sartre's schematic application of Hegel with a more rigorous translation:

We had appealed to a friend of the colored peoples, and this friend had found nothing better to do than demonstrate the relativity of their action. For once this friend, this born Hegelian, had forgotten that consciousness needs to get lost in the night of the absolute, the only condition for attaining self-consciousness. To counter rationalism he recalled the negative side, but he forgot that this negativity draws its value from a quasi-substantial absoluity [*d'une absoluité quasi substantielle*].[87]

It is tempting to read this passage as an oblique allusion to Hegel's critique of Friedrich Schelling and the latter's conceptualization of the Absolute. After all, in the preface to the *Phenomenology of Spirit*, Hegel compares Schelling's Absolute to "the night in which, as the saying goes, all cows are black."[88] However, the absolute in question is not the indifferent Absolute that drowns all particularity in the dark water of its universal container. Fanon is instead recalling the moment in the Hegelian dialectic of self-consciousness when consciousness withdraws into the absolute night of the pure "I," into "the night in which 'I' = 'I,' a night which no longer distinguishes or knows any-thing outside of it."[89] The absolute night of the pure "I" therefore represents not an indifferent whole but rather a singular subtraction from the whole, not a neutral container that includes all particularity but rather an absolute self-relating negativity.[90]

While it is true that the darkness of negativity eventually passes dialec-tically into the light of self-consciousness, Sartre's application of this dia-lectical movement to *négritude* effectively short circuits the process insofar as it relativizes a negativity that must be affirmed as absolute if, as Hegel contends, it is to push past "what circumscribes it" and "attain an existence of its own and a separate freedom."[91] In the words of Fredric Jameson, when "you anticipate resolution, you empty [contradiction] of all its negativity and generate the impression of a rigged ballot, a put-up job, a sham conflict whose outcome has already carefully been arranged in advance."[92] Fanon thus suggests that a true friend of the "colored peoples," if he were a true Hegelian, would recognize that a gesture like Sartre's constitutes the shat-tering of a *necessary* illusion, the undermining of a liberating fiction that engenders dialectical movement. As Fanon concisely states, "I *needed* not to know [*j'avais besoin* d'ignorer]."[93]

Fanon then offers an alternative account of *négritude* that attempts to reconstruct its shattered absoluity: "In terms of consciousness, black con-sciousness claims to be an absolute density, full of itself, a stage preexistent to any opening, to any abolition of the self by desire. . . . I needed to lose myself totally in negritude. . . . Black consciousness is immanent in itself. I am not a potentiality of something; I am fully what I am. I do not have to look for the universal. . . . My black consciousness does not claim to be a loss. It *is*. It merges with itself."[94] In this passage, *négritude* represents the moment when black consciousness withdraws into itself and merges with itself, affirming that "I" = "I," that "I am fully what I am." It does not have to seek out the universal because it is itself already (abstractly) universal by virtue of its abstraction from all determinations. The absolute negativity of such an affirmation, Fanon implies, is what allows black consciousness to break free from what circumscribes it and push forward the process of disalienation.

Fanon takes issue not only with Sartre's relativization of *négritude*'s absolute negativity but also with his deterministic interpretation of the movement.[95] This second defect of Sartre's argument is readily apparent in the following passage from *Black Orpheus*, which Fanon also includes in *Black Skin, White Masks*:

Will the source of Poetry silence itself? Or indeed will the great black river, despite all, color the sea into which it flows? No matter; to each epoch its poetry, for each epoch the circumstances of history elect a nation, a race, a class, to seize again the torch, by creating situations which can express or surpass themselves only through Poetry. At times the poetic élan coincides with the revolutionary élan and at times they diverge. Let us salute today the historic chance which will permit the Blacks to "raise the great Negro shout with a force that will shake the foundations of the world (Césaire)."[96]

According to Sartre, *le nègre* does not create meaning through poetry, since the meaning of poetry is already determined by history. "It is not as the wretched *nègre*," Fanon writes, "that I fashion a torch to set the world alight; the torch was already there, waiting for this historic chance."[97] This interpretation of *négritude* resonates with Hegel's discussion of the "cunning of reason," which, as previously discussed, inverts the Enlightenment notion of autonomous individuals using their faculty of reason, maintaining instead that reason uses the individual in the process of its own self-actualization.[98] Fanon nonetheless argues that Sartre once again falters not because he is too Hegelian but because he is not quite Hegelian enough. In his view, Sartre "should have opposed the unforeseeable to historical destiny. . . .

The dialectic that introduces necessity as a support for my freedom expels me from myself. It shatters my impulsive position."[99] The withdrawal of consciousness into the absolute night of the pure "I" destroys all determinations. In Hegel's analysis of religion, this moment represents the death of God, the liberation of the Subject from the certainty of a transcendent Substance cunningly determining its destiny.[100] Sartre's grounding of freedom in historical destiny, by contrast, expels the "I" from the "I," prematurely returning the Subject to its cunning substantial determination and therefore inhibiting the further dialectical movement of self-consciousness. Sartre thus disproves his own deterministic interpretation of *négritude* by grinding the dialectical process to a halt the moment he announces its inevitable movement forward.

Does *négritude*'s affirmation that it is not a potentiality of something else effectively accomplish the same thing and inhibit further dialectical movement? Fanon assures his readers that *négritude* can posit itself as absolute and at the same time "take into consideration the historical process."[101] He elaborates on this point by referring to a poem written by the Haitian Marxist Jacques Roumain. While the voice of the poem speaks to Africa of an absolute withdrawal into black particularity ("I want to be of your race alone"), the excerpt cited in *Black Skin, White Masks* concludes with the following universalist message: "We proclaim the unity of suffering / And revolt / Of all the peoples over the face of the earth / And we mix the mortar of the age of brotherhood / In the dust of idols."[102] Roumain's poem does a lot of work for Fanon's translation of Hegelian dialectics. The negativity of withdrawal is not shown to be a weak stage of relative worth that will ultimately be surpassed. It is construed, rather, as the absolute and necessary moment of dialectical negation, the particular force that joins other struggles to produce a new universal out of the ground-up materials of the past and the present.[103] The death of a divine and cunning Substance that immediately determined the Whole, be it God or an aggregate of idols, is what makes possible, as in the Christian fable, the resurrection of Substance in the form of a community of believers, a brotherhood.[104]

This dialectical movement from the particular to the universal, the negative to the positive, the internal to the external, the "I" to the "We," is a process with its own temporality. When Fanon returns to the issue of *négritude* in the sixth chapter of *Black Skin, White Masks*, he explains that the dialectical movement of disalienation cannot be rushed, lest its transformative power be attenuated. Alluding to Césaire's poem, *Notebook of a Return to the Native Land*, Fanon writes:

> One day he said: "My negritude is neither a tower . . ." And then they came to Hellenize him, to Orpheusize him . . . this black man who is seeking the universal. Seeking the universal! But in June 1950 the hotels in Paris refused to take in black travelers. . . . The black man is universalizing himself, but at the lycée Saint-Louis in Paris, they threw one out: had the cheek to read Engels. . . . How come I have barely opened my eyes they had blindfolded, and they already want to drown me in the universal? And what about the others? Those "who have no mouth," those "who have no voice." I need to lose myself in my negritude and see the ashes, the segregation, the repression, the rapes, the discrimination, and the boycotts. We need to touch with our finger all the wounds that score our black livery.[105]

This passage can be helpfully read alongside popular debates surrounding the Black Lives Matter movement, which became a national movement in the summer of 2014 in response to the widespread killing of black men and women by police and armed vigilantes across the United States.[106] Just as a deeply confused public responded to the viral tweet #BlackLivesMatter with the counter-tweet #AllLivesMatter, Sartre misses the point when he attempts to drown the particular struggle of *négritude* in the universal. The affirmation of certain particulars over others is motivated by their constitutive exclusion from a given articulation of the universal. As it is presently articulated, the abstract universal notion of "all lives" does not yet include "black lives," just as the abstract universal notion of the "human," Fanon tells us, does not yet include the dehumanized and voiceless *nègre*. Black Lives Matter and *négritude* militate against this exclusion; both movements share in common the aspiration of translating the universal, of rearticulating its contours so that it can become concrete, a "living formulation."[107]

What Sartre and those who tweet #AllLivesMatter are effectively doing is returning the particular to a universal that has not yet been transformed, which consequently perpetuates its exclusionary articulation.[108] Although the particular struggle of *négritude* may lead to the concrete universality of Roumain's brotherhood, this process must follow its own dialectical rhythm that *tarries with the negative* before a new formation can come into being. Remember Hegel on this point: "Spirit is this power only by looking the negative in the face, and tarrying with it. This tarrying with the negative is the magical power that converts it into being."[109] Fanon gives a spatial account of this prolonged rhythm with the negative when he partially redeems Sartre's allusion to Orpheus, the Greek hero who descends into the underworld to save Eurydice, and states that "Césaire *went down*. He agreed to see what was happening at the very bottom, and now he can come back up. He is ripe for the dawn."[110] The imagery here recalls that crucial passage in the introduction on the zone of nonbeing. According to Fanon, Césaire shows how *le Noir* might take advantage of descending into such a veritable hell, how this descent can turn into its opposite, an authentic upsurgence. The dialectical nature of this movement is now readily apparent, whereas its initial presentation invited divergent readings. What this movement shows is that *négritude* is not another misfire, even if at times it falls for the trap of irrationalism. It is, on the contrary, a fundamental moment in the process of disalienation, which is likewise theorized in unmistakably dialectical terms throughout the fifth and sixth chapters of *Black Skin, White Masks*.

THE STRUGGLE FOR RECOGNITION AND THE TASK OF BECOMING ACTIONAL

Fanon's analysis of *négritude* leaves the reader pondering the following questions: How does a descent into particularity change direction and rise to the height of universal brotherhood? How does a withdrawal into the self pass into self-consciousness? Fanon develops his response to these questions in a section of the seventh chapter titled "The Black Man and Hegel."[111] Building upon his earlier discussion of self-relating negativity, Fanon states that "the only way to break this vicious circle that refers me back to myself is to restore to the other his human reality, different from his natural reality, by way of mediation and recognition. The other, however, must perform a similar operation."[112] With this assertion, Fanon suggests that *le Noir* can overcome the moment in which "I" = "I" and push forward the dialectical process of disalienation by forming a relationship of mutual recognition with the other. But, as we know from Hegel, before this kind of relationship can be formed there must be a life-and-death struggle in which both sides risk their natural life for the higher, human ideal of "a world of reciprocal recognitions."[113] It appears as though *le Noir* must enter into a similar struggle. As if to verify that this is the case, Fanon goes on to maintain that black Americans are already engaged in a struggle of this kind. "In the United States," Fanon writes, "the black man fights and is fought against."[114] Sampling the title of a novel by Richard Wright, Fanon evocatively refers to "twelve million black voices" that "scream against the curtain of the sky."[115] He then concludes his brief analysis of the American conjuncture with a prophetic vision: "On the battlefield, marked out by the scores of Negroes hanged by their testicles, a monument is slowly rising that promises to be grandiose. And at the top of this monument I can already see a white man and a black man *hand in hand*."[116] This image of a monument commemorating reciprocal recognition won on the battlefield points to one way in which Fanon conceptualizes the realization of self-consciousness and universal brotherhood.

But it would seem that this path toward disalienation is open only to the black American, whereas, for the black Frenchman, it is "too late."[117] Fanon arrives at this conclusion through his analysis of the disjuncture between Hegel's conceptualization of lordship and bondage and the historical reality of slavery in the French colonial context. Fanon summarizes this disjuncture in an important and often cited footnote: "We hope we have shown that the master here is basically different from the one described by Hegel. For Hegel there is reciprocity; here the master scorns the consciousness of the slave. What he wants from the slave is not recognition but work. Likewise, the slave here can in no way be equated with the slave who loses himself in the object and finds the source of his liberation in his work. The black slave wants to be like the master."[118] Fanon thus challenges the Hegelian idea that the master was ever really concerned with gaining recognition from the other, asserting that what he really wanted all along was the other's labor. This very compelling argument is followed by a rather dubious one. Fanon takes issue with Hegel's notion that the slave negates the negation of his autonomy through his own labor, maintaining instead that the slave is too concerned with being like the master to fight for his own freedom. This leads Fanon to conclude that the abolition of slavery, at least in the French colonial context, was the master's initiative, that "historically, the black man, steeped in the inessentiality of servitude, was set free by the master. He did not fight for his freedom."[119]

As Anthony Bogues has rightly pointed out, Fanon's summation of the abolition of slavery is strange and historically inaccurate.[120] It ultimately serves as a foil for his highly critical assessment of the contemporary *Noir*, who remains too preoccupied striving to be like the white other to achieve liberation. "From time to time he fights for liberty and justice," Fanon concedes, "but it's always for a white liberty and a white justice, in other words, for values secreted by his masters."[121] From this perspective, the dialectical struggle for recognition is not an option for the black Frenchman. He remains in a now familiar deadlock, either cloistered in his own blackness or forced to serve white universalist values that do not actually extend to him. To conceive of an escape from this impasse, Fanon remarkably turns to Nietzsche for help:

> We said in our introduction that man was a *yes*. We shall never stop repeating it. Yes to life. Yes to love. Yes to generosity. But man is also a *no*. No to man's contempt. No to the indignity of man. To the exploitation of man. To the massacre of what is most human in man: freedom. Man's behavior is not only reactional [*réactionnel*]. And there is always resentment in *reaction*. Nietzsche had already said it in *The Will to Power*. To induce man to be *actional* [*actionnel*], by maintaining in his circularity respect for the fundamental values that make a world human, that is the task of utmost urgency for he who, after careful reflection, prepares to act.[122]

As in the introduction, Fanon posits that man is a "yes" but also a "no," which has the effect of blurring the conceptual boundaries between traditionally antithetical schools of thought (Nietzschean affirmation versus Hegelian-Marxian negation). Despite their coexistence in man, the emphasis is once again placed on what differentiates these positions instead of what unites them. Indeed, Fanon's call to induce man to be actional departs from and suggests an alternative to the dialectical struggle for recognition.[123] In his analysis of the United States, the actions of black Americans are depicted as a scream *against* the curtain of the sky, a collective "no" to limiting the boundless, an overcoming of that which shackles freedom. According to Fanon, this kind of action is no longer possible for the black Frenchman; it is too late, so it would seem that the urgent task is to pursue another kind of action, an actional action that is yes-saying and nondialectical.[124]

The effect of this argument is to displace the latent tension of the text and gesture toward a different kind of relationship between dialectical and nondialectical thinking insofar as their divergent theorizations of disalienating action correspond—at this moment—to divergent historical conjunctures. There appear to be at least two paths to disalienation, a bifurcation in the road after the moment of self-relating negativity, with one path leading to the Hegelian struggle for recognition and another to the Nietzschean task of becoming actional. The tension is only partially displaced, however, as it can still be felt in the previously cited passage when Fanon implicitly calls for a transvaluation of all values. This would amount to a new way of evaluating, a mode of valuation that would say "yes" to life, love, generosity, and freedom. While these values are not Nietzsche's, Fanon is clearly drawing from the author of *The Will to Power* to reflect upon how values might be created through self-affirmation rather than through the self's struggle with the other. In this way, he invites the reader to imagine a subterranean alternative to the translation of previously exclusionary values once secreted by white masters. Instead of converting their abstractly universal notions into concrete, living formulations, Fanon hints at the possibility of articulating an entirely new set of universal values from the void of nonbeing. It is therefore *not* too late for the black Frenchman; it is too late for the values of the past, too late, even, for their dialectical overcoming. But to make this argument Fanon draws from the past by translating Nietzsche. The content of the argument is therefore in tension not only with other formulations in *Black Skin, White Masks* but also with the practice of theorization that produces it. This tension between Fanon's theoretical practice and its product is reminiscent of a performative contradiction, a speech act that undermines its own assertion, and it is symptomatic of the text's generally conflicted stance on the question of change, especially with respect to the role of the past in the present realization of a disalienated future.

THE POETRY OF SOCIAL REVOLUTION

The tension between Fanon's theoretical practice and its propositional content carries over into the conclusion of *Black Skin, White Masks*. It can be felt from the very start in Fanon's choice to use the following passage from Marx's *The Eighteenth Brumaire of Louis Bonaparte* as an epigraph:

The social revolution cannot draw its poetry from the past, but only from the future. It cannot begin with itself before it has stripped itself of all its superstitions concerning the past. Earlier revolutions relied on memories out of world history in order to drug themselves against their own content. In order to find their own content, the revolutions of the nineteenth century have to let the dead bury the dead. Before, the expression exceeded the content; now the content exceeds the expression.[125]

By approvingly citing this passage, Fanon becomes entangled yet again in a kind of performative contradiction. He draws upon Marx's poetic analysis of a past social revolution to imply—and ultimately argue—that today's social revolution should not draw its poetry from the past. He turns to a memory from world history to warn against relying on such memories. The tension inherent in this kind of maneuver ought to be read as further evidence of a broader conceptual dilemma in the text, which revolves around the influence of the past or lack thereof in the revolutionary construction of a future world.[126]

Marx offers his own, unambiguously dialectical response to this dilemma in *The Eighteenth Brumaire*: "Men make their own history, but they do not make it just as they please; they do not make it under circumstances chosen by themselves, but under circumstances directly encountered, given and transmitted from the past. The tradition of all the dead generations weighs like a nightmare on the brain of the living."[127] Although the dead may not be of use when searching for the content of social revolution in the nineteenth century, Marx maintains that their determining influence is inescapable. Fanon says something similar when he asserts that "the black man, however sincere, is a slave to the past."[128] Yet Fanon does not go on to explore the dialectical implications of this statement; he does not reflect on how *le Noir* might become free precisely by overcoming the historical conditions that determine existence. Instead, he takes a more extreme position by advancing the logically contrary view just a few paragraphs later: "I am not a slave to the slavery that dehumanized my ancestors."[129] Many of the claims put forward in the remaining pages of *Black Skin, White Masks* follow suit and deviate significantly from Marx's dialectical understanding of history to argue that the past does not have the determining power with which it is commonly invested.

Fanon turns to Sartre while pursuing this line of argument and enters into an explicit dialogue with the latter's reflections on time and freedom.[130] He writes that the past *"gives form* to the individual" when inauthentically apprehended, whereas an authentic apprehension of the past reveals that

"I can also revise the past, prize it or condemn it, depending on what I choose."[131] This "also" is not dialectical but disjunctive. It signals the difference between authenticity and inauthenticity, between the recognition of one's facticity and the bad faith denial of individual freedom.[132] This distinction leads Fanon to take up the existentialist doctrine that individuals are necessarily free, which weakens, if not outright refutes, any notion of the past as dialectically conditioning one's actions in the present. Conjuring Épithalos, the explosive protagonist of *Parallel Hands*, Fanon advances a series of declarations with subtly antidialectical implications: "The density of History determines none of my acts. I am my own foundation. And it is by going beyond the historical and instrumental given that I initiate my cycle of freedom [*Et c'est en dépassant la donnée historique, instrumentale, que j'introduis le cycle de ma liberté*]."[133] This *dépassement* of the historical given does not represent a dialectical overcoming but an overcoming of dialectics, an undetermined act of freedom that lets the dead bury the dead by breaking with the density of History. Fanon's experimentation with this kind of thinking makes his selective citation of Marx all the more complicated. It is as though he is reading Marx against Marx, citing Marx to oppose him. It is tempting to see in this contradictory theoretical practice a dialectical procedure, an act of translating Marx into a new version of himself, but if this is the case, then Fanon's practice is once again at odds with its own propositional content, which attempts to name a cycle of freedom that is free from dialectical determination and from translating the poetry of the past.

Fanon also reads this translated Marx against those who drug themselves with history while attempting to achieve disalienation. Without naming names, it becomes clear that Fanon is referring to the *négritude* movement and its founders: "The discovery that a black civilization existed in the fifteenth century does not earn me a certificate of humanity. Whether you like it or not, the past can in no way be my guide in the actual state of things."[134] Fanon goes on to propose a different approach to time that nuances his critique of *négritude*: "The problem considered here is located in temporality. Disalienation will be for those Whites and Blacks who have refused to let themselves be locked in the substantialized Tower of the Past."[135] By alluding to a previously cited passage from Césaire's *Notebook*, "my negritude is *not* a tower . . ," Fanon clarifies the target of his critique, which does not encompass the entire *négritude* movement but rather certain aspects of it—from its irrationalism to its obsession with the past—that side-track the present struggle for a disalienated future.[136]

The conclusion develops this critique with another series of declarations united in their call for total rupture. It is impossible not to hear in their articulation the voice of the subterranean Fanon: "I am not a prisoner of History. I must not look for the meaning of my destiny in that direction. I must constantly remind myself that the real *leap* consists of introducing invention into existence. In the world I am heading for, I am endlessly creating myself."[137] The leap that is described here is not the kind that occurs when a given phenomenon is abolished and maintained in such a way that it "leaps" into a qualitatively new state. Instead of a dialectical leap, what is at stake is a leap that introduces into existence something that preserves nothing of the past, something that is entirely new, something that is termed "invention."[138] To introduce invention into existence is to break out of the prison of History and the tower of the Past and discover a completely different world instead of restructuring the present one. It is to initiate a cycle of freedom that consists of endless and undetermined acts of self-creation.

Fanon concludes *Black Skin, White Masks* with one final reflection on this other world and the kind of change that must occur for such a world to exist:

The black man is not. No more than the white man. Both have to move aside [*s'écarter*] the inhuman voices of their respective ancestors so that an authentic communication can be born. Before embarking on a positive voice, freedom needs to make an effort at disalienation. At the start of his existence, a man is always congested, drowned in contingency. The misfortune of man is that he was once a child. It is through an effort of recovering the self [*reprise sur soi*] and of renunciation [*dépouillement*], through a permanent tension of his freedom, that man can create the ideal conditions of existence for a human world. Inferiority? Superiority? Why not simply try to find the other, feel the other, discover each other? Was my freedom not given to me to build the world of the *You*?[139]

This is how Fanon imagines the creation of a human world—a world free from inferiority and superiority complexes, free from narcissistic particularisms and their competing universalisms, free from alienation and prejudice, free from the Manichaean relations and inhuman voices of the past. But he also imagines a world free to birth a new form of communication and create a positive voice, free to encounter, feel, and discover the other, free to form a genuine relationship with all others not as other but as You. When theorizing what kind of transformation would be needed to introduce this world into existence, Fanon advances a series of terms and images with a decidedly nondialectical resonance. Blacks and whites are called upon to move aside or depart from ("*s'écarter*") the voices of their ancestors that carry the weight of past cultures and civilizations and are too bound up with the morbid universe of colonial inhumanity to be preserved. Fanon relatedly returns to an idea that he attributes to Nietzsche in the introduction, that man's misfortune is that he was once a child.[140] This is another way of saying that man's misfortune is his own past, as well as the past that preceded him but that he inherited at the start of his existence, when he was first thrown into the world. He is from the beginning congested with this past, so disalienation entails decongestion, a clearing away of inheritance, its expulsion from the self. Fanon additionally calls for an effort of "*dépouillement*," which could be translated as "renunciation" (Philcox's choice), but the term also carries with it the notion of removal, including the removal or shedding of skin. This shedding is at the same time an effort to recover the self, not in the sense of recovering an old self but in the sense of beginning again with a new self, a clean slate. According to Fanon, the ideal conditions for a human world can be created from this tabula rasa.

The previously cited passage, like most of the passages that I have selected from the conclusion, cannot be easily reconciled with the text's predominantly dialectical account of disalienation. And yet, it is worth reflecting upon how Fanon's description of the world of the You sounds somewhat like a world of reciprocal recognition. It is as though, by the end of the book, *le Noir* finally arrives at the moment of Hegelian self-consciousness, though this occurs through a very different, Nietzschean path of actional action and affirmative self-creation. If this is the case, then the reader is encountering another example of how *Black Skin, White Masks* blurs the conceptual boundaries between traditionally antithetical schools of thought, which has the effect of partially displacing the latent tension in the text's argument. To fully appreciate this latter point, it is worth reviewing the overarching movement of the book. Despite its many twists and turns, interludes and detours, *Black Skin, White Masks* contains a basic "progressive infrastructure" of dialectical movement that passes from *le Noir*'s efforts to become white to the search for the meaning of black identity to the assumption of the universalism inherent in the human condition.[141] There are many misfires along the way, from cultural and romantic assimilationism to combatting racial prejudice with rationalism, irrationalism, and what could be described as either folkloric traditionalism or black antiquarianism. There are also instances of real transformation, from the psychoanalytic treatment that enables *le Noir* to no longer pursue hallucinatory whitening to the *négritude* movement that affirms the absolute of self-relating negativity to the struggle for recognition and the task of becoming actional that both lead to a new relationship of reciprocity with the other. When the book is read in this way, it appears as though there is a nondialectical moment located within the broader dialectical process of disalienation, a temporary suspension of dialectical movement due to the historical specificity of the French colonial context. The book's two modes of thinking about change, from this vantage point, coexist and even mutually enrich each other.

Missing from this account of *Black Skin, White Masks*, however, are all the passages that contribute to theorizing disalienation otherwise, that develop a subterranean account of change that resists being incorporated into a broader dialectical narrative and points instead toward a genuine alternative to dialectics. These passages generate a different kind of relationship between the book's distinct modes of thought, a relationship of latent and unresolved tension that intensifies and takes on a more conflictual modality as the book draws to a close. This relationship gains expression in the friction and discontinuity between a number of important concepts and ideas that are developed throughout the pages of *Black Skin, White Masks*, including, among other possible examples, contradiction and antinomy; negation and affirmation; restructuration and invention; the new as latent in the old and the new as an authentic beginning; the transformative process of overcoming and the ruptural event of complete lysis; the movement of concrete universality and the articulation of universal values from the void; the making of history under conditions inherited from the past and the clearing away of the past in order to discover an entirely new world.

Some readers may find the lack of resolution between these concepts and ideas to be rather dissatisfying. They may be tempted, as others have been before them, to systematize the text's account of disalienation by downplaying its inconsistencies or by neatly folding its discontinuities into the main thrust of the argument. I have sought to offer a different approach to reading Fanon, one that attends to the inconsistencies and discontinuities of his first book not to undermine his reputation as a great thinker but rather to confirm it, to underscore the incredible richness and complexity of his theoretical practice as well as the persistent and fascinating internal division traversing his work. My approach also aims to expose Fanon to new inquiries. Recall his "final prayer" at the very end of *Black Skin, White Masks*: "O my body, always make me a man who questions!"[142] Fanon's closing words are an opening, an appeal to his body that he be made to continue, after a long study, to question. As Fred Moten suggestively puts it, "Fanon's text is still open and it still opens."[143] This means, to borrow from Stuart Hall, that readers should not lose sight of "the unresolved arguments and the incomplete oscillations which make *Black Skin, White Masks* fundamentally an *open text*, and hence a text we are obliged to go on working *on*, working *with*."[144] It is in this spirit that I have focused on the text's distinct approaches to the problem of change instead of offering yet another commentary that willfully ignores or acrobatically resolves every conflictual statement and unexpected image in an anxious, anti-Fanonian impulse to no longer question.

Chapter Three

WRITINGS ON THE ALGERIAN REVOLUTION

RACISM, CULTURE, AND FOUNDATIONAL EXCLUSION

For three days in September 1956, intellectuals from around the world met in the Descartes lecture hall of the Sorbonne as part of the first International Congress of Black Writers and Artists. On this historic occasion, Fanon found himself in the same room with some of the most prominent cultural and political figures of Africa and the African diaspora. As part of the Martinican delegation, he was joined by Aimé Césaire, Édouard Glissant, and Louis T. Achille. Other major participants included the Senegalese cofounder of the *négritude* movement Léopold Sédar Senghor, the Malagasy poet and politician Jacques Rabemananjara, the Haitian writer and activist Jacques Stephen Alexis, the Brazilian avant-garde novelist Mário de Andrade, and the American author Richard Wright. After the opening remarks on the first day, a number of messages for the congress were read aloud from invited speakers who could not attend the event (e.g., George Padmore, W. E. B. Du Bois) as well as from writers and artists who wished to express their solidarity with the congress proceedings (e.g., Claude Lévi-Strauss, Michel Leiris, Pablo Picasso).[1]

One message from the latter group must have been particularly meaningful for Fanon. Signed by Jean Sénac, Henri Krea, and Kateb Yacine, the message was written on behalf of numerous cultural producers in Algeria and sought to establish a connection between the political spirit of the congress and the ongoing armed struggle for Algerian independence.[2] Although Fanon had been invited to the congress as a representative of Martinique, he was living and working in Algeria at the time and had already made contact with the Algerian National Liberation Front (Front de Libération Nationale or FLN). Just four months later, in January 1957, he would be forced into exile after resigning from his post at the Blida-Joinville Psychiatric Hospital to protest colonialism's "systematized de-humanization" of the Algerian people.[3] He would relocate to Tunisia where he would write for the FLN newspaper, *El Moudjahid*, while continuing to practice medicine in Tunis. He would also travel around Africa as a spokesperson for the Algerian Revolution and for international solidarity against colonial domination.

The congress in Paris thus took place during a transitional moment in Fanon's life, when his focus was steadily shifting from Martinique to Algeria, from the French Caribbean to North Africa, and from the transformational process of disalienation to the violent struggle for decolonization.[4] Yet throughout this transition Fanon remained the deeply divided thinker who wrote *Parallel Hands* and *Black Skin, White Masks*, split between an explicitly declared and developed project of dialectical analysis and a more implicit, subterranean current of nondialectical and sometimes antidialectical thought. This chapter will reflect upon the continuity of Fanon's internal division while also exploring how it acquires new dimensions as he directs his gaze toward a new set of historical circumstances.

Fanon's paper for the congress, titled "Racism and Culture," is perhaps the paradigmatic text of this transitional moment. It returns to a number of major themes from *Black Skin, White Masks* to develop them in a direction that anticipates subsequent writings on the Algerian Revolution. Although the Algerian Revolution is never mentioned by name, its influence is pivotal, so much so that it arguably functions as the absent center around which the entire paper circulates. In the broadest terms, "Racism and Culture" charts a series of transformations that occur in the colony at the level of culture from the early days of colonization to the full achievement of independence. Fanon conceptualizes these transformations as occurring in and through a dialectical process that contains three moments: "There is first affirmed the existence of human groups having no culture; then of a hierarchy of cultures; and finally, the notion of cultural relativity. From overall negation to singular and specific recognition. It is precisely this fragmented and bloody history that we must sketch on the level of cultural anthropology."[5] As this passage implies, "Racism and Culture" is loosely organized around a modified Hegelian dialectic of self-consciousness. To arrive at the moment of reciprocal recognition, colonized peoples must pass through a bloody life-and-death struggle that, among other accomplishments, negates the negation of their cultural existence.[6]

Notwithstanding this Hegelian framework, the paper also translates major ideas and categories of Marxist thought to advance some of Fanon's most explicitly materialist arguments to date. This is clearly evinced in his unwavering rejection of the notion that racism is "a psychological flaw" or an aberration of the individual psyche.[7] He argues, on the contrary, that racism is a "cultural element" that fits "into a well-defined system," "one element of a vaster whole: that of the systematized oppression of a people."[8] The colonial system that Fanon has in mind materially exploits and inferiorizes the native population, so racism, rather than the deviation of a few bad apples, is the system's logically consistent cultural expression. The dialectical interpenetration of material exploitation and racism leads Fanon to conclude that "the racist in a culture with racism is therefore normal. He has achieved a perfect harmony of economic relations and ideology."[9] This is not to say that racism is merely an epiphenomenal reflection of the material conditions of colonization. While expressing material conditions in the cultural realm, racism also reproduces these conditions by providing a justification for them, by functioning as "the emotional, affective, sometimes intellectual explanation of this inferiorization." Careful to distance himself from mechanical materialism, Fanon adds: "The idea that one forms of man, to be sure, is never totally dependent on economic relations."[10] Culture is accordingly theorized as a relatively autonomous realm of the societal whole that maintains a relationship of mutual dependence with all other realms of that same whole. As a consequence of this understanding of culture, Fanon is able to account for the emergence of contradictions within the system, such as the formation of anti-racist attitudes and practices within a thoroughly racist society.

Before addressing these contradictions, however, Fanon delves into the first moment of his dialectical analysis, which corresponds to the early days of the violent historical process known as colonization:

The social panorama is destructured; values are flaunted, crushed, emptied. . . . In their stead a new system of values is imposed, not proposed but affirmed, by the heavy weight of cannons and sabers. The setting up of the colonial system does not of itself bring about the death of the native culture. Historic observation reveals, on the contrary, that the aim sought is rather a continued agony than a total disappearance of the pre-existing culture. This culture, once living and open to the future, becomes closed, fixed in the colonial status, caught in the yoke of oppression.[11]

The above passage clarifies Fanon's reference to an "overall negation" of native culture, which is not to be conflated with its total disappearance. The phrase refers, instead, to a process of "deculturation," whereby precolonial traditions and ways of being are abolished and maintained in a state of fixed agony, an immobile condition that Fanon terms "cultural mummification."[12] The imposition of acculturation accompanies deculturation, as new values are brought over from the metropole and imposed on the native population with the threat and often use of force.

During this initial phase of colonization, racism is blatant and simplistic and grounded in pseudoscientific claims. It nonetheless remains more open and fluid than the rigidified culture of the native population and endures modifications throughout the course of colonial history. "Racism has not managed to harden," Fanon writes. "It has had to renew itself, to adapt itself, to change its appearance. It has had to undergo the fate of the cultural whole that informed it."[13] To explain what necessitates these changes, Fanon turns once again to some basic categories of Marxist thought:

The evolution of techniques of production, the industrialization, limited though it is, of the subjugated countries, the increasingly necessary existence of collaborators, impose a new attitude upon the occupant. The complexity of the means of production, the evolution of economic relations inevitably involving the evolution of ideologies, unbalance the system. Vulgar racism in its biological form corresponds to the period of crude exploitation of man's arms and legs. The perfecting of the means of production inevitably brings about the camouflage of the techniques by which man is exploited, hence of the forms of racism.[14]

Roughly describing the transition from a feudal to a semifeudal or proto-capitalist mode of production under colonial rule, Fanon notes that this material transformation creates an imbalance between the colony's base and its superstructure. An outmoded ideology becomes a fetter on the new economy, occasioning racism's translation, the overcoming of its limits, so as to create a subtler, camouflaged form of racist culture that more adequately corresponds to the new material reality. At this moment in the dialectical process, the overall denial of the existence of native culture passes into the positing of a cultural hierarchy that construes the colonizer's culture as superior to all others.

According to Fanon, the material development of the colony also proletarianizes the native, who acquires new skills and new forms of knowledge as a result of this process. Yet racial prejudice stubbornly persists throughout these changes. The colonizer continues to treat the native as inferior, even after the native successfully adapts to modern labor conditions. In Fanon's words: "Developing his technical knowledge in contact with more and more perfected machines, entering into the dynamic circuit of industrial production, meeting men from remote regions in the framework of the concentration of capital, that is to say, on the job, discovering the assembly line, the team, production 'time,' in other words yield per hour, the oppressed is shocked to find that he continues to be the object of racism and contempt."[15] This shock marks the beginning of a radical transformation in consciousness. As a result of proletarianization, the native comes to the infuriating realization that no amount of acculturation, not even the mastery of the colonizer's techniques and knowledge of production, will be sufficient in dismantling colonial racism. In this way, Fanon taps into the same kind of dialectical reasoning that led the writers of *The Communist Manifesto* to assert that the bourgeoisie produces its own gravediggers.[16] "Racism and Culture" likewise reveals how the contradictory material development of the colony puts the proletarianized native in a position to reject the legitimacy of the colonizer's legitimating ideology.

The colony's material development and the obstinance of its racist cultural hierarchy propel the native population to enter a new phase of the dialectical process, a "passion-charged, irrational, groundless phase" that develops its own cultural hierarchy through a return to and celebration of precolonial tradition.[17] For Fanon, this return is irrational and groundless because native culture, as a result of its mummification, is even more outmoded with respect to contemporary historical conditions than the vulgar racism of the early colonizers. Fanon explains: "This falling back on archaic positions having no relation to technical development is paradoxical. The institutions thus valorized no longer correspond to the elaborate methods of action already mastered. The culture put into capsules, which has vegetated since the foreign domination, is revalorized. It is not reconceived, grasped anew, dynamized from within. It is shouted."[18] The reader will notice in this passage certain recurrent themes central to *Black Skin, White Masks*. As discussed in the previous chapter, Fanon identifies a number of inadequate approaches to combatting racial prejudice and alienation, including efforts to oppose European rationalism with irrationalism and Eurocentric accounts of history with the recovery of black antiquity.[19] Instead of rehearsing this argument in abbreviated form, "Racism and Culture" combines the two approaches into one, underscoring the irrationality of valorizing a mummified culture of the past in lieu of creating a new version of that culture, a renewed culture that would correspond with the colony's new material conditions. Fanon thus alludes to a practice of translation that is not yet available to the native, but, as in *Black Skin, White Masks*, he suggests that such a practice represents an alternative to the opposition between either assimilationism or traditionalism, meekly accepting the colonizer's cultural hierarchy or rejecting it in the name of outmoded cultural practices.

And yet, Fanon is more sympathetic toward the traditionalist position than in his first book and even defends the native's return to precolonial customs and ways of being as a key moment in the struggle for liberation: "This rediscovery, this absolute valorization almost in defiance of reality, objectively indefensible, assumes an incomparable and subjective importance. On emerging from these passionate espousals, the native will have decided . . . to fight all forms of exploitation and of alienation of man."[20] Fanon makes a similar argument with respect to *négritude*, which is theorized in *Black Skin, White Masks* as an illusory withdrawal into the self and an affirmation of absolute negativity that, despite its illusory quality, plays a necessary role in setting the dialectical process of disalienation in motion and in making possible an opening toward universal brotherhood.[21] Fanon relatedly suggests in "Racism and Culture" that the native's turning inward so as to passionately valorize their culture is followed by a turning outward, a decision to fight on a "human level" against exploitation and alienation in all of its forms.[22]

For Fanon, this universalist commitment must gain expression in concrete sites. Clearly drawing inspiration from the Algerian Revolution, he argues that "the logical end of this will to struggle is the total liberation of the national territory. In order to achieve this liberation, the inferiorized man brings all his resources into play, all his acquisitions, the old and the new, his own and those of the occupant." The native establishes this new relationship with culture upon emerging from "the plunge into the chasm of the past."[23] Instead of defiantly affirming the superiority of precolonial culture over the culture of the colonizer, which merely inverts the latter's cultural hierarchy, the native grasps both cultures anew and dynamizes them from within in order to translate them into weapons of liberation. As though to participate in or model what he is describing, Fanon performs this same practice of translation throughout his paper, drawing from the resources of Hegelian and Marxian thought to elaborate his critical analysis of racism and colonialism.

The paper closes with a number of abrupt and extremely suggestive formulations concerning the final phase of the dialectical process, the moment of cultural relativity:

In the course of struggle the dominating nation tries to revive racist arguments but the elaboration of racism proves more and more ineffective. . . . Those who were once unbudgeable, the constitutional cowards, the timid, the eternally inferiorized, stiffen and emerge bristling. The occupant is bewildered. The end of racism begins with a sudden incomprehension. The occupant's spasmed and rigid culture, now liberated, opens at last to the culture of people who have really become brothers. The two cultures can face each other, enrich each other. In conclusion, universality resides in this decision to nurture [*prise en charge*] the reciprocal relativism of different cultures, once the colonial status is irreversibly excluded [*une fois exclu irréversiblement le statut colonial*].[24]

As the native population intensifies its opposition, the colonizer's certainty of native inferiority is challenged and transforms into bewildering confusion. For Fanon, this is the beginning of the end of racism. It points toward the potential for mutual enrichment between cultures, a new relationship of fraternal reciprocity and exchange that is entirely other to the colonial imposition of European values with the heavy weight of cannons and sabers. It consequently foreshadows the emergence of a universal condition that nurtures the equality of all cultures, what Fanon terms reciprocal relativism.

Yet it is important to note that Fanon's vision for realizing such a universal condition is *founded on exclusion*. He is unambiguous on this point: universality only emerges "once the colonial status is irreversibly excluded." This claim, which appears at the very end of a thoroughly dialectical analysis, is doubly jarring. The paper's narrative of dialectical movement is jarringly interrupted right at the moment of its culmination, which jars the expectations of the reader. Instead of sublation, the negation of negation, or overcoming, Fanon concludes with what appears to be a call for nondialectical rupture that would completely void a prior form of relation, that would result, to read Fanon's words against the grain, "in the total disappearance of the pre-existing culture."[25] It is tempting to try to resolve this latent tension in the argument, to fold Fanon's concluding imperative of exclusion into the classic Hegelian movement that passes from abstract universality, which is founded on exclusion, to concrete or "actual" universality, a universality that "renders thematic the exclusions on which it is grounded."[26] Such an interpretive maneuver is nonetheless foreclosed by the temporality of the exclusion, its conceptualization as an irreversible event. Rather than implying a future reflexive moment of dialectically renegotiating the exclusion, the phrase *"une fois exclu irréversiblement"* evokes a stark before and after that is more reminiscent of what I have been referring to as the Nietzschean will to "break the history of the world in two."[27]

This same Nietzschean will can be found in *Parallel Hands* and *Black Skin, White Masks*, but it acquires a new dimension in "Racism and Culture" through the theme of exclusion. Recall how Fanon defends *négritude* in his first book for its efforts to militate against the exclusion of the dehumanized *nègre* from the abstractly universal notion of the "human."[28] In his paper for the congress, a different kind of exclusion is articulated, an exclusion that is praised rather than critiqued, militantly asserted rather than militated against. As the reader will come to appreciate, this same affirmation of foundational exclusion is a major topos of Fanon's final work, *The Wretched of the Earth*. Before discussing that text, however, it will be helpful to explore earlier works that anticipate its nondialectical and antidialectical formulations. These writings reveal how a subterranean mode of thought will continue to gain expression, as it does in the final lines of

Fanon's paper for the congress, by interrupting the dominant form of analysis with images and terms that refer to another kind of change, the kind that exceeds dialectical reason.

REAL CONTRADICTION AND TOTAL INDEPENDENCE

Exiled from Algeria, Fanon remained committed to supporting the revolutionary efforts of its people. He expressed this commitment in a number of ways, including through his journalistic work with the FLN newspaper *El Moudjahid*. Between 1957 and 1960, he wrote a series of short essays and polemics for the paper while living in neighboring Tunisia. Many of these unsigned texts were anthologized shortly after Fanon's death in *Toward the African Revolution*, with additional material appearing in the recently published volume, *Alienation and Freedom*.[29] These texts, which rarely receive the attention that they deserve, play an important role in Fanon's intellectual and political trajectory insofar as they represent his first explicit theoretical reflections on the armed struggle in Algeria and its future. As *El Moudjahid*'s chief editor, Rédha Malek, explains in a letter to Fanon's publisher, François Maspero, "*The Wretched of the Earth* is basically a development and deepening of topics that are treated in *El Moudjahid* and that were elaborated from day to day by our editorial board (notably topics concerning the dialectical relations between the total character of oppression and the no less total character of struggle, between the war of liberation and the transformation of collective awareness, etc.)."[30] In line with Malek, I read the articles of *El Moudjahid* as experiments in dialectical thinking that are predominantly concerned with theorizing relations of contradictory movement, especially between oppression and resistance and between practice and consciousness. But this should not overshadow how these articles experiment with nondialectical and antidialectical approaches to theorizing these same issues, which—as previously stated—are also developed and deepened in *The Wretched of the Earth*. Accordingly, in this section of the chapter, I will underscore the persistent instability of these texts from *El Moudjahid*, their uneasy and conflicted vacillation between different schools of thought.[31]

I begin with one of Fanon's earliest articles for the newspaper, "Algeria Face to Face with the French Torturers." The focus of this article, as the title suggests, is the dialectical nature of the relationship between the Algerian people and colonial oppression. In a subsection of the article, titled "The Real Contradiction," Fanon introduces an important distinction in an effort to define this relationship: "Wars of national liberation are often presented as expressing the internal contradictions of the colonialist countries. The Franco-Algerian war, while it takes its place in a historic context characterized by the simultaneous and successive outbreak of movements of national liberation, has its own particularities."[32] The aim of this passage is to emphasize the importance of attending to the specificity of the Algerian Revolution, which is to be distinguished from other national liberation movements even as it takes place within a broader, international context of struggle. Fanon is concerned, in other words, with the particularity of Algeria's contradictions, a recurrent theme that will appear in later articles as well. In this text, however, he goes on to argue that Algeria is not only a site of internal contradictions but also, and more importantly, one aspect of a broader contradiction, that the *real contradiction* of the Franco-Algerian war is not to be found within Algeria but between Algeria and "the entire French nation."[33]

In the following extended passage, Fanon develops the implications of this contradictory relationship and addresses the kind of antagonistic movement that it generates:

In reality, the attitude of the French troops in Algeria fits into a pattern of police domination, of systematic racism, of dehumanization rationally pursued. Torture is inherent in the whole colonialist configuration. The Algerian Revolution, by proposing the liberation of the national territory, is aimed both at the death of this configuration and at the creation of a new society. The independence of Algeria is not only the end of colonialism, but the disappearance, in this part of the world, of a gangrene germ and of a source of epidemic. The liberation of the Algerian national territory is a defeat for racism and for the exploitation of man; it inaugurates the unconditional reign of Justice.[34]

Much like his discussion of racism at the congress in Paris, Fanon offers a systemic and structural analysis of colonialism in the previously cited passage. Violence toward Algerians is not an aberration of the colonialist configuration but rather an organic expression of it. As Fanon puts it, "the colonialist structure rests on the necessity of torturing, raping, and committing massacres."[35] Colonialism therefore cannot be reformed; its very foundation is violence. The dialectical antagonism between this infrastructure of violence and the Algerian people sets in motion the struggle for liberation, a transformative process of overcoming that moves toward the negation of colonial racism and exploitation. In this way, the particular fight in Algeria contributes to the realization of a new universal order, what Fanon calls the reign of Justice.

If this passage highlights Fanon's dialectical analysis of colonialism and of its overcoming, it nonetheless also deploys images and terms that hint at a divergent understanding of the relationship between France and Algeria as well as a divergent theorization of the struggle for liberation and its aims. This is the case, for example, when colonialism is likened to an epidemic that spreads by killing healthy tissue and turning it gangrenous. The metaphor suggests that the only effective treatment is surgical removal, a complete cutting away of anything infected by the colonial relation. As Fanon goes on to assert, "the demand that we make—our objective—is from the outset [d'emblée] total and absolute."[36] Independence is the name Fanon proposes for this demand that entails the immediate death of the whole colonial configuration, not its overcoming but its total and absolute disappearance. In another article for *El Moudjahid*, Fanon extends his vision of what must disappear to include precolonial societal configurations as well, arguing that Algerian liberation requires both "the destruction of colonial structures and a rupture with precolonial structures or what remains of them."[37] To destroy present structures and rupture with the remaining structures of the past is to be left with a void. It is from this void that an entirely new society can be created, inaugurating with it an entirely new universal order. When read in this way, the above extended passage implies that the opposition between France and Algeria cannot be dialectically sublated and that no higher unity between its aspects is possible. It would seem, in fact, that the real contradiction of the Franco-Algerian war is actually an antinomy of two heterogeneous entities and that both of these entities must be wiped out or cleared away before a fundamentally different relationship between fundamentally different entities can emerge.

This latent tension between divergent theorizations of colonial domination and the struggle for liberation intensifies and becomes more conflictual in a series of three articles for *El Moudjahid*, collectively titled "French Intellectuals and Democrats and the Algerian Revolution." Fanon is once again concerned with the historical particularity of contradiction in these articles, focusing this time on the specificity of colonial society: "Within a nation it is usual and commonplace to identify two antagonistic forces: the working class and bourgeois capitalism. In a colonial country this distinction proves totally inadequate. What defines the colonial situation is rather the undifferentiated character that foreign domination presents."[38] Here Fanon challenges any dogmatic application of Marxism to the colonial situation by refuting that the contradiction between labor and capital plays the primary role in every historical context. The defining feature of colonial countries, he maintains, is actually the undifferentiated domination of the colonizer over the colonized. While some might hastily read this argument as evidence of Fanon breaking with Marxism, it would be advantageous to recall that Mao came to a very similar conclusion in his canonical essay, "On Contradiction," when he affirmed the primacy in semi-colonial China of the antagonism between Japanese imperialism and the Chinese liberation struggle.[39] If Marxism is not a dogma but, as Mao argues, paraphrasing Lenin, "the concrete analysis of concrete conditions," then, in certain historical contexts, it would actually go *against* Marxism to rigidly uphold as primary the contradiction between labor and capital.[40] In such instances, it would be necessary, as Fanon does here and elsewhere, to translate Marxist thought, reformulating its basic premises in light of different concrete circumstances. Fanon engages in this kind of Marxist analysis while theorizing the particularity of contradiction in colonial society.

Yet Fanon's theorization of the undifferentiated character of foreign domination feels somewhat antidialectical in its dialectical reasoning. Would a more thoroughly dialectical analysis not recognize the internal contradictions of the foreign presence? Is the notion of the colonizer's undifferentiated domination not, in Hegel's words, a kind of "abstraction made by understanding" that results in "a forcible insistence on a single aspect, and a real effort to obscure and remove all consciousness of the other attribute which is involved"?[41] In sum, is this view of colonial power not overly simplistic in its stable one-sidedness? Fanon's rejoinder, in anticipation of such a critique, is that it would actually be simplistic *to deny* the undifferentiated character of French colonial domination. Claiming that "all Frenchmen in Algeria are not colonialists" or "that there are different degrees of colonialism" is "over-simple imagery" because it psychologizes and individualizes a relationship of domination that can only gain full comprehension at the systemic and structural level.[42] As Fanon argues:

The Algerian resents the whole of French colonialism, not out of simplemindedness or xenophobia but because in reality every Frenchman in Algeria maintains, with reference to the Algerian, relations that are based on force. The evocation of special cases of Frenchmen who are abnormally nice to Algerians does not modify the nature of the relations between a foreign group that has seized the attributes of national sovereignty and the people which finds itself deprived of the exercise of power.[43]

Fanon's language is unequivocal. How Algerians *feel* is not a reflection of ignorance or prejudice but rather, quite the contrary, a reflection of *how things really are*. This series of articles concludes that it is actually the French intellectuals and democrats, so often paternalistically presented in colonial settings as the sole bearers of knowledge, who have something to learn from the Algerian people. Instead of attempting to distinguish between kind Frenchmen and oppressive French colonialists, instead of approaching colonialism as a contradictory phenomenon, Fanon calls upon the intellectuals and democrats of France to offer their unqualified, indeed undifferentiated, condemnation of "colonization as a whole."[44] While this series of articles continues to frame the colonial relation as a contradiction between two antagonistic forces, certain formulations imply that the dialectical overcoming of this contradiction would not go far enough in overthrowing colonial society. When this occurs, the reader encounters the seeds of an antidialectical argument that will be further developed in *The Wretched of the Earth*.

This is also the case for "Decolonization and Independence," an article published in *El Moudjahid* that takes on colonialism's attempt to "maintain itself as a value," which is to say, its efforts to construe colonial subjugation as ultimately—or even partially—beneficial for Algeria. On behalf of the FLN, Fanon writes: "We rob French colonialism of its legitimacy, its would-be incorporation into Algerian reality. Instead of integrating colonialism, conceived as the birth of a new world, in Algerian history, we have made of it an unhappy, execrable accident, the only meaning of which was to have inexcusably retarded the coherent evolution of the Algerian society and nation."[45] To give this passage some context, it will be helpful to recall Hegel's assertion in *The Philosophy of History* that European colonialism represents a necessary moment in the development of Spirit, such that, in his own words, "it is the necessary fate of Asiatic Empires to be subjected to Europeans."[46] This is an archetype of colonialist thinking that has been utilized to justify the subjugation of non-European peoples from around the world. "Decolonization and Independence" opposes this way of thinking by offering a very different perspective on the legacy of colonial domination in Algeria. Instead of necessarily contributing to historical progress, colonialism achieves the very opposite as an unhappy accident that impedes Algeria's organic development and growth.[47]

Although Fanon enacts a kind of dialectical inversion of Hegel in the previous passage, whereby necessity becomes contingency and change becomes stasis, the main thrust of his argument represents a subtle but significant challenge to dialectical thinking as such. Colonialism is not conceptualized as a historical phenomenon whose negative features can take on a positive valence in a moment of dialectical reversal.[48] Colonialism is construed, rather, as "fundamentally inexcusable," as absolutely irredeemable and containing no latent potential.[49] Colonialism did not give birth to a new world, and it has absolutely no future in the world to come. Independence will be total insofar as it entails "the execution of the colonial system," "its liquidation as a style of contact with other peoples."[50] Fanon's dialectical mind, his transformation of colonialism's self-justification into its opposite, thus leads him to formulate a position of total rupture that ruptures with himself, that breaks with his dominant theoretical framework in the name of a future completely severed from the colonial past and present.

The article adds a further dimension of complexity to Fanon's theorization of independence by addressing its temporality: "This refusal of progressive solutions, this contempt for the 'stages' that break the revolutionary torrent and cause the people to unlearn the unshakable will to take everything into their hands at once in order that everything may change [*de tout prendre en main tout de suite afin que tout change*], constitutes the fundamental characteristic of the struggle of the Algerian people."[51] Not unlike the Haitian Revolution's rejection of a gradualist overturning of slavery, its demand for immediate and universal emancipation, Fanon describes the radical torrent of the Algerian Revolution as demanding immediate and total independence and refusing to slow its pace for progressive or partial solutions.[52] This extremely significant formulation cannot be reduced to the kind of heterodox Marxist thinking that problematizes the unilinear conception of history, which holds that historical development necessarily passes through certain fixed stages.[53] Instead of presenting an alternative path of development that would pass through a different set of stages, Fanon describes a revolutionary outpouring that rejects all paths of development by calling for everything (*tout*) to change immediately (*tout de suite*). To develop this point, he introduces a distinction that he will later abandon, maintaining that the "FLN does not aim at achieving a decolonization of Algeria or a relaxation of the oppressive structure. What the FLN demands is the independence of Algeria."[54] The historical process of decolonization is rejected for the transitionless rupture of independence. If the relaxation or "*assouplissement*" of oppressive structures is never equated with their dialectical overcoming, it would seem that the latter kind of change should also be rejected insofar as it, too, entails a historical process rather than an instantaneous transformation.[55]

And yet, despite its implicitly antidialectical formulations, "Decolonization and Independence" stands out for its more explicit development of a concept that will become a cornerstone of Fanon's dialectical thought in future works—namely, the concept of *mutation*. Fanon turns to this concept when reflecting on how the armed struggle contributes to the subjective transformation of the native population, which is to say, how collective political practice in Algeria dialectically transforms collective awareness. Fanon characterizes this transformation as "a vertiginous mutation [*une mutation vertigineuse*]," in which the Algerian "acquires a new quality [that] develops in and through combat."[56] By participating in the struggle, Fanon adds, "the Algerian has brought into existence a new, positive, efficient personality, whose richness is provided . . . by his certainty that he embodies a decisive moment of the national consciousness."[57] Like Épithalos's act in *Parallel Hands*, the Algerian's lived experience of such a drastic and sweeping mutation is one of dizzying vertigo.[58] But the mutation is not immediate or instantaneous. It is, on the contrary, a transformative process that develops and takes shape over time; it is a moment in the dialectical progression of national consciousness. The result of this process, moreover, is not the creation of an entirely new entity but rather the qualitative transformation of the Algerian, the latter's acquisition of a new quality and a new personality.

It follows that Fanon's analysis of the struggle for liberation entails a struggle of its own in which a notion of change as a historical process and of the new as a dialectical mutation of the old collides with a notion of change as an immediate and total rupture and of the new as completely severed from the old. The persistent instability of the *El Moudjahid* articles with respect to these distinct modes of thinking about change and the new corresponds to a persistent internal division that traverses Fanon's oeuvre. If the relationship between these modes of thought is typically one of latent and unresolved tension, the *El Moudjahid* articles veer toward a more antagonistic modality of relation insofar as they experiment with antidialectical formulations in addition to nondialectical ones and imply that dialectical change may not be enough when confronting the colonial situation. Instead of continuing to pursue this line of argument, however, Fanon's second book-length publication, which was written around the same time as these articles, complicates it by introducing yet another modality of relation. *A Dying Colonialism* (originally published as *L'An V de la révolution algérienne* or *Year Five of the Algerian Revolution*) likewise includes moments of tension between its predominantly dialectical form of analysis and a subterranean alternative to dialectics, but the text gestures toward how these modes of thought might work in tandem as well, how they might contribute to describing different aspects or moments of the struggle for liberation rather than competing accounts of the struggle as such. The remainder of this chapter will attempt to substantiate these claims by turning to *A Dying Colonialism* and examining the dynamic relationship between its different approaches to the question of change.

THE MUTATIONS OF REVOLUTION

Perhaps above all else, *A Dying Colonialism* is a sustained reflection on the multitude of mutations that occur within the context of the Algerian Revolution. As Fanon explains in one programmatic statement: "We shall have occasion to show throughout this book that the challenging of the very principle of foreign domination brings about essential mutations in the consciousness of the colonized, in the manner in which he perceives the colonizer, in his situation as man in the world."[59] To rephrase this passage in more formal terms, Fanon will demonstrate how the armed struggle for liberation sets in motion mutational processes on at least three different levels: consciousness, perception, and existence, or, construed differently, the self's relationship with the self, with the other, and with the world. Because of these mutations, Fanon maintains that "the old Algeria is dead.

All the innocent blood that has flowed onto the national soil has produced a new humanity."[60] The same language of death and the new, so prevalent in the articles for *El Moudjahid*, is utilized to convey the radical change that is occurring in Algeria. But these terms take on a more dialectical significance when deployed in *A Dying Colonialism*. The old, although dead, lives on to the extent that it nourishes the growth of a new humanity with its own blood. Old Algeria is negated yet preserved in a qualitatively new form; it mutates into a new nation just as the colonized mutate into a new humanity.

Fanon is also concerned with how the Algerian Revolution engenders mutations in the realm of culture: "This trial of strength not only remodels [*remodèle*] the consciousness that man has of himself, the idea that he forms of his previous conquerors or of the world that is at last within reach. This struggle at different levels also renews [*renouvelle*] the symbols, the myths, the beliefs, the emotional responsiveness of the people. We witness in Algeria a starting up again of man [*une remise en marche de l'homme*]."[61] The language Fanon uses here is telling. Instead of introducing into existence something entirely new, the Algerian Revolution remodels and renews what already exists so that it can become fundamentally different, a translated version of itself. Given Fanon's focus on how this occurs in the realm of culture, *A Dying Colonialism* can and ought to be read as an elaboration of the main argument put forward in his paper for the first International Congress of Black Writers and Artists. The book is a rich and detailed account of what the congress paper more schematically presents as the dialectical transformation of the native's relationship with culture during the historical transition from colonization to independence. When the two texts are read together in this way, it becomes clear that the *remise en marche* of man refers to the moment in the armed struggle when the natives overcome colonialism's mummification of their culture such that it can finally be grasped anew and dynamized from within along with the potentially liberatory elements of the colonizer's culture. Indeed, *A Dying Colonialism* explores mutations in how Algerians relate to their own culture, from the institution of the veil to traditional family structures, as well as mutations in how Algerians relate to the culture of the colonizers, including European technological innovation, the French language, and the Western science of medicine. But *A Dying Colonialism* can be read alongside Fanon's paper for the congress in yet another sense, for it likewise contains interruptions in its argument that make way for the examination of transformations that exceed dialectical reason. When this occurs, new terms and images are introduced that diverge from yet coexist with the logic of mutation. As I will attempt to demonstrate in what follows, this happens at very precise moments in the book, when the Algerian Revolution challenges Fanon's usual way of thinking, or, put differently, when dialectical analysis appears to be incapable on its own of fully accounting for the kind of change taking place in Algeria.

THE "HISTORIC DYNAMISM" OF THE VEIL
AND THE BIRTH OF ALGERIAN TRAGEDY

The most discussed chapter from *A Dying Colonialism* is undoubtedly its first, titled "Algeria Unveiled," or, perhaps more accurately, "Algeria Unveils Herself [*L'Algérie se dévoile*]."[62] The chapter focuses on the evolving significance of wearing the veil in Algeria during the period of armed struggle. Once a relatively uninteresting cultural phenomenon among others, Fanon maintains that the veil becomes a special site of contestation in the early days of anticolonial resistance due to the colonizer's aggressive campaign of cultural assimilation. This is how Fanon describes the situation:

The colonialist's relentlessness, his methods of struggle were bound to give rise to reactional behavior [*comportements réactionnels*] on the part of the colonized. In the face of the violence of the occupier, the colonized is driven to define a principled position with respect to a formerly inert element of the native cultural configuration. It was the colonialist's frenzy to unveil the Algerian woman, it was his gamble on winning the battle of the veil at whatever cost, that provoked the native's bristling resistance [*l'arc-boutant de l'autochtone*]. The deliberately aggressive intentions of the colonialist with respect to the *haïk* gave a new life to this dead element of the Algerian cultural stock—dead because stabilized, without any progressive change in form or color. We here recognize one of the laws of the psychology of colonization. In an initial phase, it is the action, the plans of the occupier that determine the centers of resistance around which a people's will to survive becomes organized. It is the white man who creates the *nègre*. But it is the *nègre* who creates *négritude*. To the colonialist offensive against the veil, the colonized opposes the cult of the veil.[63]

In this passage, Fanon returns to certain Nietzschean categories deployed in *Parallel Hands* and *Black Skin, White Masks*—the actional and the reactional—to analyze cultural movements like *négritude* and the cult of the veil. Recall that for Nietzsche the strong and noble human type pursues creative and affirmative *action*, whereas the weak and slavish human type is characteristically limited to resentfully *reacting* to the actions of the strong.[64] Although Fanon does not exactly embrace Nietzsche's positive valuation of the strong human type, since colonial violence and oppression embody that position at this initial phase in the process, he does draw a polemical parallel between the reactional personality of Nietzsche's slave and the rigidly principled, flying-buttress-like-resistance of the colonized subject.

The passage also makes clear that, for Fanon, there is nothing inherently special about the veil. It was once an inert cultural element like all the rest, mummified by the violent and ongoing legacy of colonization. Yet, because the colonizer seeks to eliminate the veil as part of an assimilationist project, it is reactively invested with new meaning and vitality. Wearing the veil mutates into a timeless principle, a "mechanism of resistance," and a symbol of the "maintenance of cultural, hence national, originality."[65] The veil is paradoxically translated so that it cannot be further translated, grasped anew so that it can remain the same, altered so that it can be preserved in a supposedly original, fixed state. Fanon contends that this cultural maneuver, like the affirmation of *négritude*, is ultimately the product of a defense mechanism proper to the historically conditioned psychology of colonization. The mechanism's strategy of resistance is to cling to the opposite of whatever the colonizer seeks to impose. As a result, at the very moment when the colonized attempts to escape the influence of the colonizer, that influence becomes fully determining.

Perhaps because "Algeria Unveils Herself" was not—like "Racism and Culture"—meant to be read in front of the founders of *négritude*, there is little effort on Fanon's part to defend these cultural movements by presenting them as contributing in some important way to the dialectical process of liberation. Could this be read as yet another sign of Nietzsche's influence on the chapter's argument? Could it be said that Fanon is looking for something more actional than the cult of the veil, something beyond what Gilles Deleuze refers to as "lukewarm affirmations that carry the negative within themselves"?[66] While it is undeniable that the chapter promotes breaking with reactional impulses, Fanon does not (yet) go so far as to depart from the dialectical framework of the book. Instead, he highlights the positive and negative valences of the cult of the veil so as to reveal how it strengthens and weakens the revolution at the same time: "The tenacity of the occupier in his endeavor to unveil the women, to make of them an ally in the work of cultural destruction, had the effect of strengthening the traditional patterns of behavior. These patterns, which were essentially positive in the strategy of resistance to the corrosive action of the colonizer, naturally had negative effects. . . . This relatively cloistered life, with its known, categorized, regulated comings and goings, made any immediate revolution seem a dubious proposition."[67] This passage demonstrates how, in the words of Diana Fuss, "the veil can . . . signify doubly, as a mode of defying colonialism and as a means of ensuring patriarchal privilege."[68] Fanon's point, in fact, is that this double signification is dialectical in nature. He underscores the contradictory significance of an anticolonial practice, how it can prolong colonialism even as it resists colonialism to the extent that it rests on a foundation of patriarchal traditionalism. Put another way, insofar as the cult of the veil reinforces traditional gender norms, including "a rigid separation of the sexes," it also weakens the revolution, since these norms inhibit women from joining and participating in the armed struggle.[69]

According to Fanon, women were virtually barred from anticolonial militancy until 1955, and it was only because of "the urgency of total war" that their male counterparts gradually opened up to the notion of women playing a more active role in the resistance effort.[70] This implies that the traditionalist division of labor within the liberation struggle was not abandoned because of its misogynist underpinnings or because of a change of heart among the male leaders of the FLN. It was abandoned, rather, because of the exigency of the moment and the strategy's unintended negative consequences on the struggle. For Fanon, in other words, the change in policy regarding women's participation in the fight for national liberation was not in itself a sign that *women's liberation* had been recognized as an integral aspect of the battle. This is an important—though subtle and often overlooked—criticism of the revolution and its limits during the first phase of its development.

Fanon's account of the next phase of the revolution, when women were officially integrated into the organized struggle against French colonial rule, finally does depart from dialectical thinking in an unambiguous way:

It is without apprenticeship, without briefing, without fuss, that [the Algerian woman] goes out into the street with three grenades in her handbag or the activity report of an area in her bodice. She does not have the sensation of playing a role she has read about ever so many times in novels or seen in motion pictures. There is not that coefficient of play, of imitation, almost always present in this form of action when we are dealing with a Western woman. What we have here is not the bringing to light of a character known and frequented a thousand times in imagination or in stories. *It is an authentic birth in a pure state, without preliminary instruction.* There is no character to imitate. On the contrary, there is an intense dramatization, a continuity [*une absence de jour*] between the woman and the revolutionary. The Algerian woman rises immediately [*d'emblée*] to the level of tragedy.[71]

If the aim of *A Dying Colonialism* is to trace various mutations of previously existing attitudes and practices during the struggle for liberation, the book interrupts its dialectical analysis of these mutational processes to consider an event of authentic birth.[72] Fanon presents the exigencies of the war as the conditions of possibility for such an event, but he describes the event as introducing into existence something *entirely* new, something so unprecedented that it can only be understood when detached from all prior historical conditioning. His strange and problematic depiction of the Western woman, as almost always afflicted by a kind of Bovarism, serves as a foil to highlight, in a quasi-mythical fashion, the genuine beginning of the revolutionary Algerian woman.[73] If the Western woman's life imitates art, life is art itself for the Algerian woman engaged in combat. At this precise moment, the battlefield becomes her stage, and she assumes her role in the tragedy of armed struggle.

To account for this event, Fanon again turns to Nietzschean thought, especially as it is developed in *The Birth of Tragedy*.[74] In the aforementioned work, Nietzsche details how ancient Greek tragedy is born from the mysterious combination of antagonistic tendencies within art—namely, Dionysian music and Apollonian sculpture. This understanding of tragedy leads Nietzsche to develop an aesthetic conceptualization of existence, such that, in the words of one critic, "the world is a tragic play of opposites."[75] Fanon draws from these ideas to theorize another birth, what could be called the birth of Algerian tragedy.[76] This birth ushers into existence a militant subject that combines Algerian femininity and revolutionary commitment, which are held to be starkly antagonistic forces in a world of patriarchal norms and traditions. There is no gestation period, no tarrying with the negative, and no process of mutation that contributes to her emergence. She is, for Fanon, self-affirmation in a pure state, the immediate ascendance of the new.

If the colonized reactively mutate the veil into a timeless principle to protect it from further mutation under colonial rule, the birth of Algerian tragedy allows the colonized to break with this defense mechanism and imagine new possibilities for the veil's mutation. Once women militants emerge onto the scene, the veil is no longer stubbornly preserved in its supposedly original state but rather "manipulated, transformed into a technique of camouflage, into a means of struggle."[77] Fanon describes this as the "second phase" of the veil's dialectical development, at which point women militants strategically wear the veil or remove it depending on what is most advantageous in the fight against colonialism.[78] Before moving on to consider this second phase of development, it is worth pausing to reflect on the transition that occurs between phases. Not unlike certain points in Fanon's psychiatric papers, a nondialectical event that ruptures with the existing state of things appears to play a role in the generation of further dialectical movement.[79] The authentic birth of the revolutionary Algerian woman jolts a stalled dialectic into motion, allowing the veil to take on new forms beyond its status as a cult object. Fanon does not further elaborate upon this idea, but, as in other works, it suggests the potential for dialectical and nondialectical thinking to form a non-antagonistic relationship and even mutually enrich each other by contributing to the theorization of different aspects or moments of the same revolutionary process.

During his discussion of the second phase in the veil's development, Fanon focuses on Algerian women who choose to remove the garment when crossing the border which separates the predominantly Arab sector of the city of Algiers from its European quarters. Since the police authorities on patrol associate the veil with anticolonial resistance, its removal helps these women avoid detection and searches. A strategic translation of appearance thus enhances movement. "Carrying revolvers, grenades, hundreds of false identity cards or bombs," Fanon writes, "the unveiled Algerian woman moves like a fish in the Western waters."[80] The dialectical logic of this strategy is readily apparent. Under conditions of heightened surveillance, revealing one's face can be the best form of coverage and passing as

European—or at least Europeanized—can be the most effective method of fighting European colonialism.

Strategically electing to remove the veil necessitates further mutations, which develop in and through what Fanon calls a "new dialectic of the body and of the world." He explains:

The absence of the veil distorts the Algerian woman's corporal pattern. She quickly has to invent new dimensions for her body, new means of muscular control. She has to create for herself an attitude of unveiled-woman-outside. She must overcome all timidity, all awkwardness (for she must pass for a European), and at the same time be careful not to overdo it, not to attract notice to herself. The Algerian woman who walks stark naked into the European city relearns her body, reestablishes it in a totally revolutionary fashion.[81]

Although Fanon mobilizes the language of invention in this passage, the new corporal patterns of the Algerian woman are not really invented at all. They are, on the contrary, based on certain preexisting gestures, attitudes, and modes of appearance associated with European femininity. Unburdened by a reactional defense mechanism, women militants allow this inherited model of femininity to influence the way they move their bodies through the world, not in an effort to assimilate the colonizer's culture but rather in an effort to dialectically repurpose it for new, anticolonial ends. In this way, Fanon once again describes a practice of translation that represents an alternative to assimilationism and traditionalism, meekly accepting the imposition of European values and stubbornly rejecting them in an ineffectual way.

If Fanon focuses on examples of strategic unveiling, he also considers when the veil reappears in response to changing historical conditions and explains how its presence—like its absence before—can mutate into a weapon of liberation. What conditions this mutation is the discovery by police authorities that Algerians who appear Europeanized, and even some Europeans living in Algeria, are participating in the armed struggle against colonial rule. After this discovery, everyone is viewed as a potential enemy combatant and therefore anyone can be searched. This new situation undermines the effectiveness of removing the veil, but it also reveals new possibilities for the veil's use. In response to the heightened suspicion of the police, "a new technique must be learned: how to carry a rather heavy object . . . under the veil and still give the impression of having one's hands free, that there is nothing under this *haïk*, except a poor woman or an insignificant young girl."[82] When everyone is a suspect, a traditional garment can become an "instrument" for the covert circulation of illegal materials.[83] Translating the veil into such an instrument "helped the Algerian woman to meet the new problems created by the struggle."[84]

Fanon also discusses how women militants contribute to mutating traditional gender norms in Algeria while recruiting others to the cause. In his view, they become a kind of vanguard group on these two fronts: "Behind the daughter, the whole family—even the Algerian father, the authority for all things, the founder of every value—following in her footsteps, becomes committed to the new Algeria."[85] This idea is developed in a subsequent chapter of *A Dying Colonialism* that analyzes the impact of the liberation effort on the Algerian family structure. There Fanon argues that, as a result of women participating in the armed struggle, Algerian society "renews itself [*se renouvelle*] and develops new values governing sexual relations. The woman ceases to be a complement for man. *She literally forges a new place for herself by her sheer strength*."[86] To forge this new place, the revolutionary Algerian woman confronts the real and symbolic authority of the father within the family. She "who enters the agitated arena of history urges her father to undergo a kind of mutation, to wrench himself free of himself."[87] She contributes, in this way, to the overcoming of the father's authority, which permits him to form new relationships with himself, with others, and with the world. The revolutionary Algerian woman is accordingly depicted, in this instance like in many others, as a militant translator engaged in dialectically renewing herself, those around her, and her culture in an effort to dialectically renew all of Algerian society.

Although Fanon theorizes the "historic dynamism" of the veil as passing through a series of phases, it is important to note that he does not conceive of this dynamism as a linear progression that only moves in one direction. He notes that French colonial authorities, at a very advanced point in the struggle, redeploy their campaign in favor of strict assimilation, which leads the colonized to revert back to old patterns of reactional behavior. "Spontaneously and without being told," Fanon laments, "the Algerian women who had long since dropped the veil once again donned the *haïk*. . . . Behind these psychological reactions . . . we again see the overall attitude of rejection of the values of the occupier." Fanon describes this response as "a turning back, a regression," and argues against its effectiveness for addressing the exigencies of the war.[88] While this claim reaffirms his critique of reactional anticolonial resistance, it also subtly complicates some of his prior formulations. If the authentic birth of the revolutionary Algerian woman is construed as a nondialectical event of rupture with the past, Fanon implies that this rupture is not—or is not yet—total. It can, in fact, be spontaneously undone by the ebb and flow of the struggle. This historical lesson from the Algerian Revolution renders problematic the vision of irreversible change developed here and in other texts. But Fanon does not go so far as to renounce the notion of an authentic birth. Instead, the chapter closes with a vague sense of latent and unresolved tension between its distinct modes of thinking about change, despite also gesturing toward their potential collaboration.

LANGUAGE AND TECHNOLOGY IN THE EPIC "BATTLE OF THE AIRWAVES"

If the struggle for liberation mutates how Algerians relate to their own culture, it also mutates how they relate to the culture of the colonizer. Fanon focuses on this latter issue in his chapter on the radio, a technological import from the metropole that received very little attention from the native population before the onset of the Algerian Revolution. This attitude of generalized disinterest, according to Fanon, led some to speculate that a problem of translation was at play, that the hegemonic French programming of *Radio-Alger* alienated non-Western audiences with crass humor, sexual innuendo, and unknown cultural references. From this perspective, the radio "threatens . . . traditional types of sociability; the reason invoked being that the programs in Algeria, undifferentiated because they are copied from the Western model, are not adapted to the strict, almost feudal type of patrilineal hierarchy, with its many moral taboos, that characterizes the Algerian family."[89] This kind of explanation is a frequent trope in theories of cultural exchange. When existing values and customs clash with and inhibit the adoption of something new, translation is presented as a practice that can bridge the gap separating the familiar from the foreign, the traditional from the modern.[90]

This understanding of the situation somewhat resembles the self-critique that Fanon and Jacques Azoulay develop in response to their experimentation with French social therapy in Blida-Joinville.[91] Fanon and Azoulay maintain that their experiment failed because they did not translate their psychiatric method to account for the specificity of its new site of implementation. In a paper detailing the experiment, they argue that an "authentic sociological study" must be carried out, one that, utilizing the terminology of Marcel Mauss, explores the "totality" of the "North African social fact" so as to better inform and adapt "western-inspired" treatment practices to "a framework that is still feudal in many respects."[92] The paper also notes that one of its authors is preparing such a study, an investigation into "the complexity of North African society, which is currently undergoing extremely deep structural modifications."[93] This last remark could very well be referring to A Dying Colonialism. Yet in the five-year period that separates the coauthored paper from the book's publication, Fanon nuances his position on the translation of Western culture in non-Western sites and arguably engages in a subtle self-critique of his prior self-critique. Indeed, he is very adamant in distinguishing his understanding of the radio's reception in Algeria from those who blame native disinterest in radio on the inadaptation of its programming: "As we describe the drastic changes that have occurred in [the realm of technology], in connection with the national war, we shall see how artificial such a sociological approach is, what a mass of errors it contains."[94] The sociological approach, as Fanon now conceives it, gets things wrong from the start because of its underappreciation of the determining role of colonial domination in Algerian society.[95] Without grasping the significance of this relationship of violence, the true meaning behind local disinterest in the radio will remain unintelligible.

Fanon argues that a more properly political and psychopathological explanation is required to comprehend this phenomenon. Not unlike Walter Benjamin, he conceives of the radio device as a kind of prosthesis that enhances the human perceptual and cognitive apparatus.[96] He posits that, "in the limited sense, the radio receiving set develops the sensorial, intellectual, and muscular powers of man in a given society."[97] But this is a limited or inadequate understanding of the radio for Fanon because it does not take into account the particular historical conditions of the device's reception.[98] To move past this abstract view of technology, Fanon offers what could be called a "phenomenology of reception," which attends to the specific politico-psychical significance of the radio as it is lived by the native population in Algeria.[99] This allows him to appreciate why "the radio, as a symbol of French presence, as a material representation of the colonial configuration, is characterized by an extremely important negative valence. The possible intensification and extension of sensorial or intellectual powers by the French radio are implicitly rejected or denied by the native."[100] Since the radio is spontaneously associated with French colonialism, the native necessarily cathects it with negative affective energy. Its material presence, Fanon reasons, functions metonymically as a reminder of the presence of the colonizer.

As a result, before the armed struggle, it is nearly impossible for Algerians to recognize the potentially positive valence of the radio. "The communication is never questioned," Fanon writes, "but is simply refused, for it is precisely the opening of oneself to the other that is organically excluded from the colonial situation. Before 1954, in the psychopathological realm, the radio was an evil object, anxiogenic and accursed."[101] Fanon thus offers another example of how the actions of the colonizers generate a reactional defense mechanism in the colonized. In this instance, said mechanism gains expression when Algerians respond to undifferentiated copies of Western culture and technology with anxious, defiant, and indeed undifferentiated rejection. This missed encounter between the radio and the native does not stem from the inadaptation of the radio programming or from the modern technological medium of its circulation but rather from what both represent in the context of colonized Algeria. The implication here is that the translation of culture is not a sufficient solution to the problem at hand. Producing radio programming sensitive to cultural difference while leaving colonial rule intact is an artificial response to the situation. Accordingly, if the psychiatric paper from Fanon's days in Blida-Joinville emphasizes the importance of translating an inherited method for its new site of implementation, the radio essay nuances this position by forefronting the limits of such a practice when unaccompanied by a broader transformation of society.

This is not to imply that the radio's incorporation into Algerian culture, as well as some mode of opening oneself up to the influence of the other, depends upon the full achievement of independence. Rather, the process of struggling for liberation creates the conditions of possibility for a series of mutations that will affect the radio, the listener, and their relationship. Fanon singles out November 1, 1954, the FLN's official start date for the

Algerian Revolution, as the moment when "the most important mutations occurred in the defining of new attitudes toward this specific technique for the dissemination of news."[102] As skirmishes with colonial forces proliferated, the native population sought information about what was happening. New historical circumstances produced a new need, which print culture could not easily satisfy because of the country's high level of illiteracy. During these early days of the revolution, the radio was not yet embraced as an alternative resource for obtaining the news, but the armed struggle generated a real desire among the native population to organize its own news distribution system.

This set the stage for what Fanon calls "the true mutation" that occurred in 1956 when the anticolonial radio programming of the *Voice of Algeria* burst onto the scene.[103] This radical alternative to *Radio-Alger* allowed Algerians to overcome their reactional defense mechanism, to dialectically transform their attitude of rejection into its opposite, and seize the radio as a weapon of liberation.[104] Alluding to the well-known metaphor of cultural anthropophagy, Fanon summarizes this transformational moment of incorporation accordingly: "The foreign technique, 'digested' in connection with the national struggle, became a fighting instrument for the people."[105] What makes the radio a weapon of liberation, beyond its dissemination of the news, is its capacity to function as an instrument for political organization, for "consolidating and bringing together [*prise en masse*] the people."[106] To explain how the radio functions in this way, Fanon focuses less on *what* the *Voice of Algeria* says and more on *how* it says it. He asserts that "the use of the Arab, Kabyle, and French languages . . . had the advantage of developing and of strengthening the unity of the people."[107] In other words, when a single voice—the *Voice of Algeria*—speaks in different languages, it does not so much address an already existing people as constitute a people that is both one and plural.[108] The mutation of the radio into a weapon therefore contributes to the mutation of the colonized into a people. This latter mutation entails a fundamental transformation at the level of consciousness, the formation of a collective awareness of shared struggle across ethnic, cultural, and linguistic differences. The radio foments this understanding of the situation by turning "scattered acts . . . into a vast epic," by elaborating upon the greater significance of the many individual battles taking place, such that "the Kabyles are no longer 'the men of the mountains,' but the brothers who, with Ouamrane and Krim, make things difficult for the enemy troops."[109]

The radio, and particularly the *Voice of Algeria*, also frees the French language from the colonizer by transforming it into one of the many languages that are used to communicate and organize the armed struggle. As a result, Algerians come to associate French with their own liberation, whereas previously it could only be associated with foreign domination and colonial rule. For Fanon, this once again points to "a mutation, a radical change of valence, . . . a dialectical overcoming [*un dépassement dialectique*]."[110] Instead of undifferentiated rejection, a new relationship with the other is formed through language, one that is "open to the signs, the symbols, in short to a certain influence of the occupier."[111] Fanon vividly expands upon this idea in the following passage:

The broadcasting in French of the programs of *Fighting Algeria* was to liberate the enemy language from its historic meanings. The same message transmitted in three different languages unified the experience and gave it a universal dimension. The French language lost its accursed character, revealing itself to be capable also of transmitting, for the benefit of the nation, the messages of truth that the latter awaited. Paradoxical as it may appear, it is the Algerian revolution, it is the struggle of the Algerian people, that is facilitating the spreading of the French language in the nation.[112]

Regarded for so long as exclusively the language of the colonizer, French is translated into a language of the Algerian people, a resource for disseminating the truth of the revolution. Yet, as a result of this process, French does not become—like colonial "advocates of integration" propose—"the sole practical means of communication," nor is French granted "the role of *Logos*."[113] On the contrary, the revolution's message of truth is communicated in the many languages of the people, and this multilingual communication of the same truth generates a kind of universality, a universal dimension that only gains expression in and through multiplicity. In Fanon's words, the radio helps to forge a common idiom, the "new language of the nation," that "makes itself known through multiple meaningful channels."[114]

Once police authorities catch on to the *Voice of Algeria* and its contributions to the revolutionary cause, its subversive programming is jammed so that it cannot be easily heard. The "battle of the airwaves" begins, and its soldiers on the front lines are those listeners who sit closest to the radio set and attempt to decode its crackling noises and fragmented messages for everyone else in the room.[115] The following extended passage describes such a scene of collective listening and interpretation:

Very often only the operator, his ear glued to the receiver, had the unhoped-for opportunity of hearing the *Voice*. The other Algerians present in the room would receive the echo of this voice through the privileged interpreter who, at the end of the broadcast, was literally besieged. Specific questions would then be asked of this incarnated voice. Those present wanted to know about a particular battle mentioned by the French press in the last twenty-four hours, and the interpreter, embarrassed, feeling guilty, would sometimes have to admit that the *Voice* had not mentioned it. But by common consent, after an exchange of views, it would be decided that the *Voice* had in fact spoken of these events, but that the interpreter had not caught the transmitted information. A real task of production [*d'élaboration*] would then begin. Everyone would collaborate, and the battles of yesterday and the day before would be reconstructed in accordance with the deep aspirations and the unshakable faith of the group. The listener would compensate for the fragmentary nature of the news by an autonomous creation of information [*par une création autonome de l'information*].[116]

The function of the radio operator is to use their voice to broadcast the *Voice*. The operator orally reproduces a message that is itself already an oral and technological reproduction of the events of war. The consequences of this parallel are very significant. If, at the beginning of the chapter, the radio is theorized as a kind of prosthesis for the listener, the jamming of the program dialectically inverts this relationship. The operator now mutates into an extension of the radio, a speaker for the radio's amplification. Repetition generates further repetition as information travels through an echo chamber of conversations and debates until "every Algerian . . . emits and transmits the new language" and becomes "a reverberating element of the vast network of meanings born of the liberating combat."[117] The epic battle of the airwaves thus continually reproduces the universal condition of a united yet plural people, such that every Algerian becomes an amplification device that plugs into the revolution's network of signification.

Yet these human amplifiers are not limited to passive automatism, the mechanical repetition of identical messages. Since very little can be heard from the radio, listeners participate in an active and collaborative process of autonomous creation. In this way, the *Voice*, rather than a centralized vanguard that issues orders to its listeners, becomes the scene for many voices to collectively produce the meaning of the revolution through consensus.[118] The collective empowers itself to invent any relevant information that is either unheard or unsaid during the broadcasts. While reconstructing past events, new details are produced to fill in the gaps of the narrative. The radio's message of truth is consequently replaced with a lie. However, not unlike in the psychoanalytic interpretation of dreams, Fanon maintains that it is a "true lie," a fiction that acquires "a dimension of truth" insofar as it expresses the real desire and revolutionary commitment of the Algerian people.[119] There is also a performative element to this fiction, since a collective voice inventing tales of struggle against colonial domination is itself an example of struggle against colonial domination and the latter's goal of silencing the *Voice* of the revolution.[120] When spinning partially fictitious tales of past battles, in other words, the radio's audience engages in a true battle of its own.

Note how this scene of reconstruction *and* autonomous creation subtly interrupts and complicates the book's account of mutational change, the kind of change that dialectically transforms existing attitudes and practices. The act of autonomously creating a true lie, of inventing information when it cannot be reconstructed, resonates more directly with the notion of an authentic birth, since it implies a kind of newness that is detached from prior historical conditions, that emerges on its own as if from a void. The conceptual divergence between reconstruction and autonomous creation represents another example of a broader divergence in the book—and in Fanon's oeuvre as a whole—between distinct modes of thinking about change. But the previously cited passage does not go so far as to construe these concepts as irreconcilably at odds with each other. On the contrary, they are deployed to describe different aspects of the same phenomenon, which suggests that the modes of thought to which they correspond can work in tandem and in fact must do so to give a fully comprehensive account of the Algerian Revolution.

Something similar occurs toward the end of the chapter, where Fanon offers some final reflections on the radio's anticolonial programming and on the kind of change that it contributes to precipitating. He writes:

The national struggle and the creation of *Free Radio Algeria* provoke a fundamental mutation at the core of the people.... We see a drastic change [*un bouleversement*] from top to bottom of the means of perception, of the very world of perception. In Algeria, it is true to say that there never was, with respect to the radio, receptive conduits, adhesion, or acceptance. Insofar as mental processes are concerned, we see, starting in 1956, a *quasi-invention of the technique*. The *Voice of Algeria*, created from nothing [*créée de rien*], brought the nation into existence and endowed every citizen with a new status.[121]

What is of primary importance in this passage is Fanon's theorization of the *Voice* as something *created from nothing*. Although dismissed as an insignificant moment of "hyperbole" by one prominent critic, ex nihilo creation is another way of describing an event of authentic birth, the genuine beginning of something entirely new.[122] Such an event, in conjunction with the armed struggle, triggers a fundamental mutation at the core of the Algerian people, which includes a total *"bouleversement"* of their perception and of their existence in the world. Despite the absence of receptive conduits among the Algerian people, the emergence of the *Voice* also triggers the radio technique's quasi-invention, not its ex nihilo creation but rather its transformation into something qualitatively new. If ex nihilo creation and quasi-invention imply different kinds of change, they nevertheless complement each other, insofar as they signal how a nondialectical event might contribute to jumpstarting dialectical movement, to provoking a sweeping mutational process. It follows, once again, that the distinct modes of thought to which these concepts pertain are not necessarily antagonistic, that their relationship can be one of coexistence and even of mutual enrichment insofar as they contribute to illuminating different aspects of the same struggle for liberation.

DIFFERENTIATION

If *A Dying Colonialism* can be read as an elaboration of the main argument put forward in "Racism and Culture," it can also be read as a text that maintains an uneasy and conflicted relationship with certain ideas developed in the *El Moudjahid* articles. The notions of undifferentiated rejection and total independence, hailed in the FLN newspaper as the only adequate response to the colonial system, are frequently regarded in *A Dying*

Colonialism as exemplary of a reactional form of anticolonial politics that is, in the final analysis, no less subservient to colonial domination than the politics of assimilation that it seeks to oppose. The alternative to both of these approaches, as the reader will no doubt have guessed, is the translational politics of mutation, which at one point in the book is construed as synonymous with a process of *differentiation*: "Gone were the days when mechanically switching on the radio amounted to an invitation to the enemy. For the Algerian, the radio, as a technique, becomes differentiated [*se différencie*]."[123] The radio-technique, once held to be an undifferentiated element of the whole colonialist configuration, becomes differentiated from this configuration through its mutation into a weapon of liberation. The French language passes through a similar movement, and Fanon dedicates an entire chapter to analyzing how certain forms of Western medicine, "taken for granted before the struggle for liberation," are likewise remade for the purposes of the struggle.[124]

The most noteworthy and surprising differentiation, however, appears in the final chapter of *A Dying Colonialism*, "Algeria's European Minority." This section of the book is dedicated to what David Macey has characterized as a "remarkably generous" discussion of settler colonialism in Algeria, a discussion that differentiates between European settlers who maintain an exploitative relationship with the colony and European settlers who become part of the united yet plural Algerian people.[125] Such generosity does not lead Fanon to completely abandon his call for exclusion: "The Algerian people need not restate their position with respect to these men who have considered Algeria and the Algerians as their private reserve. The people have excluded them from the Algerian nation and they must not hope to be 'taken back.'"[126] Yet this exclusion is significantly qualified, its reach far more limited than before, as it only applies to a subset of European settlers rather than to everyone whose status as settler maintains the colonial relation of violence.

Much of Fanon's argument hinges on a (self-)critique of the initial phase of the Algerian Revolution. He asserts that, during those early days of the liberation effort, "the European minority was perceived *en bloc* within the framework of the colonial situation. On November 1, 1954, there was therefore an extreme oversimplification. The outlines and antinomies of the world stood out in sudden sharpness."[127] At the outbreak of the armed struggle, popular perception placed European settlers and Algerian natives on opposite sides of a stark antinomy, a Manichaean opposition between two heterogeneous groups. Fanon arguably contributed to this popular perception of the situation when he put forward the following thesis in *El Moudjahid*: "What defines the colonial situation is . . . the undifferentiated character [*le caractère indifférencié*] that foreign domination presents."[128] *A Dying Colonialism* complicates the notion of undifferentiated domination throughout its final chapter by detailing how some settlers, instead of supporting colonial rule, stand in solidarity with the revolutionaries, treat them medically, and even fight beside them. According to Fanon, these internal contradictions among the European minority in Algeria contribute to a radical mutation in how they are perceived by the native population. As the armed struggle advances toward achieving independence, the unitary perception of European settlers divides in two and becomes differentiated along the lines of comrade and counterrevolutionary.

To fully appreciate what is at stake here, it will be helpful to contrast Fanon's newfound generosity toward Algeria's European minority with the following passage from "French Intellectuals and Democrats and the Algerian Revolution," which I analyzed in a previous section of this chapter:

The Algerian resents the whole of French colonialism, not out of simplemindedness or xenophobia, but because in reality every Frenchman in Algeria maintains, with reference to the Algerian, relations that are based on force. The evocation of special cases of Frenchmen who are abnormally nice to Algerians does not modify the nature of the relations between a foreign group that has seized the attributes of national sovereignty and the people which finds itself deprived of the exercise of power.[129]

This passage is unapologetically categorical regarding the European presence in Algeria. Some Frenchmen may exist in contradiction with their structural position, but their position still contributes to the systematic reproduction of a relationship that is violent in nature. What is the reader to make of Fanon's seeming divergence from this point of view? Could it be said that Fanon's reflections on Algeria's European minority signal a fundamental mutation in his own thinking and a departure from his call for total independence?

Fanon partially responds to these questions when he alludes to and defends the previously cited passage from his article for *El Moudjahid* while continuing to affirm the importance of differentiation:

It has often been claimed that the FLN made no distinction among the different members of Algeria's European society. Those who make such accusations fail to take into account both the policy long defined by the Front with respect to Algeria's Europeans, and the constant support that hundreds and hundreds of European men and women have brought to our units and to our political cells. What we have said is that the Algerian people are spontaneously aware of the importance of the European population which expresses itself through its oppressive system and especially through the silence and inactivity of the French democrats in Algeria in the face of the affirmed and total violence of the colonialists.[130]

In this complicated passage, Fanon attempts to ease the tension between two seemingly incompatible arguments. It appears to be a matter of strategic emphasis. On the one hand, when French intellectuals and democrats fail to denounce the atrocities of colonialism or when they attempt to distinguish between good and bad aspects of colonial rule, Fanon strategically emphasizes the systemic nature of domination and the way it structurally implicates all settlers in colonial violence. On the other hand, when critics of the Algerian Revolution attempt to discredit the FLN as an extremist organization that is anti-European rather than simply anticolonial, Fanon places strategic emphasis on the revolution's contribution to mutating popular perception, which makes possible the differentiation of Algeria's European minority and the recognition of its internal contradictions.

Rather than a fully satisfying argument that answers all lingering questions, this passage reads more like a disavowal of the subtle yet undeniable internal dividedness that traverses Fanon's oeuvre. The inherent tension between undifferentiated rejection and mutational differentiation cannot be resolved as a matter of strategic emphasis, for they refer to divergent theoretical frameworks and competing political programs. The reader is thus confronted with a particularly striking example of the kind of conceptual friction that can occur when dialectical and nondialectical thinking discrepantly rub against each other.[131] But to say this is not to advocate for a rigid periodization of Fanon's writings on the Algerian Revolution, which would construe *A Dying Colonialism* as marking a major shift in emphasis or even a complete departure from the *El Moudjahid* articles. It is true that nondialectical and antidialectical formulations are more prevalent in the articles than in the book; however, in both cases, terms and images are introduced that do not straightforwardly align with the dominant form of analysis. What characterizes the aggregate of these writings on the Algerian Revolution, in other words, is not a definitive mutation in thought but rather thought's definitive division, a pattern of vacillation between distinct modes of thinking that maintain a multifaceted and dynamic relationship with each other. If it is often a relationship of latent and unresolved tension, the relationship becomes more collaborative at times and leads to the development of a shared account of the Algerian Revolution and its different kinds of change. And yet, on other occasions, the relationship becomes blatantly antagonistic, resulting in a truly explosive confrontation between warring positions. The reader catches a glimpse of this confrontation in the *El Moudjahid* articles, but, as I will demonstrate in the remaining two chapters of this book, it is a defining feature of Fanon's final work, *The Wretched of the Earth*.

Chapter Four

THE WRETCHED OF THE EARTH (PART I)

DECOLONIZATION AND THE EXCESS OF DECISION

Originally published in May 1961 in *Les Temps Modernes*, and then slightly revised for its republication later that same year as the first chapter of *The Wretched of the Earth*, "On Violence" is Fanon's most widely discussed and debated piece of writing.[1] The attention that this essay has received stems in part from the complexity of its argument, in part from its unapologetic stance on revolutionary violence, and in part from the programmatic quality of its account of decolonization. In its opening pages, it sets out to define decolonization with a series of axiomatic claims. Fanon reflects upon the difficulty of this endeavor later in the essay: "Because decolonization has taken on multiple forms, reason hesitates and abstains from saying what is an instance of true decolonization and what is an instance of false decolonization."[2] Yet Fanon does not respond to this dilemma by dwelling in a space of indecision or by relativizing his earlier statements. Instead, he declares that "urgent decisions need to be made on means and tactics, which is to say, on direction and organization."[3] In light of this passage, I propose reading the claims that open "On Violence" as decisions, as Fanon's attempt to intervene in the urgent debate surrounding what must occur to achieve decolonization.[4] As I will soon demonstrate, however, Fanon decides only then to decide the contrary, vacillating between discrepant arguments concerning the nature of decolonization as such. Rather than approaching such vacillation as evidence of Fanon's inability to decide, I see in it the staging of an excess of decision, of an explosive struggle between conflicting decisions. Fanon's decisions, in other words, split him in two, pitting him against himself.

The opening sentence of "On Violence" is the exception that sets the rule. It justifies the specific focus of the essay by affirming that "decolonization is *always* a violent phenomenon."[5] The universally violent character of decolonization is the only major claim in the essay that Fanon does not at some point qualify, reconsider, or outright contradict by advancing a competing claim.[6] Although it is possible for a country to become formally independent without a proper armed struggle, and colonial authorities sometimes even grant independence as part of a pacifying "strategy of containment," such a transition of power is never tantamount to decolonization, since a relationship of colonial domination and exploitation will invariably remain intact.[7] To achieve decolonization, according to Fanon, the colonized must violently smash the whole colonial system to pieces. This is, of course, not a glorification of violence in itself, as some have erroneously argued, but rather a recognition of its necessity, which follows from a specific understanding of the structure and functioning of colonialism.[8] As Fanon explains, "Colonialism is not a machine capable of thinking, a body endowed with reason. It is naked violence and only gives in when confronted with greater violence."[9]

The next two claims of the essay, which address the temporality and the end result of decolonization, are just as categorical as the first. It is stated that "decolonization is quite simply the substitution of one 'species' of man for another 'species' of man. *Without transition*, this substitution is total, complete, absolute."[10] Bracketing for a later chapter all the complications that arise the day after such a transformation, Fanon adds that the focus of this essay is delimited to "the kind of *tabula rasa* which from the outset defines any decolonization."[11] Immediate and all-encompassing, decolonization is by definition an event of starting over, of creating a blank slate, of completely erasing a species of the past and replacing it with an entirely new species. Decolonization is therefore a special kind of event, one that happens not so much in history as to history, rupturing with one history to begin a different one. It is yet another expression of the Nietzschean will that I have been discussing throughout this book, which seeks to "break the history of the world in two."[12] In Fanon's words, the colonized "decides to put an end to the history of colonization and the history of despoliation in order to bring to life the history of the nation, the history of decolonization."[13]

Almost immediately, however, Fanon introduces a discrepant characterization of decolonization's temporality, as if to oppose his prior claims with a more dialectical form of reasoning: "Decolonization, which sets out to change the order of the world, is clearly an agenda for absolute disorder. But it is not the result of a magical intervention, a natural cataclysm, or a gentleman's agreement. Decolonization, we know, is a historical process. In other words, it can only be understood, it can only find its intelligibility and become transparent to itself insofar as the historicizing movement [*mouvement historicisant*] which gives it form and substance is perceived."[14] Decolonization goes so deeply against the grain of established reality, so thoroughly defies the rules and logic of the world, that it might seem like some sort of magical force is behind it. But this is obviously not the case, just as decolonization is not a natural phenomenon or the product of reasoned compromise. Decolonization can only be understood, according to this passage, as a process that gains form and substance through a movement of historical becoming.[15] What was to shatter history in two is thus placed back into history. As a result, the reader of "On Violence" is confronted with what could be called the "double temporality" of decolonization.[16] If Fanon initially characterizes decolonization as an event of transitionless substitution, another Fanon implicitly challenges this view by asserting that decolonization can only be properly grasped as a historical process, as a violent period of revolutionary transition.

The essay goes on to show how the dynamic relationship that the colonized maintain with violence contributes to shaping the historical form and substance of the decolonization process. Like other texts from Fanon's oeuvre that map out dialectical movement, this process is divided into three key moments: (1) During the colonial situation, the colonized repress, mystify, and sublimate violent impulses in various ways, from practicing symbolically violent rituals to misdirecting violent acts toward fellow colonized subjects.[17] (2) The nationalist parties and the colonized intellectuals—despite their many limitations—eventually "stir up subversive feelings" and contribute to formulating the minimal demands of the colonized, generating what Fanon terms an "atmosphere of violence."[18] (3) Colonial authorities respond to this atmospheric violence with intimidation tactics and repression, but this has the unintended consequence of strengthening the resolve of the colonized and "setting violence in motion."[19] The essay relatedly distinguishes between the first "insurrectional phase" of decolonization and "the second phase, i.e. nation building."[20] Much of "On Violence" is dedicated to fleshing out the details of how the colonized pass from one moment to the next and transition between phases. But the essay never fully accounts for its competing characterization of decolonization as a movement that occurs without transition, that takes place without moments or phases. To attend to this alternative conceptualization of change is to catch a glimpse of a subterranean alternative to dialectics, which construes decolonization as an instantaneous rupture rather than a historical process.

Something similar is at stake when "On Violence" expands upon the notion of substituting one species of man for another species of man. The reader is told that decolonization "introduces into being a rhythm specific to a new generation of men, a new language, and a new humanity. Decolonization is truly the creation of new men."[21] The use of repetition in this passage, its emphasis on the thoroughly *new* character of the rhythm, language, and humanity that is introduced into being, recalls the description of decolonization as a tabula rasa. If, by definition, decolonization is a kind of clearing, an event of starting over again with a blank slate, then it follows that the new men of decolonization are effectively created from nothing, that their emergence constitutes the authentic birth of an entirely new kind of being, of a species of man with no ties to the previous species. This would explain why the substitution is described as total, complete, and absolute. However, Fanon immediately nuances his account of these new men and their creation, which has the effect of introducing into the argument—once again—a discrepant characterization of decolonization: "But such a creation cannot be attributed to a supernatural power: The 'thing' colonized becomes a man through the very process of his self-liberation. Decolonization, therefore, implies the urgent need to thoroughly challenge the colonial situation. Its definition can, if we want to describe it accurately, be summed up in the well-known words: 'The last shall be first.' Decolonization is the verification of this phrase."[22] According to this passage, something is not supernaturally created from nothing during decolonization, since the colonized "thing" becomes the new man by passing through a historical process of self-liberation, of negating the negation of humanity in order to (re)create humanity. Yet this view of change implicitly challenges the essay's prior association of decolonization with a tabula rasa, since the colonized thing is not so much erased as dialectically transformed into the opposite of a thing, substituted for a qualitatively new, translated version of the self. Once again opposing his own, more subterranean propositions with dialectical thinking, Fanon suggests that there is no authentic birth in decolonization, since a collective entity persists throughout the redemptive, quasi-biblical movement from last to first.

Another major issue in "On Violence" that pits Fanon against himself is the opposition between the colonizer and the colonized and the overcoming of this opposition. Early in the essay, Fanon posits that "decolonization is the encounter between two congenitally antagonistic forces that in fact owe their originality to the kind of substantification secreted and nurtured by the colonial situation. Their first confrontation was colored by violence and their cohabitation—or rather the exploitation of the colonized by the colonizer—continued at the point of the bayonet and under cannon fire."[23] This passage, as with many others from *The Wretched of the Earth*, ought to be read alongside Jean-Paul Sartre's *Critique of Dialectical Reason*.[24] In the latter work, which had a major impact on Fanon, Sartre theorizes colonialism as a praxis and a process.[25] Sartre's notion of praxis can be telegraphically summarized as a form of willful action that contributes to a project, which transforms existing material conditions in the service of an end.[26] Applying this general definition to the specific case of colonialism, Sartre contends that a violent praxis of domination and settlement creates the material conditions for the end goal of colonialist superexploitation, a process that institutionalizes and continuously reproduces its founding praxis.[27] In the passage from "On Violence," Fanon describes the colonial situation in analogous terms, noting how a violent confrontation produces a relation of exploitation sustained by the continual threat and use of further violence. The forces "colonizer" and "colonized" are secretions of this situation, products of the colonial "practico-inert."[28] This explains why the next few pages of the essay offer such a striking and detailed account of the "compartmentalized world" of colonial society.[29] The spatial distribution of the colony, its compartmentalization into two opposing zones, is the material embodiment of violent colonialist praxis, and this congealed violence *substantifies* those who inhabit it, conditioning—without wholly determining—their actions.[30] In Fanon's analysis, these conditions foster a contradictory relationship of conflictual cohabitation between the colonizer and the colonized, what Sartre describes as a relationship of "antagonistic reciprocity."[31] The encounter of decolonization is a subsequent moment of this same dynamic relationship, which entails its own "absolute praxis" of violence that sets in motion a new process consisting of nation building.[32]

This dialectical account of the opposition between the colonizer and the colonized is complicated when "On Violence" addresses the Manichaeanism of these congenitally antagonistic forces. According to Fanon, colonialism is "the organization of a Manichaean world" that secretes the colonizer as the pinnacle of what is good and the colonized as the incarnation of "absolute evil."[33] The careful reader will note a structural similarity between this description of the colonial situation and Fanon's discussion in *Black Skin, White Masks* of "a genuinely Manichaean notion of the world," which opposes white superiority to black inferiority. This earlier text considers how *le Noir* responds to such an opposition, either by attempting to become white, by affirming blackness, or by rejecting both poles of the opposition. The colonized of "On Violence" pursues a slightly different path. In Fanon's account, the colonized inverts colonial Manichaeanism and declares that it is in fact the colonizer who embodies absolute evil. In this way, Fanon elaborates upon and develops Sartre's understanding of violence as a "structure of human action under the sway of Manichaeism," which always "presents itself as *counter-violence*, that is to say, as a retaliation against the violence of the Other."[34] For Fanon, decolonizing violence is precisely a kind of Manichaean "counter-violence" that responds in a reciprocal manner to the Manichaean violence of the colonizer. By treating the colonized as the Other, as non-human and as absolutely evil, the colonizer becomes—for the colonized—what he sees in the colonized.[35] Or, as Fanon more concisely puts it, "the Manichaeanism of the colonist produces a Manichaeanism of the colonized. The theory of the 'absolute evil of the colonist' is in response to the theory of the 'absolute evil' of the native."[36]

This idea somewhat resonates with Fanon's examination in *A Dying Colonialism* of how foreign domination and colonial rule produce in the native a reactional attitude of undifferentiated rejection toward all things European, including the European settler community living in Algeria. As the reader will recall, Fanon argues that the armed struggle makes possible the differentiation of Algeria's European minority, such that the native's attitude of absolute rejection mutates into the recognition that some set-tlers are actually comrades in the fight against colonialism.[37] In "On Vio-lence," however, it appears that no such transformation takes place during the struggle: "The Manichaeanism that first governed colonial society is maintained intact during the period of decolonization. In fact the colonist never ceases to be the enemy, the antagonist, in plain words public enemy number one [*très précisément l'homme à abattre*]."[38] Decolonization is accordingly a persistent battle, from start to finish, between opposing Manichaeanisms. The colonized respond to colonialism's absolute nega-tion of their humanity (the colonized = an absolutely evil thing) with abso-lute negation (the colonizer = *l'homme à abattre*, the man to cut down or slaughter).

The absolute quality of this double negation has led Nick Nesbitt to con-vincingly argue that "On Violence" is not only in critical dialogue with Sar-tre's *Critique* but also with Alexandre Kojève's reinterpretation of the Hegelian master-slave dialectic.[39] Recall that for Kojève the slave becomes free through the "'dialectical,' or better, revolutionary, overcoming of the World," which presupposes its *absolute* negation."[40] And yet, as I have sug-gested in previous chapters, Fanon typically conceives of Manichaean oppositions as nondialectical, such that the relationship between these antagonistic forces tends to be one of strict heterogeneity rather than con-tradictory interpenetration. This is not to say that Fanon ought to be read against Kojève but rather that we ought to appreciate their elective affinity on an even deeper level. To do this is to reflect upon the inverted commas that Kojève places over the word "dialectical" before advancing "revolution-ary" as a more precise term in describing the slave's absolute negation of the World. Without obsessing over the question of influence, whether direct or indirect, it is worth appreciating how Fanon applies pressure on the exact same point as Kojève, placing—in his own way—inverted commas over any straightforwardly dialectical account of the life-and-death struggle between the colonizer and the colonized.

Consider first how Kojève reinterprets the master-slave dialectic in an extraordinarily important footnote that can be found toward the end of his book on Hegel's *Phenomenology of Spirit*:

In truth, only the Slave "overcomes" his "nature" and finally becomes Citizen. . . . The final fight, which transforms the Slave into Citizen, overcomes Mastery in a *nondialectical* fashion: the Master is simply killed, and he dies as Master. . . . Therefore one can say that Aristotle correctly described the Master. He erred only in believing that the Master is Man in general—that is, in denying the humanity of the Slave. He was right in saying that the Slave as Slave *is* not truly human; but he was wrong in believing that the Slave could not *become* human.[41]

The fundamental idea of this passage bears repeating: the slave's revolutionary overcoming of the master is *nondialectical*. The process does not lead to an overcoming of the contradiction but rather to the total elimination of one of its aspects. As Fredric Jameson has observed, whereas the slave, through labor, engages in the "determinate Negation of matter, which produces specific works and physical objects," this must be "sharply distinguished from the absolute Negation which produces only death and destruction."[42] Kojève reserves this latter form of negation for the Master in the Slave's becoming Citizen-Human.

Now consider how Fanon recasts the antagonistic relationship between the colonizer and the colonized in "On Violence": "The zone inhabited by the colonized is not complementary to the zone inhabited by the colonizers. The two zones confront each other, but not in the service of a higher unity. Governed by a purely Aristotelian logic, they follow the principle of mutual exclusion: There is no conciliation possible, one of the terms is superfluous."[43] Completely defying the expectations generated by his prior statements, Fanon affirms, like Kojève, that the Manichaean opposition between the colonizer and the colonized cannot find a dialectical resolution and that Aristotle ultimately got it right. The contradictory poles are actually contrary opposites in the strict Aristotelian sense, opposites that, in Aristotle's words, "are not in any way interdependent, but are contrary one to the other. The good is not spoken of as the good *of the bad*, but as *the contrary of the bad*, nor is the white spoken of as the white *of the black*, but as *the contrary of the black*."[44] The colonizer and the colonized, from this standpoint, only relate to each other on the basis of mutual exclusion. In more Kantian terms, to recall Fanon's vocabulary in previous works, the contradiction is shown to be an antinomy.[45]

It would be tempting to follow the lead of some of Fanon's most dedicated readers and restrict the implications of the previous passage from "On Violence" to the colonial situation. It could then be argued that a dialectical overcoming of the opposition between the colonizer and the colonized is indeed possible but only when their relationship enters the second moment of its becoming, the decolonizing moment during which the colonial integument is burst asunder.[46] This interpretation remains plausible even when Fanon asserts that, throughout the armed struggle, "every colonist reasons on the basis of simple arithmetic" and "envisages rather arithmetically the disappearance of the colonized."[47] Although the colonizers remain tied to an Aristotelian outlook during the struggle, Fanon includes an essential footnote on this issue, which cites Sartre's *Critique* and argues—in good Hegelian fashion—that the colonizer cannot completely eliminate the colonized because the master is ultimately dependent upon the slave.[48] Eliminating the slave would eliminate the conditions of possibility for the master's own existence qua master. It follows that, for the colonizer, absolute negation is a self-defeating fantasy, since it would ensure the colonizer's own disappearance with the disappearance of the colonized.

Fanon nevertheless breaks with this dialectical mode of thinking when he asserts that, unlike the colonizers, the colonized *can* exercise the kind of arithmetic reason governed by Aristotelian logic insofar as they *do* seek to completely destroy the colonial masters. As though returning to the argument for exclusion at the end of "Racism and Culture,"[49] Fanon theorizes decolonization as an operation of subtraction: "The colonial context, as we have said, is characterized by the dichotomy it inflicts on the world. Decolonization unifies this world by a radical decision to remove its heterogeneity."[50] Stated differently, the colonized do not request inclusion; they decide to exclude. Decolonization therefore cannot be understood as an appeal to "the famous principle that all men are equal."[51] This is the wrongheaded approach of the colonized intellectuals, those who "have followed the colonizer onto the plane of the abstract universal."[52] Instead of appealing to an abstract notion of universal equality and endeavoring to make it concrete, the subtractive procedure of decolonization constitutes as its effect a unification without heterogeneity, an *in situ* embodiment of a competing form of universal equality.[53] This explains Fanon's complicated assertion that "challenging the colonial world" entails "the untidy affirmation of an originality posed as absolute."[54] What is affirmed in the frenzy and disorder of decolonizing violence is absolutely severed from the colonial world; it is the vision of an original, totally independent, and entirely new world founded subtractively on the exclusion of the colonial status and its attendant abstract universalism.

Fanon will intermittently reiterate this point by underscoring the importance of "annihilating the colonist" and "ejecting him outright from the picture."[55] As Michael Hardt and Antonio Negri put it, Fanon's decolonizing violence is "open negativity," a relation of force that "does not lead to any dialectical synthesis" but rather "poses a separation from colonialist domination."[56] This entails, for Fanon, decimating the colonial practico-inert that secretes the colonizers as a reciprocally antagonistic force: "To destroy the colonial world means nothing less than demolishing the colonizer's zone, burying it deep within the earth or banishing it from the territory."[57] Passages like these contribute to undermining any notion of overcoming the antagonistic encounter dialectically, for the unity of decolonization is built on the disappearance of both sides of the encounter. The new man of decolonization is not the sublation of the colonizer-colonized opposition but rather, to reiterate, the result of subtraction (in terms of the colonizer) and substitution (in terms of the colonized).

Fanon nevertheless toggles back to dialectical thinking when he addresses the relationship between colonizing violence and decolonizing violence: "The very same people who had it constantly drummed into them that the only language they understood was that of force, now decide to express themselves with force. In fact the colonist has always shown them the path they should follow to liberation. The argument chosen by the colonized was conveyed to them by the colonist, and by an ironic twist of fate [*retour de choses*] it is now the colonized who state that it is the colonizer who only understands the language of force."[58] Just as the contradictory nature of capitalism produces its own gravediggers, so too does colonialism's violence "boomerang" on itself, contributing in this way to its own negation.[59] Sartre's *Critique* articulates a similar position in its analysis of the Algeria War, maintaining that "the violence of the rebel *was* the violence of the colonialist; there was never any other."[60] For Sartre, the rebel's violence—as a negation of the negation that is colonialism—is also an affirmation, the positive constitution of an independent Algeria, "whose content would be defined in struggle."[61] Fanon likewise considers how negating violence, when wielded by the colonized, takes on "positive, formative features"—including elevating the level of consciousness, de-inferiorizing the psyche, and contributing to the formation of group unity and collective responsibility—such that "the second phase, i.e. nation building, is facilitated by the existence of this mortar kneaded with blood and rage."[62] When Fanon is read alongside Sartre, the extent to which both thinkers exercise an emphatically dialectical mode of thinking becomes clearer. Such parallels complicate the characterization of decolonizing violence as open negativity without, in the words of Hardt and Negri, "the upbeat that will be resolved in a future harmony."[63] To be clear, my point is not that this nondialectical summation of decolonizing violence is wrong but rather that it is only half of the story. The challenge is to keep both Fanons in view at the same time so that their conflict in the text is not rendered illegible. Along with the discrepancy between an instantaneous rupture and a historical process and between ex nihilo creation and dialectical transformation, this conflict gains expression through the related discrepancy between the ultimately Aristotelian or Hegelian-Marxian nature of decolonizing violence and the colonizer-colonized opposition.

But it is worth noting that this conflict in the text gains expression in other ways as well, not only through discrepant claims but also through the underlying tension between said claims and the theoretical practice that produces them. An especially salient example of this kind of tension occurs when Fanon examines the relationship between race and class in colonial society:

Looking at the immediacies of the colonial context, it is clear that what divides this world is first and foremost what species, what race one belongs to. In the colonies the economic infrastructure is also a superstructure. The cause is effect: You are rich because you are white, you are white because you are rich. This is why Marxist analyses should always be slightly stretched [*doivent être toujours légèrement distendues*] when it comes to addressing the colonial problem. . . . It is not the factories, the estates, or the bank account which primarily characterize the "ruling class." The ruling species is first and foremost the outsider from elsewhere, different from the indigenous population, "the others."[64]

As I discussed in the introduction to this book, Fanon's analysis of the colonial situation performs the stretching that he prescribes, insofar as the passage dialectically translates certain abstractly universal categories associated with Marxism—infrastructure, superstructure, class—so that they may take on a new, concrete form. As a result, Marxist analysis becomes slightly stretched, distended, or dilated, made to swell and expand from within. Fanon thus participates in a long tradition of the best Marxist thinkers, those who remain faithful to Marxism by "betraying" its most basic categories, which is to say, by reinventing these categories in response to changing historical conditions.[65] Yet, in another sense, Fanon stretches some of these categories to the breaking point, such that the product of his theoretical practice ruptures with Marxism's dialectical kernel. If a society's infrastructure and superstructure are standardly thought to form a relationship of contradictory interpenetration, as captured by various metaphors that are deployed throughout the Marxist tradition (e.g., reflection, expression, relative autonomy, last-instance determination), Fanon suggests that under colonialism the relationship between these two realms is actually one of strict identity (cause = effect). Put another way, instead of a unity of opposites, Fanon appears to be describing a relationship of unity without opposition. He also stretches the contradictory relationship between classes to encompass a division between races or species, but, as previously discussed, "On Violence" often presents this relationship as one of mutual exclusion and heterogeneity. When this is the case, such a relationship likewise does not constitute a unity of opposites. It is, on the contrary, an opposition without unity, the inverse of the relationship between the infrastructure and superstructure of colonial society. Accordingly, in both cases, Fanon's claims appear to break with dialectical thinking even as he is dialectically translating basic categories from Marxism to produce said claims. The inconsistency between Fanon's theoretical practice and its product thus mirrors the essay's primary object of analysis, for decolonization likewise vacillates in and out of dialectics.

This raises some pressing questions about the role of European culture and thought in decolonization. Can ideas and values inherited from Europe, like Europe's colonizing violence, be dialectically transformed into weapons of decolonization? Or are they to be submitted to an absolutely subtractive procedure along with the colonizer and the colonizer's zone? To address these questions, it is worth noting that, for Fanon, any discussion of cultural life in the colony must begin with colonialism's unrelenting campaign of assimilation and acculturation. As Fanon puts it, "the colonist only quits undermining the colonized once the latter have proclaimed loud and clear that white values reign supreme."[66] The values that Fanon has in mind, which he also terms "Mediterranean values," include individualism, enlightenment, beauty, and the abstract ideal of human dignity.[67] If this understanding of the colonial situation resonates with how it is construed in earlier works, Fanon offers a divergent account of how the colonized *respond* to the imposition of foreign values. In *A Dying Colonialism*, for example, Fanon describes how European cultural elements are "'digested' in connection with the national struggle" and repurposed as anticolonial instruments of war.[68] He now advances a very different view, sustaining that the colonized actually purge themselves of everything that colonialism has forced them to internalize: "In the period of decolonization, the colonized masses thumb their noses at these very values, insult them, and *full-throatedly vomit them up*."[69]

This vivid imagery of total elimination, of getting everything out that has forced its way in rather than digesting it, submits white Mediterranean values to the same Aristotelian logic of mutual exclusion that removes the colonizer and demolishes the colonizer's zone. "Whenever an authentic liberation struggle has been fought," Fanon concludes, "there is an effective eradication of the superstructure borrowed . . . from the colonialist bourgeois circles."[70] It may be that a socialist revolution in the metropole can dialectically overcome the existing bourgeois superstructure, but, when this superstructure travels to the colony, an authentic liberation struggle cannot respond to its translation with translation but must opt instead for a complete break with translation. At the same time, an underlying tension persists between Fanon's claims and the theoretical practice that produces them, since the theorization of decolonization as the suspension of translation includes a translation of the Marxist notion of superstructure. Much like the performative contradictions of *Black Skin, White Masks*, Fanon's enunciation in "On Violence" of the eradication of a borrowed superstructure is at the same time the preservation, in dialectically modified form, of an element from a borrowed superstructure.

But perhaps a distinction needs to be made between the vomiting up of bourgeois European values and the translation of anti-bourgeois European thought. While Fanon's own engagement with Marxism supports this distinction, it becomes less convincing once his ancient Greek and Christian references are taken into account. Indeed, no such distinction is ever explicitly stated or developed in "On Violence." Fanon instead describes a more Manichaean division that absolutely opposes the values of the colonized to the values of the colonizer. With respect to the former set of values, Fanon emphasizes "first and foremost the land" as a value, which provides both bread and dignity, though this dignity "has nothing to do" with the abstract

European ideal of human dignity.[71] He also mentions the collectivist value of shared responsibility, exemplified in militant action and in the "African institution" of group self-criticism.[72]

For some readers, it may be surprising that Fanon turns to African tradition at this point in his argument, since he typically harbors great skepticism toward such cultural elements, convinced that they are invariably mummified and distorted during the process of colonization. In fact, "On Violence" reiterates this point on various occasions, maintaining, for example, that "the arrival of the colonist signified syncretically the death of indigenous society, cultural lethargy, and petrification of the individual. For the colonized, life can only materialize from the rotting cadaver of the colonist."[73] Given the prevalence of passages like this one, it would be a mistake to read Fanon's allusion to self-criticism as an uncritical celebration of African tradition or as an invitation to return to precolonial times. It is far more likely that Fanon is attempting to reclaim the practice, "which has been much talked about recently," from its narrow presentation as a European discovery.[74] The image of the colonizer's cadaver, on the other hand, seems to capture where Fanon ultimately places his confidence: in the birth of new values that emerge from the absolute negation of the colonial world.

But, as I have argued throughout this book, what it means to describe something as "new" is a major site of contention for Fanon, and this remains the case in how "On Violence" approaches new and old cultures and values. While the essay translates ancient Greek, Christian, and Hegelian-Marxian ideas to theorize decolonization, its propositional content leaves their fate uncertain. Will these ideas persist in the decolonized world to come or will they, too, be full-throatedly vomited up and eradicated? It is also unclear what the future holds for traditional African institutions. Can certain rituals be translated in the service of the new man of decolonization or will the new man exhibit, as Fanon puts it, "a singular loss of interest in these rituals"?[75] Although referring specifically to the formation of a decolonized economy, the following passage—which represents an exceptional moment of indecision among a multitude of decisions—could be read as a more general, subterranean statement concerning what constitutes decolonization as such: "Everything has to be started over again, everything has to be rethought. . . . Perhaps everything has to be started again."[76] Perhaps.

THE *DÉCALAGES* OF POLITICAL ORGANIZATION AND
THE ENCOUNTERS OF SPONTANEITY

In many respects, the second chapter of *The Wretched of the Earth* departs from the first by developing a generally consistent, dialectical account of decolonization. The challenge is to determine how to read the two chapters together. One popular approach is to frame the second chapter, titled "Grandeur and Weakness of Spontaneity," as a "reflexive and revisionary commentary" on the inaugural claims of "On Violence."[77] If "the unmasking of antinomy as contradiction . . . constitutes truly dialectical thinking as such,"[78] the aforementioned approach to reading Fanon argues that the aim of "Grandeur and Weakness of Spontaneity" is to reveal how the putatively antinomical oppositions of "On Violence" are actually dialectical contradictions in disguise. But even if this were the case, it would still be worth considering whether any discrepancies or inconsistencies stubbornly persist in Fanon's writing, which would destabilize such attempts to construe *The Wretched of the Earth* as a text that gradually resolves the internal conflict of its opening chapter in favor of dialectical thinking. To fully address this issue, however, it will be necessary to trace Fanon's new account of the historical process of decolonization in an effort to appreciate what is reaffirmed from "On Violence" and what is discarded. Once this necessary detour is complete, I will propose an alternative interpretation of the relationship between the first two chapters of *The Wretched of the Earth* that will inform my reading of the remainder of Fanon's final work.

"Grandeur and Weakness of Spontaneity" begins somewhat unexpectedly with a discussion of the weaknesses that typically plague the leadership and political organizations of the colonized. In other words, far from one-sidedly criticizing spontaneity in favor of its opposite, a significant section of the chapter is dedicated to highlighting the limits of existing organizational forms and their leaders within the colonial context. The main weakness that Fanon identifies is the recurrent missed encounter between the urban cadre of the nationalist parties and the rural peasant masses.[79] Instead of mutually enriching each other in the struggle for liberation within the framework of a united political organization, Fanon identifies a "gap [*décalage*]" between these groups, which he also describes as a "difference of rhythm" and a "gulf [*fossé*]" of separation.[80] While the groups under discussion immediately evoke a spatial division between town and country, the term "*décalage*" suggests that the division is more temporal in nature, that the gap is a kind of "time lag."[81] Indeed, the two sides maintain a relationship of non-correspondence at least in part because they expect change to occur at different rhythms. Whereas the masses "demand an immediate and total improvement of their situation, . . . the cadres, gauging the difficulties likely to be created by employers, limit and put a restraint on their demands."[82] The *décalage* thus partially stems from the divergence between instantaneous rupture—what "On Violence" theorizes as a transitionless substitution—and gradualist reform.

Fanon will return to this important distinction later in his argument. For now, he focuses on other contributing factors to the *décalage* between the urban nationalists and the rural masses, such as the former group's failure to translate the modern organizational form of the party in light of the colony's uneven historical development. Consider how Fanon portrays this situation:

The birth of nationalist parties in the colonized countries is contemporary with the constitution of an intellectual and business elite. These elites attach primordial importance to the organization as such, and the fetishism of organization often takes priority over a rational study of colonial society. The notion of the party is a notion imported from the metropole. This instrument of modern resistance is plastered as is onto a protean, unbalanced reality where slavery, bondage, barter, cottage industries, and stock transactions exist side by side.[83]

Fanon's description of the uneven or unbalanced ("*déséquilibrée*") reality of the colony gestures toward another kind of *décalage*, one between interrelated yet staggered and conflicting temporalities associated with distinct modes of production and exchange.[84] Modern industry booms to the point of creating a class of intellectual and business elites, a nascent bourgeoisie, while "the rural masses still live in a feudal state whose overbearingly medieval structure is nurtured by the colonial administrators and army."[85] Since the modern party form historically develops out of industrial capitalism, the colony's budding industrialization establishes the material conditions of possibility for the formation of local, nationalist parties. Yet such organizations, when plastered onto colonial reality, are out of joint with the unevenness of their new surroundings. As a consequence, another *décalage* emerges, this time between the untranslated party form and the colony. This is because the historical contradictions of colonial reality do not correspond to the historical contradictions that produced this instrument of modern resistance. Not unlike his stance on implementing European methods of psychiatric treatment in North Africa, Fanon concludes that "innovations and adaptations should have been made as to the type of organization" that would be adequate for the temporal disequilibrium of the colony, that the party form should have been translated in accordance with colonial reality rather than fetishistically copied without modification from the metropole.[86]

How does the *décalage* between the party form and the colony contribute to sustaining the *décalage* between the urban nationalists and the rural masses? For Fanon, the former group's fetishism of organization principally affects the party platform, such that a concrete analysis of colonial society is exchanged for an ahistorical idealization of the proletariat:

The great mistake, the inherent flaw of most of the political parties in the underdeveloped regions has been traditionally to address first and foremost the most politically conscious elements: the urban proletariat, the small tradesmen and civil servants, i.e., a tiny section of the population which represents barely more than one percent. . . . In colonial territories the proletariat is the kernel of the colonized people most pampered by the colonial regime. The embryonic urban proletariat is relatively privileged. In the capitalist countries, the proletariat has nothing to lose and possibly everything to gain. In the colonized countries, the proletariat has everything to lose.[87]

The final two lines of this passage evoke the famous closing statement of *The Communist Manifesto*, which maintains that the proletariat has nothing to lose but their chains and a world to win.[88] Fanon posits that this may be true of the proletarian masses in capitalist Europe, but in the uneven historical context of colonized Africa the proletariat is still a small segment of the population that partially benefits from the colonial regime. Fanon thus departs from his argument in "Racism and Culture" that proletarianization plays a major role in advancing the struggle for liberation.[89] Such a view is now presented as the mistaken position of the imported political parties.

Their obsession with the proletariat leads them to neglect the rural masses and thus perpetuate the missed encounter that constitutes one of their greatest organizational weaknesses.

How are we to understand Fanon's departure from the standard Marxist position that "the proletariat alone is a really revolutionary class"?[90] When read by itself and out of context, the above extended passage from *The Wretched of the Earth* could easily be interpreted as evidence of Fanon *provincializing* Marxism by demarcating the historical limits of its analysis.[91] Marxism's purportedly universal categories and notions, one could argue, are nothing but generalizations of European historical experience that have no bearing on the reality of non-European countries. Yet, when Fanon's discussion of the colonial proletariat is read in conjunction with a related passage from "On Violence," it becomes clear that he is actually performing a different theoretical maneuver. As he states in the previous chapter, "The peasantry is systematically left out of most of the nationalist parties' propaganda. But it is obvious that in colonial countries only the peasantry is revolutionary. It has nothing to lose and everything to gain."[92] Notice how this passage stretches rather than restricts the closing statement of *The Communist Manifesto*. It sustains that the negative universality of having nothing to lose, which can dialectically transform into the positive universality of a new world, is a feature of the peasantry rather than the proletariat in the colonial context.[93] This is why Fanon ought to be read as contributing to the *deprovincialization* of Marxism, to the overcoming of its historical limits, insofar as he translates Marxism's abstractly universal categories and notions so that they can take on a new, concrete form in the colony.[94]

This is precisely what the nationalist parties fail to do. Along with idealizing the urban proletariat, their platforms consistently disregard the rural masses and underestimate their revolutionary potential. According to Fanon, such an outlook toward the peasantry is likewise imported directly from the metropole. He relates that "the history of bourgeois revolutions and the history of proletarian revolutions have demonstrated that the peasant masses often represent a curb on the revolution."[95] As though paraphrasing Marx's *The Eighteenth Brumaire of Louis Bonaparte*, Fanon also acknowledges that in industrialized countries the peasantry standardly exhibits "reactionary behavior" characterized by "individualism, lack of discipline, the love of money, fits of rage, and deep depression."[96] If the nationalist parties fetishistically copy this analysis from the metropole,

Fanon goes on to argue that in the colony it is actually "within the burgeoning proletariat that we find individualistic behavior," whereas the peasants exhibit great "discipline" when defending the traditional collectivism of their "community-minded" social structures.[97] While Fanon continues to use certain Marxian categories inherited from the metropole (e.g., proletariat, peasantry), they are stretched to include new characteristics specific to the colony. The reader thus encounters more evidence of Fanon deprovincializing Marxism by translating its key terms and concepts in an effort to challenge the dogmatically provincial platform of the nationalist parties.

The theoretical limitations of this kind of platform have practical effects that intensify the *décalage* between the urban nationalists and the rural masses. When the nationalist parties attempt to extend their reach beyond the urban centers, Fanon notes that they "are unable to implant their organization within the countryside."[98] He continues:

Instead of using the existing structures in order to invest them with nationalist or progressive elements, they are intent on disrupting traditional existence within the context of the colonial system. . . . They do not place their theoretical knowledge at the service of the people, but instead try to regiment the masses according to an *a priori* schema. Consequently, they parachute into the villages inexperienced or unknown leaders from the capital who, empowered by the central authorities, endeavor to manage the *douar* or the village like a company committee. The traditional chiefs are ignored, sometimes bullied. Instead of integrating the history of the village and conflicts between tribes and clans into the people's struggle, the history of the future nation has a singular disregard for minor local histories and tramples on the only thing relevant to the nation's actuality.[99]

The rural masses are expected to conform to the nationalist parties and blanketly accept that this new form of organization will replace their traditional social structures and leaders. Fanon describes this replacement as a parachuting of foreign ideas and people into the villages of the countryside, which suggests that, like French paratroopers, the nationalist parties invade native territory.[100] The comparison is an apt one because the imposition of untranslated European political forms, the attempt to take power from indigenous authorities, and the general disregard for local histories and traditions cannot but enact a kind of internal colonization.[101] To achieve independence, in other words, the rural masses are told to exchange the colonial relation for its neocolonial cousin. This of course convinces no one and the party fails to make inroads in the countryside. Instead of learning from this failure and recognizing it as a sign of the deep limitations of their approach to organizing, the urban nationalists view it as a confirmation of their suspicion that the peasants are condemned to backwardness.

This is not to say that Fanon sheds his own skepticism toward tradition and now calls for its uncritical defense and preservation. On the contrary, he argues that the colonizers often use longstanding customs and rituals for their own ends in order to further entrench the *décalage* between the urban nationalists and the rural masses. To develop this point, Fanon focuses on the antagonism between traditional leaders and the party leaders who seek to replace them. The colonizers find ways to prop up the authority of the local chiefs and elders, not out of respect for indigenous ways of life but rather because these figures, in their attempt to preserve their authority, "form a barrier between the young Westernized nationalists and the masses."[102] In this way, tradition is used to deepen the division between groups that could be working together to fight for their shared independence. The lesson here is not only that tradition can be easily manipulated as part of colonialism's broader strategy to divide and conquer. Fanon is also revealing how the nationalist parties, by antagonistically combatting tradition, by attempting to supplant rather than incorporate traditional social structures and local histories, play directly into the hands of colonial rule and make a united front against colonialism nearly impossible. To the opposition between preserving tradition or combatting it, Fanon implicitly proposes and later explores a third option of translation, which would entail dynamizing tradition from within, imbuing it with new life and progressive elements so that it could contribute to the struggle for liberation.

At this point in the chapter, Fanon presents two possible paths to independence, as well as minor variations of these paths. The first path entails the anticolonial propaganda of the nationalist parties resonating with the rural masses despite the *décalage* separating the two groups. The propaganda is effective because "the memory of the precolonial period is still very much alive in the villages."[103] The dialectical interplay of collective memory and revolutionary propaganda contributes to fomenting what the previous chapter termed an atmosphere of violence, and, just as before, Fanon reaffirms that colonial repression sets this atmospheric violence in motion, catalyzing the outbreak of a spontaneous insurrection.[104] When this occurs, due to the grave limitations of the existing political parties, the urban nationalists "make no attempt to organize the insurrection. They do not dispatch agents to the interior to politicize the masses, to enlighten their consciousness or raise the struggle to a higher level. . . . There is no contamination of the rural movement by the urban movement. Each side evolves according to its own dialectic."[105] The colonizers then pit the urban dialectic against the rural dialectic so as to cement their *décalage*. Faced with widespread revolt among the peasants, the colonizers break ties with the traditional authorities of the villages and begin working with the most easily coopted members of the nationalist parties. This new alliance quells the insurrection and negotiates a peaceful transfer of power that results in formal independence and the imposition of a neocolonial economy and state.

Given the failure of this path to realize decolonization, Fanon spends much of the rest of the chapter describing an alternative route that might avoid the replacement of colonialism with neocolonialism. His discussion of this alternative starts with the emergence of "two lines of action" from within the nationalist parties.[106] The first line of action refers to intellectuals who "criticize the ideological vacuum of the national party and its dearth of strategy and tactics."[107] These intellectuals, isolated and discredited by the party leadership, are wary of electoral politics, dissatisfied with the party's abstract nationalism, and want a clearer vision of independence and the means necessary for achieving it. Fanon's second line of action is composed of highly committed and courageous party members who are "uncomfortable with the party's exacerbated legalism" and consequently participate in subversive and illegal activities that make them the target of repression.[108] These two lines of action, in a seemingly aleatory way, swerve to "encounter" each other, leading to "the formation of a clandestine party, parallel to the official party."[109] As repression intensifies and the party leadership grows closer to compromising with the colonizers, the clandestine party is forced to "retreat to the interior, the mountains, and deep into the rural masses."[110]

This relocation of the clandestine party makes possible another encounter that contributes to overcoming the *décalage* between the urban nationalists and the rural masses. Fanon's description of this moment is particularly striking:

Understandably, the encounter between these militants, hounded by the police, and these restless, instinctively rebellious masses can produce an explosive mixture [*un mélange détonant*] of unexpected power. The men from the towns enter the school of the people and at the same time offer courses for the people on political and military training. The people sharpen their weapons. In fact, the courses do not last long, for the masses, getting back in touch with the intimacy of their own muscles, push the leaders to speed things up. The armed struggle is triggered.[111]

The explosive encounter in the countryside principally educates the educators, those who formerly dismissed the peasantry in theory and in practice. While teaching in the school of the people, the clandestine party members "realize at last that change does not mean reform, that change does not mean improvement. . . . They discover that the rural masses have never ceased to pose the problem of their liberation in terms of violence, of taking back the land from the foreigners, in terms of *national struggle* and armed insurrection."[112] To overcome the *décalage*, in other words, the urban militants of the clandestine party are pushed to shed the old rhythm of gradualist reform so that they can catch up with the rural masses. The former gulf of separation gives way to an alliance that triggers a new, shared dialectic of armed struggle. Fanon goes on to assert that the struggle spreads throughout the countryside as local groups spontaneously rise up against colonial authorities and take back their land. The insurrection grows and expands until it eventually enters the cities. Stretching Marxist analysis once again, Fanon deems the notoriously controversial lumpenproletariat to be the "urban spearhead" of insurrection, even characterizing this sector of society as "one of the most spontaneously and radically revolutionary forces of a colonized people."[113]

While describing such an explosive moment in the struggle, certain subterranean claims from "On Violence" return and interrupt Fanon's otherwise consistently dialectical analysis. It is said, for example, that the "*jacqueries*" or peasant revolts follow "a simple doctrine: The nation must be made to exist. There is no program, no discourse, there are no resolutions, no factions. The problem is clear-cut: the foreigners must leave."[114] Here the struggle is conceived once more in terms of the absolute subtraction of the colonizers and the creation of a new world in their absence. This is a moment of true grandeur insofar as it delivers a series of rapid blows to the colonial system while engendering a euphoric sense of victory, unity, and confidence among those involved in the struggle. It appears as though the rural masses are in the midst of accomplishing their demand for immediate and total change.

To emphasize the all-encompassing nature of this change, its enactment of a kind of tabula rasa, the reader is told that rival families of the countryside "decide to erase everything, to forget everything. Reconciliations abound. Deep-buried, traditional hatreds are dug up, the better to root them out."[115] Whereas Fanon previously maintained that memory and tradition could contribute to the struggle for liberation and should not be ignored by the nationalist parties, he now hails the quasi-Nietzschean decision of the peasants to forget the past and uproot tradition for the sake of action and the flourishing of a new life.[116] These are, of course, not necessarily irreconcilable positions if they apply to different aspects of the past (memories of life without the colonizers versus memories of precolonial rivalry) and to different aspects of tradition (collectivism versus tribalism). But the assertion that *everything* is erased and forgotten, not by a colonizing force but by the collective decision of the colonized, cannot but evoke similar statements made in "On Violence." It is as though, in its explosive excess, this claim subtly articulates a politics of rupturing with history to begin a new history, of voiding the past to invent the future. As John Drabinski alluringly puts it, the kind of temporal dynamic that Fanon is describing "wants not just to suspend unruly memories but, instead, to entomb them in a past that is surpassed in the complete break from history and memory."[117] In other words, while it is true that Fanon generally theorizes the moment of spontaneous revolt from within a dialectical framework, he also gestures toward a different understanding of time and change that unsettles the overarching logic of the chapter.

THE LIMITS OF SPONTANEITY AND THE REDISCOVERY OF POLITICS

Toward the end of the second chapter of *The Wretched of the Earth*, it is revealed that the explosive moment of widespread spontaneous violence is not enough on its own to achieve decolonization. Instead, it sets the stage for a new moment in the dialectic of armed struggle during which the colonialist forces launch a counterattack in an effort to regain their position of authority. The colonized fight just as before, surging head-on toward the enemy with rash confidence, but they are met with heavy machinegun fire and many lives are lost. The peasant rebels hold their ground and refuse to retreat, as though "their own mountain peak [were] the nation." Casualties multiply as a result and those who survive are plagued with doubt; the intense suffering "throws the euphoria and idyll of the first period into question."[118]

It is worth pausing to reflect upon the similarities between this moment in the armed struggle and the dilemma that Épithalos faces in *Parallel Hands*.[119] After his explosive act of violence, he too is surrounded by death and suffering, and his steadfast conviction toward the significance of his act is shaken. In both cases, the same questions arise: Was the act that promised a complete and total change destined to fail? Does the revolutionary event merely contribute to completing another revolution of the same tragic circle that leads from order to disorder to order again? Was the euphoria of the struggle the product of an illusion? Fanon begins to answer these questions in *The Wretched of the Earth* when he transitions from a focus on the grandeur of spontaneity to a critical account of its various weaknesses. This is also the moment when he implicitly refers to and problematizes a number of claims put forward in "On Violence" during his conflicted account of decolonization.

Fanon's critique of spontaneity begins with a discussion of its voluntarism: "This spectacular voluntarism . . . [has] proved in light of experience to be a very great weakness. As long as he imagined passing, *without transition*, from the state of the colonized to the state of the sovereign citizen of an independent nation, as long as he believed in the mirage of the immediacy of his muscles, the colonized achieved no real progress along the road of knowledge."[120] Notice how this passage calls into question Fanon's previous claim that decolonization constitutes a transitionless substitution of the colonized thing for the new man. When the peasant masses spontaneously revolt, they believe that this kind of change is possible and that the exertion of brute force is its guarantee. But Fanon maintains that experience reveals this belief to be a voluntarist illusion of spontaneity. The colonized may demand an immediate exchange of one kind of being for another, but history moves at a different rhythm. It should be clear, however, that Fanon is not calling for a return to gradualist reformism but rather for a dialectical overcoming of transitionless substitution. In Fanon's words, "This voluntarist impetuosity that intends to immediately [*tout de suit*] resolve its destiny with the colonial system is condemned, as a doctrine of instantaneity [*doctrine de l'instantanéisme*], to negate itself. . . . The basic instinct of survival calls for a more flexible, more agile response."[121]

The demand for instantaneous change *"tout de suit,"* so prevalent in the articles Fanon wrote for *El Moudjahid*, is now presented as a transitional moment within an ongoing historical movement.[122] If the spontaneous peasant revolts are to avoid defeat, if they are to prevent the military onslaught from reestablishing colonial rule, they must negate themselves to survive in a modified form. The reader will recall that, according to one possible interpretation of *Parallel Hands*, Épithalos passes through this same movement of self-negation. This analogy suggests that the doctrine of instantaneity is not so much a tragic illusion as a dialectically necessary one. Like *négritude*'s "absoluity" in *Black Skin, White Masks*, it is a liberating fiction that propels the dialectic forward.[123] Accordingly, whereas the temporality of decolonization in "On Violence" is split between an instantaneous rupture and a historical process, the final pages of "Grandeur and Weakness of Spontaneity" weave these divergent temporalities together, converting the voluntarist demand for immediate and total change into a preliminary stage of decolonization's historical becoming.

In Fanon's view, the insurrectional phase of the decolonization process must enter a "second period" by passing from spontaneous peasant revolts to the more flexible and agile strategy of organized guerilla warfare.[124] This more advanced stage of the armed struggle entails a different approach in both spatial and temporal terms. Guerilla fighters are mobile rather than static; they do not attempt to defend a specific mountain peak as though it were the nation itself but rather "[carry] the soil of the homeland to war between [their] bare toes."[125] Likewise, guerilla warfare is not a single event but rather "a succession of local struggles" that contribute to a broader process of change.[126] For this transition in strategy to occur, Fanon argues that the urban militants, now the leaders of the insurrection, must assist the rural masses in their progression along the road of knowledge:

The leaders of the insurrection realize that their units need enlightening, instruction, and indoctrination; an army needs to be created, a central authority established. . . . The leaders who had fled the futile atmosphere of urban politics rediscover politics, no longer as a sleep-inducing technique or a means of mystification, but as the sole means of fueling the struggle and preparing the people for clear-sighted national leadership. The leaders of the insurrection notice that peasant revolts, even grandiose ones, need to be controlled and guided. The leaders are driven to negate the movement as peasant revolt and transform it into a revolutionary war. They discover that the success of the struggle depends on a clear set of objectives, a well-defined methodology, and above all the recognition by the masses of the temporal dynamic of their efforts. One can hold out for three days, three months at most, using the masses' pent-up resentment, but one does not win a national war, one does not rout the formidable machine of the enemy or transform men if one neglects to raise the consciousness of the combatant.[127]

As previously discussed, the spontaneous peasant revolts must be negated so that they can survive in a modified form, so that a new moment in the struggle can emerge, the moment of revolutionary war. For this dialectical movement to occur, politics needs to be rediscovered, not necessarily as a "politics without party" but certainly as a politics without the mystifying nationalist parties.[128] Fanon calls for the short-lived classes of the clandestine party to be resumed so that the insurrection can enter a heightened stage of consciousness and combat. These urban militants, reeducated as a result of their encounter with the peasant rebels, are now in a position to supply the rural masses with military training, political instruction, and the creation of a centralized organizational structure.[129] This is how the voluntarist illusion of transitionless substitution through spontaneous violence can pass into a more nuanced understanding of the objectives, methodology, and temporality of the struggle.

The above extended passage importantly concludes by pointing to another major weakness of spontaneity, which is its dependence on affective sentiments of resentment and hatred toward the oppressor. While these sentiments can inspire bursts of explosive violence, Fanon maintains that their intensity fades over time and is insufficiently motivating for the colonized to endure a lengthy revolutionary war. Fanon also observes that affective sentiments, not unlike local traditions, can be easily manipulated by the enemy. Once it becomes clear that heighted repression emboldens the colonized, the colonizer "can phase out the violent aspects of his presence" and engage in "psychological warfare," disarming the colonized through "psychological devices [that] defuse their hatred."[130] Politeness, formal respect, symbolic acts of generosity, monetary gifts, and minor concessions can all contribute to the psychoaffective pacification of the colonized. In the absence of a conscious political program, such a systematic diffusion of animosity makes compromise more appealing. In Fanon's words, "The violent, unanimous demands of the revolution, which once lit up the sky, now shrink to more modest proportions."[131] But the flagging radicalism of the struggle only serves to strengthen colonial power, for "certain concessions are in fact shackles."[132] Fanon reasons that "the militant must be supplied with further, more searching explanations so that the enemy's concessions do not pull the wool over his eyes."[133] To safeguard the armed struggle and its longevity, in other words, political education must reveal the deeper meaning of violence beyond its expression of resentment and hatred.

In passages like these, Fanon sometimes sounds as if he is advocating for replacing the grassroots spontaneity of the rural masses with a kind of top-down urban vanguardism. Some readers might even be tempted to search for parallels between Fanon's vision of political leadership and the failed leadership of the nationalist parties, which contributed to the organizational weaknesses of these groups and their missed encounter with the peasantry. The following excerpt from *The Wretched of the Earth* nevertheless elucidates how Fanon's understanding of the relationship between the urban and rural elements of the armed struggle avoids reproducing the *décalage* that opens the chapter:

All this clarification, these successive illuminations of consciousness, and this progression on the road to understanding the history of societies can only be achieved within the framework of an organization, by guiding the people. This organization is established by the revolutionary elements arriving from the towns at the beginning of the insurrection and those who make their way to the interior as the struggle intensifies. It is this core which constitutes the embryonic political organism of the insurrection. But, as for the peasants who develop their understanding through experience, they prove apt to lead [*à diriger*] the popular struggle. A wave of edification and reciprocal enrichment flows between the nation on a war footing and its leaders [*ses dirigeants*]. Traditional institutions are reinforced, expanded, and sometimes literally transformed. The tribunal for local conflicts, the *djemaas*, and the village assemblies are transformed into revolutionary tribunals, into politico-military committees.[134]

For Fanon, urban elements make up the political core of the revolutionary war and provide leadership and guidance during the struggle. However, the peasants, through the development of experiential knowledge, assume the role of the struggle's vanguard. When Fanon refers to a movement of reciprocal enrichment between the nation and its leaders, one might assume that he is referring to a new relationship between the urban nationalists and the rural masses beyond their standard missed encounter. But, given how the above passage deploys the verb "*diriger*" and the pluralized noun "*dirigeants*," I take Fanon to be arguing that the leadership of the insurrection is actually comprised of both urban and rural elements. In other words, both the urban political core and the rural peasant vanguard make up the leaders that enrich and are enriched by the nation on a war footing.

This notion of shared leadership between the urban and rural elements of the struggle, combined with an emphasis on reciprocal enrichment between the leaders and the masses, is what primarily distinguishes Fanon's vision of the liberation process from the top-down vanguardism of the urban nationalist parties. But he diverges from their approach in yet another important way. Whereas the urban nationalists distrust traditional social structures and seek to impose their own form of organization, which is merely an untranslated copy of the European party form, Fanon suggests, in contrast, that the urban and rural elements of the struggle each contribute to the development of new forms of organization. The urban core translates their clandestine party into an organism of political education, while traditional institutions from the countryside like the *djemaas* and the village assemblies take on a new, translated form as revolutionary tribunals and committees. In this way, Fanon departs from the idea that everything is to be forgotten in the tabula rasa of decolonization and returns to the notion that existing phenomena can be dialectically transformed into weapons of liberation. As Nigel Gibson memorably puts it, "the peasantry is not a tabula rasa but rather an archive" containing latently revolutionary organizational forms and practices.[135]

Along with subtly challenging prior statements concerning the temporality of decolonization and the role of the past and the present in effecting change, Fanon complicates his prior assessment of the Manichaeanism of the colonized. This mostly occurs during his critique of a politics that is dependent on affective sentiments:

The pride of the peasant . . . served as a permanent reminder that he opposed his own dichotomy to the dichotomy of the colonist. Antiracist racism and the determination to defend one's skin, which is characteristic of the colonized's response to colonial oppression, clearly represent sufficient reasons to join the struggle. But one does not sustain a war, one does not endure massive repression or witness the disappearance of one's entire family in order for hatred or racism to triumph. Racism, hatred, resentment, and "the legitimate desire for revenge" alone cannot nurture a war of liberation. These flashes of consciousness which fling the body into a zone of turbulence, which lunge it into a virtually pathological dreamlike state where . . . my death through mere inertia calls for the death of the other, this great passion of the first hours disintegrates if it is left to feed on itself.[136]

The antiracist racism of the colonized, according to Fanon, is a response to the racism of the colonizer, mirroring in inverted form the colonizer's Manichaean logic of good versus evil, superior versus inferior, us versus the others. The reader may recall that "antiracist racism" is a formulation that Sartre deploys in *Black Orpheus* to describe *négritude*.[137] In Sartre's analysis, *négritude* is to be understood as a necessary but insufficient response to white supremacy, an antithetical "moment of negativity" that must ultimately be surpassed in the struggle to overcome racial prejudice and discrimination.[138] As I discussed previously, in *Black Skin, White Masks*, Fanon is very critical of Sartre's analysis of *négritude* because he prematurely relativizes its negativity, whereas said negativity must be posited as absolute and self-sufficient if it is not to lose all of its dialectical force.[139] By returning to Sartre's formulation at this moment in the dialectic of armed struggle, Fanon appears to be saying that the absolute negativity of decolonizing violence has served its purpose and now is precisely the time for its relativization.

When Fanon asserts that antiracist racism is a *resentful* response to oppression, he likewise evokes *A Dying Colonialism* and its Nietzschean diagnosis of the psychology of colonization.[140] In this previous work, Fanon maintains that native Algerians are primarily reactive during the colonial period and counter the colonizer's campaign of forced assimilation with the undifferentiated rejection of everything foreign, including the presence of foreign settlers. This perception of the settlers nevertheless undergoes a process of mutation during the armed struggle. Native Algerians begin to embrace a more dialectical view toward the European minority in Algeria, one that differentiates between comrades and enemies, insofar as some settlers join the revolutionary cause and even give their lives fighting against colonialism. Fanon implies in the previously cited passage from *The Wretched of the Earth* that a similar kind of transformation occurs among the colonized during the revolutionary war. Indeed, he goes on to observe that, at this advanced stage in the struggle, "the colonist is no longer simply public enemy number one [*l'homme à abbatre*]. Some members of the colonialist population prove to be closer, infinitely closer, to the nationalist struggle than certain native sons. The racial and racist dimension is transcended [*est dépassé*] on both sides. Not every black or Muslim is automatically given a vote of confidence. One no longer grabs a gun or a machete every time a colonist approaches. Consciousness stumbles upon partial, finite, and shifting truths."[141] Notice how Fanon challenges yet another claim from "On Violence" by stating that the colonizer is no longer simply *l'homme à abbatre*. During the struggle for decolonization, a mutation occurs in how the colonized perceive the colonizer, such that their Manichaean outlook is dialectically transcended and the truth of the colonizer's absolute evil is revealed to be only partial, finite, and shifting. This puts into crisis the logic of Aristotelian subtraction. It would seem that mutual exclusion, like transitionless substitution, is another illusion of spontaneity that must ultimately pass into a new understanding of the relationship between the colonizer and the colonized, one that attends to the internally contradictory nature of both sides of the opposition.

How are we to read Fanon's implicit and sometimes explicit critique of a number of claims made in "On Violence"? Within Fanon studies, Ato Sekyi-Otu has developed the most influential approach to answering this question.[142] As I discussed in the introduction to this book, Sekyi-Otu maintains that *The Wretched of the Earth* narrates a dialectical movement whereby the colonized subject's overly simplistic apprehension of colonization and decolonization develops through experience into a richer and more complicated comprehension of the existing world and its overcoming. From this viewpoint, the nondialectical claims of "On Violence" should not be read as propositional statements on Fanon's part but rather as a strategic staging and ventriloquy of the "immediate knowledge" of the colonized, which endures a process of revision and "bewildering enlightenment" during the armed struggle.[143] The movement from the beginning of the first chapter to the conclusion of the second chapter thus performs a major development in the dialectic of experience of the colonized, a progression from the demand for instantaneous rupture to the recognition that decolonization is a protracted historical process, from the desire to clear the slate and create something entirely new to the methodical practice of translating existing phenomena, and from a Manichaean worldview to an appreciation of colonial society's internal contradictions.

Construing the relationship between the first two chapters in this way nevertheless begs the question: Why would Fanon publish "On Violence" by itself in *Les Temps Modernes* if its claims remain overly simplistic, their role in his broader argument ultimately unintelligible, without the counterpart essay, "Grandeur and Weakness of Spontaneity"? A look at the May 1961 issue of *Les Temps Modernes* reveals that the publication offers no indication that "On Violence" is an excerpt from a forthcoming book.[144] The essay therefore *can be* and *was* read as a standalone piece. Of course, "On Violence" can and ought to be read alongside "Grandeur and Weakness of Spontaneity" as well, but such a reading should not eclipse the historical context in which these essays were produced, published, and circulated. Keeping this history in mind allows for an alternative interpretation of the second chapter of *The Wretched of the Earth*, as a self-critique of the non-dialectical and antidialectical excesses of prior statements on decolonization, not only in the essay for *Les Temps Modernes* but also in *A Dying Colonialism* and the articles for *El Moudjahid*. But this implies a fundamentally different understanding of Fanon, as a divided thinker rather than a consistently dialectical one, as a theorist who is at war with himself rather than a theorist who consistently develops a unified dialectical narrative. In other words, while I agree with Sekyi-Otu and his followers that *The Wretched of the Earth* engages in a "reflexive and revisionary commentary" on its own inaugural claims, I read this commentary as further evidence of Fanon's dividedness rather than as evidence of its resolution in favor of dialectical thinking. Indeed, as I will demonstrate in the final chapter of this book, Fanon's dividedness persists throughout the remainder of *The Wretched of the Earth* and even intensifies in its concluding pages. While predominantly working within dialectical reason, Fanon also experiments with terms and images that cannot be easily incorporated into or subsumed under such a framework. To study these moments in the text, rather than obscure them or attempt to explain them away, is to grapple with the underground theory of radical change that traverses *The Wretched of the Earth* and Fanon's work as a whole.

Chapter Five

THE WRETCHED OF THE EARTH (PART II)

THE DAY AFTER: IMITATE EUROPE, START FROM SCRATCH, OR BUILD BRIDGES?

Upon completing a thorough analysis of the insurrectional phase of decolonization, Fanon turns his attention in the third chapter of *The Wretched of the Earth* to what happens "the day after," at that liminal moment when formal independence has been achieved but the future of the new nation and its relationship with Europe remains unclear. Building upon "Grandeur and Weakness of Spontaneity," which outlined two possible paths to independence, "The Trials and Tribulations of National Consciousness" considers where these paths might lead by exploring two potential routes for the newly independent nation. Drawing on multiple historical examples from Africa and Latin America, Fanon describes the first route as a transfer of power from the colonizers to the national bourgeoisie. Due to the many weaknesses and limitations of the national bourgeoisie as a class, when this transfer of power occurs, the former colonizers ultimately maintain their influence and independence gives way to the formation of a neocolonial economy and state. The second path that Fanon describes, more aspirational than historically grounded, consists of a mass revolutionary party barring the national bourgeoisie from taking power so that the party can itself lead the nation in a direction not channeled by neocolonialism.

While the first pathway is one of many trials and tribulations ("*mésaventures*" in the original French), the second leads to full decolonization. But, for countries that have already traveled down the road of neocolonialism, all is not lost. Fanon briefly gestures toward how these countries might finally break with their neocolonial status and open up a new way forward.

In what follows, I will consider each of these historical trajectories and demonstrate how Fanon's response to the dilemma of neocolonialism creates another kind of dilemma, insofar as his vision for the future is torn between a dialectical conceptualization of change and a subterranean alternative. As the reader will soon come to appreciate, this continues to be the case for the remainder of *The Wretched of the Earth*. Despite what some critics have argued, the nondialectical and antidialectical formulations of "On Violence" are not progressively abandoned after the self-critical conclusion of "Grandeur and Weakness of Spontaneity."[1] Instead, a kind of "return of the repressed" takes place, as similar formulations are subtly put forward and developed throughout the rest of the book, formulations that maintain an uncertain relationship—one of latent and unresolved tension—with the text's overarching dialectical framework.[2] In this chapter, I will focus on how the aforementioned formulations introduce further discrepancies and inconsistencies in the argumentation of *The Wretched of the Earth* so as to complete my discussion of the internal division that traverses not just Fanon's final work but his entire oeuvre.

To begin, let us turn to Fanon's examination of the national bourgeoisie and its contribution, once in power, to the creation of a neocolonial society. He posits that shortly after formal independence is achieved the national bourgeoisie reveals its "incapacity . . . to fulfil its historic role as bourgeoisie."[3] The role that Fanon has in mind stems from the traditional Marxist understanding of the bourgeoisie as the class that spearheads industrialization, capitalist accumulation, proletarianization, and the creation of a bourgeois state and bourgeois culture. This is the bourgeoisie that Marx and Engels describe in *The Communist Manifesto* as "constantly revolutionizing the instruments of production, and thereby the relations of production, and with them the whole relations of society."[4] According to Fanon, in formerly colonized countries, the national bourgeoisie lacks such dynamism and simply preserves intact the colonial economy that it inherits during the transfer of power. Instead of building up industry and transforming the nation's conditions of production, the bourgeois elites remain focused on producing the same agricultural products and extracting the same raw materials for export to the former colonizers. Hedonistic, prideful, lacking ambition, and constantly scheming for petty financial gain, the national bourgeoisie "mimics the Western bourgeoisie in its negative and decadent aspects without having accomplished the initial phases of exploration and invention."[5] The national bourgeoisie is thus an "underdeveloped bourgeoisie," a weak imitation of its counterparts in Europe.[6]

This blistering critique of the class that typically rises to power after independence recalls an often-cited passage from Marx's *The Eighteenth Brumaire of Louis Bonaparte*, a text that had a major impact on Fanon's thinking throughout his life.[7] The passage that I have in mind reads accordingly: "Hegel remarks somewhere that all facts and personages of great importance in world history occur, as it were, twice. He forgot to add: the first time as tragedy, the second time as farce. Caussidière for Danton, Louis Blanc for Robespierre, the Montagne of 1848 to 1851 for the Montagne of 1793 to 1795, the Nephew for the Uncle. And the same caricature occurs in the circumstances attending the second edition of the Eighteenth Brumaire."[8] In *The Wretched of the Earth*, Fanon analogously reflects upon the second edition of the Western bourgeoisie, that nephew class that exhibits, in his own words, "the psychology of a businessman, not that of a captain of industry."[9] Even though the national bourgeoisie "has learned by heart what it has read in the manuals of the West," the result is that it "subtly transforms itself not into a replica of Europe but rather its caricature."[10]

As a farcical caricature of the European model, the national bourgeoisie displays its ineptitude and lack of dynamism not only economically but at all levels of society. In the realm of ideology, for example, Fanon maintains that this underdeveloped class fails to introduce bourgeois principles of abstract universal liberty, equality, and fraternity and instead clings to the undifferentiated nationalism of the pre-independence moment and promotes the empty slogan, "Replace the foreigners!"[11] Bourgeois elites draw on nationalist sentiments as part of their effort to fill positions of power previously held by the colonizers, but when proletarians, small artisans, and the lumpen follow suit, their nationalism in the postindependence era gets redirected as hostility toward African workers of other nationalities, who are viewed as the primary source of competition for these groups. Nationalism then mutates into "ultranationalism, chauvinism, and racism. There is a general call for these foreigners to leave, their shops are burned, their

market booths torn down and some are lynched."[12] As this chauvinism continues to intensify, it can even turn against itself and subdivide into opposing tribalisms that splinter the nation along ethnic, regional, and religious
lines. What this demonstrates for Fanon is that the national bourgeoisie is
"incapable of implementing a program with even a minimum humanist
content" and cannot "maintain a pretense of universal democratic ideas."[13]

Fanon depicts the national bourgeoisie as equally inept at the level of politics. The underdeveloped class tends to disregard traditional parliamen-
tary rule and instead favors a single-party dictatorship led by a popular
leader. This anti-democratic impulse stems from the national bourgeoisie's
failure "to establish coherent social relations based on the principle of class
domination."[14] To rectify this situation, a leader is installed as the head of
the party, someone who can pacify discontent and garner widespread support by incessantly recalling his militant past and his heroic participation
in the struggle for liberation. The leader, in this way, "constitutes a screen
between the people and the grasping bourgeoisie. . . . He lends his support
to this caste and hides its maneuvers from the people, thus becoming its
most vital tool for mystifying and numbing the senses of the masses."[15] As
a result, any former reciprocity between the masses and the party leadership during the armed struggle degenerates into a strictly top-down relationship. "That productive exchange between the rank and file and the
higher echelons and vice versa, the basis and guarantee of democracy in a
party, no longer exists," writes Fanon. "On the contrary, the party now
forms a screen between the masses and the leadership."[16] By converting both
the leader and the party into screens ("*écrans*"), the national bourgeoisie
momentarily safeguards its recently acquired power.[17] However, the dispar-
ity between the wealth of the bourgeoisie and the wretchedness of the
masses grows to the point that these screens no longer serve their purpose
and the state must implement more authoritarian tactics, such as calling
upon the army to quell popular unrest and regain control over the citizenry.
Since the military is trained and supervised by foreign advisers and the
national bourgeoisie remains dependent on the European market, independence is merely formal, and the metropole "governs indirectly."[18] The utter
incompetence of the national bourgeoisie allows history to repeat itself, with
colonialism returning as neocolonialism.

Throughout this section of the chapter, Fanon sometimes sounds like he
accords the status of universal model to Europe's particular instantiation

of the bourgeoisie. When he states that the national bourgeoisie is incapable of fulfilling its historic mission, for instance, it could be argued that he equates the *specific* accomplishments of the Western bourgeoisie with the historic task of the bourgeoisie *as such*. At its core, however, Fanon's theorization of the national bourgeoisie fundamentally breaks with such a Eurocentric conception of class and such a unilinear understanding of historical development.[19] Much like his discussion of the proletariat and the peasantry in the colonial situation, his treatment of the bourgeoisie in the context of neocolonial underdevelopment stretches Marxist analysis by translating some of its most basic ideas and concepts so that they can take on a qualitatively new form. Put another way, Fanon's theoretical practice concretizes the abstractly universal notion of the bourgeoisie, such that any future account of its characteristics would remain provincial and incomplete if limited to the historical traits of its European form.

Fanon's critical assessment of what bourgeois rule looks like under neocolonialism leads him to the following conclusion:

In the underdeveloped countries the bourgeoisie should not find conditions conducive to its existence and fulfilment. In other words, the combined efforts of the masses, regimented by a party, and of keenly conscious intellectuals, armed with revolutionary principles, should bar the way to this useless and harmful bourgeoisie. The theoretical question, which has been posed for some fifty years when addressing the history of the underdeveloped countries, i.e., whether the bourgeois phase can be skipped [*être sautée*], must be resolved through revolutionary action and not through reasoning.[20]

This passage introduces the second possible route to follow after independence, a route paved by the efforts of a mass revolutionary party and closed off to the national bourgeoisie. In theorizing this alternative trajectory, Fanon—like others before him, including the late Marx—further stretches the Marxist analysis of historical development.[21] The bourgeois phase is not regarded as a moment in history through which all countries, "on pain of extinction," must necessarily pass.[22] On the contrary, for Fanon, this is precisely what should be prevented from happening in underdeveloped countries: "Barring the way to the national bourgeoisie is a sure way of avoiding the pitfalls of independence, the trials and tribulations of national unity, the decline of morals, the assault on the nation by corruption, an economic downturn and, in the short term, an antidemocratic regime relying on force and intimidation. But it also means choosing the only way to go forward."[23] Fanon nevertheless maintains that the theoretical question of skipping or leaping over a certain phase of development ultimately requires a practical answer, so, instead of offering a reasoned argument for why bypassing bourgeois rule is a historical necessity for underdeveloped countries, much of the remaining chapter reads like a revolutionary handbook on how to build a political organization that could accomplish such a feat.

Before turning to Fanon's discussion of the party form and its historic role in staving off neocolonialism, it is worth pausing to consider what he has to say about the future of countries in which the national bourgeoisie do take power and set up a neocolonial social structure after independence. Although not a major focus of the chapter, this matter is addressed in one of the chapter's most memorable passages:

Once [the national bourgeoisie] has been annihilated, swallowed up by its own contradictions, it will be clear to everyone that no progress has been made since independence, that everything has to be started over again, that it is necessary to begin from scratch [*qu'il faut tout reprendre, qu'il faut repartir de zéro*]. The conversion [*reconversion*] will not occur at the level of the structures set in place by the bourgeoisie during its reign, since this caste has done nothing else but take up without modification the heritage of the colonial economy, thinking, and institutions.[24]

While the national bourgeoisie must be overthrown, Fanon suggests that its own contradictions will weaken it to such an extent that it will virtually remove itself from power. The history of postcolonial African countries after the publication of *The Wretched of the Earth* reveals this prediction to be overly optimistic, but this is perhaps what is least interesting about the passage. What deserves further reflection, on the other hand, is Fanon's reuse of a phrase from "On Violence"—"everything has to be started over again [*il faut tout reprendre*]"—to once more announce the need for a kind of tabula rasa.[25] Fanon extends this logic to the future *reconversion*, which will not take place at the level of existing structures, since these structures are inherited directly from the colonial period. He suggests, in other words, that dialectically overcoming the extant colonial economy, political institutions, and ideology would be an insufficient response to the situation. Instead, the *reconversion* must be a universal restructuring that begins not from what already exists but from nothing, from zero, from the void. A subterranean Fanon gains expression in this passage's call to wipe the slate clean and start from scratch. As is often the case, however, this alternative conceptualization of change is not developed further once it is introduced. Instead, the chapter's focus quickly shifts back to the national bourgeoisie's internal contradictions, returning in this way to the dominant language of dialectics.

When Fanon shifts his attention to countries that can still bypass the neocolonial route, he fervently argues for placing a mass revolutionary party at the helm. This is where he expands upon his vision of the dialectically reciprocal relationship between the masses and the party leadership. At times, he construes this relationship in rather traditional terms as consisting of a thinking head and a laboring body, such as when he speaks of the "revolutionary principles" of "keenly conscious intellectuals" that will guide the "efforts of the masses."[26] But, on other occasions, he challenges the notion of the party as an organization that issues decrees from above, such that, instead of a thinking head, the party operates as "an instrument in the hands of the people."[27] Fanon similarly draws from a common notion of the party as an organization that represents the collective will and interests of the masses, while also gesturing toward a more horizontal and participatory model. He states, for example, that "the party must be the direct expression of the masses," which entails setting aside "the very Western, very bourgeois, and hence very disparaging idea that the masses are incapable of governing themselves [*de se diriger*]."[28] Nigel Gibson helpfully points out that Fanon also transitions from an insistence on the centralization of the party's authority in the previous chapter of *The Wretched of the Earth* to a call for thorough decentralization.[29] This shift in strategy corresponds to a shift in historical conditions. If, during the armed struggle, a central authority is necessary to organize the dispersed spontaneity of the peasant rebellions, after independence is achieved a network of decentralized "regional bureaus" more adequately facilitates grassroots participation and national unity by simultaneously inhibiting the creation of an isolated political clique in the capital and blocking the proliferation of tribalisms in the interior.[30]

This argument for a directly democratic and decentralized form of political organization has led Reiland Rabaka to posit that Fanon is engaged in a "repudiation of the Marxist-Leninist theory of the vanguard party."[31] Nick Nesbitt has intriguingly put forward an argument that is the exact opposite of Rabaka's, maintaining that Fanon "conforms to a neo-Jacobin, Leninist model of enlightened avant-gardism" and even "a top-down model of Kantian enlightenment."[32] While Fanon's more traditional statements on the party lend credence to this latter interpretation, Nesbitt bases his assessment on Fanon's insistence that the task of the revolutionary intellectual is to "politicize the masses." Such politicization, Fanon explains, "is not meant to infantilize" the masses "but rather to make them mature [*les rendre adultes*]."[33] And yet, even if politicization is a process of maturation rather than infantilization, such a view presupposes an infantilized mass in need of instruction and guidance.

Though diametrically opposed, my sense is that both Nesbitt and Rabaka illuminate aspects of Fanon's approach to political organization and leadership. Fanon's allusions to a more directly democratic and decentralized party can indeed be read as a kind of translation, if not outright repudiation, of the Marxist-Leninist vanguard party form. His notion of politicization, on the other hand, as something that keenly conscious intellectuals do to the masses and not vice versa, does signal a certain sympathy for enlightened vanguardism.[34] As Fanon goes on to state, now including himself among the revolutionary intellectuals tasked with politicization: "We must elevate the people, expand their minds, equip them, differentiate them, and humanize them."[35] These seemingly irreconcilable views nevertheless converge when Fanon explains that politicizing the masses is necessary precisely so that they can more fully participate in the decision-making process, so that enlightened vanguardism can wither away and be replaced with a more horizontal experience.[36] The goal of politicization is "not that three hundred people understand and decide but that all understand and decide, even if it takes twice or three times as long," because, as Fanon affirms, "the successful outcome of any decision depends on the conscious, coordinated commitment of the people as a whole."[37] Along with making mass participation possible, in other words, politicization aims to "make the masses understand" that their participation is in fact decisive, "that everything depends on them, that if we stagnate the fault is theirs, and that if we progress, they too are responsible."[38]

To further develop the notion of politicization, Fanon offers the memorable example, rich with conceptual meaning and symbolism, of building a bridge. He writes:

If the building of a bridge does not enrich the consciousness of those working on it, then don't build the bridge, and let the citizens continue to swim across the river or use a ferry. The bridge must not be parachuted in [*être parachuté*], it must not be imposed on the social panorama by a *deus ex machina*. On the contrary, it must be the product of the citizens' brains and muscles. And of course architects and engineers, foreigners for the most part, will probably be needed, but the local party leaders must see to it that the technique seeps into the cerebral desert of the citizen, that the bridge in its entirety and in every detail can be seized, understood, and assumed [*soit repris, conçu et assumé*]. It is necessary for the citizen to appropriate the bridge. Then, and only then, is everything possible.[39]

Just as Fanon condemned parachuting inexperienced leaders and foreign organizational forms into the interior during the armed struggle, he now argues against parachuting in techniques like bridge building and imposing them on the citizenry of the newly independent nation. A given technique may be of foreign origin or require foreign guidance for its implementation, but what determines if it should be introduced into a new reality is not its foreignness or lack thereof but rather its capacity to enrich the consciousness of those who would perform the technique.

For the enrichment of consciousness to occur, a double translation is required. Local party leaders must first translate the foreign technique so that it can seep into the so-called cerebral desert of the masses. The masses must then actively seize or take up (*reprendre*) the technique as their own and in that way translate it again. To politicize the masses, in other words, is not to elevate their consciousness for them while they remain passive. Rather, according to Fanon, politicization introduces certain techniques to the masses so that the masses may elevate their own consciousness through activity that is at once intellectual and practical. If Fanon's reference to the barren, desert-like intellect of the masses remains problematic, it is clear that revolutionary intellectuals are not supposed to think for the masses but are to facilitate spaces in which the masses may think for themselves. Put another way, the party's leadership must build a bridge between the masses and the technique of bridge building. Once the masses cross that bridge, once they seize the technique as their own, they have at that precise moment also built a bridge to a new level of consciousness. Fanon thus uses the example of building a bridge to conceptualize the dialectical movement of consciousness after independence, a double movement of politicization and appropriation. The condition of possibility for this movement, it bears repeating, is the formation of a revolutionary party that bridges the traditional *décalage* between the masses and the party leadership.[40]

As Fanon suggests through the repetition of the category of "citizen" in the previously cited passage, bridge building is tied to nation building, and consciousness is understood at this moment in its development as national consciousness. Consider, in this light, how Fanon introduces the technique of building bridges:

Since individual experience is national, since it is a link in the national chain, it ceases to be individual, narrow and limited in scope, and can lead to the truth of the nation and the world. Just as every fighter clung to the nation during the period of armed struggle, so during the period of nation building every citizen must continue in his everyday concrete action to combine with the nation as a whole [*l'ensemble de la nation*], to embody the perpetually dialectical truth of the nation, and to will here and now the triumph of man in his totality [*le triomphe de l'homme total*].[41]

This passage refers the reader back to a memorable claim in "On Violence"— namely, Fanon's assertion that the "violent praxis" of the colonized "is totalizing, since each individual represents a violent link in the great chain. . . . Groups recognize each other and the future nation is already indivisible."[42] Both passages from *The Wretched of the Earth* also allude to Jean-Paul Sartre's notion of totalizing group praxis as he develops it in his *Critique of Dialectical Reason*. According to Sartre, totalizing group praxis constitutes an activity that "makes each part an expression of the whole and relates the whole to itself through the mediation of its parts."[43] Fanon's example of building a bridge is therefore not only a metaphor but also a real, concrete activity, which, like decolonizing violence, is a form of totalizing praxis.[44] To participate in building a bridge is to embody the dialectical truth of the nation, to become a link in the national chain, to fuse with the group of citizens.

For Fanon, this collective ensemble, whether it is called the nation, the citizenry, or the people, is not a prepolitical or essentialized unity based on racial or ethnic belonging, cultural heritage, religious faith, or birthplace. It is, rather, a (particularly large) group that fuses on the basis of shared activity.[45] In *A Dying Colonialism*, Fanon argues that listening to the radio contributes to forming such a group, whereas now he extends this argument to other activities.[46] A preexisting people does not engage in decolonizing violence; those who engage in decolonizing violence become a people. Preexisting citizens do not build bridges; those who build bridges become citizens. These political categories, in Fanon's reworking of them, name specific kinds of doing rather than naturalized attributes or stable identities, specific kinds of "action rather than a status to which one might petition for inclusion."[47] It follows that bridge building is nation building and that national consciousness is consciousness of the collective ensemble that emerges from such a totalizing praxis. But the activity of building bridges will have none of these effects if it is foisted upon the masses in an artificial way. A dialectically reciprocal relationship must form between knowledge and action, theory and practice. As Fanon puts it, "bourgeois leadership of the underdeveloped countries confines the national consciousness to a sterile formalism. Only the massive commitment by men and women to *enlightened* and *productive* tasks gives content and density to this consciousness."[48]

If national consciousness is to move past sterile formalism, if it is to take on positive content and density, the undifferentiated nationalism of the armed struggle must finally be differentiated along class lines. This is what Fanon means when he suggests that politicization must not only educate but also *differentiate* the people. "If we really want to safeguard our countries from regression, paralysis, or collapse," Fanon argues, "we must rapidly switch from a national consciousness to a social and political consciousness. The nation can only come into being in a program elaborated by a revolutionary leadership and enthusiastically and lucidly seized [*repris*] by the masses."[49] Like the technique of bridge building, the party program cannot be imposed on the masses as if by a *deus ex machina*. While the program is the creation of the revolutionary party, the masses must translate it so as to make it their own. This double movement builds the bridge from national consciousness to social and political consciousness. Once this bridge is crossed, the national bourgeoisie, in Fanon's words, no longer seem to be "respectable men but flesh-eating beasts, jackals and ravens who wallow in the blood of the people."[50] This is how a mass revolutionary party might bar the national bourgeoisie from taking power after independence, which would in turn make possible an alternative trajectory of historical development, one that would not pass through neocolonialism.

While the party program must address the particular historical circumstances of the newly independent nation, Fanon maintains that it contains a universalist dimension as well. Recall that totalizing praxis leads not only to the truth of the nation but also to "the truth of the world" and that the citizen, by fusing with the national ensemble, wills the triumph of *l'homme total*. It follows that enlightened and productive tasks, in building toward the culmination of a national group formation, also build toward this group's dialectical overcoming. On this point, Fanon may once again be in dialogue with Sartre, who claims in his *Critique of Dialectical Reason* that "the worker will be saved from his destiny only if the human multiplicity as a whole is permanently changed into a group *praxis*."[51] As though reflecting on how to realize such a world transformation, in which all of humanity would fuse on the basis of shared activities, Fanon sustains that the party must develop "not only an economic program but also . . . a conception of man, a conception of the future of humanity," adding that nationalism leads to an impasse "if it does not very quickly transform into a social and political consciousness, into humanism."[52] This is the other aspect of politicization: differentiation but also humanization, class consciousness but also a universalist worldview. This may, in fact, be one way of understanding Fanon's notion of mass democratic participation, as a conception of the future of human multiplicity, which, if lucidly seized by the masses, could become a kind of totalizing group praxis for all of humankind.

Before moving on, I want to call attention to how the keyword *reprendre* takes on a new signification during Fanon's discussion of the mass revolutionary party, one that recuperates it for a very different mode of thinking about change.[53] Whereas the word is initially used to describe a total clearing of the slate, it comes to signify the dialectical mutation of preexisting phenomena and, more specifically, their appropriation by the masses. Instead of inventing the technique of bridge building from scratch, instead of creating a party platform ex nihilo, the masses take up existing versions of these phenomena and reinvent them as their own. This distinction holds significant conceptual implications for the chapter's overall argument. For example, if to build a bridge is to build a nation then it would seem that the nation is likewise not an entirely new creation that emerges from the tabula rasa of decolonization but rather the result of a historical process that translates an extant social reality. The same could be said for Fanon's vision of a new humanity and the new way of thinking that corresponds to it. Formerly construed as the immediate outcome of decolonizing violence, as the result of a transitionless substitution, the future humanity now appears to emerge out of a dialectical progression from the colonized thing to the independent citizen to *l'homme total*. The future way of thinking appears to be the result of a similar progression from undifferentiated nationalism to national consciousness to social and political consciousness and humanism. The final pages of the third chapter of *The Wretched of the Earth* thus function much like the final pages of the previous chapter. They depart from the book's earlier, subterranean moments and place the reader solidly within the dominant theoretical framework of dialectical change. However, as I will demonstrate in what follows, an underground alternative to this framework intermittently resurfaces throughout the rest of the book, which has the effect of significantly complicating the straightforward series of progressions just outlined.

THE COLONIZED INTELLECTUAL

The fourth chapter of *The Wretched of the Earth*, "On National Culture," consists of a long essay written between the spring and early summer of 1961 and a shorter essay titled "Reciprocal Foundations for National Culture and Liberation Struggles," which was first delivered as a paper in March 1959 at the second International Congress of Black Writers and Artists in Rome, Italy.[54] "On National Culture" alludes to and expands upon "Racism and Culture," Fanon's paper for the first International Congress of Black Writers and Artists held in Paris in September 1956. Along with certain thematic similarities and various shared conclusions, both texts narrate a dialectical process that passes through three moments or phases.[55] In the 1956 text, Fanon considers how the colony endures a series of transformations at the level of culture—passing from the overall denial of native culture and the violent imposition of the colonizer's culture to the hierarchization of these cultures to their relativization—during the historical transition from colonization to independence. Fanon narrows his focus in the fourth chapter of *The Wretched of the Earth* to examine the three phases of the colonized intellectual, how the colonized intellectual maintains a dynamic and shifting relationship with foreign and local culture, during the same historical trajectory. Such a focus allows Fanon to build upon the previous chapter's discussion of the intellectual's role in politicizing the masses. But, as the adjective suggests in the designation "colonized intellectual," Fanon casts his gaze back in this chapter to consider what kind of transformative process must take place before an intellectual can pursue the revolutionary task of politicization. While there is accordingly a logic in the movement from the third chapter to the fourth chapter of Fanon's final work, this logic is not one of forward dialectical movement, as in the transition from the second chapter to the third. Rather, it may be characterized as a dialectically reflexive movement that returns to an earlier moment in the process of decolonization so as to elucidate how the colonized intellectual assumes a position of leadership within this process.

It should also be noted that Fanon's discussion of the colonized intellectual shuffles back and forth between different phases of development rather than treating each of them sequentially as in "Racism and Culture." Fanon begins, for example, with an extended discussion of the second phase of the colonized intellectual and only later clarifies that he has three phases in mind and that what has been presented thus far "corresponds approximately" to the second one.[56] This discrepancy between the overall dialectical narrative of the chapter and the scattered organization of the text's claims invites various possible interpretations. One could speculate that perhaps Fanon's battle with leukemia, which ultimately took his life in December 1961, left him without the time and energy to properly revise his work. Or it could be argued that Fanon began with a critical assessment of the second phase of the colonized intellectual, which corresponds with the emergence of the *négritude* movement, so as to highlight his divergence from figures like Aimé Césaire, Léopold Sédar Senghor, and others who spoke at the aforementioned international congresses. A third possibility would be to read the discrepancy between the chapter's overall narrative and the organization of its claims as yet another sign of the persistent friction in Fanon's oeuvre between a dominant mode of thinking about change and an underground mode of thought that interrupts and unsettles the flow of dialectical movement. I favor this latter interpretation and will take it as my point of departure in presenting further evidence of the often subtle but significant tensions and discontinuities permeating *The Wretched of the Earth*.

The three phases of the colonized intellectual can be telegraphically summarized as assimilationist, traditionalist, and revolutionary. To map the dialectical movement between these phases, Fanon begins with colonialism's "obliteration" of native culture,[57] what was described at the Paris congress as the "overall negation" of the native's cultural dynamism and the "mummification" of precolonial traditions and customs.[58] In response to this situation of loss and petrification, the colonized intellectual searches for a substitute cultural attachment and "hurls himself frantically into the frenzied acquisition of the occupier's culture."[59] Fanon compares the condition of colonized intellectuals at this phase in their development to adopted children seeking psychical reassurance after the loss of their birth parents.[60] If it is common to find "Parnassians, Symbolists, and Surrealists among the colonized writers," this is because the aim is "full assimilation" with the new literary family.[61]

Fanon consistently presents the first phase of the colonized intellectual as coinciding with the colonial period before the outbreak of the armed struggle. He is less consistent, however, in his presentation of the historical context corresponding to the second phase. He suggests at one point that the colonized intellectual may enter the next phase of development once independence is achieved; however, he tends to favor depicting the colonized intellectual's transition out of assimilationism as taking place much earlier, "when the nationalist parties mobilize the people in the name of national independence."[62] During these early days of struggle, the colonized intellectual "rejects his accomplishments, suddenly feeling them to be alienating."[63] This simultaneous recognition and rejection of alienation ushers in a new phase of development, during which anti-assimilationist cultural movements like *négritude* proliferate.

In "Racism and Culture" and *Black Skin, White Masks*, Fanon describes the passage from assimilation to *négritude* as a passion-charged retraction into the self and an irrational recovery of archaic cultural traditions. "On National Culture" similarly refers to a "movement of withdrawal" comparable to "a muscular contraction," and a "passionate quest for a national culture prior to the colonial era."[64] Extending Fanon's metaphor of the adopted child, it is as though colonized intellectuals reject the new family in order to deny the loss of their prior familial ties. To shore up this denial, they recover anything that predates the traumatic event of separation, or at least their consciousness of it. "Old childhood memories will resurface, old legends will be reinterpreted," but, as though unable to fully break free from the prior moment of assimilation, colonized intellectuals relate to these legends "on the basis of a borrowed aesthetic, and a concept of the world discovered under other skies."[65] Fanon describes this impassioned yet incomplete rejection of the new European family as "normal," "justified," and even "necessary."[66] But he also portrays it as ultimately leading to a "dead end [*cul-de-sac*]" and an "impasse."[67] The limits of the colonized intellectual, which I will discuss in further detail below, must be overcome so as to pass into a third phase of development. The intensification of the liberation struggle "into open, organized rebellion" and "the advances made by national consciousness among the people" are the historical conditions of possibility for this overcoming.[68] These conditions shift the colonized intellectual's focus from precolonial legends to the new reality, from the history of the people to the people making history, from yesterday's tradition to today's revolution. Once this shift occurs, the colonized intellectual is ready to take on the task of politicizing the masses and becomes "a galvanizer of the people" whose work "inspires concerted action."[69]

To clarify what distinguishes a galvanizer of the people from those whom Fanon polemically refers to as "the bards of negritude," much of "On National Culture" is dedicated to a thorough examination of the second phase of the colonized intellectual.[70] Building off of themes explored in previous works, especially *A Dying Colonialism*, Fanon shows how, at this moment in the process, colonized intellectuals maintain a reactive relationship with colonialism that leads them to mirror what they oppose in inverted form. When the colonizers denigrate African culture on a continental scale, for example, colonized intellectuals respond by affirming African culture on an equally continental scale. The problem with this response, for Fanon, is that it accepts the colonialist notion that there is a single African culture rather than a multiplicity of cultures spanning the continent. To defend African culture as such is to "obey the same rules of logic" governing colonial reason's blanket dismissal of African culture.[71] Something similar occurs due to colonialism's "racialization of thought," its insistence on "placing white culture in opposition to the other noncultures."[72] Colonized intellectuals respond by insisting that "a Negro culture [*une culture nègre*]" does indeed exist, but this leads them to embrace rather than challenge the colonialist logic of racialization.[73] As a result, colonized intellectuals take for granted the intelligibility of categories like "Negro culture" or "African culture," while making illegible the significant differences between various groups that are subsumed under these categories.

The "historicization of men," the recognition of the specific historical deter-minations that differentiate groups of people, reveals the limits of such generalizations and demonstrates, according to Fanon, that "every culture is first and foremost national."[74]

What exactly constitutes national culture and how Fanon distinguishes it from yet another generalization will be discussed in the next section of this chapter. For now, it should be noted that Fanon does *not* equate national culture with the precolonial traditions and customs of the colonized, though colonized intellectuals turn precisely to these relics of the past when break-ing with their former assimilationism. This traditionalist stance once more constitutes a reactive response to colonialism and the latter's distor-tion of precolonial African history as nothing but prehistorical barbarism. Fanon explains how colonialism "is not content merely to impose its law on the colonized country's present and future" but also seeks to control the colony's past in an effort to colonize the native's unconscious, to implant the idea that, without the enlightenment and civilization of the colonizers, the native would regress back to darkness and savagery.[75] Colonized intel-lectuals in the second phase of their development respond by passionately searching for evidence of great civilizations prior to the colonial conquest to prove to themselves and to others that the colonialist narrative of his-tory is a lie. However, according to Fanon, there are hidden motivations driving this obsession with the past. Beyond any conscious project of undo-ing colonialist distortions, Fanon suggests that what ultimately propels the traditionalist worldview is the unconscious "self-hatred" of colonized intellectuals, the shame that they feel due to the colony's "current state of barbarity," as well as "the secret hope of discovering beyond the present wretchedness . . . some magnificent and shining era that redeems us in our own eyes and those of others."[76] Colonized intellectuals are "terrified by the void, the mindlessness, and the savagery" they see around them, so they shield themselves from this condition of wretchedness by turning their backs on the present to gaze into the glorious past of precolonial African civilizations.[77]

Although devastating, Fanon's critical assessment of traditionalism and its underlying motivations should not be confused with one-sided con-demnation. Fanon insists that recovering the past "triggers a mutation of *fundamental importance* in the psycho-affective equilibrium of the colo-nized."[78] Self-hatred gives way to pride and confidence, as well as, most importantly, a sense of grounding and belonging. Colonized intellectuals who fail to "wrench" themselves from assimilation tend to "collect all the historical determinations which have conditioned them and place themselves in a thoroughly 'universal perspective.'"[79] As a result, they expose themselves to "extremely serious psycho-affective mutilations" and become "individuals without anchorage, without limit, colorless, stateless, rootless, a body of angels."[80] Colonized intellectuals who reject assimilationism by reclaiming the past, in contrast, protect themselves psychically from drowning in an abstract universalism without content. Fanon also suggests that a traditionalist stance, "though historically limited," can contribute to the struggle for liberation.[81] By celebrating precolonial African civilizations with significant cultural achievements, colonized intellectuals contribute to invalidating colonialism's self-presentation as a necessary, civilizing force. This loosens colonialism's grip on the native's unconscious and makes it easier to imagine a world without colonial domination. Even if proving the existence of "a once mighty Songhai civilization does not change the fact that the Songhais today are undernourished," Fanon understands such a practice of cultural memory as transformative at the subjective or psychical level, if not at the objective level of material conditions.[82]

That being said, the colonized intellectual's obsession with the past—like the continentalization of culture and the racialization of thought—ultimately marks another limit that must be overcome in order to keep pace with the rapidly escalating struggle for liberation. At this phase in the process, the colonized intellectual exchanges abstract universalism for an "inventory of particularisms," and, like a tourist in one's own country, confuses "exoticism" with "cultural authenticity" and "mummified fragments" with "a more fundamental substance beset with radical changes."[83] This more fundamental substance refers to the cultural transformations taking place from within the armed struggle. Just as he argued in *A Dying Colonialism*, Fanon reaffirms that, when the colonized participate in revolutionary activity, "traditions change meaning. What was a technique of passive resistance," like wearing the veil, speaking only Arabic, refusing to purchase a radio, or rejecting Western medicine, "may, in this phase, be radically doomed. Traditions in an underdeveloped country undergoing armed struggle are fundamentally unstable and crisscrossed by centrifugal forces. This is why the intellectual often risks being out of step [*à contretemps*]."[84] Put another way, the traditionalism of the colonized intellectuals unwittingly introduces a *décalage* between themselves and the people engaged in combat. While these intellectuals are stuck in the past, recovering yesterday's customs, the people have already drastically reconfigured these cultural phenomena for today's battle.

Once Fanon reaches this point in *A Dying Colonialism*, he explains that the colonized no longer reactively reject European culture but rather decide to translate it for qualitatively new, anticolonial purposes. The colonized intellectuals of "On National Culture," on the other hand, have only just wrenched themselves from assimilation and are not yet ready to develop a new, nonreactive relationship with all things European. It follows that they are out of step with the people in terms of local *and* foreign culture. Their belatedness leads them to "forget that modes of thought, diet, modern techniques of communication, language, and dress have dialectically reorganized the mind of the people and that the abiding features that acted as safeguards during the colonial period are in the process of undergoing enormous radical mutations."[85] If colonized intellectuals attempt to break with Europe and renew contact with their people and their culture by searching for both in an uncontaminated, precolonial past, Fanon explains that anything that remains of that historical moment is already completely transformed and inextricably intertwined with modern European culture. It follows that, to catch up to the people and to truly join the struggle for liberation, colonized intellectuals will need to overcome their traditionalism by developing a new relationship with the various cultures that surround them.

As the reader will have noticed, Fanon's analysis of the colonized intellectual is eminently dialectical in its reasoning. His critique of traditionalism does not reach the conclusion that all ties should be severed with the past but rather that a different approach to the past is necessary, one that attends to how phenomena from the past live on in the present in their radically mutated form. He similarly construes modern European culture not as something to be completely rejected but rather as something that, when translated, can play a positive role in the struggle for liberation. He also frames the second phase of the colonized intellectual as a necessary moment of development within a broader dialectical progression. The reciprocal relationship between culture and the liberation struggle appropriately drives the dialectical helix forward: the outbreak of the struggle leads to the formation of cultural movements like *négritude* that contribute subjectively to the advancement of that very same struggle, which in turn makes possible a new kind of revolutionary national culture that reciprocally galvanizes the people and heightens the struggle even further.

And yet, when Fanon offers another gloss on the transformation of the colonized intellectual, his rhetoric, in its excess, introduces a subtle discrepancy at the heart of his treatment of European culture, signaling in this way a fissure or rift in his thinking:

We cannot go resolutely forward unless we first become conscious of our alienation. We have taken *everything* from the other side. Yet the other side has given us *nothing* except to sway us in its direction through a thousand detours, except lure us, seduce us, and imprison us by ten thousand devices, by a hundred thousand tricks. To take also means on several levels being taken. It is not enough to try and disentangle ourselves by accumulating proclamations and denials. It is not enough to reunite with the people in a past where they no longer exist. We must rather reunite with them in their recent counter movement which is going to suddenly *call everything into question*; we must focus on that zone of occult disequilibrium where the people can be found, for let there be no mistake, it is here that their souls are crystallized and their perception and respiration illuminated.[86]

Although not always legible in translation, this extended passage contains many examples of wordplay that add much conceptual nuance to the argument. Fanon states that to take ("*prendre*") means on several levels to be taken ("*être pris*"), and to disentangle oneself or get untaken ("*se déprendre*") requires something more than denying cultural alienation or attempting to escape it by turning to the past. It requires colonized intellectuals to first become conscious ("*prend d'abord conscience*") of their alienation, or consciously take hold of it, so as to break its hold on them by joining the people in the toppling-over movement ("*mouvement basculé*") that calls everything into question.[87]

As though performing what is being described, Fanon calls everything into question when he asserts that *everything* taken from the other side has done *nothing* for colonized intellectuals except to alienate them in thousands, tens of thousands, and even hundreds of thousands of ways. Gone is the dialectical recognition of European culture's capacity to positively contribute to the liberation struggle, and in its place is a more Manichaean relationship of mutual exclusion between "we" the colonized intellectuals and "the other side." The notion of disentanglement returns the reader to "On Violence" and the essay's construal of decolonization as an event of total elimination, absolute subtraction, and full-throated vomiting. It also recalls Fanon's claim that "whenever an authentic liberation struggle has been fought, . . . there is an effective eradication of the superstructure borrowed by these intellectuals from the colonialist bourgeois circles."[88] If colonized intellectuals have truly taken everything from the other side, then getting untaken would transform them into a kind of blank slate. Fanon suggests that colonized intellectuals become this void as they join the people's struggle for liberation. From that zone of occult disequilibrium, a new culture is born.

NATIONAL CULTURE AND UNIVERSALIZING VALUES

Fanon refers to the new culture that the colonized intellectual both takes on and contributes to producing as national culture. He reiterates that national culture is not to be conflated with precolonial tradition and criticizes the kind of "abstract populism" that would present "folklore" or "some congealed mass of noble gestures" as "the truth of the people."[89] He then offers the chapter's most concise definition of the phenomenon in question: "National culture is the ensemble of efforts made by a people at the level of thought to describe, justify, and extol the action whereby the people have constituted themselves and persisted [*s'est constitué et s'est maintenu*]. National culture in the underdeveloped countries, therefore, must lie at the very heart of the liberation struggle these countries are waging."[90] To speak of national culture in Fanon's sense is to speak of a people's efforts to give cultural expression to their own action, which constitutes them as a people. In the context of colonialism, the totalizing praxis of decolonizing violence actively constitutes such a group formation. Accordingly, national culture—far from a collection of outmoded beliefs and rituals—describes, justifies, and extols the totalizing praxis of a people as it unfolds in the present. It follows that there is no national culture without the liberation struggle, just as there is no "people" without the activity of decolonizing violence. In Fanon's words, "the struggle for nationhood unlocks culture and opens the doors of creation."[91] Abstract populism fails to grasp this lesson of the struggle and confuses national culture with the customs of the past, just as it confuses the people actively engaging in combat with the passive series of colonized individuals.

Like the notion of "the people," Fanon maintains that national culture names a contradictory unity, "the outcome of tensions internal and external to society as a whole and its multiple layers."[92] It is an amalgam of sometimes conflicting values, preferences, taboos, and models that take shape during the liberation struggle. But national culture is not simply an effect or result of the struggle. As mentioned earlier, it dialectically intervenes in the activity that serves as its condition of possibility. Fanon even goes so far as to posit that a "nation born of the concerted action of the people . . . depends on exceptionally productive cultural manifestations for its very existence."[93] With this statement, he clarifies what it means to conceive of national culture and the liberation struggle as "reciprocal foundations" of each other.[94] This is the case insofar as they mutually serve as the basis for the other's elaboration and growth. In other words, if there is no national culture without the liberation struggle, Fanon insists that the inverse is also true, that there is no liberation struggle without incredibly fecund experimentations with culture.

The final pages of the chapter expand on this point by detailing how a veritable cultural renaissance accompanies the overthrow of colonialism. Fanon writes, for instance, that "oral literature, tales, epics, and popular songs, previously classified and frozen in time, begin to transform [during the struggle]. The storytellers who recited inert episodes revive them and introduce increasingly fundamental modifications."[95] Once stalwarts of tradition, storytellers become translators who reinvent their cultural heritage; they breathe new life into the mummified fragments of the past so that these fragments can speak to a new situation. Fanon notes that "the same mutations" occur in "the fields of dance, song, rituals, and traditional ceremonies."[96] This statement stands in stark contrast with the claim in "On Violence" that the colonized, when fighting for decolonization, exhibit "a singular loss of interest" in such rituals.[97] In the final pages of "On National Culture," tradition and custom are presented as uninteresting only insofar as they remain closed off from the radical transformation taking place at every level of society. "When the colonized intellectual writing for his people uses the past," Fanon explains, "he must do so with the intention of opening up the future, of spurring [the people] into action and fostering hope."[98]

This is not to say that "On National Culture" comes to a close with an exclusively dialectical account of past cultural phenomena and their potential contribution to the future. Although this is the general tendency, there are some notable exceptions that deserve further consideration. When Fanon expands upon his discussion of the storyteller, for example, he returns to a familiar site of tension in his oeuvre between mutation and invention, translating the old into something qualitatively new and creating something entirely new from scratch:

Every time the storyteller narrates a new episode, the public is treated to a real invocation. The existence of a new type of man is revealed to the public. . . . The story-teller once again gives free rein to his imagination, innovates, and makes creative work. It even happens that unlikely characters for such a transmutation, social misfits such as outlaws or drifters, are taken up again and remodeled [*soient reprises et remodelées*]. . . . The storyteller responds to the expectations of the people by trial and error and searches for new models, national models, apparently on his own, but in fact with the support of his audience. Comedy and farce disappear or else lose their appeal.[99]

This passage offers a vivid description of the storyteller as someone capable of conjuring up a form of humanity that does not yet exist, that must be invented and then revealed to the audience. The liberation of the storyteller's imagination anticipates the ultimate liberation of the colonized, the latter's transmutation into a new type of man. Whereas this depiction of change resonates with the notion of decolonization as an absolute substitution of one species of man for another, Fanon goes on to explain that the storyteller takes up and remodels already existing types of men to create the new type. Fanon also extends the wordplay deployed earlier in the chapter, as though to suggest that once colonized intellectuals get untaken, the new content that they take up is in fact old content that is *taken up again* and modified for the present. In this way, Fanon returns the reader to a keyword (*reprendre*) that is used in the previous chapter of *The Wretched of the Earth* to theorize the dialectical appropriation of preexisting phenomena. Yet the passage provides a glimmer of an even more radical conception of newness when it implicitly contrasts what is remodeled with the new models that the storyteller and the audience discover together. The reader is told that old models, such as comedy and farce, are not taken up again and remodeled, that they do not pass through a process of mutation. Instead, they are forgotten as they lose their appeal (like the rituals of "On Violence") and disappear. They are then replaced with alternatives that are just being introduced into existence.

Although distinct modes of thinking about change gain expression in Fanon's discussion of the storyteller, he does not delve into the relationship between them or whether they can be reconciled. They come together in the passage, despite their divergent logics, in a seemingly non-conflictual way; however, their relationship quickly becomes laden with unresolved tension in the chapter's final paragraphs. To appreciate how this occurs, we must first consider Fanon's theorization of national culture as contributing to the realization of a new universal condition. He begins to develop this idea by arguing that "the national character of culture" is not what separates one culture from another but rather what "makes it permeable to other cultures and enables it to influence and penetrate them."[100] The national thus takes on a very precise meaning for Fanon: it names the possibility of a new form of relation with other cultures that transcends the limits of the colonial relation. The dialectical movement of this process is unmistakable. After passing through assimilation and anti-assimilation, one-sided incorporation and one-sided rejection, national culture emerges as the moment of mutual permeability and interpenetration.

To develop this point, Fanon recasts the notions of permeability and interpenetration in more explicitly Hegelian terms: "Self-consciousness does not mean closing the door on communication. Philosophy teaches us on the contrary that it is its guarantee. National consciousness, which is not nationalism, is alone capable of giving us an international dimension."[101] In this passage, Fanon evokes Hegel's understanding of self-consciousness as necessarily relational, as requiring, for its own realization, reciprocal recognition from another self-consciousness qua self-consciousness.[102] Fanon translates this notion of the intersubjective dimension of self-consciousness to theorize the international dimension of national consciousness. He accordingly distinguishes nationalism from national consciousness insofar as nationalism is a closing off of the group from other groups, an absolute self-relating negativity, whereas national consciousness is an opening of the group to reciprocal communication, a new way of relating to the collective self through mutual (read: international) recognition. "Far then from distancing it from other nations," Fanon concludes, "it is national liberation that puts the nation on the stage of history. It is at the heart of national consciousness that international consciousness establishes itself and thrives."[103]

Just as there is an international dimension to national consciousness, Fanon posits that there is a "universal dimension" to national culture.[104] Although carrying different connotations, the international and the universal play synonymous roles in Fanon's theorization of consciousness and culture respectively. They both name that which goes beyond yet resides within the national-particular. Given that the colonized intellectual passes through the abstract universalism of assimilation and *négritude*'s inventory of particularisms to arrive at this phase of development, Fanon appears to be drawing from another Hegelian motif to theorize national culture as the moment of concrete universality. The dialectical movement of this process is once again unmistakable. If traditionalist particularism negates the abstract universalism of assimilation, national culture negates the negation so that universality can become concrete, thereby sublating the contradiction between the (abstractly) universal and the particular.[105]

It is worth examining in this light how Fanon theorizes the dual emergence of national culture and humanism during the liberation struggle:

The liberation struggle does not restore to national culture its former values and configurations. This struggle, which aims at a fundamental redistribution of relations between men, cannot leave intact either the form or content of this people's culture. After the struggle is over, there is not only the disappearance of colonialism, but also the disappearance of the colonized. This new humanity, for itself and for others, inevitably defines a new humanism. This new humanism is prefigured in the objectives and methods of the struggle.[106]

Fanon insists here as elsewhere that decolonization cannot be confused with a traditionalist movement of restitution that would restore precolonial values and configurations to their previous form. This is why I find David Scott's claim misleading that in "the Fanonian story . . . the colonized are alienated from a harmonious identity" and the "redemptive project of overcoming colonialism is to return the natives to themselves."[107] For Fanon, on the contrary, there can be absolutely no return to a prior, harmonious identity. The historical process of decolonization so radically transforms everything in existence—including the colonized and their customs—that a new humanity is created along with a new culture that is at once particular and universal, national and humanist, for itself and for others. Or, as Peter Hallward puts it, the "actively decoloniz*ing* subject is not endowed, in advance, with an innate freedom that need only be exposed through elimination of colonial constraints: the subject *qua* subject only comes into being *through* and as a result of the militant process of decolonization as such."[108]

The previously cited passage from *The Wretched of the Earth* also complicates Judith Butler's suggestion, in an important essay on Fanon and Sartre, that "the struggle for a new universality . . . begins, perhaps, precisely when decolonization ends."[109] Although the colonized do not fully disappear until after the liberation struggle is complete, Fanon tells us that the defining of a new, humanist universality begins *during* the very process of decolonization itself. Recall his argument in *A Dying Colonialism*, which he makes five years into an ongoing revolutionary process, that the Algerian nation "is no longer the product of hazy and phantasy-ridden imaginations. It is at the very center of the new Algerian man. . . . The thesis that men change at the same time that they change the world has never been so manifest as it is now in Algeria."[110] The fight for independence wages on, but the nation to some extent already exists; the colonized have not completely disappeared, yet a new man has come into being. Fanon extends this line of reasoning in *The Wretched of the Earth* to the new humanity and the new humanism of the liberation struggle. In this way, his notion of humanism resonates with how Marx and Engels understand communism, not as "an *ideal* to which reality [will] have to adjust itself" but rather as "the *real* movement which abolishes the present state of things."[111] The new humanism of the new humanity is not some far-off utopia, a promise of something that, in the words of Samira Kawash, "is always, like justice, to come."[112] For Fanon, more precisely, the new humanism is like communism, the real movement abolishing the present colonial state of things. It is not something (only) of the future but (also) something already here, prefigured in the objectives and the methods of the struggle. Fanon is thus pointing to what could be called the *actuality* of the new humanism.[113]

If my reading of the aforementioned passage comfortably fits within a dialectical framework, it must be stressed that the word "disappearance," used to describe the fate of colonialism and of the colonized, rings out within this framework like a dissonant note. It would be tempting to read "disappearance" as a euphemism for determinate negation, but the notion more directly recalls Fanon's concluding argument in "Racism and Culture" that the universality of cultural relativism is founded on the irreversible exclusion of the colonial status. As I argued in the third chapter of this book, if an exclusion can be dialectically taken up again at a later moment of reflexivity, the *irreversibly* excluded is to disappear forever. Fanon's description of the fate of colonialism and of the colonized carries this subterranean residue of permanent and absolute subtraction with it. Fanon's description also returns the reader to his use of the word "disappearance" just a few paragraphs earlier to detail how certain models for telling stories become uninteresting and are replaced with newly discovered models as their substitutes. When the notion of disappearance is construed in this way, it is as though Fanon is reaffirming the thesis in "On Violence" that decolonization is a substitutional replacement of the colonized thing for an entirely new species. If this is the case, might the new humanism of the new humanity be what Natalie Melas describes as "quite emphatically *new*, previously unseen and unexperienced and in no way therefore a restoration of lost certainties or even a materialization of Enlightenment (or any other Western) promises of emancipation"?[114] Might the actuality of the new humanism, in other words, be irreducible to the dialectical negation and preservation of cultural beliefs and values corresponding to an inhuman condition?

Fanon points in this direction when he enigmatically states at the end of the chapter that nation building coincides with "the discovery and advancement of universalizing values."[115] Here "discovery" does not signal an unearthing of something that already exists, like the precolonial values that colonial domination sought to bury and suppress. The kind of discovery in question likewise seems to diverge from what the previous chapter of *The Wretched of the Earth* describes as the discovery of a universalist worldview at the culmination of a dialectical progression from undifferentiated nationalism to humanism. At this moment in the text, on the contrary, Fanon alludes to a more esoteric notion of discovery as the emergence of an entirely new set of values that prefigure the entirely new world without colonialism and the entirely new humanity without the colonizer and the colonized. Departing from the dominant Fanonian narrative of preexisting cultural phenomena enduring a process of dialectical mutation, the text gestures toward something more obscure that is, according to Fanon, already underway—namely, the emergence of universalizing values from the void of irreversible exclusion and disappearance, an affirmative creation coinciding with the tabula rasa of decolonization.

UNTIMELY MEDITATIONS FROM THE CLINIC

Despite their various differences, the third and fourth chapters of *The Wretched of the Earth* conclude in an analogous way, with a vision of a new world and a new humanity that defines a new humanist value system. "But the war goes on," Fanon states at the opening of the fifth chapter, as if to remind the reader that much suffering and inhumanity still lie ahead.[116] Titled "Colonial War and Mental Disorders," the majority of the chapter consists of case studies that detail how the traumatic events of the armed struggle produce psychotic reactions, cortico-visceral illnesses, and psychosomatic disorders in both the colonized and the colonizers. The chapter also offers a thorough critique of the colonialist myth, backed by the pseudoscientific research of the Algiers School of psychiatry, that "criminality" is biologically congenital to North African peoples rather than, as Fanon argues, "the direct result of the colonial situation."[117]

Fanon concedes early in the chapter that his psychiatric notes may seem "out of place and especially untimely [*inopportunes et singulièrement déplacées*]" in *The Wretched of the Earth* but goes on to assert that "there is absolutely nothing we can do about that."[118] While it is true that the scientific language and schematic presentation of Fanon's case studies diverge from the rest of the book, the untimely and out-of-place quality of the chapter—the extent to which it runs counter to and acts upon one of the main thrusts of the book—can be felt at a deeper level as well.[119] Thus far, *The Wretched of the Earth* has presented colonialism as the root cause of various psychological complexes and decolonizing violence as the only effective treatment in such instances. Fanon memorably explains in the first chapter of the book how the violence of decolonization operates as "a cleansing force. It rids the colonized of their inferiority complex, of their passive and despairing attitude. It emboldens them and restores their self-confidence."[120] Fanon embraces this same line of reasoning in the fifth chapter, positing that "the liberation struggle's rehabilitation of man fosters a process of reintegration that is extremely productive and decisive. The victorious combat of a people . . . procures them substance, coherence, and homogeneity."[121] Yet now, for perhaps the first time in *The Wretched of the Earth*, Fanon high-lights a negative valence of the violent struggle against colonialism: "Today the all-out national war of liberation waged by the Algerian people for seven years has become a breeding ground for mental disorders."[122] This charac-terization of the struggle, as contributing to new psychological trauma at the same time that it cleanses the colonized of prior psychological trauma, is what is so out of place and untimely about the case studies of the fifth chapter. Mental disorders are shown to be not only a target of the war but also one of its side effects. It would seem that violence is a kind of *pharma-kon*, both remedy and poison.[123]

Attuned to this dilemma, Butler's aforementioned essay on Fanon and Sartre encourages its readers "to ask whether violence itself, said to efface the marks of violence, does not simply make more such marks, leaving new legacies of violence in its wake."[124] In this way, Butler challenges Sartre's assertion in the preface to *The Wretched of the Earth* that "no indulgence can erase the marks of violence: violence alone can eliminate them."[125] Later in the same text, Sartre reiterates this idea: "Violence, like Achilles' spear, can heal the wounds it has inflicted."[126] Since Sartre's preface is almost uni-versally accused of falsely embellishing Fanon's views on violence, it is pertinent to ask if these claims correspond with the position that Fanon develops in *The Wretched of the Earth*. The short—though incomplete—answer is yes, Fanon is in agreement with Sartre when, for example, he theorizes decolonizing violence as the dialectical inversion of colonialist violence, as colonialist violence boomeranging back at the colonizers while taking on "positive, formative features" for the colonized.[127]

If Fanon continues to look to the healing properties of violence in "Colo-nial War and Mental Disorders," he sometimes presents the outcome of the struggle—not unlike in "On Violence"—in a way that exceeds dialec-tical reason. He writes, for instance, that the "combat waged by a people for their liberation leads them, depending on the circumstances, either to reject or explode the so-called truths sown in their consciousness by the colonial regime, military occupation, and economic exploitation. And only the armed struggle can effectively exorcize these lies about man that subordinate and literally mutilate the more conscious-minded among us."[128] Notice how Fanon uses the language of rejection, explosion, and exor-cism to describe the armed struggle as a force that wipes out colonialist falsehoods, totally clearing them from the psyche. This idea also gains expression when Fanon describes how colonialist "seeds of decay . . . must be relentlessly tracked down and rooted out [*extirper*] from our land and from our minds."[129] It is as though decolonizing violence operates as a kind of annihilation therapy, an electrical jolt to the system that results in the total dissolution of a personality that was formed in and through the violence of colonization.[130] Fanon and Sartre thus share the view that violence can eliminate the marks of violence; however, Fanon's account of this elimination, throughout *The Wretched of the Earth*, is less stable in its reasoning, vacillating between a movement of dialectical overcoming and a procedure of complete lysis.

But, to return to Butler's question, what of the *new* marks of violence, those out-of-place and untimely marks that appear *because of* the struggle for liberation? This is not an issue that Sartre addresses in his preface, since he restricts his focus to how the colonized are "cured of colonial neurosis" by participating in violent revolutionary activity.[131] For Fanon, on the other hand, this issue is a major concern, and it even forces him to consider the limits of violence as a remedy.[132] He explores this point subtly at first, though an attentive reader will immediately recognize the weighty implications of the following statement: "And for many years to come we shall be bandaging the countless and sometimes indelible wounds inflicted on our people by the colonialist onslaught."[133] According to Fanon, during the liberation struggle, colonialist forces sometimes inflict *indelible* wounds, wounds that can never fully heal, that leave a permanent mark on the body but also the psyche of the colonized even after decolonization has been achieved. This raises some serious doubts about the total, complete, and absolute nature of decolonization. How can decolonization be a tabula rasa if some marks of colonialist violence cannot be wiped clean by decolonizing violence? Fanon's case studies show that these marks are not only permanent but also, in many cases, malignant, which leads him to conclude: "In all evidence the future of these patients is compromised."[134] When Fanon gives the fatal prognosis, he could not be further away from his vision of an entirely new humanity living in an entirely new world in which every trace of colonial domination has been eliminated.[135] Drucilla Cornell aptly describes what is at stake here when she observes that "Fanon sometimes writes as if those who have participated in the revolution might never be able to heal enough from the trauma to be part of this new world."[136]

It is important to note that Fanon attributes the indelible wounds of the armed struggle to the colonialist onslaught rather than to decolonizing violence. He does not yet go so far as to characterize this latter form of violence as a potential source of harm for the colonized. This occurs later, when Fanon discusses a "patriot and former resistance fighter" from a now independent African country whom Fanon treats for insomnia, anxiety attacks, and obsessional thoughts of suicide. Fanon relates that these ailments afflict the patient at a very specific time of the year: "The critical date corresponded to the day he had been ordered to place a bomb somewhere. Ten people had perished during the attack. This militant, who never for a moment had thought of recanting, fully realized the price he had had to pay in his person for national independence."[137] Even though the militant's participation in decolonizing violence greatly injured his psyche, Fanon contends that he willingly made that sacrifice for independence and never renounced his decision when facing its consequences. Fanon is uninterested in moralizing such cases of armed struggle. Instead, he highlights how decolonizing violence, while remedying the colonial situation, precipitates the militant's pathological condition.

Fanon expands on this point in one of his characteristically indispensable footnotes. Allow me to reproduce it in full:

The circumstances surrounding the symptoms [of the militant] are interesting for several reasons. Several months after his country gained independence he had made the acquaintance of nationals from the former colonizing nation. They became friends. These men and women welcomed the newly acquired independence and unhesitatingly paid tribute to the courage of the patriots in the national liberation struggle. The militant was then overcome by a kind of vertigo. He anxiously asked himself whether among the victims of his bomb there might have been individuals similar to his new acquaintances. It was true the bombed café was known to be the haunt of notorious racists, but nothing could stop any passerby from entering and having a drink. From that day on the man tried to avoid thinking of past events. But paradoxically a few days before the critical date the first symptoms would break out. They have been a regular occurrence ever since. In other words, our actions never cease to haunt us. The way they are ordered, organized, and reasoned can be a posteriori radically transformed. It is by no means the least of the traps history and its many determinations set for us. But can we escape vertigo? Who dares claim that vertigo does not prey on every life?[138]

If a Manichaean logic of good versus evil and us versus them justified the militant's actions, this same logic is challenged when the militant realizes, standing before his new European friends, that they are not evil and yet someone just like them could have wandered into the café before the bomb went off. Fanon thus returns to issues that he explored in *A Dying Colonialism* and in the second chapter of *The Wretched of the Earth*—the differentiation of the colonizers and the overcoming of Manichaeanism—so as to consider their existential and psychological ramifications.

The militant in question is intriguingly reminiscent of Épithalos in *Parallel Hands*, who likewise finds himself dizzy with vertigo in the wake of his explosive act.[139] But here the direct intertextual referent is not Nietzsche's *Thus Spoke Zarathustra* but the early Sartre of *Being and Nothingness* insofar as Fanon is concerned with the militant's existential anxiety in the face of the past and his vertigo before the abyss of freedom.[140] The militant remains steadfast in his conviction that his sacrifice was worth it, that he would not trade independence for relief from his current ailments. But he is not as steadfast as he once was regarding his sacrifice of others, those who were once regarded as the undifferentiated embodiment of absolute evil. Once his core beliefs are shaken in this way, the militant apprehends that past convictions cannot offer him a sturdy foundation but must be freely recreated at every moment. Consciousness of this freedom produces anxiety and vertigo because it forces the militant to face the possibility that one day he might not recreate his convictions and that, as a consequence, his past actions would lose their former justification. Standing before his new friends, he does not trust himself to reaffirm what he once held to be absolute. He is like Sartre's gambler, someone who decides never to gamble again but one day finds himself before the gambling table, at which point, defeated, "all his resolutions melt away."[141] Sartre's account of the gambler's lived experience of anxiety in the face of the past is instructive: "It seemed to me that I had established a *real barrier* between gambling and myself, and now I suddenly perceive that my former understanding of the situation is no more than a memory of an idea, a memory of a feeling."[142] Analogously, it seems to the militant that his understanding of the situation is just as unbudgeable, until he suddenly perceives the idea and the feeling of Manichaeanism as no more than a memory, as something that, in Sartre's words, "stands behind [him] like a boneless phantom."[143]

When Manichaeanism becomes a phantom-like memory, the memory of planting a bomb becomes a haunting psychological nightmare. The militant tries to avoid thinking of the past, but Fanon explains that forgetting is ultimately not possible, that repression will only lead to a return of the repressed.[144] The anniversary of the bombing necessarily triggers a myriad of symptoms. It is therefore not decolonizing violence *as such* that causes the militant's existential and psychological duress but rather his violent actions combined with the postindependence transformation of their significance for him. From this it follows that decolonizing violence can take on a negative valence as the militant's consciousness overcomes Manichaeanism. This is not to say, however, that the chapter is organized around a miniature dialectic of experience, in which its more extreme formulations progressively give way to the views just outlined. Instead, "Colonial War and Mental Disorders" is jaggedly split between calling for absolute and total elimination (when it comes to colonialist falsehoods) and recognizing the impossibility of such an absolute and total endeavor (when it comes to certain wounds and memories).

For Fanon and Sartre, vertigo may be something that everyone is condemned to experience at some point because of the kind of freedom that comes with existence. Yet, as Fanon suggests toward the end of his footnote, it is precisely this condition of freedom that opens up the possibility of transforming once more how the militant attributes meaning to his past actions, such that he would no longer suffer from the symptoms currently plaguing him. These are the thoughts of a hopeful Fanon who continues to believe, despite how he sometimes writes, that the patriots and resistance fighters who have participated in the struggle will one day heal enough so that they can truly join the new, decolonized world. If we read between the lines and with the chapter's main theme in mind, it appears as though Fanon is calling for a renewed psychiatric practice, a kind of treatment that will help militants work through the underlying causes of their symptoms so that they can dialectically transform how their past actions are ordered, organized, and reasoned. Although he does not go so far as to explicitly frame his discussion of war and mental disorders in these terms, he does offer a series of reflections on the importance of militants collectively establishing a new relationship with the past as part of their struggle for liberation. "Fighting for the freedom of one's people is not the only necessity," Fanon insists throughout the chapter. "You must retrace the paths of history, the history of man damned by other men, and initiate, make possible, the encounter between your own people and other men."[145] Fanon implies that working through the past in this way is a necessary precondition for such an encounter of mutual recognition to occur, an encounter that does not, like in the case of Fanon's patient, send one side spiraling into vertigo and anxiety. Such an endeavor could very well play an important role in the emergence of the new humanity that Fanon envisions at the end of the previous two chapters of *The Wretched of the Earth*.

If Fanon's patient hails from a country that has already gained independence, Fanon appears to be interested in determining how to avoid the proliferation of similar cases in the future when he sustains that working through the past must take place during—rather than after—the liberation struggle:

We must not wait for the nation to produce new men. We must not wait for men to change imperceptibly during the perpetual revolutionary renewal. It is true both processes are important, but it is consciousness that needs help. If revolutionary practice is meant to be totally liberating and exceptionally productive, everything must be accounted for. The revolutionary feels a particularly strong need to totalize events, to handle everything himself, to settle everything, to be responsible for everything. Consciousness then does not balk at going back or marking time, if need be. This is the reason why as a combat unit progresses in the field the end of an ambush does not mean cause for respite but the very moment for consciousness to go one step further since everything must work in unison.[146]

Those who participate in the liberation struggle cannot allow a temporal *décalage* to disarticulate the dual dialectic of the new nation and the new man, such that the transformation of consciousness would lag behind the transformation of society. To allow this to occur would be to inhibit revolutionary practice from being totally liberating, which would then open the door to mental disorders, anxiety, and vertigo. However, as Nigel Gibson points out, Fanon is not calling for consciousness to endure "constant forward movement," but rather to pass through a dialectically reflexive process, one that draws back into the past so as to catapult into the future.[147]

As Gibson also underscores, there is a "tension" in the above passage "between the revolution as 'totally liberating' and the revolutionary's will to 'totalize events.'"[148] Whereas the latter phrase draws from late Sartrean terminology to recast the idea of the militant dialectically working through the past, the former phrase resonates more clearly with the subterranean Fanon's call for a complete break with the past that would inaugurate the tabula rasa of decolonization. This tension becomes significantly more palpable in the final lines of the chapter:

Once again, the colonized subject fights in order to put an end to domination. But he must also ensure that all the untruths planted within him by the oppressor are liquidated. . . . Total liberation involves every facet of the personality. The ambush or the skirmish, the torture or the massacre of one's comrades entrenches the determination to win, renews the unconscious and nurtures the imagination. When the nation in its totality is set in motion, the new man is not an a posteriori creation of this nation, but coexists with it, matures with it, and triumphs with it. This dialectical requirement explains the reticence to adapted forms of colonization or to superficial reforms. Independence is not a word to exorcize but rather an indispensable condition for the existence of truly free men and women, which is to say, masters of the material resources that make possible the radical transformation of society.[149]

Just as he previously called for the rejection, explosion, and exorcism of colonialist falsehoods, Fanon now calls for their liquidation. This would constitute a total liberation; untruths would be banished from the personality of the colonized rather than dialectically reorganized. Amazingly, after dedicating an entire chapter to graphically depicting how the horrors of war negatively affect the psyche of the colonized, Fanon states that the torture and massacre of one's comrades can *renew* the unconscious and *nurture* the imagination. With this untimely assertion in an already untimely chapter, Fanon vacillates back toward dialectical reason by replacing the total rejection of a phenomenon with the search—even in the case of an atrocity— for its latent potential. This leads Fanon to reiterate that the dual dialectic of the new nation and the new man must advance in unison. He also theorizes the culmination of this dialectical process as the beginning of a new one by construing independence as the condition of possibility for a radical transformation of society. As a result, the careful reader cannot but experience a sense of déjà vu, insofar as what is centrally at stake in this passage and throughout the chapter is the dialectical or nondialectical nature of decolonization. Far from neatly resolving all the discrepancies and inconsistencies that permeate the opening formulations of *The Wretched of the Earth*, in other words, "Colonial War and Mental Disorders" acts as a kind of prelude for their full return.

NEW SKIN

The conclusion of *The Wretched of the Earth* reads like a short manifesto that brings the work to a close with an uncontained and uncontainable explosion. Such an intense flash of light appropriately starts with a call for collective awakening:

Now, comrades, now is the time to change sides. We must shake off the great mantle of night which has enveloped us, we must get out from under it. The new day which is dawning must find us determined, shrewd, and resolute. We must abandon our dreams and say farewell to our old beliefs and former friendships. Let us not lose time in useless laments or nauseating mimicry. Let us leave this Europe which never stops talking of man yet massacres him wherever he is encountered, at every one of its street corners, at every corner of the world.[150]

With imagery reminiscent of *Parallel Hands*, Fanon construes the radical change ahead as the dawning of a new day after the dark night of Europe's reign over the world. To prepare for this new day, the dream of being like Europe must be abandoned. This is not because a former colony of Europe can never hope to realize such a dream; Fanon will go on to discuss the United States and its ascent to power so as to demonstrate the contrary.[151] The dream must be abandoned, rather, because Europe is not as it appears in the dream. Fanon thus urges his comrades to join him in shaking off the great mantle of night that inhibits all who are under it from seeing that former friend, that supposedly humanist Europe, for what it has been all along: a force of murderous destruction that for centuries "has brought the progress of other men to a halt and enslaved them for its own purposes and glory."[152]

Once Europe is seen in this light, its incessant talk of man, its universalist rhetoric and musings, can no longer mystify and obscure its deeply anti-universalist legacy of acting out of self-interest while brutalizing the rest of the world. What concerns Fanon, however, is not so much the inconsistency between what Europe says and what it does, how it talks and how it acts. He wants to demonstrate that Europe's appeal to the universal is in fact intertwined with its conquest of the world. He forcefully makes this point by alluding to Hegel's *Philosophy of History*, a text that presents European colonialism as a necessary moment in the development of Spirit.[153] "It is in the name of Spirit," Fanon writes, "meaning the spirit of Europe, that Europe justified its crimes and legitimized the slavery in which it held four fifths of humanity."[154] When Fanon qualifies Hegel's Spirit as the spirit of Europe, he provincializes a philosophical notion that is standardly articulated as universal. This critical gesture sheds light on how Europe's historical development gets conflated with historical development as such, how European history gets conflated with Universal History.[155] Such conflations, Fanon maintains, serve as the basis for a philosophical justification of halting the progress of others, indeed of enslaving the overwhelming majority of humanity, so that Europe may progress in the attainment of its own "spiritual victories."[156]

It must nevertheless be emphasized that when Fanon critiques Europe's colonialist form of universalism, he is not suggesting that universalism is itself a product of the European colonial enterprise. This popular notion among today's critics is simply Eurocentrism disguised as its opposite. What could be more Eurocentric, after all, than to assume that the universal is European property, as if other parts of the world were incapable of articulating their own universalisms?[157] Fanon, on the other hand, denies that Europe has a monopoly over the claim to universality. He does so not by looking to non-European traditions for alternative worldviews but rather by inciting his comrades to undertake a new universalist project: "Let us decide not to imitate Europe and let us tense our muscles and our brains in a new direction. Let us endeavor to invent a man in full, something which Europe has been incapable of achieving."[158] These statements tap into an underground current of thinking that I have discussed throughout the present book, the same kind of thinking that envisions the colonized fullthroatedly vomiting up the values that have been forced down their throats so as to clear the way for the creation of entirely new values that correspond to an entirely new species of man. As Fanon explains, "The human condition, the projects of man, the collaboration between men on tasks that strengthen the totality of man are new problems which require veritable invention."[159] These may sound like old problems inherited from that supposedly humanist Europe, but, according to Fanon, they are new problems to the extent that they were never really Europe's problems, since Europe was willing to enslave the rest of humanity to enrich itself. Europe's colonialist form of universalism has been and remains of no use in solving problems that are truly universal in scope. Fanon insists: "Come, comrades, the European game is definitively over, we must find something else."[160] This something else is what requires veritable invention.

And yet, the conclusion's experimentation with this decidedly nondialectical conceptualization of change is quickly interrupted when Fanon offers an important qualification: "It is all too true, however, that we need a model, schemas and examples. For many of us the European model is the most elating."[161] Here the dominant theoretical framework of Fanon's oeuvre returns as the reader is told that something cannot be created from nothing, that the new emerges not from the void of a tabula rasa but from the dialectical mutation of preexisting schemas and examples. While imitating the European model must be rejected as an inviable and ultimately undesirable path for the Third World, the previously cited passage implies that elements from this model, what Fanon also describes as the "occasional prodigious theses" of Europe, ought to be translated and thus deprovincialized in the service of a universalist project that would truly extend to all of humanity.[162]

Fanon, now in open disagreement with his subterranean self, argues that this was actually Europe's task all along but that it failed to complete its historic mission:

All the elements for a solution to the major problems of humanity existed at one time or another in European thought. But the Europeans did not act on the mission that was designated them and which consisted of violently weighing these elements, modifying their configuration, their being, of changing them and finally taking the problem of man to an incomparably higher plane. Today we are witnessing a stasis of Europe. Comrades, let us flee this immobile movement where the dialectic has gradually transformed into a logic of equilibrium. Let us take up again the question of man [*Reprenons la question de l'homme*].[163]

Notice how the problems of humanity are no longer construed as new problems that require veritable invention. Instead, they are problems that already could have been solved with existing elements of European thought if these elements had undergone the kind of dialectical transformation necessary so that they could be reconfigured on a higher, incomparably less provincial plane. At this point in the conclusion, Fanon depicts Europe and its universalist thought as contradictory phenomena that still contain a latent and not yet realized potential. Likely alluding to Marx and Sartre, among others, Fanon even mentions how certain Europeans attempted to steer Europe away from its current stasis but that the European workers, convinced that "they too were part of the prodigious adventure of the European Spirit," did not heed the call.[164]

If the elements needed to solve the major problems of humanity already exist, it would seem that Fanon's comrades do not need to start from scratch, that they can take up the mission that their European counterparts failed to complete and reinvent it as their own. Fanon suggests as much when he once more deploys the keyword *reprendre* to encourage the examination of a question that has been posed before but has not yet been satisfactorily answered. If Europe was ultimately unsuccessful in resolving the question of man, Fanon encourages his comrades to take up the question again and overcome the limits of previous responses to it.[165] What appeared like a stark antinomy between Europe and the Third World is converted into a contradictory relationship that engenders movement and growth. Fanon goes on to describe this relationship accordingly: "The Third World is today facing Europe as one colossal mass whose project must be to try and solve the problems this Europe was incapable of finding the answer to."[166]

There is nonetheless an important moment of ambiguity in the previous extended passage that deserves further contemplation. What does Fanon mean when he calls upon his comrades to "flee this immobile movement where the dialectic has gradually transformed into a logic of equilibrium"? When read with the sentence that immediately precedes it, Fanon seems to be saying that the dialectic has definitively stalled in Europe and that it is the task of the Third World to set the dialectic back in motion. The sentence reads very differently, however, if it is considered alongside Fanon's closing statement:

If we want humanity to advance one notch, if we want to take humanity to a different level than the one where Europe has placed it, then we must invent, we must discover. If we want to respond to the expectations of our peoples, we must look elsewhere besides Europe. . . . For Europe, for ourselves, and for humanity, comrades, we must make new skin, develop a new thought, attempt to put in place a new man.[167]

Together these passages gesture once more toward a subterranean Fanon who is inviting his comrades to *flee* the dialectic, to break with it rather than jump-start it.[168] Europe, that real-life Lébos, offers only more of the same. To take humanity to a *different* level, rather than a higher level as stated previously, not even the dialectical mutation of European thought will do. The new humanity in formation is so unprecedented that it requires the discovery, invention, and development of an entirely new kind of thought.[169]

With its striking appeal to also make new skin, the last line of *The Wretched of the Earth* returns the reader to Fanon's first book, *Black Skin, White Masks*.[170] This is a very appropriate ending, since the last section of Fanon's last work showcases the internal division that was there all along, from the very beginning, and that traverses his short life as a writer, psychiatrist, and revolutionary. Throughout this study, I have argued that Fanon splits in two when grappling with the question of change, and I have demonstrated how this results in a dynamic and multifaceted relationship between distinct modes of thought that manifests itself differently at different moments in his writings. Sometimes Fanon can appear openly conflictual and antagonistic toward his own ideas, whereas at other moments seemingly irreconcilable formulations coexist and even mutually enrich each other. More frequently, however, the characteristic dividedness of Fanon's oeuvre gains expression through the introduction of a term, image, or metaphor that reads like a symptomatic slip, revealing an underground current of thought flowing through the entirety of his writings.

In the first chapter of *Black Skin, White Masks*, Fanon describes two dimensions of *le Noir*, how *le Noir*'s being-for-others is divided between a being-for-blacks and a being-for-whites. Fanon characterizes this condition as marked by "scissiparity," which is to say that *le Noir* experiences a kind of fission and—like when a single cell endures a process of fission—is split in two.[1] To explain why this occurs, Fanon states that it is "no doubt whatsoever . . . a direct consequence of the colonial undertaking."[2] But, as he goes on to argue, it is not enough to study *le Noir*'s divided being-for-others as a product of colonialism: "Once we have taken note of the situation, once we have understood it, we consider the job done. How can we not hear that voice again tumbling down the steps of History: 'It's no longer a matter of knowing the world, but of transforming it.' This question is terribly present in our lives."[3] Fanon is referring to and paraphrasing Marx's eleventh thesis on Feuerbach: "The philosophers have only *interpreted* the world in various ways; the point is to *change* it."[4] Vulgar readings of this thesis sustain that Marx is calling for action instead of thinking, that he is undialectically opposing change to interpretation. Of course, if Marx really held such a view, he would not have spent much of his life thinking about and developing an interpretation of the historical tendencies of capital. But, as his critique of Feuerbach suggests, Marx pursued this research program with the hope that it would play a role in capital's overcoming. The same is true for Fanon. His point is that interpreting the world, analyzing the enduring legacy of colonization in the lived experience of *le Noir* loses all of its meaning if it is not pursued with the intention of contributing to the world's transformation, to its decolonization. The question of change is therefore terribly present in Fanon's life; it haunts him, like Marx's specter. And it leads him not to abandon thinking but to produce what Achille Mbembe calls "metamorphic thought," the kind of thought that can be "deployed like an artillery shell aimed at smashing, puncturing, and transforming the mineral and rocky wall and interosseous membrane of colonialism."[5]

Yet, as I have argued throughout this book, the question of change is at the core of Fanon's internal division, so his metamorphic thought is ultimately split between two distinct modes of thinking about change. What are we to make of *this* scissiparity, of the dominant and subterranean dimensions in Fanon's oeuvre now that their major features have been explored? Could it not be said that the process of fission that occurs within Fanon's thought is also a direct consequence of the colonial undertaking? Indeed, throughout his body of work, we can see how the ruthless violence of colonialism forces Fanon to reflect on whether anything tied to its legacy can be preserved, even in the form of dialectical negation. He searches for what it would take to break free from the colonial world and create new subjectivities and new relationships, new cultures and new ways of thinking, new political institutions and new economic conditions, all while grappling with historical occurrences that stretch and even exceed the limits of his inherited theoretical frameworks. Issues like these pull Fanon in different directions, or, more exactly, they contribute to the formation of two Fanons.

My primary aim for this book has been to make a case for the existence of these two Fanons, to examine their different understandings of change, and to trace the multifaceted and dynamic relationship between them. Borrowing from the words of Gary Wilder, it has been my goal "to break through the crust encasing" Fanon, who is "more frequently talked about than listened to, more likely to be invoked instrumentally than read closely."[6] This has meant developing an interpretation of Fanon's dividedness rather than ignoring it, explaining it away, or attempting to resolve it for him. This has also meant doing my best to meet Fanon on his own terms instead of anxiously transcoding his language and ideas so that they appear more in line with the newest intellectual trend, theoretical school, or disciplinary debate. For these reasons, I have consciously stayed close to Fanon's texts and avoided detours into discussions that did not and likely would not have concerned him. To conclude this study, however, I do want to signal how we might begin to think with Fanon, beyond Fanon, by transitioning from a focus on his internal division to a preliminary and necessarily incomplete reflection on its broader stakes for contemporary politics. More specifically, I want to gesture toward the kinds of questions that can emerge when we inhabit Fanon's internal division rather than one side of it, questions that might contribute, in some small and modest way, to the ongoing efforts to think about and ultimately bring about radical change.

Consider, along these lines, an aphorism coined by Audre Lorde that has become a kind of motto among many of today's activists: "For the master's tools will never dismantle the master's house."[7] If you have participated in recent social movements like Occupy Wall Street or Black Lives Matter, you have likely heard this phrase many times and perhaps even joined others in parsing out its meaning and significance. In my experience, these conversations often revolve around identifying the master's tools and reflecting on how wielding such tools will not usher in what Lorde refers to as "genuine change" but only the kind of reform that allows individuals to provisionally beat the master at his own game, to ease one's own oppression but also perpetuate it while extending, if not intensifying, the oppression of others.[8] Typically these conversations get more complicated when someone poses the inevitable follow-up question: If the master's tools will not dismantle the master's house, which ones will? Here is where we might turn to Fanon, not because he gives us a definitive answer to this question but because his internal division invites us to pose further questions that can nuance our perspective on the matter and help reveal its stakes. For example, in light of Fanon's dividedness, we might ask: Can the master's tools be translated in such a way that they no longer function as his tools? Can they be dialectically transformed into the tools needed to dismantle the master's house or are completely different tools needed? Do such tools already exist, passed down from traditions that predate and will perhaps postdate the master, or do entirely new tools need to be invented? That Fanon's internal division does not always result in the development of irreconcilable positions, that the distinct modes of thinking in his oeuvre are just as often complementary as they are antagonistic, invites further questions: Can we think translation and invention together? In other words, to realize genuine change, could it be the case that some tools must be totally abolished whereas others must be abolished and maintained, negated yet preserved in an elevated form? Finally, the dynamic nature of Fanon's internal division raises the issue of how fluid or mobile we should be when responding to these questions. Can they be answered in an a priori and principled way or must they be continually rethought from within specific conjunctures, such that different historical situations will necessitate different approaches to the master's tools? I do not claim to have ready-made answers to these questions, and, what's more, my sense is that these are the kinds of questions that can only be decided collectively and on the ground. But what I want to underscore is how Fanon's internal division, far from a defect or flaw in his thinking, provides us with the means to pose these questions and explore different responses to them as part of a larger undertaking to gather the tools necessary to dismantle the master's house.

This is not to say that dismantling the master's house is the only objective of today's social movements. People march in the streets, occupy parks and buildings, hold demonstrations and sit-ins, practice mutual aid and experiment with new forms of assembly, direct action, and decision-making because they—we—want to build a new society, to create a new world without masters. Or, in the words of Robin D. G. Kelley, "Although we still need to overthrow all vestiges of the old colonial order, destroying the old is just half the battle."[9] The other half of the battle will require an immense effort of collective creativity, imagination, and organization aimed at developing a vision of this world to come and a program for its realization. Insofar as this has been and will be a battle occurring on a world scale, and not just in an isolated pocket of the world, it will also require—as Fanon knew—grappling with the question of universality. But to approach the question in this way will mean freeing ourselves from a certain fear of universality that has become commonplace within both academic and activist circles. This is how Judith Butler describes the situation: "The question of universality has emerged perhaps most critically in those Left discourses which have noted the use of the doctrine of universality in the service of colonialism and imperialism. The fear, of course, is that what is named as universal is the parochial property of the dominant discourse, and that 'universalizability' is indissociable from imperial expansion."[10]

To some extent, Fanon is a precursor of these Left discourses. He critiques the many ways in which Europe attempts to elevate its particular values, beliefs, and customs to the level of the universal, to what holds true for all cultures throughout time, and he challenges notions of the human that constitutively exclude racialized and colonized groups so as to justify their enslavement and exploitation. However, similar to Butler, Fanon holds that it is possible to think universality otherwise, that we need not fear universality as such. This aspect of his thought has been lost among those who equate any universalist project with domination and the erasure of difference. The irony is that such a universal condemnation of universality contributes to erasing the very differences that distinguish oppressive forms of universalism from the universalist demands and formulations that have historically emerged out of the struggle against oppression and represent the greatest threat to the universalizing drives of colonialism and imperialism.[11]

My emphasis throughout this book on Fanon's commitment to an emancipatory universality is meant to recover what gets lost in the unexamined dismissal of all universalist thinking and politics. In this way, I build upon contemporary scholarship that explores a long and vibrant tradition of universalism within black radical theory and practice.[12] By returning to the work of figures like Fanon, Aimé Césaire, Suzanne Césaire, C. L. R. James, and Claudia Jones, among many others, it becomes possible to shift the terms of contemporary debate so that, instead of arguing for or against universalism, we can engage in a more nuanced discussion of different kinds of universalism and their different effects.[13] The question of universality would thus become the question of *universalities*. Here is where we might once again turn to Fanon's internal division and consider how it can further nuance the conversation. If our starting point is the distinction between oppressive forms of universalism and emancipatory alternatives, Fanon's dividedness pushes us to reflect more deeply on the relationship between these alternatives. Are distinct articulations of universality inherently in conflict or in tension with each other, even when they are emancipatory in nature, insofar as they imply competing visions of the world and its future? Or can emancipatory articulations of universality coexist within a space of compossibility and form a kind of alliance or coalition based on certain shared aims and goals?[14]

These are questions that Fanon never explicitly poses, but they naturally follow from his internal division between a dialectical notion of universality and a nondialectical or even antidialectical alternative. They are also crucial questions for today's social movements, since these movements likewise contain distinct articulations of universality within themselves—anarchist, black radical, communist, feminist, indigenous, and queer, to name just a few—and the challenge will be to determine their relationship and negotiate their differences and disagreements in a way that does not return to the colonizing or imperialist form of universality, of one articulation dominating the others.[15] This is perhaps what is at stake in that famous demand of the Zapatistas, which has become another motto in recent years among a multitude of activists: "The world we want is one in which many worlds fit [*El mundo que queremos es uno donde quepan muchos mundos*]."[16] What kind of transformation is necessary to bring such a world of many worlds into existence? This is the question of change. And if Fanon cannot answer this question for us, how can we not hear his voice impelling us to ask it?

NOTES

INTRODUCTION

1. For the classic overview of Fanon studies, see Lewis R. Gordon, T. Denean Sharpley-Whiting, and Renée T. White, "Introduction: Five Stages of Fanon Studies," in *Fanon: A Critical Reader*, ed. Lewis R. Gordon, T. Denean Sharpley-Whiting, and Renée T. White (Cambridge: Blackwell, 1996), 1–8. See also Nigel Gibson, introduction to *Rethinking Fanon: The Continuing Dialogue* (New York: Humanity, 1999), 9–46; Henry Louis Gates Jr., "Critical Fanonism," in *Tradition and the Black Atlantic* (New York: BasicCivitas, 2010), 83–112; Magali Bessone, "Introduction: Frantz Fanon, en équilibre sur la *color line*," in Frantz Fanon, *Oeuvres* (Paris: La Découverte, 2011), 37–43; Anthony C. Alessandrini, *Frantz Fanon and the Future of Cultural Politics: Finding Something Different* (Lanham, MD: Lexington, 2014), 19–47; and Lewis R. Gordon, *What Fanon Said: A Philosophical Introduction to His Life and Thought* (New York: Fordham University Press, 2015), 1–7.
2. Frantz Fanon, *Écrits sur l'aliénation et la liberté*, ed. Jean Khalfa and Robert J. C. Young (Paris: La Découverte, 2015). Frantz Fanon, *Alienation and Freedom*, ed. Jean Khalfa and Robert J. C. Young, trans. Steven Corcoran (London: Bloomsbury, 2018).
3. For an introductory discussion of this material, see Jean Khalfa's and Robert J. C. Young's essays at the beginning of each major section of *Alienation and Freedom*. See also Nigel Gibson and Roberto Beneduce, *Frantz Fanon, Psychiatry, and Politics* (London: Rowman & Littlefield, 2017); and David Marriott, *Whither Fanon? Studies in the Blackness of Being* (Stanford, CA: Stanford University Press, 2018).
4. For the best intellectual biographies on Fanon, see David Macey, *Frantz Fanon: A Biography* (London: Verso, 2012); and Alice Cherki, *Frantz Fanon: A Portrait*, trans. Nadia Benabid (Ithaca, NY: Cornell University Press, 2006). Other notable biographies that have been published recently include: Joby Fanon, *Frantz Fanon, My Brother: Doctor, Playwright, Revolutionary*, trans. Daniel Nethery (Lanham,

MD: Lexington, 2014); Peter Hudis, *Frantz Fanon: Philosopher of the Barricades* (London: Pluto, 2015); and Christopher Lee, *Frantz Fanon: Toward a Revolutionary Humanism* (Athens: Ohio University Press, 2015).

5. Achille Mbembe, *Critique of Black Reason*, trans. Laurent Dubois (Durham, NC: Duke University Press, 2017), 170.

6. On this point, see Homi Bhabha, "Foreword: Framing Fanon," in Frantz Fanon, *The Wretched of the Earth*, trans. Richard Philcox (New York: Grove, 2004), vii–lxii; and David Scott, *Refashioning Futures: Criticism and Postcoloniality* (Princeton, NJ: Princeton University Press, 1999), 190–220. Gary Wilder complicates this assessment of anticolonial movements, focusing on the way they historically imagined futures not tied to the nation-state. See *Freedom Time: Negritude, Decolonization, and the Future of the World* (Durham, NC: Duke University Press, 2015).

7. Grant Farred, "Imperative of the Now," *South Atlantic Quarterly* 112, no. 1 (Winter 2013): 2.

8. For Fanon's take on political organization and intellectual leadership, see Frantz Fanon, *The Wretched of the Earth*, trans. Richard Philcox (New York: Grove, 2005), 63–144. For some helpful accounts of how contemporary social movements challenge the traditional role of political organization and intellectual leadership, see, among many other possible titles, Raúl Zibechi, *Dispersing Power: Social Movements as Anti-State Forces*, trans. Ramor Ryan (Oakland, CA: AK Press, 2010); Marina Sitrin, *Everyday Revolutions: Horizontalism and Autonomy in Argentina* (New York: Zed, 2012); Mark Bray, *Translating Anarchy: The Anarchism of Occupy Wall Street* (Winchester: Zero, 2013); and Marina Sitrin and Dario Azzelini, *They Can't Represent Us! Reinventing Democracy from Greece to Occupy* (London: Verso, 2014).

9. On Fanon and the Arab / African Spring, see Alessandrini, *Frantz Fanon and the Future of Cultural Politics*, 163–187; and Yasser Munif, "Frantz Fanon and the Arab Uprisings: An Interview with Nigel Gibson," *Jadaliyya*, August 17, 2012, https://jadaliyya.com/Details/26906. On Fanon and Occupy, see Lewis R. Gordon, George Ciccariello-Maher, and Nelson Maldonado-Torres, "Frantz Fanon, Fifty Years On: A Memorial Roundtable," *Radical Philosophy Review* 16, no. 1 (2013): 307–324; and Nicholas Mirzoeff, "Mindful Occupation," *Occupy 2012: A Daily Observation on Occupy*, May 5, 2012, https://nicholasmirzoeff.com/O2012/2012/05/05/mindful-occupation/. On Fanon and Idle No More, see Glen Sean Coulthard, *Red Skin, White Masks: Rejecting the Colonial Politics of Recognition* (Minneapolis: University of Minnesota Press, 2014). On Fanon and Rhodes Must Fall, see Achille Mbembe, "The State of South African Political Life," *Africa Is a Country*, September 19, 2015, https://africasacountry.com/2015/09/achille-mbembe-on-the-state-of-south-african-politics; Nigel Gibson, "The Specter of Fanon: The Student Movements and the Rationality of Revolt in South Africa," *Social Identities* 23, no. 5 (2017): 579–599; and Thierry M. Luescher, "Frantz Fanon and the #MustFall Movements in South Africa," *International Higher Education*, no. 85 (Spring 2016): 22–24. On Fanon and Black Lives Matter, see, among other possible references, Jared Ball, Todd Steven Burroughs, Hate, and Frank B. Wilderson III, "Irreconcilable Anti-Blackness and Police Violence," *iMWiL!*, October 2014, https://imixwhatilike.org/2014/10/01/frankwildersonandantiblackness-2/; Robin D. G. Kelley, Fred Moten, and Maisha Quint, "Do Black Lives Matter? Robin DG Kelley and Fred Moten in Conversation,"

Critical Resistance Event, Oakland, California, December 13, 2014, http://criticalresis tance.org/do-black-lives-matter-robin-dg-kelley-and-fred-moten-in-conversation/; and Jared Sexton, "Unbearable Blackness," *Cultural Critique*, no. 90 (Spring 2015): 159–178.

10. For an account of the #BlackLivesMatter demand and its development into a movement, see Alicia Garza, "A Herstory of the #BlackLivesMatter Movement," *Feminist Wire*, October 7, 2014, https://thefeministwire.com/2014/10/blacklivesmatter-2/. See also Barbara Ransby, *Making All Black Lives Matter: Reimagining Freedom in the 21st Century* (Oakland: University of California Press, 2018); and Keeanga-Yamahtta Taylor, *From #BlackLivesMatter to Black Liberation* (Chicago: Haymarket, 2016).

11. I have been unable to determine who or what group first attributed these sentences to Fanon. For discussions of the (creative mis)attribution, see Nigel Gibson, "Why Frantz Fanon Still Matters: Failure and Reciprocity," *The Critique*, June 14, 2016, http://thecritique.com/articles/why-frantz-fanon-still-matters/; and Jean-Thomas Tremblay, "Being Black and Breathing: On 'Blackpentecostal Breath,'" *Los Angeles Review of Books*, October 19, 2016, https://lareviewofbooks.org/article/being-black -and-breathing-on-blackpentecostal-breath/.

12. See, for example, Tony Webster's photograph of a banner with these sentences on it that was displayed outside the Minneapolis Fourth Precinct Police Station at a demonstration protesting the ultimately fatal shooting of Jamar Clark. The photograph is included in Sara Salem, "A Revolutionary Lifeline: Teaching Fanon in a Postcolonial World," *Historical Materialism* blog, August 16, 2017, http://historical materialism.org/blog/revolutionary-lifeline-teaching-fanon-postcolonial-world.

13. Frantz Fanon, *Black Skin, White Masks*, trans. Richard Philcox (New York: Grove, 2008), 201. Unless otherwise specified, I will refer to Philcox's translation of this text instead of Charles Lam Markmann's translation. For the latter version, see Frantz Fanon, *Black Skin, White Masks*, trans. Charles Lam Markmann (London: Pluto, 2008).

14. On the distinction between the victim and the vanquished, see Enzo Traverso, *Left-Wing Melancholia: Marxism, History, and Memory* (New York: Columbia University Press, 2017).

15. Cedric Robinson, "The Appropriation of Frantz Fanon," *Race & Class* 35, no. 1 (1993): 79.

16. Fanon, *Wretched*, 5 (my emphasis, translation modified). For the original, see Fanon, *Oeuvres*, 455.

17. Anthony Alessandrini makes a similar point when he writes that Fanon's thought "is at all times the enemy of stasis. This is one thing that links his entire oeuvre." Alessandrini, *Frantz Fanon and the Future of Cultural Politics*, 191.

18. Mbembe, *Critique of Black Reason*, 162.

19. Karl Marx, "Capital: A Critique of Political Economy, Volume I," in *Collected Works*, vol. 35 (New York: International, 1996), 19.

20. See Fredric Jameson, "The Three Names of the Dialectic," in *Valences of the Dialectic* (London: Verso, 2010), 3–4.

21. Or, as Slavoj Žižek puts it in one of his many discussions of dialectics, "The wound is already in itself its own healing." Slavoj Žižek, *The Ticklish Subject: The Absent Centre of Political Ontology* (London: Verso, 2000), 71.

22. See, along these lines, Jameson's discussion of how "to turn our current problem—the presentation of the dialectic—into a solution in its own right," as well as his reflections on the sine qua non of Marxism, in "The Three Names of the Dialectic," 4, 15.

23. Fredric Jameson, "Persistencies of the Dialectic: Three Sites," in *Valences of the Dialectic*, 288.

24. "Every actual thing involves a coexistence of opposed elements. Consequently to know, or, in other words, to comprehend an object is equivalent to being conscious of it as a concrete unity of opposed determinations." G. W. F. Hegel, *Hegel's Logic*, trans. William Wallace (Oxford: Oxford University Press, 1975), 78.

25. G. W. F. Hegel, *Science of Logic*, trans. A. V. Miller (New York: Routledge, 2010), 439.

26. See Bertolt Brecht, "A Short Organum for the Theatre," in *Brecht on Theatre: The Development of an Aesthetic* (New York: Hill and Wang, 1964), 179–205; C. L. R. James, *Notes on Dialectics: Hegel, Marx, Lenin* (Westport, CT: Lawrence Hill, 1981); and Mao Tse-Tung, "On Contradiction," in *On Practice and Contradiction* (London: Verso, 2007), 67–102. See, relatedly, Fredric Jameson, *Brecht and Method* (London: Verso, 1998).

27. Marx, "Capital, Volume I," 19.

28. See Hegel's remark on the term "sublation" in *Science of Logic*, 106–108. See also the entry for *Aufheben* in Barbara Cassin, ed., *Dictionary of Untranslatables: A Philosophical Lexicon*, trans. Steven Rendall, Christian Hubert, Jeffrey Mehlman, Nathanel Stein, and Michael Syrotinski (Princeton, NJ: Princeton University Press, 2014), 71–76. And see Jacques Derrida's discussion of the term and his "translation" of it in "What is a 'Relevant' Translation?," trans. Lawrence Venuti, *Critical Inquiry* 27, no. 2 (Winter 2001): 174–200.

29. On Fanon's relationship to Kojève, see Nick Nesbitt, *Caribbean Critique: Antillean Critical Theory from Toussaint to Glissant* (Liverpool: Liverpool University Press, 2013), 192–215; and Ethan Kleinberg, "Kojève and Fanon: The Desire for Recognition and the Fact of Blackness," in *French Civilization and Its Discontents: Nationalism, Colonialism, Race*, ed. Tyler Edward Stovall and Georges Van den Abbeele (Lanham, MD: Lexington, 2003), 115–28. See, relatedly, Bruce Baugh, *French Hegel: From Surrealism to Postmodernism* (New York: Routledge, 2003); and Michael S. Roth, *Knowing & History: Appropriations of Hegel in Twentieth-Century France* (Ithaca, NY: Cornell University Press, 1988).

30. Alexandre Kojève, *Introduction to the Reading of Hegel: Lectures on the Phenomenology of Spirit*, trans. James H. Nichols Jr. (Ithaca, NY: Cornell University Press, 1969), 15; Alexandre Kojève, *Introduction à la lecture de Hegel* (Paris: Gallimard, 1980), 21.

31. Kojève, *Introduction to the Reading of Hegel*, 14.

32. Kojève, *Introduction to the Reading of Hegel*, 15 (emphasis in original). The standard English translation of this passage reads: "the negation coming from consciousness, which supersedes in such a way as to preserve and maintain what is superseded, and consequently survives its own supersession." G. W. F. Hegel, *Phenomenology of Spirit*, trans. A. V. Miller (Oxford: Oxford University Press, 1977), 114–115.

33. "Man achieves his true autonomy, his authentic freedom, only after passing through Slavery." Kojève, *Introduction to the Reading of Hegel*, 27.

34. Nigel Gibson underlines the centrality of the concept of "mutation" in Fanon's work in "Radical Mutations: Fanon's Untidy Dialectic of History," in *Rethinking Fanon*, 408–446. Gibson offers another gloss on this issue in a chapter titled "Radical Mutations: Toward a Fighting Culture" in *Fanon: The Postcolonial Imagination* (Cambridge: Polity, 2003), 127–156.

35. Fanon, *Wretched*, 5; Fanon, *Oeuvres*, 455.

36. On translation contributing to the afterlife of the original, see Walter Benjamin, "The Task of the Translator," in *Selected Writings*, vol. 1, *1913–1926*, ed. Marcus Bullock and Michael W. Jennings (Cambridge, MA: Harvard University Press, 1996), 253–263. See also Jacques Derrida, "Roundtable on Translation," in *The Ear of the Other*, trans. Peggy Kamuf (Lincoln: University of Nebraska Press, 1985), 93–162.

37. Antonio Gramsci, *Further Selections from the Prison Notebooks*, ed. Derek Boothman (London: Lawrence & Wishart, 1995), 306.

38. In what follows, I am deeply indebted to the work of Sandro Mezzadra and Brett Neilson, who discuss Gramsci's interpretation of this speech in *Border as Method, or, the Multiplication of Labor* (Durham, NC: Duke University Press, 2013), 270–276.

39. Lenin, as cited in Mezzadra and Neilson, *Border as Method*, 272.

40. José Carlos Mariátegui, "Anniversary and Balance Sheet," in *José Carlos Mariátegui: An Anthology*, ed. Harry E. Vanden and Marc Becker (New York: Monthly Review, 2011), 130. For Mariátegui's multifaceted theorization of translation, see Gavin Arnall, "Hacia una teoría de la práctica teórica: Mariátegui, marxismo y traducción," *Escrituras americanas* 2, no. 2 (December 2017): 43–80.

41. Aimé Césaire, "Letter to Maurice Thorez," trans. Chike Jeffers, *Social Text* 28, no. 2 (Summer 2010): 149–150.

42. Césaire, "Letter to Maurice Thorez," 149.

43. Mezzadra and Neilson, *Border as Method*, 270.

44. Aimé Césaire, *Discourse on Colonialism*, trans. Joan Pinkham (New York: Monthly Review, 2000), 51–52; Aimé Césaire, "Discours sur le colonialisme," in *Poésie, Théâtre, Essais et Discours*, ed. Albert James Arnold (Paris: Planète libre, 2013), 1460.

45. On Césaire's politics of *dépassement*, see Wilder, *Freedom Time*, 35, 49, 169, 281n86.

46. Siri Nergaard and Robert J. C. Young, "Interview with Robert J. C. Young," *translation: a transdisciplinary journal*, http://translation.fusp.it/interviews/interview-with-robert-j.c.-young (accessed January 30, 2018). See, relatedly, Robert J. C. Young, "Frantz Fanon and the Enigma of Cultural Translation," *translation: a transdisciplinary journal* (Summer 2012): 1–10; and Robert J. C. Young, *Postcolonialism: A Very Short Introduction* (Oxford: Oxford University Press, 2003), 142–144.

47. Slavoj Žižek, "Holding the Place," in Judith Butler, Ernesto Laclau, and Slavoj Žižek, *Contingency, Hegemony, Universality: Contemporary Dialogues on the Left* (London: Verso, 2000), 316.

48. Slavoj Žižek, "Mao Tse-Tung, the Marxist Lord of Misrule," in Mao Tse-Tung, *On Practice and Contradiction*, 2. Recent scholarship on Marx shows how he "betrayed" himself or revised and altered his views on historical development over the course of his life. It would therefore be more accurate to say that Lenin's betrayal of Marx refers to a specific Marx, the Marx of Marxist orthodoxy. For the best account of Marx's changing views on historical change, see Kevin Anderson, *Marx at the Margins: On Nationalism, Ethnicity, and Non-Western Societies* (Chicago: University of Chicago Press, 2010).

49. Antonio Gramsci, "The Revolution Against *Capital*," in *Pre-Prison Writings*, ed. Richard Bellamy, trans. Virginia Cox (Cambridge: Cambridge University Press, 1994), 39–42.

50. Žižek, "Mao Tse-Tung," 2 (emphasis in original).

51. Žižek, "Mao Tse-Tung," 4.

52. For his classic discussion of traveling theory, see Edward Said, *The World, the Text, and the Critic* (Cambridge, MA: Harvard University Press, 1983), 226–247. See also his subsequent commentary on this text in light of Fanon's work in Edward Said, "Traveling Theory Reconsidered," in Gibson, *Rethinking Fanon: The Continuing Dialogue*, 197–214.

53. Žižek, "Mao Tse-Tung," 4 (emphasis in original).

54. Žižek, "Mao Tse-Tung," 2.

55. Karl Marx, *Grundrisse: Foundations of the Critique of Political Economy (Rough Draft)*, trans. Martin Nicolaus (New York: Penguin, 1993), 101.

56. Žižek likely opts to describe this movement as a process of reinvention rather than of translation because he associates the latter term with "postcolonial critiques of universality," which, in his view, arrive at the same conclusions as liberal multiculturalism: the tolerance of difference, the ideal of neutrality between particular groups, etc. While I am sympathetic to Žižek's argument, it does not exhaust all possible theorizations of translation, including those, like my own, that draw from a more militant and Marxist tradition of theorizing the concept and practice. For Žižek's take on translation, see his *Welcome to the Desert of the Real: Five Essays on September 11 and Related Dates* (London: Verso, 2002), 65–66. See also Slavoj Žižek, "Da Capo Senza Fine," in Butler, Laclau, and Žižek, *Contingency, Hegemony, Universality*, 214–217.

57. Here I take my cue, once again, from Gramsci, who invites thinking about a dialectical process of translation alongside the movement of concrete universality in the following passage from his *Prison Notebooks*: "The problem arises of whether a theoretical truth, whose discovery corresponded to a specific practice, can be generalized and considered as universal for a historical epoch. The proof of its universality consists precisely 1. in its becoming a stimulus to know better the concrete reality of a situation that is different from that in which it was discovered . . . 2. in its capacity to incorporate itself in that same reality as if it were originally an expression of it. It is in this incorporation that its real universality lies. . . . It can further be deduced that every truth, even if it is universal, and even if it can be expressed by an abstract formula of a mathematical kind (for the sake of the theoreticians), owes its effectiveness to its being expressed in the language appropriate to specific concrete situations." Antonio Gramsci, *Selections from the Prison Notebook*, ed. Quintin Hoare and Geoffrey Nowell Smith (New York: International, 1971), 201. See also Mezzadra and Neilson, *Border as Method*, 272–273. For an early attempt to elaborate upon the relationship between translation and universality, see Gavin Arnall, "Alejo Carpentier's *El siglo de las luces*: The Translation of Politics and the Politics of Translation," *Journal of Latin American Cultural Studies* 21, no. 1 (April 2012): 87–102.

58. Fanon, *Wretched*, 4 (translation modified). For the original, see Fanon, *Oeuvres*, 454.

59. Aristotle, as cited in Ato Sekyi-Otu, *Fanon's Dialectic of Experience* (Cambridge, MA: Harvard University Press, 1996), 55 (emphasis in original).

60. Fanon, *Wretched*, 6.

61. Fanon, *Wretched*, 1.

62. Frantz Fanon, *A Dying Colonialism*, trans. Haakon Chevalier (New York: Grove, 1965), 50.

63. Fanon, *Black Skin, White Masks*, 197. Robert J. C. Young contextualizes Fanon's interest in Nietzsche as tied to his reading of Césaire and Karl Jaspers. See "Fanon, Revolutionary Playwright," in Fanon, *Alienation and Freedom*, 47–48. For Césaire's Nietzscheanism, see A. James Arnold, *Modernism & Negritude: The Poetry and Poetics of Aimé Césaire* (Cambridge, MA: Harvard University Press, 1998).

64. Here I have in mind Bhabha's attempt, via Fanon and others, to develop a theory of translation without sublation in *The Location of Culture* (New York: Routledge, 1994).

65. Here I am borrowing from Louis Althusser's discussion of "a philosophy of the *void*: . . . a philosophy which *creates the philosophical void* [*fait le vide philosophique*] in order to endow itself with existence: a philosophy which, rather than setting out from the famous 'philosophical problems' (why is there something rather than nothing?), *begins by evacuating all philosophical problems*." Louis Althusser, "The Underground Current of the Materialism of the Encounter," in *Philosophy of the Encounter: Later Writings, 1978–1987*, trans. G. M. Goshgarian (London: Verso, 2006), 174 (emphasis in original). While Fanon and Althusser could both be construed as thinkers of the void, this comparison can only be made with the important caveat that they diverge drastically on other issues, including on the merits of Hegelian and Sartrean thought.

66. Fanon, *Wretched*, 180.

67. Althusser, "The Underground Current of the Materialism of the Encounter," 167.

68. Emilio de Ípola, *Althusser, The Infinite Farewell*, trans. Gavin Arnall (Durham, NC: Duke University Press, 2018). De Ípola's method of reading takes it cue from the "object" he reads, which is to say, from Althusser's own theorization of reading. See Louis Althusser, "From *Capital* to Marx's Philosophy," in *Reading Capital* (London: Verso, 2006), 13–69. De Ípola also borrows from Leo Strauss, who was interested in how writers might evade persecution by writing at two different levels, an exoteric level (for a general audience) and an esoteric level (for readers "in the know"). See Leo Strauss, *Persecution and the Art of Writing* (Chicago: University of Chicago Press, 1980).

69. De Ípola, *Althusser, The Infinite Farewell*, 8, 13 (emphasis in original).

70. De Ípola, *Althusser, The Infinite Farewell*, 13, 14.

71. Here I am deploying a phrase that Henry Louis Gates Jr. uses to describe Fanon's intellectual project in "Critical Fanonism," 111.

72. Stuart Hall, "The After-life of Frantz Fanon: Why Fanon? Why Now? Why *Black Skin, White Masks*?," in *The Fact of Blackness: Frantz Fanon and Visual Representation*, ed. Alan Read (Seattle: Bay Press, 1996), 34. Here I am slightly stretching Hall's original formulation since he considers three of Fanon's dialogues—his critical conversation with psychiatry and psychoanalysis, Sartre and Hegel, and *négritude*—whereas my focus is on the dialogue between dialectical and nondialectical thinking, which is a dialogue that traverses these other dialogues, that occurs within and between each of them, and that takes on multiple forms while doing so (i.e., dialogue as antagonism, dialogue as form of mutual enrichment, and dialogue as generator of tension).

73. Timothy Brennan relatedly posits that arguments over Fanon's relationship to Hegel "divide the field down the middle." See Brennan, *Borrowed Light: Vico, Hegel, and the Colonies* (Stanford, CA: Stanford University Press, 2014), 84–85.

74. Alessandrini, *Frantz Fanon and the Future of Cultural Politics*, 51–52.

75. For an introduction to the theoretical debates of postcolonialism, see Ania Loomba, *Colonialism / Postcolonialism* (New York: Routledge, 2015); and Robert J. C. Young, *Postcolonialism: An Historical Introduction* (Cambridge: Blackwell, 2001).

76. Jini Kim Watson and Gary Wilder, "Introduction: Thinking the Postcolonial Contemporary," in *The Postcolonial Contemporary: Political Imaginaries for the Global Present*, ed. Jini Kim Watson and Gary Wilder (New York: Fordham University Press, 2018), 4.

77. Homi Bhabha, "Remembering Fanon: Self, Psyche, and the Colonial Condition," in Frantz Fanon, *Black Skin, White Masks*, trans. Charles Lam Markmann (London: Pluto, 2008), xxii, xxiii; Bhabha, *The Location of Culture*, 57. In subsequent citations of this essay, I will refer to the version that appears in *The Location of Culture*. For a discussion of Bhabha's revisions to his original foreword, see Alessandrini, *Frantz Fanon and the Future of Cultural Politics*, 30-36.

78. Bhabha, *Location of Culture*, 88 (emphasis in original).

79. Hall, "The After-life of Frantz Fanon," 25.

80. Bhabha, *Location of Culture*, 58.

81. Bhabha, *Location of Culture*, 88 (emphasis in original).

82. Robinson, "The Appropriation of Frantz Fanon," 79.

83. Neil Lazarus, "Disavowing Decolonization: Fanon, Nationalism, and the Question of Representation in Postcolonial Theory," in *Frantz Fanon: Critical Perspectives*, ed. Anthony C. Alessandrini (New York: Routledge, 1999), 164; Benita Parry, "Problems in Current Theories of Colonial Discourse," *Oxford Literary Review* 9, nos. 1/2 (1987): 32; Sekyi-Otu, *Fanon's Dialectic of Experience*, 45.

84. At an event featuring Bhabha, Hall, bell hooks, and Gilane Tawadros, an anonymous attendee gave this characterization of Bhabha's reading of Fanon. See the "Dialogue" section in Alan Read, ed., *The Fact of Blackness: Frantz Fanon and Visual Representation* (Seattle: Bay Press, 1996), 41.

85. Hall, "The After-life of Frantz Fanon," 25.

86. Anne McClintock, *Imperial Leather: Race, Gender, and Sexuality in the Colonial Contest* (New York: Routledge, 1995), 363. There is a vast body of scholarship that critically engages with Fanon's understanding of gender and sexuality. Some canonical texts include Rey Chow, "The Politics of Admittance: Female Sexual Agency, Miscegenation, and the Formation of Community in Frantz Fanon," in Alessandrini, *Frantz Fanon*, 34–56; Diana Fuss, *Identification Papers: Readings on Psychoanalysis, Sexuality, and Culture* (New York: Routledge, 1995), 141–172; T. Denean Sharpley-Whiting, "Fanon and Capécia," in Alessandrini, *Frantz Fanon*, 57–74; T. Denean Sharpley-Whiting, "Fanon's Feminist Consciousness and Algerian Women's Liberation: Colonialism, Nationalism, and Fundamentalism," in Gibson, *Rethinking Fanon*, 329–353; and Hortense Spillers, *Black, White, and in Color: Essays on American Literature and Culture* (Chicago: University of Chicago Press, 2003), 376–427. For more recent examples, see Amey Victoria Adkins, "Black / Feminist Futures: Reading Beauvoir in *Black Skin, White Masks*," *South Atlantic Quarterly* 112, no. 4 (Fall 2013): 697–723; Alessandrini, *Frantz Fanon and the Future of Cultural Politics*, 36–47; and

Julietta Singh, *Unthinking Mastery: Dehumanism and Decolonial Entanglements* (Durham, NC: Duke University Press, 2018).

87. McClintock, *Imperial Leather*, 362, 364.

88. Benita Parry, *Postcolonial Studies: A Materialist Critique* (London: Routledge, 2004), 48.

89. "At a time when dialectical thinking is not the rage amongst colonial discourse theorists, it is instructive to recall how Fanon's interrogation of European power and native insurrection constructs a process of cultural resistance *and* cultural disruption, participates in writing a text that *can* answer colonialism back, *and* anticipates a condition beyond imperialism." Parry, *Postcolonial Studies*, 27 (emphasis in original).

90. Sekyi-Otu, *Fanon's Dialectic of Experience*, 25. For Sekyi-Otu's discussion of how Fanon's dialectic of experience diverges from Hegel's, even as it shares the same basic structure, see pages 26–30.

91. Sekyi-Otu, *Fanon's Dialectic of Experience*, 3–4.

92. Sekyi-Otu, *Fanon's Dialectic of Experience*, 25.

93. Sekyi-Otu gives a helpful summary of Fanon's dialectic of experience and its various moments in *Fanon's Dialectic of Experience*, 237.

94. Fanon, *Wretched*, 95.

95. Alessandrini makes a similar point when he argues that "what gets lost in [Sekyi-Otu's] analysis is the opportunity to understand [Fanon's] moments of discontinuity symptomatically—more specifically, as signs of Fanon's particular political and intellectual struggles as they are carried on in his writing." Alessandrini, *Frantz Fanon*, 52.

96. Sekyi-Otu, *Fanon's Dialectic of Experience*, 4.

97. Sekyi-Otu, *Fanon's Dialectic of Experience*, 22, 25.

98. Sekyi-Otu, *Fanon's Dialectic of Experience*, 26, 217.

99. Fanon, *Black Skin, White Masks*, 161.

100. See, Sekyi-Otu, *Fanon's Dialectic of Experience*, 182–184, 201, 225, 233.

101. Gibson, *Fanon: The Postcolonial Imagination*, 2–3. According to Gibson, his argument draws from Sekyi-Otu's book, *Fanon's Dialectic of Experience*, as well as Gordon's famous study, *Fanon and the Crisis of European Man: An Essay on Philosophy and the Human Sciences* (New York: Routledge, 1995). In my reading, this latter text does not clearly fit within either of the two tendencies that I have been describing, although, in general, Gordon's scholarship tends to emphasize what he evocatively refers to as Fanon's "ice-cold dialectical logic." Gordon, *What Fanon Said*, 112. See, relatedly, Gordon's discussion of Sekyi-Otu and Gibson in *What Fanon Said*, 116–117.

102. For Gibson's account of his divergence from Sekyi-Otu, see Gibson, *Fanon: The Postcolonial Imagination*, 2–9. See also Nigel Gibson, "Fanon and the Pitfalls of Cultural Studies," in Alessandrini, *Frantz Fanon*, 122n15.

103. Gibson, *Fanon: The Postcolonial Imagination*, 6.

104. Gibson, *Fanon: The Postcolonial Imagination*, 8.

105. Gibson, *Fanon: The Postcolonial Imagination*, 2.

106. Nelson Maldonado-Torres, "Fanon and Decolonial Thought," in *Encyclopedia of Educational Philosophy and Theory*, ed. Michael A. Peters (Singapore: Springer, 2017), 800. See, relatedly, Walter D. Mignolo and Catherine E. Walsh,

On Decoloniality: Concepts, Analytics, Praxis (Durham, NC: Duke University Press, 2018).

107. See, for instance, Walter Mignolo's emphasis on how Fanon departs from Marx and Freud in *Local Histories / Global Designs: Coloniality, Subaltern Knowledges, and Border Thinking* (Durham, NC: Duke University Press, 2012), 85–87. Mignolo relatedly claims, in an article for *Al Jazeera*, that "we, decolonial intellectuals, if not philosophers, 'have better things to do' as Fanon would say, than being engaged with issues debated by European philosophers." See Walter D. Mignolo, "Yes, We Can: Non-European Thinkers and Philosophers," *Al Jazeera*, February 19, 2013, https://aljazeera.com/indepth/opinion/2013/02/20132672747320891.html.

108. Nelson Maldonado-Torres, *Against War: Views from the Underside of Modernity* (Durham, NC: Duke University Press, 2008), 16, 106. It is worth noting that although Maldonado-Torres recognizes Sekyi-Otu's approach to reading Fanon as "outstanding," he emphasizes that his own treatment of Fanon "takes a different direction," one that does not attempt "to illuminate dimensions of Fanon's work with reference to modes of argumentation related to the general outlines of Hegel's philosophy of Spirit." Maldonado-Torres, *Against War*, 281n21.

109. Maldonado-Torres seems to be making this stronger claim about Fanon's decolonial thought when his reading leans on the work of Kierkegaard and Emmanuel Levinas. See, in particular, his discussion of how Fanon reinterprets the relationship between master and slave as operating under "the logic of the gift," as well as his argument concerning Fanon's "ethical and de-colonial suspension of the universal." Maldonado-Torres, *Against War*, 142, 158.

110. Maldonado-Torres, *Against War*, 282n.25 (my emphasis). The following passage likewise suggests a narrower claim, that Fanon's decolonial thought is an alternative, non-Hegelian form of dialectical thinking: "The Fanonian critique of ontology gives expression to a most fascinating reversal: while for Hegel the dialectic of master and slave becomes a moment in the development of Spirit and cannot be properly understood without reference to it, for Fanon, it is precisely the existence of relations of subordination *akin to this dialectic* that makes reference to Spirit and subordination to its logic inadequate." Maldonado-Torres, *Against War*, 105 (my emphasis).

111. Maldonado-Torres tends to oppose universality and particularity, the abstract and the concrete, in an undialectical way, which makes the Hegelian movement of concrete universality unintelligible. As a result, he often misconstrues Fanon's attempt to concretize rather than "suspend" the universal. Maldonado-Torres, *Against War*, 152. For a wayward but intriguing discussion of the tendency among decolonial theorists to think in these terms, see Zahi Zalloua, "Decolonial Particularity or Abstract Universalism? No, Thanks!: The Case of the Palestinian Question," *International Journal of Žižek Studies* 13, no. 1 (2019): 83–120.

112. George Ciccariello-Maher, *Decolonizing Dialectics* (Durham, NC: Duke University Press, 2017), 13, 50, 53.

113. Ciccariello-Maher, *Decolonizing Dialectics*, 6, 13, 70.

114. Jared Sexton and Daniel Colucciello Barber, "On Black Negativity, or the Affirmation of Nothing," *Society & Space*, September 18, 2017, http://societyand space.org/2017/09/18/on-black-negativity-or-the-affirmation-of-nothing/. On Afro-Pessimism, I have found this text especially helpful: Jared Sexton,

"Afro-Pessimism: The Unclear Word," *Rhizomes: Cultural Studies in Emerging Knowledge*, no. 29 (2016), http://rhizomes.net/issue29/sexton.html. See also Frank B. Wilderson III, *Red, White & Black: Cinema and the Structure of U.S. Antagonisms* (Durham, NC: Duke University Press, 2010).

115. Marriott, *Whither Fanon?*, 200.

116. For some of the most important texts from this exchange, see Fred Moten, "Black Op," *PMLA* 123, no. 5 (2008): 1743–1747; Fred Moten, "The Case of Blackness," *Criticism* 50, no. 2 (Spring 2008): 177–218; Fred Moten, *The Universal Machine* (Durham, NC: Duke University Press, 2018), 140–246; Jared Sexton, "Ante-Anti-Blackness: Afterthoughts," *Lateral: Journal of the Cultural Studies Association*, no. 1 (2012), https://doi.org/10.25158/L1.1.16; and Jared Sexton, "The Social Life of Social Death: On Afro-Pessimism and Black Optimism," *InTensions Journal*, no. 5 (2011): 1–47.

117. Sometimes, however, Fanon is presented more one-sidedly, as if he were an undivided thinker that consistently deploys a single conceptual framework. This occurs, for example, when Calvin Warren reads Fanon against Hegel in general, and against the Hegelian negation of negation in particular, without acknowledging the importance of both in Fanon's thought. See Calvin L. Warren, *Ontological Terror: Blackness, Nihilism, and Emancipation* (Durham, NC: Duke University Press, 2018), 92.

118. In "Afro-Pessimism: The Unclear Word," Sexton alludes to a different division in Fanon's thought. He writes that "Afro-Pessimism entails a certain motivated reading or return to Fanon, an attention to Fanon the theorist of racial slavery and 'negrophobia' more so than Fanon the theorist of metropolitan colonialism" (no page number). It is worth pondering if selectively privileging Fanon's theorization of racial slavery over his theorization of colonialism might lead to a misunderstanding of both, since these phenomena, for Fanon, are only intelligible when thought in tandem. Sexton actually makes this same point in an earlier essay co-authored with Huey Copeland when he refers to "a tension often left unremarked in Fanon between the specificity of his analysis of Negrophobia and the generality of his comments on the dehumanization of the native, the colonized, 'the wretched of the earth.' The challenge, of course, is to think both at once." Jared Sexton and Huey Copeland, "Raw Life: An Introduction," *Qui Parle* 13, no. 7 (Spring/Summer 2003): 57–58. See, relatedly, Wilderson's distinction between "the Fanon of the Slave and the Fanon of the postcolonial subject" in *Red, White, & Black*, 338.

119. For a more sustained engagement with how Afro-Pessimists read Fanon, as well as an attempt to read Fanon *against* Afro-Pessimism, see Annie Olaloku-Teriba, "Afro-Pessimism and the (Un)Logic of Anti-Blackness," *Historical Materialism* 26, no. 2 (2018), http://historicalmaterialism.org/index.php/articles/afro-pessimism-and-unlogic-anti-blackness.

120. Sexton and Colucciello Barber, no page number.

121. Sekyi-Otu, *Fanon's Dialectic of Experience*, 181.

122. Sekyi-Otu, *Fanon's Dialectic of Experience*, 182.

123. Hegel, *Phenomenology of Spirit*, 21.

124. Sexton and Colucciello Barber, no page number.

125. This is not to imply that Fanon holds an exclusively dialectical view of humanism. On the contrary, as I will show throughout this book, humanism is yet another

important site of internal division for Fanon. Natalie Melas has contributed greatly to my thinking on this point. See her article, "Humanity/Humanities: Decolonization and the Poetics of Relation," *Topoi* 18 (1999): 13–28. For related discussions of Fanon's humanism, see Alessandrini, *Frantz Fanon*, 75–100; and Marriott, *Whither Fanon?*, 2–7, 200–289.

126. Recall Bhabha's dismissive characterization of Fanon's humanism as "banal" and "beatific." Bhabha, *Location of Culture*, 87.

127. Sexton and Coluicciello Barber, no page number.

128. Sexton and Coluicciello Barber, no page number. Sexton is alluding to the following article: David Marriott, "Whither Fanon?," *Textual Practice* 25, no. 1 (2011): 33–69.

129. Marriott, "Whither Fanon?," 42. See also Marriott, *Whither Fanon?*, 12. For Marriott's extended discussion of invention, see *Whither Fanon?*, 237–276.

130. On this point, see Rebecca Comay's argument for reading Hegel as a thinker of ex nihilo creation in *Mourning Sickness: Hegel and the French Revolution* (Stanford, CA: Stanford University Press, 2010).

131. Moten describes it as a "pre-optical optimism" in *The Universal Machine*, 145.

132. Moten, *Universal Machine*, 181, 216.

133. Fred Moten in Stefano Harney and Fred Moten, *The Undercommons: Fugitive Planning and Black Study* (New York: Minor Compositions, 2013), 132.

134. Harney and Moten, *Undercommons*, 132.

135. Fanon, *Black Skin, White Masks*, xiv. Moten discusses the concept of lysis throughout his work on Fanon. See, for example, Moten, *Universal Machine*, 194–227. Harney and Moten relatedly discuss critique in terms of its threat to "the sociality it is supposed to defend"; however, they do so not to engage in a critique of critique but rather in what they refer to as a "takedown" of critique. See Harney and Moten, *Undercommons*, 19.

1. THE PSYCHIATRIC PAPERS AND *PARALLEL HANDS*

1. Tosquelles notes that there is an "annoying confusion" surrounding these and other related terms in one of his coauthored papers with Fanon. While the terms are generally thought to be synonymous, it is noteworthy that Tosquelles preferred "institutional psychotherapy," whereas Fanon typically used "social therapy" (*socialthérapie*) to describe his own method of treatment. For Tosquelles's take on this issue, see François Tosquelles and Frantz Fanon, "Indications of Electroconvulsive Therapy Within Institutional Therapies," in Frantz Fanon, *Alienation and Freedom*, ed. Jean Khalfa and Robert J. C. Young, trans. Steven Corcoran (London: Bloomsbury, 2018), 296. See also Frantz Fanon and Jacques Azoulay, "Social Therapy in a Ward of Muslim Men: Methodological Difficulties," in Fanon, *Alienation and Freedom*, 353–371. For an excellent introduction to Tosquelles and the politics of institutional psychotherapy, see Camille Robcis, "François Tosquelles and the Psychiatric Revolution in Postwar France," *Constellations* 23, no. 2 (June 2016): 212–222.

2. Frantz Fanon, "Day Hospitalization in Psychiatry: Value and Limits," in *Alienation and Freedom*, 475.

3. For a discussion of Fanon's experimentation with the method of social therapy in France and later in Algeria, see Alice Cherki, *Frantz Fanon: A Portrait*, trans. Nadia Benabid (Ithaca, NY: Cornell University Press, 2006); and David Macey, *Frantz Fanon: A Biography* (London: Verso, 2012). See also Hussein Abdilahi Bulhan, *Frantz Fanon and the Psychology of Oppression* (New York: Plenum, 1985); Jock McCulloch, *Black Soul, White Artifact: Fanon's Clinical Psychology and Social Theory* (Cambridge: Cambridge University Press, 1983); Françoise Vergès, "To Cure and to Free: The Fanonian Project of 'Decolonized Psychiatry,'" in *Fanon: A Critical Reader*, ed. Lewis R. Gordon, T. Denean Sharpley-Whiting, and Renée T. White (Cambridge: Blackwell, 1996), 93–96; Françoise Vergès, "Chains of Madness, Chains of Colonialism: Fanon and Freedom," in *The Fact of Blackness: Frantz Fanon and Visual Representation*, ed. Alan Read (Seattle: Bay Press, 1996), 48–52; and Irene Gendzier, *Frantz Fanon: A Critical Study* (New York: Pantheon, 1973), 61–116.

4. Tosquelles asserts that "the psychiatric hospital must be an institution of disalienation" in the discussion section of a paper coauthored with Fanon: Tosquelles and Fanon, "Indications of Electroconvulsive Therapy," 298.

5. Tosquelles and Fanon, "Indications of Electroconvulsive Therapy," 295.

6. François Tosquelles and Frantz Fanon, "On Some Cases Treated with the Bini Method," in Fanon, *Alienation and Freedom*, 285.

7. Frantz Fanon, "Mental Alterations, Character Modifications, Psychic Disorders, and Intellectual Deficit in Spinocerebellar Heredodegeneration: A Case of Friedreich's Ataxia with Delusions of Possession," in *Alienation and Freedom*, 272. Jean Khalfa's introduction to the section of *Alienation and Freedom* containing Fanon's psychiatric papers makes a strong case for reading the dissertation as the foundation of Fanon's subsequent research in psychiatry. See his essay, "Fanon, Revolutionary Psychiatrist," in Fanon, *Alienation and Freedom*, 167–202.

8. Fanon, "Mental Alterations," 215, 247.

9. Tosquelles and Fanon, "Indications of Electroconvulsive Therapy," 294.

10. Tosquelles and Fanon, "On Some Cases Treated," 288.

11. Tosquelles and Fanon, "Indications of Electroconvulsive Therapy," 294.

12. Tosquelles and Fanon, "On Some Cases Treated," 289.

13. Tosquelles and Fanon, "Indications of Electroconvulsive Therapy," 294.

14. Tosquelles and Fanon, "On Some Cases Treated," 289.

15. Tosquelles and Fanon, "Indications of Electroconvulsive Therapy," 294.

16. Tosquelles and Fanon, "On Some Cases Treated," 289; François Tosquelles and Frantz Fanon, "Sur quelques cas traités par la méthode de Bini," in Frantz Fanon, *Écrits sur l'aliénation et la liberté*, ed. Jean Khalfa and Robert J. C. Young (Paris: La Découverte, 2015), 241.

17. Tosquelles and Fanon, "Indications of Electroconvulsive Therapy," 294; François Tosquelles and Frantz Fanon, "Indications de la thérapeutique de Bini dans le cadre des thérapeutiques institutionnelles," in Fanon, *Écrits sur l'aliénation et la liberté*, 245.

18. Tosquelles and Fanon, "On Some Cases Treated," 290.

19. Tosquelles, in Tosquelles and Fanon, "Indications of Electroconvulsive Therapy," 298. In this section of the paper, Tosquelles also refers to the "dialectic" of the doctor's presence during treatment and to "the dialectical game" that advances toward a cure (297–298).

20. Tosquelles, as cited in Robcis, "François Tosquelles," 218.
21. Khalfa, "Fanon, Revolutionary Psychiatrist," 184; Robert J. C. Young, "Fanon, Revolutionary Playwright," in Fanon, *Alienation and Freedom*, 73.
22. Tosquelles and Fanon, "On Some Cases Treated," 289.
23. The phenomenological concept of "lived experience" plays an important role in many of Fanon's works. See my discussion of lived experience and its philosophical basis in chapter 2. I also discuss Fanon's notion of an "authentic birth" at length in chapter 3.
24. On this point, see François Tosquelles and Frantz Fanon, "On an Attempt to Rehabilitate a Patient Suffering from Morpheic Epilepsy and Serious Character Disorders," in Fanon, *Alienation and Freedom*, 299–305.
25. Frantz Fanon, "Yesterday, Today, and Tomorrow," in *Alienation and Freedom*, 282–283.
26. Fanon, "Yesterday, Today, and Tomorrow," 283 (translation modified). For the original, see Frantz Fanon, "Hier, aujourd'hui et demain," in Fanon, *Écrits sur l'aliénation et la liberté*, 235.
27. Alexandre Kojève, *Introduction to the Reading of Hegel: Lectures on the Phenomenology of Spirit*, trans. James H. Nichols, Jr. (Ithaca, NY: Cornell University Press, 1969), vi; Alexandre Kojève, *Introduction à la lecture de Hegel* (Paris: Gallimard, 1980), 7.
28. Walter Benjamin, "The Task of the Translator," *Selected Writings*, vol. 1, *1913–1926*, ed. Marcus Bullock and Michael W. Jennings (Cambridge, MA: Harvard University Press, 2004), 254.
29. Friedrich Nietzsche, *Thus Spoke Zarathustra: A Book for All and None*, ed. Adrian del Caro and Robert B. Pippin (Cambridge: Cambridge University Press, 2006), 162.
30. Nietzsche, *Thus Spoke Zarathustra*, 163; Friedrich Nietzsche, *Also sprach Zarathustra: ein Buch für Alle und Keinen* (Leipzig: C. G. Naumann, 1893), 293.
31. Friedrich Nietzsche, *Ainsi parlait Zarathoustra: Un livre pour tout le monde et personne*, trans. Henri Albert (Paris: Société du 'Mercure de France,' 1898), 288. For details on the passage that Fanon cites from Albert's translation of *Thus Spoke Zarathustra*, see Fanon, *Alienation and Freedom*, 746.
32. Nietzsche, *Thus Spoke Zarathustra*, 5; Nietzsche, *Also sprach Zarathustra*, 9; Nietzsche, *Ainsi parlait Zarathoustra*, 8.
33. Gilles Deleuze, *Nietzsche and Philosophy*, trans. Hugh Tomlinson (New York: Columbia University Press, 2006), 163.
34. Nietzsche, *Thus Spoke Zarathustra*, 14, 90.
35. Deleuze, *Nietzsche and Philosophy*, 163 (emphasis in original).
36. The Nietzschean theme of active forgetting and its benefits for life and growth is most famously articulated in Friedrich Nietzsche, "On the Uses and Disadvantages of History for Life," in *Untimely Meditations*, ed. Daniel Breazeale (Cambridge: Cambridge University Press, 1997), 57–124. As previously mentioned, Fanon had a French translation of *Untimely Meditations* in his library. See Fanon, *Alienation and Freedom*, 746. For a reading of Fanon that recognizes the importance of Nietzschean forgetting for his political project, see Zahid Chaudhary, "Subjects in Difference: Walter Benjamin, Frantz Fanon, and Postcolonial Theory," *differences* 23, no. 1 (May 2012): 170.
37. On this moment in Fanon's life, see Macey, *Frantz Fanon*, 197–201.

38. Frantz Fanon, "Letter to Maurice Despinoy," in *Alienation and Freedom*, 349; Cherki, *Frantz Fanon*, 62.

39. Fanon and Azoulay, "Social Therapy in a Ward of Muslim Men," 353–371.

40. Fanon and Azoulay, "Social Therapy in a Ward of Muslim Men," 371.

41. Fanon and Azoulay, "Social Therapy in a Ward of Muslim Men," 362 (translation modified). For the original, see Frantz Fanon and Jacques Azoulay, "La socialthérapie dans un service d'hommes musulmans: Difficultés méthodologiques," in Fanon, *Écrits sur l'aliénation et la liberté*, 305.

42. Fanon and Azoulay, "Social Therapy in a Ward of Muslim Men," 362.

43. Charles Geronimi, who also worked as Fanon's intern, has claimed that Fanon actually anticipated the experiment's failure but felt that the failure would be instructive, that it would demonstrate to his colleagues (and confirm for himself) that social therapy could not be blanketly applied outside of Europe and that it needed to be reinvented in and for North Africa. While this is certainly plausible, I try—as a rule—not to indulge in speculation about Fanon's real intentions. Instead, my treatment of the text focuses on its internal, self-critical logic. For Geronimi's account of his exchange with Fanon, see Cherki, *Frantz Fanon*, 71–72. See also Khalfa, "Fanon, Revolutionary Psychiatrist," 189–190.

44. On provincialization, see Dipesh Chakrabarty, *Provincializing Europe: Postcolonial Thought and Historical Difference* (Princeton, NJ: Princeton University Press, 2000).

45. Fanon and Azoulay, "La socialthérapie," 305 (my translation). The English translation of this text renders the original phrase, "*sortir de l'impasse*," as "exit the deadlock." See Fanon and Azoulay, "Social Therapy in a Ward of Muslim Men," 362.

46. Fanon and Azoulay, "Social Therapy in a Ward of Muslim Men," 362, 363 (translation modified). For the original, see Fanon and Azoulay, "La socialthérapie," 305. The English translation eliminates all dialectical connotation from the French verb "*passer*" by rendering it as "to go from." The more literal translation, "to pass," is a better choice when Fanon is describing dialectical movement.

47. Fanon and Geronimi similarly decide to "develop a projection test with Maghrebi Muslims in mind" after a failed experiment with the Thematic Apperception Test (TAT) on a large group of Muslim women patients. Fanon and Geronimi, "TAT in Muslim Women: Sociology of Perception and Imagination," in Fanon, *Alienation and Freedom*, 432.

48. On deprovincialization, see Harry Harootunian, *Marx After Marx: History and Time in the Expansion of Capitalism* (New York: Columbia University Press, 2015), 1–20; and Gary Wilder, *Freedom Time: Negritude, Decolonization, and the Future of the World* (Durham, NC: Duke University Press, 2015), 9–10, 258. See, relatedly, Achille Mbembe, *Critique of Black Reason*, trans. Laurent Dubois (Durham, NC: Duke University Press, 2017), 8.

49. Fanon and Azoulay, "Social Therapy in a Ward of Muslim Men," 363 (translation modified). For the original, see Fanon and Azoulay, "La socialthérapie," 306.

50. Many of Fanon's subsequent psychiatric papers can be read as contributing to grasping the North African social fact in its totality. See Frantz Fanon and Jacques Azoulay, "Daily Life in the Douars," in Fanon, *Alienation and Freedom*, 373–384; Frantz Fanon, "Ethnopsychiatric Considerations," in *Alienation and Freedom*, 405–408; Frantz Fanon and Raymond Lacaton, "Conducts of Confession in North

Africa (1)," in Fanon, *Alienation and Freedom*, 409–412; Frantz Fanon, "Conducts of Confession in North Africa (2)," in *Alienation and Freedom*, 413–416; and Frantz Fanon and François Sanchez, "Maghrebi Muslims and Their Attitude to Madness," in Fanon, *Alienation and Freedom*, 421–425.

51. G. W. F. Hegel, *Phenomenology of Spirit*, trans. A. V. Miller (Oxford: Oxford University Press, 1977), 6. See V. I. Lenin, "Conspectus of Hegel's book *The Science of Logic*," in *Collected Works*, vol. 38 (Moscow: Progress Publishers, 1976), 123; and C. L. R. James, *Notes on Dialectics: Hegel, Marx, Lenin* (Westport CT: Lawrence Hill, 1981), 99–100.

52. The editors of *Alienation and Freedom* make a similar point in a footnote added to another one of Fanon's psychiatric papers. They suggest that the shift from Antoine Porot's "colonialist constitutionalism" to Fanon's "scientific outlook" is "not a dialectical movement," since "nothing is to be retained . . . of the essentialism of the Algiers School." See Fanon and Geronimi, "TAT in Muslim Women," 431n9.

53. Fanon and Azoulay, "Social Therapy in a Ward of Muslim Men," 367.

54. This is how Fanon defines communication in one of his editorials for *Trait d'Union*. See Fanon, *Alienation and Freedom*, 282 (emphasis in original).

55. Fanon and Azoulay, "Social Therapy in a Ward of Muslim Men," 367–368 (translation modified). For the original, see Fanon and Azoulay, "La socialthérapie," 310. Fanon describes the experience of using an interpreter in similar terms in Frantz Fanon, "The 'North African Syndrome,'" in *Toward the African Revolution: Political Essays*, trans. Haakon Chevalier (New York: Grove, 1967), 3–16.

56. Diana Fuss, *Identification Papers: Readings on Psychoanalysis, Sexuality, and Culture* (New York: Routledge, 1995), 162 (emphasis in original).

57. Fanon and Azoulay, "Social Therapy in a Ward of Muslim Men," 368 (translation modified). For the original, see Fanon and Azoulay, "La socialthérapie," 310.

58. Fanon and Azoulay, "Social Therapy in a Ward of Muslim Men," 367.

59. Frantz Fanon, "Letter to the Resident Minister (1956)," in *Toward the African Revolution*, 53.

60. For a helpful introduction to Fanon's thinking about day hospitalization, see Bulhan, *Frantz Fanon*, 243–249. See also Nigel Gibson, *Fanon: The Postcolonial Imagination* (Cambridge: Polity, 2003), 91–92.

61. Frantz Fanon, "Day Hospitalization in Psychiatry," 473–494; Frantz Fanon and Charles Geronimi, "Day Hospitalization in Psychiatry: Value and Limits. Part Two: Doctrinal Considerations," in Fanon, *Alienation and Freedom*, 495–509.

62. Fanon, "Day Hospitalization in Psychiatry," 475.

63. Fanon and Geronimi, "Day Hospitalization in Psychiatry," 508.

64. Fanon and Geronimi, "Day Hospitalization in Psychiatry," 499, 500.

65. Fanon and Geronimi, "Day Hospitalization in Psychiatry," 496; Frantz Fanon and Charles Geronimi, "L'hospitalisation de jour en psychiatrie, valeur et limites. Deuxième partie: considérations doctrinales," in Fanon, *Écrits sur l'aliénation et la liberté*, 418.

66. Fanon and Geronimi, "Day Hospitalization in Psychiatry," 501 (translation modified). For the original, see Fanon and Geronimi, "L'hospitalisation de jour en psychiatrie," 423.

67. Fanon and Geronimi, "Day Hospitalization in Psychiatry," 504; Fanon and Geronimi, "L'hospitalisation de jour en psychiatrie," 425.

68. Fanon and Geronimi, "Day Hospitalization in Psychiatry," 502.
69. Fanon, "Day Hospitalization in Psychiatry," 474–475; Frantz Fanon, "L'hospitalisation de jour en psychiatrie, valeur et limites," in *Écrits sur l'aliénation et la liberté*, 398.
70. Fanon and Geronimi, "Day Hospitalization in Psychiatry," 501, 503–504; Fanon and Geronimi, "L'hospitalisation de jour en psychiatrie," 422, 424–425.
71. Fanon and Geronimi, "Day Hospitalization in Psychiatry," 504.
72. Fanon and Geronimi, "Day Hospitalization in Psychiatry," 497 (translation modified). For the original, see Fanon and Geronimi, "L'hospitalisation de jour en psychiatrie," 419.
73. See Hegel, *Phenomenology of Spirit*, 111–119; and Kojève, *Introduction to the Reading of Hegel*, 3–30.
74. Kojève, *Introduction to the Reading of Hegel*, 27.
75. I would like to extend a special thanks to Antonio de Ridder-Vignone for his help in working through and retranslating some of the more complicated and tangled passages of *Parallel Hands*.
76. Young, "Fanon, Revolutionary Playwright," 69, 75.
77. Frantz Fanon, *Parallel Hands*, in *Alienation and Freedom*, 114, 115, 117, 119, 123, 155.
78. Frantz Fanon, *Parallel Hands*, 116–117, 119 (translation modified). For the original, see Frantz Fanon, *Les Mains parallèles*, in *Écrits sur l'aliénation et la liberté*, 93–94, 96.
79. Friedrich Nietzsche, "The Birth of Tragedy," in *Basic Writings of Nietzsche*, trans. Walter Kaufmann (New York: Random House, 2000), 35.
80. Fanon, *Parallel Hands*, 116.
81. Nietzsche, "The Birth of Tragedy," 72.
82. Fanon, *Parallel Hands*, 135–136 (translation modified). For the original, see Fanon, *Les Mains parallèles*, 110.
83. Fanon, *Parallel Hands*, 155 (my emphasis).
84. Fanon, *Parallel Hands*, 162. On the distinction between attack and revenge in Nietzsche's thought, see Deleuze, *Nietzsche and Philosophy*, 3.
85. Friedrich Nietzsche, "Letter to Strindberg, 8 December 1888," in *Selected Letters of Friedrich Nietzsche*, ed. Christopher Middleton (Indianapolis, IN: Hackett, 1996), 330. For a helpful discussion of this passage, see Alain Badiou, "Who Is Nietzsche?," *Pli* 11 (2001): 1–11. See also Alain Badiou, *The Century*, trans. Alberto Toscano (Cambridge: Polity, 2007), 31–34; Alenka Zupančič, *The Shortest Shadow: Nietzsche's Philosophy of the Two* (Cambridge, MA: MIT Press, 2003); and Bruno Bosteels, "Radical Antiphilosophy," *Filozofski Vestnik* 29, no. 2 (2008): 155–187.
86. Fanon, *Parallel Hands*, 133.
87. Fanon, *Parallel Hands*, 137 (translation modified). For the original, see Fanon, *Les Mains parallèles*, 111. There is nevertheless one moment in the play when Épithalos, by challenging Fate, seems to be accepting his own personal fate. In his words, "the light, magical wonder detected at the core of BEING, fixes my fate" (129 [translation modified]). For the original, see Fanon, *Les Mains parallèles*, 105. While this may sound like an outright contradiction given the everyday notion of fate (i.e., fatalism), Greek tragedy developed a much more complicated and multifaceted understanding of the notion that may have influenced how Fanon deals with the theme in *Parallel Hands*. For a helpful discussion of fate in Greek tragedy, see Hanna M. Roisman, ed., *The Encyclopedia of Greek Tragedy* (Oxford: Wiley-Blackwell, 2012), 502–506.

88. Fanon, *Parallel Hands*, 154 (my emphasis, translation modified). For the original, see Fanon, *Les Mains parallèles*, 100, 125.

89. These ideas, developed throughout Nietzsche's later works, are most famously advanced in Friedrich Nietzsche, *On the Genealogy of Morality*, trans. Maudemarie Clark and Alan J. Swensen (Indianapolis: Hackett, 1998). See also Friedrich Nietzsche, *The Will to Power*, ed. Walter Kaufmann (New York: Vintage, 1968).

90. Nietzsche, *Thus Spoke Zarathustra*, 48.

91. Nietzsche, *Thus Spoke Zarathustra*, 13.

92. Fanon, *Parallel Hands*, 131 (translation modified). For the original, see Fanon, *Les Mains parallèles*, 107.

93. As Young notes in his introduction, Fanon's library contained a copy of Michel Carrouges's *La mystique du surhomme*. See Young, "Fanon, Revolutionary Playwright," 60n153.

94. Fanon, *Parallel Hands*, 139.

95. Fanon, *Parallel Hands*, 139–140. Here and in other passages the question of the relationship between the leader and the masses is obliquely raised, inviting comparisons with how C. L. R. James approaches this same question through the tragic. See, on this issue, Jeremy Matthew Glick, *The Black Radical Tragic: Performance, Aesthetics, and the Unfinished Haitian Revolution* (New York: New York University Press, 2016).

96. Fanon, *Parallel Hands*, 131.

97. Deleuze, *Nietzsche and Philosophy*, 17.

98. Nietzsche, "The Birth of Tragedy," 58–59.

99. Fanon, *Parallel Hands*, 113 (translation modified). For the original, see Fanon, *Les Mains parallèles*, 91.

100. Young also discusses this double negative structure in "Fanon, Revolutionary Playwright," 78.

101. Nietzsche's shadow may still linger over Fanon's use of the verb "*transmuer.*" Recall that *transmutation* is the nominalization of both *transmuer* and the related verb *transmuter*. This is important because Nietzsche's notion of *Umwertung*, as in "*Umwertung aller Werte* [revaluation/transvaluation of all values]," is often rendered as "*transmutation*" in French. If Fanon had referred to human values rather than human thought in the above passage, the connection to francophone Nietzscheanism would be undeniable. For the translation of "*Umwertung*" as "*transmutation*," see, for example, Friedrich Nietzsche, *La Volonté de puissance: Essai d'une transmutation de toutes les valeurs: Études et fragments*, trans. Henri Albert (Paris: Librairie Générale Française, 1991).

102. Fanon, *Parallel Hands*, 126 (translation modified). For the original, see Fanon, *Les Mains parallèles*, 102.

103. Fanon, *Parallel Hands*, 141; Fanon, *Les Mains parallèles*, 115. On *hamartia*, see Aristotle, *Poetics*, trans. Malcolm Heath (New York: Penguin, 1997).

104. Fanon, *Parallel Hands*, 132 (translation modified). For the original, see Fanon, *Les Mains parallèles*, 107.

105. Fanon, *Parallel Hands*, 161 (translation modified). For the original, see Fanon, *Les Mains parallèles*, 130.

106. Fanon, *Parallel Hands*, 122.

107. Fanon, *Parallel Hands*, 141 (my emphasis, translation modified). For the original, see Fanon, *Les Mains parallèles*, 115.
108. Fanon, *Parallel Hands*, 142.
109. Fanon, *Parallel Hands*, 152.
110. On eternal return, see, for example, Nietzsche, *Thus Spoke Zarathustra*, 123–130.
111. The tension in the play between exploding repetition and explosion as repetition can be fruitfully read alongside Kara Keeling's discussion of explosion in *Black Skin, White Masks*. See "'In the Interval': Frantz Fanon and the 'Problems' of Visual Representation," *Qui Parle* 13, no. 2 (2003): 103–110.
112. This is Keith Ansell-Pearson summarizing the argument of Erich Heller in Keith Ansell-Pearson, *An Introduction to Nietzsche as Political Thinker* (Cambridge: Cambridge University Press, 1994), 117. See also Erich Heller, *The Importance of Nietzsche: Ten Essays* (Chicago: University of Chicago Press, 1988). It should be noted that many readers of Nietzsche, Deleuze and Ansell-Pearson among them, reject that Nietzsche's notion of eternal return can be reduced to what Deleuze calls "the cyclical hypothesis." See Deleuze, *Nietzsche and Philosophy*, 49; and Ansell-Pearson, *Introduction to Nietzsche*, 110. While I find Heller's reading of Nietzsche compelling, what interests me here is less what Nietzsche "really meant" and more Fanon's Nietzscheanism.
113. Fanon, *Parallel Hands*, 149.
114. Fanon, *Parallel Hands*, 144.
115. Fanon, *Parallel Hands*, 141.
116. Fanon, *Parallel Hands*, 159; Fanon, *Les Mains parallèles*, 129.
117. Young mentions a similar instance of wordplay between "*mort*," "*amour*," and "*mot*" in Young, "Fanon, Revolutionary Playwright," 60.
118. Fanon, *Les Mains parallèles*, 129.
119. Fanon, *Parallel Hands*, 153.
120. Fanon, *Parallel Hands*, 163–164.
121. Nietzsche, "The Birth of Tragedy," 131. Young turns to this same passage in his reading of *The Drowning Eye*. See Young, "Fanon, Revolutionary Playwright," 45.
122. Fanon, *Parallel Hands*, 164.
123. Fanon, *Parallel Hands*, 164.
124. Nietzsche, *Thus Spoke Zarathustra*, 103–104.
125. Joby Fanon, as cited in Young, "Fanon, Revolutionary Playwright," 11n1. See also Joby Fanon, *Frantz Fanon, My Brother: Doctor, Playwright, Revolutionary*, trans. Daniel Nethery (Lanham, MD: Lexington, 2014), 61.
126. See Alain Badiou, *Metapolitics*, trans. Jason Barker (London: Verso, 2005), 124–140.
127. I discuss melancholic leftism in Gavin Arnall, "Repeating Translation, Left and Right (and Left Again): Roberto Bolaño's *Between Parentheses* and *Distant Star*," *CR: The New Centennial Review* 17, no. 3 (Winter 2017): 237–263. See also Wendy Brown, "Resisting Left Melancholia," in *Loss: The Politics of Mourning*, ed. David L. Eng and David Kazanjian (Berkeley: University of California Press, 2003), 458–466. For a discussion of the related defeatism that characterizes the repentant Left, see Gavin Arnall, "Remembering the Sixties: On Julio Cortázar's *Hopscotch* and Time," *MLN* 134, no. 2 (March 2019): 360–381.
128. Fanon, *Parallel Hands*, 162 (translation modified). For the original, see Fanon, *Les Mains parallèles*, 131.

129. For more on the negation of the negation in these terms, see Slavoj Žižek, *In Defense of Lost Causes* (London: Verso, 2009), 189.

130. Fanon, *Parallel Hands*, 162.

131. Hegel, *Phenomenology of Spirit*, 21.

132. Here I have in mind Raymond Williams's classic study on the relationship between revolution and tragedy. See the section titled "The Tragedy of Revolution" in Raymond Williams, *Modern Tragedy* (Stanford, CA: Stanford University Press, 1966), 77–84. Presumably without access to *Parallel Hands*, Lewis Gordon came to a strikingly similar conclusion over twenty years ago in his reading of *The Wretched of the Earth* and "tragic revolutionary violence." See Lewis R. Gordon, *Fanon and the Crisis of European Man: An Essay on Philosophy and the Human Sciences* (New York: Routledge, 1995), 70.

133. Nietzsche, *Thus Spoke Zarathustra*, 125 (original emphasis).

134. Fanon, *Parallel Hands*, 161.

135. Nietzsche, *Thus Spoke Zarathustra*, 130.

136. Nietzsche, *Thus Spoke Zarathustra*, 130 (emphasis in original).

137. Frantz Fanon, *Black Skin, White Masks*, trans. Richard Philcox (New York: Grove, 2008), 89 (my emphasis).

138. Merleau-Ponty, as cited in Macey, *Frantz Fanon*, 164. I discuss this point further in chapter 2.

139. For the original French passage, see Frantz Fanon, *Oeuvres* (Paris: La Découverte, 2011), 153.

2. BLACK SKIN, WHITE MASKS

1. Frantz Fanon, *Black Skin, White Masks*, trans. Richard Philcox (New York: Grove, 2008), xi.

2. Aimé Césaire, *Discourse on Colonialism*, trans. Joan Pinkham (New York: Monthly Review, 2000), 55.

3. René Descartes, as cited in Césaire, *Discourse on Colonialism*, 56.

4. According to his brother Joby, Fanon's favorite philosopher while working in Blida-Joinville was Descartes. He even demonstrated particular enthusiasm toward Descartes's *Discourse on Method* during Joby's visit to Algeria. See Joby Fanon, *Frantz Fanon, My Brother: Doctor, Playwright, Revolutionary*, trans. Daniel Nethery (Lanham, MD: Lexington, 2014), 74.

5. Césaire, as cited in Fanon, *Black Skin, White Masks*, xi.

6. Fanon, *Black Skin, White Masks*, xii, xiii; Frantz Fanon, *Oeuvres* (Paris: La Découverte, 2011), 65. One unfortunate choice of Richard Philcox's translation is that it homogenizes three different terms in *Peau noire, masques blancs*—*le Noir, le nègre*, and *l'homme noir*—by translating each interchangeably, though not consistently, as "the black man." While Fanon sometimes uses these terms interchangeably, the reader familiar with francophone language and culture will immediately sense the difference between them. To be more precise in my own analysis of the text, I refer to Fanon's main concept, *le Noir*, in the original French throughout this chapter. Lewis Gordon has also taken issue with Philcox's English translation by arguing that rendering *le Noir* as "the black man" misleadingly genders Fanon's concept

and argument. While I take Gordon's point, I think it passes too quickly over the implicit gender politics of Fanon's generic universalist terms. To offer one example, in *Peau noire, masques blancs*, the masculine generic term *le Noir* is often followed by the gendered term *homme*. Le Noir, for Fanon, is therefore to some extent already entangled in a masculinist formulation of universality even if, when considered on its own, in abstraction, this does not appear to be the case. Judith Butler has helpfully pointed out that Fanon remains caught in the equivocation of "*homme*" as both "human" and "man" at the same time that his thought seeks to reach "beyond the strictures of gender." See Judith Butler, "Violence, Nonviolence: Sartre on Fanon," in *Senses of the Subject* (New York: Fordham University Press, 2015), 182, 195–196. See also Lewis R. Gordon, *What Fanon Said: A Philosophical Introduction to his Life and Thought* (New York: Fordham University Press, 2015), 22.

7. Fanon, *Black Skin, White Masks*, xiii, xiv.

8. Fanon, *Black Skin, White Masks*, xv.

9. Fanon, *Black Skin, White Masks*, xiv; Fanon, *Oeuvres*, 65.

10. Fanon, *Black Skin, White Masks*, xii.

11. Césaire's universalism is far too multivalent to be equated with Enlightenment universalism, but the latter tradition does play a very important role in some of his formulations. See, especially, Aimé Césaire, *Toussaint Louverture: La Révolution française et le problème colonial* (Paris: Présence Africaine, 2000). On Césaire's universalism, see Achille Mbembe, *Critique of Black Reason*, trans. Laurent Dubois (Durham, NC: Duke University Press, 2017); Gary Wilder, *Freedom Time: Negritude, Decolonization, and the Future of the World* (Durham, NC: Duke University Press, 2015); and Nick Nesbitt, *Caribbean Critique: Antillean Critical Theory from Toussaint to Glissant* (Liverpool: Liverpool University Press, 2013).

12. For a related reading of inhumanism in Fanon's *The Wretched of the Earth*, see Nesbitt, *Caribbean Critique*, 192–215.

13. Fanon, *Black Skin, White Masks*, xii.

14. See Fanon, *Oeuvres*, 64.

15. Fanon, *Black Skin, White Masks*, xvi.

16. Fanon, *Black Skin, White Masks*, xii; Fanon, *Oeuvres*, 63–64.

17. On this point, see Étienne Balibar, *The Philosophy of Marx*, trans. Chris Turner (London: Verso, 2017), 39–40.

18. Fanon, *Black Skin, White Masks*, xiv-xv.

19. This is a running theme in much of the critical literature on Fanon. For some early examples that set the stage for the broad acceptance of this periodization, see Jock McCulloch, *Black Soul, White Artifact: Fanon's Clinical Psychology and Social Theory* (Cambridge: Cambridge University Press, 1983), 85; and Irene Gendzier, *Frantz Fanon: A Critical Study* (New York: Pantheon, 1973), 64. For a sustained criticism of this approach to reading Fanon's oeuvre, see Anthony C. Alessandrini, *Frantz Fanon and the Future of Cultural Politics: Finding Something Different* (Lanham, MD: Lexington, 2014).

20. See Frantz Fanon and Jacques Azoulay, "Social Therapy in a Ward of Muslim Men: Methodological Difficulties," in Frantz Fanon, *Alienation and Freedom*, ed. Jean Khalfa and Robert J. C. Young, trans. Steven Corcoran (London: Bloomsbury, 2018), 353–371. I discuss this paper at length in chapter 1.

21. Fanon, *Black Skin, White Masks*, xv.

22. This interpretation of Fanon draws inspiration from Slavoj Žižek's call to repeat Lenin, to repeat "in the present worldwide conditions, the Leninist gesture of reinventing the revolutionary project in the conditions of imperialism and colonialism." See Slavoj Žižek, "Introduction: Between Two Revolutions," in V. I. Lenin, *Revolution at the Gates: A Selection of Writings from February to October 1917*, ed. Slavoj Žižek (London: Verso, 2004), 11. See, relatedly, Sylvia Wynter's trailblazing analysis of sociogeny in "Towards the Sociogenic Principle: Fanon, Identity, the Puzzle of Conscious Experience, and What It Is Like to Be 'Black,'" in *National Identities and Sociopolitical Changes in Latin America*, ed. Mercedes F. Durán-Cogan and Antonio Gómez-Moriana (New York: Routledge, 2001), 30–66.

23. Fanon, *Black Skin, White Masks*, xvii; Fanon, *Oeuvres*, 67.

24. For the distinction between an antinomy and the more properly dialectical notion of contradiction, see Fredric Jameson, *The Seeds of Time* (New York: Columbia University Press, 1994), 1–8. See also Fredric Jameson, "Three Names of the Dialectic," in *Valences of the Dialectic* (London: Verso, 2010), 3–74.

25. Fanon, *Oeuvres*, 65. For a classic discussion on the length of analysis, see Sigmund Freud, "Analysis Terminable and Interminable," in *Standard Edition of the Complete Psychological Works of Sigmund Freud*, vol. 23 (London: Vintage, 2001), 211–253.

26. Fanon, *Oeuvres*, 64.

27. Fanon, *Black Skin, White Masks*, xii.

28. On "disjunctive synthesis" as a "non-dialectical couple," see Alain Badiou, *The Century*, trans. Alberto Toscano (Cambridge: Polity, 2007), 36–37. See also Alain Badiou, *Deleuze: The Clamor of Being*, trans. Louise Burchill (Minneapolis: University of Minnesota Press, 2000); and Gilles Deleuze and Félix Guattari, *Anti-Oedipus: Capitalism and Schizophrenia*, trans. Robert Hurley, Mark Seem, and Helen Lane (Minneapolis: University of Minnesota Press, 2005).

29. Friedrich Nietzsche, as paraphrased by Badiou in *The Century*, 31. I discuss this idea at length in the previous chapter of this book. For the original passage, see Friedrich Nietzsche, "Letter to Strindberg, 8 December 1888," in *Selected Letters of Friedrich Nietzsche*, ed. Christopher Middleton (Indianapolis: Hackett, 1996), 330.

30. Fanon, *Black Skin, White Masks*, 1–2 (translation modified). For the original, see Fanon, *Oeuvres*, 71. Fanon anticipates Jacques Derrida's discussion of Marx and specters, though his emphasis on processes of actualization, which I will develop at other moments in this book, is ultimately at odds with Derrida's theorization of spectrality. See Jacques Derrida, *Specters of Marx: The State of the Debt, the Work of Mourning and the New International*, trans. Peggy Kamuf (New York: Routledge, 1994). On actuality versus spectrality, see Bruno Bosteels, *Badiou and Politics* (Durham, NC: Duke University Press, 2011), 231–237.

31. See Karl Marx, "Theses on Feuerbach," in *Collected Works*, vol. 5, *Marx and Engels, 1845–1847* (New York: International, 1975), 5.

32. Fanon, *Black Skin, White Masks*, 12 (translation modified). For the original, see Fanon, *Oeuvres*, 79.

33. See Frantz Fanon, "Mental Alterations, Character Modifications, Psychic Disorders and Intellectual Deficit in Spinocerebellar Heredodegeneration: A Case of Friedreich's Ataxia with Delusions of Possession," in *Alienation and Freedom*, 203–275.

34. Fanon, *Black Skin, White Masks*, 7.

35. Fanon, *Black Skin, White Masks*, 2.

36. Fanon, *Black Skin, White Masks*, 6–7; Fanon, *Oeuvres*, 75. Gordon's most recent study on Fanon takes as one of its focal points the latter's analysis of misfires in *Black Skin, White Masks*. See *What Fanon Said*, 1–74.

37. Fanon, *Black Skin, White Masks*, 20.

38. Michel Leiris, as cited in Fanon, *Black Skin, White Masks*, 23. For the original, see Fanon, *Oeuvres*, 88.

39. Fanon, *Black Skin, White Masks*, 27–28 (my emphasis).

40. Fanon, *Black Skin, White Masks*, xii, 25, 90.

41. On competing universalisms intrinsic to distinct particularisms, see Judith Butler, "Competing Universalities," in Judith Butler, Ernesto Laclau, Slavoj Žižek, *Contingency, Hegemony, Universality: Contemporary Dialogues on the Left* (London: Verso, 2000), 136–181.

42. Fanon, *Black Skin, White Masks*, 41.

43. Fanon, *Black Skin, White Masks*, 29–30. This issue unites Fanon's theorization of romantic relationships between black men and white women and between black women and white men; however, Rey Chow has importantly argued that there are also many differences that cut across sexual difference in Fanon's treatment of masculine and feminine agency and sexuality. See Rey Chow, "The Politics of Admittance: Female Sexual Agency, Miscegenation, and the Formation of Community in Frantz Fanon," in *Frantz Fanon: Critical Perspectives*, ed. Anthony C. Alessandrini (London: Routledge, 1999), 34–56.

44. Fanon, *Black Skin, White Masks*, 40.

45. Fanon, *Black Skin, White Masks*, 27. Here is how Fanon describes this translation of Hegel's master-slave dialectic: "I was to be recognized not as *Black*, but as *White*. But—and this is the form of recognition that Hegel never described—who better than the white woman to bring this about? By loving me, she proves to me that I am worthy of a white love. I am loved like a white man. I am a white man." Fanon, *Black Skin, White Masks*, 45. For Hegel's account of the master-slave dialectic, see G. W. F. Hegel, *Phenomenology of Spirit*, trans. A. V. Miller (Oxford: Oxford University Press, 1977), 111–119.

46. For a related reading of Fanon on nondialectical recognition and love, see David Marriott, *Haunted Life: Visual Culture and Black Modernity* (New Brunswick, NJ: Rutgers University Press, 2007), 33–65.

47. Fanon, *Black Skin, White Masks*, 44.

48. Fanon, *Black Skin, White Masks*, 44; Fanon, *Oeuvres*, 107.

49. Fanon, *Oeuvres*, 65.

50. Fanon, *Black Skin, White Masks*, 63 (translation modified). For the original, see Fanon, *Oeuvres*, 125.

51. Fanon, *Black Skin, White Masks*, 80.

52. Fanon, *Black Skin, White Masks*, 80 (emphasis in original).

53. Fanon, *Black Skin, White Masks*, 89; Fanon, *Oeuvres*, 151.

54. See David Macey, *Frantz Fanon: A Biography* (London: Verso, 2012), 162–164.

55. Maurice Merleau-Ponty, as cited in Macey, *Frantz Fanon*, 162.

56. Fanon, *Black Skin, White Masks*, xvii–xviii.

57. Fanon, *Black Skin, White Masks*, 161.

58. Although his reflections often stray greatly from Fanon's own ideas, Homi Bhabha's work remains the starting point for any non-essentialist discussion of Fanon on identity and identification. See *The Location of Culture* (London: Routledge, 1994). See also Diana Fuss, *Identification Papers: Readings on Psychoanalysis, Sexuality, and Culture* (New York: Routledge, 1995), 141–172. On Fanon's existentialist phenomenology, see, for example, Lewis R. Gordon, *Existentia Africana: Understanding Africana Existential Thought* (New York: Routledge, 2000); Paget Henry, "Africana Phenomenology: Its Philosophical Implications," *CLR James Journal* 11, no. 1 (Summer 2005): 79–112; Reiland Rabaka, *Forms of Fanonism: Frantz Fanon's Critical Theory and the Dialectics of Decolonization* (Lanham, MD: Lexington, 2010), 49–96; and Jean Khalfa, *Poetics of the Antilles: Poetry, History and Philosophy in the Writings of Perse, Césaire, Fanon and Glissant* (Oxford: Peter Lang, 2016), 183–208. Many works that discuss Fanon's critique of ontology have been published in recent years. See, especially, Frank B. Wilderson III, *Red, White & Black: Cinema and the Structure of U.S. Antagonisms* (Durham, NC: Duke University Press, 2010); and David Marriott, *Whither Fanon? Studies in the Blackness of Being* (Stanford, CA: Stanford University Press, 2018).

59. Fanon, *Black Skin, White Masks*, 98.

60. Sartre, as cited in Fanon, *Black Skin, White Masks*, 98.

61. Étienne Balibar helpfully frames this point for readers of Hegel, noting that the German philosopher "was acutely aware of the conflict . . . between *two realizations of universality*: the religious and the national-popular. In a sense it could be said that Hegel's dialectic of history had no other object than precisely explaining how one great historical 'fiction,' that of the universalistic church, could be substituted by another historical 'fiction,' that of the secular, rational institutions of the state (in practice, the nation-state), with equally universalistic aims. To be sure, Hegel's view of this process was associated with the idea that historical development necessarily leads from religious universality to political universality (in Hegelian terms, religious universality is 'rational' only *an sich*, or in alienated form, whereas political universality is 'rational' *für sich*, or consciously). In other words, he saw it as an irreversible *progress*. Therefore political universality, notwithstanding its fictive character, should appear as an absolute." Étienne Balibar, "Ambiguous Universality," in *Politics and the Other Scene*, trans. Christine Jones, James Swenson, Chris Turner (London: Verso, 2002), 156 (emphasis in original).

62. Regarding the absolute quality of the state, Hegel asserts in his *Philosophy of Right*: "The state is absolutely rational inasmuch as it is the actuality of the substantial will which it possesses in the particular self-consciousness once that consciousness has been raised to consciousness of its universality. This substantial unity is an absolute unmoved end in itself, in which freedom comes into its supreme right." He goes on to discuss the role of individuals in the historical dialectic of Spirit's actualization: "All actions, including world-historical actions, culminate with individuals as subjects giving actuality to the substantial. They are the living instruments of what is in substance the deed of the world mind." G. W. F. Hegel, *Hegel's Philosophy of Right*, trans. T. M. Knox (Oxford: Oxford University Press, 1967), 155–156, 218.

63. For this point in Hegel's dialectic of history, see the section titled, "Classification of Historic Data," in G. W. F. Hegel, *The Philosophy of History*, trans. J. Sibree (Amherst, NY: Prometheus, 1991), 103–110.

64. Fanon, *Black Skin, White Masks*, 99; Fanon, *Oeuvres*, 161.

65. This reading of Fanon, which alludes to a subtle elective affinity with the work of Theodor Adorno and Max Horkheimer on Enlightenment reason and dialectics, is inspired by the important efforts of Natalie Melas and Paul Fleming to bring together postcolonial theory and Frankfurt School thought in a two-part conference series that was held at Cornell University, "Critical Theory and (Post)Colonialism." Compare Fanon's arguments about rationalization with the opening "fragment" in Theodor W. Adorno and Max Horkheimer, *Dialectic of Enlightenment: Philosophical Fragments*, trans. Edmund Jephcott (Stanford: Stanford University Press, 2002), 1–34.

66. Fanon, *Black Skin, White Masks*, 101. I modified the brackets in this passage to parentheses in order to avoid confusion between Fanon's writing and my own modifications to the text, which appear uniformly throughout this book in brackets.

67. Césaire develops a similarly critical analysis of the circular dialectic of Enlightenment. He notes in *Discourse on Colonialism* that colonialist intellectuals of so-called Western civilization participate in a "barbaric repudiation" of Descartes while maintaining that their own claims are "based on the firmest rationalism." See Césaire, *Discourse on Colonialism*, 56.

68. Gary Wilder, *The French Imperial Nation-State: Negritude and Colonial Humanism Between the Two World Wars* (Chicago: University of Chicago Press, 2005), 260.

69. Fanon, *Black Skin, White Masks*, 102.

70. Fanon, *Black Skin, White Masks*, 101.

71. Fanon, *Black Skin, White Masks*, 106–107; Fanon, *Oeuvres*, 166–167.

72. Although this theme is more prevalent in Senghor's work than in Césaire's, Fanon does not draw such a distinction when discussing the strategy of irrationalism.

73. Fanon, *Black Skin, White Masks*, 105–106.

74. Fanon, *Black Skin, White Masks*, 108–109.

75. Fanon, *Black Skin, White Masks*, 63.

76. Fanon, *Black Skin, White Masks*, 109.

77. Fanon, *Black Skin, White Masks*, 109.

78. Fanon, *Black Skin, White Masks*, xviii.

79. Senghor, as cited in Fanon, *Black Skin, White Masks*, 106.

80. Fanon, *Black Skin, White Masks*, 111.

81. Fanon, *Black Skin, White Masks*, 116.

82. Fanon, *Black Skin, White Masks*, 116–117.

83. Fanon, *Black Skin, White Masks*, 111.

84. Sartre, as cited in Fanon, *Black Skin, White Masks*, 111–112 (translation modified). For the original, see Fanon, *Oeuvres*, 170.

85. Paige Arthur helpfully contextualizes *Black Orpheus* in relation to Sartre's other works from the same period in *Unfinished Projects: Decolonization and the Philosophy of Jean-Paul Sartre* (London: Verso, 2010), 31–41.

86. For recent examples of this line of argument, see Reiland Rabaka, *The Negritude Movement: W. E. B. Du Bois, Leon Damas, Aimé Césaire, Leopold Senghor, Frantz Fanon, and the Evolution of an Insurgent Idea* (Lanham, MD: Lexington, 2015), 277; George Ciccariello-Maher, *Decolonizing Dialectics* (Durham, NC: Duke University Press, 2017), 66–73; and David Marriott, *Whither Fanon?*, 328–363.

87. Fanon, *Black Skin, White Masks*, 112–113 (translation modified). For the original, see Fanon, *Oeuvres*, 171.

88. Hegel, *Phenomenology of Spirit*, 8.
89. Hegel, *Phenomenology of Spirit*, 476. Nigel Gibson is one of the few critics to recognize Fanon's allusion to Hegel's conceptualization of the pure "I" in his response to Sartre. See *Fanon: The Postcolonial Imagination* (Cambridge: Polity, 2003), 75. Peter Hudis more generally alludes to this moment in *Frantz Fanon: Philosopher of the Barricades* (London: Pluto, 2015), 49.
90. As Slavoj Žižek explains, the pure "I" entails "absolute negation of all determinate content; it is the void of radical abstraction from *all* determinations." Slavoj Žižek, *Less Than Nothing: Hegel and the Shadow of Dialectical Materialism* (London: Verso, 2012), 365–366 (emphasis in original).
91. Hegel, *Phenomenology of Spirit*, 18–19. These lines are extracted from Hegel's discussion of the faculty of Understanding: "The activity of dissolution is the power and work of the *Understanding*, the most astonishing and mightiest of powers, or rather the absolute power.... But that an accident as such, detached from what circumscribes it, what is bound and is actual only in its context with others, should attain an existence of its own and a separate freedom—this is the tremendous power of the negative; it is the energy of thought, of the pure 'I.'"
92. Jameson, *Seeds of Time*, 5.
93. Fanon, *Black Skin, White Masks*, 114 (emphasis in original); Fanon, *Oeuvres*, 172 (emphasis in original).
94. Fanon, *Black Skin, White Masks*, 113–114 (emphasis in original).
95. Lewis Gordon helpfully discusses this aspect of Fanon's critique of Sartre in Lewis R. Gordon, *Fanon and the Crisis of European Man: An Essay on Philosophy and the Human Sciences* (New York: Routledge, 1995), 32–33. See also Gibson, *Fanon: The Postcolonial Imagination*, 73–78.
96. Sartre, as cited in Fanon, *Black Skin, White Masks*, 113.
97. Fanon, *Black Skin, White Masks*, 113 (translation modified). For the original, see Fanon, *Oeuvres*, 172.
98. See Hegel, *Philosophy of History*, 32–33.
99. Fanon, *Black Skin, White Masks*, 113–114.
100. Hegel's argument regarding the death of God and the pure "I" can be found in *Phenomenology of Spirit*, 475–476. Žižek offers a helpful discussion of this aspect of Hegel's analysis of religion in Slavoj Žižek, *Tarrying with the Negative: Kant, Hegel, and the Critique of Ideology* (Durham, NC: Duke University Press, 1993), 169–171.
101. Fanon, *Black Skin, White Masks*, 114.
102. Fanon, *Black Skin, White Masks*, 114–115.
103. Fanon may have first learned this lesson from another born Hegelian: Aimé Césaire. As Césaire once observed, "When the French translation of the *Phenomenology* first came out, I showed it to Senghor, and said to him 'Listen to what Hegel says, Léopold: to arrive at the Universal, one must immerse oneself in the Particular!'" Césaire, as cited in Nick Nesbitt, *Voicing Memory: History and Subjectivity in French Caribbean Literature* (Charlottesville: University of Virginia Press, 2003), 120.
104. Žižek on this point: "With regard to Christianity, this means that the death of Christ is simultaneously a day of grief and a day of joy: God-Christ had to die in order to be able to come to life again in the shape of the community of believers

(the 'Holy Spirit'). Instead of the 'substance' qua God-Master, the inscrutable Fate which reigns in its Beyond, we obtain the 'substance' qua community of believers. In this precise sense, 'the wound is healed only by the spear that smote you': the death of God *is* his resurrection, the weapon that killed Christ *is* the tool that created the Christian community of the Holy Spirit." See Žižek, *Tarrying with the Negative*, 170–171.

105. Fanon, *Black Skin, White Masks*, 163–164. For the reference to Césaire, see Aimé Césaire, "Notebook of a Return to the Native Land," in *The Collected Poetry*, trans. Clayton Eshleman and Annette Smith (Berkeley: University of California Press, 1983), 67.

106. For an account of the important organizing work that went into building this movement before it went viral, see Alicia Garza, "A Herstory of the #BlackLivesMatter Movement," *The Feminist Wire*, October 7, 2014, https://thefeministwire.com/2014/10/blacklivesmatter-2/. See also Barbara Ransby, *Making All Black Lives Matter: Reimagining Freedom in the 21st Century* (Oakland: University of California Press, 2018); and Keeanga-Yamahtta Taylor, *From #BlackLivesMatter to Black Liberation* (Chicago: Haymarket, 2016).

107. Consider Judith Butler on this point: "If we jump too quickly to the universal formulation, 'all lives matter,' then we miss the fact that black people have not yet been included in the idea of 'all lives.' That said, it is true that all lives matter (we can then debate about when life begins and ends). But to make that universal formulation concrete, to make that into a living formulation . . . we have to foreground those lives that are not mattering now, to mark that exclusion, and militate against it. Achieving that universal, 'all lives matter,' is a struggle, and that is part of what we are seeing on the streets." See George Yancy and Judith Butler, "What's Wrong with 'All Lives Matter'?," *New York Times*, January 12, 2015. http://opinionator.blogs.nytimes.com/2015/01/12/whats-wrong-with-all-lives-matter/.

108. To Sartre's credit, he later critiqued this precise intellectual maneuver and, in that way, implicitly critiqued a former version of himself: "One of the principal traps an intellectual must avoid in this enterprise is to universalize too fast. I have seen some who were in such a hurry to pass over to the universal that during the Algerian war they condemned Algerian terrorism in exactly the same breath as French repression. Such a judgement was the very patter of a false bourgeois universality. What these intellectuals failed to understand was that the Algerian rebellion—an insurrection of the poor, disarmed and hunted by a police regime—could not but choose *guerilla war and the use of bombs*. Thus, the true intellectual, in his struggle against himself, will come to see society as the arena of a struggle between particular groups (particularized by virtue of their structure, their position and their destiny) for the statute of universality." Jean-Paul Sartre, "A Plea for Intellectuals," in *Between Existentialism and Marxism*, trans. John Matthews (London: Verso, 2008), 250 (emphasis in original).

109. Hegel, *Phenomenology of Spirit*, 19.

110. Fanon, *Black Skin, White Masks*, 172 (emphasis in original).

111. Fanon, *Black Skin, White Masks*, 191.

112. Fanon, *Black Skin, White Masks*, 192.

113. Fanon, *Black Skin, White Masks*, 193.

114. Fanon, *Black Skin, White Masks*, 196.

115. Fanon, *Black Skin, White Masks*, 196. See Richard Wright, *12 Million Black Voices* (New York: Basic Books, 2002).

116. Fanon, *Black Skin, White Masks*, 196 (emphasis in original).

117. Fanon, *Black Skin, White Masks*, 196.

118. Fanon, *Black Skin, White Masks*, 195n10.

119. Fanon, *Black Skin, White Masks*, 191, 194 (translation modified). For the original, see Fanon, *Oeuvres*, 238, 240.

120. Anthony Bogues, *Empire of Liberty: Power, Desire, & Freedom* (Hanover, NH: Dartmouth College Press, 2010), 113.

121. Fanon, *Black Skin, White Masks*, 195.

122. Fanon, *Black Skin, White Masks*, 197 (emphasis in original, translation modified). For the original, see Fanon, *Oeuvres*, 242–243.

123. On this point in Nietzsche's work, see especially Friedrich Nietzsche, *The Will to Power*, ed. Walter Kaufmann (New York: Vintage, 1968); and Friedrich Nietzsche, *On the Genealogy of Morality*, trans. Maudemarie Clark and Alan J. Swensen (Indianapolis, IN: Hackett, 1998).

124. Glen Sean Coulthard is particularly attentive to Fanon's "practical reworking of Hegel's master/slave relation in contexts where the possibility of achieving affirmative relations of mutual recognition appears foreclosed." The solution for Fanon, according to Coulthard's argument, is "a quasi-Nietzschean form of personal and collective *self*-affirmation," which is also intriguingly theorized by Coulthard as "*self-recognition*." See Glen Sean Coulthard, *Red Skin, White Masks: Rejecting the Colonial Politics of Recognition* (Minneapolis: University of Minnesota Press, 2014), 43, 139 (emphasis in original). See, for a related discussion of Fanon on recognition, Sergio Villalobos-Ruminott, *Heterografías de la violencia. Historia, Nihilismo, Destrucción* (Buenos Aires: La Cebra, 2016), 92–96.

125. Marx, as cited in Fanon, *Black Skin, White Masks*, 198.

126. For a related discussion of Fanon and temporality, see Kara Keeling, *Queer Times, Black Futures* (New York: New York University Press, 2019), 81–82.

127. Karl Marx, "The Eighteenth Brumaire of Louis Bonaparte," in *Collected Works*, vol. 11, *Marx and Engels 1851–1853* (New York: International, 1979), 103.

128. Fanon, *Black Skin, White Masks*, 200. Tony Martin offers further examples of Fanon converging with Marx's *The Eighteenth Brumaire* in "Rescuing Fanon from the Critics," in *Rethinking Fanon: The Continuing Dialogue*, ed. Nigel Gibson (New York: Humanity, 1999), 86–87.

129. Fanon, *Black Skin, White Masks*, 205.

130. Fanon's library contained a number of works by Sartre that were heavily underlined and annotated. For more information on these texts and their annotations, see Fanon, *Alienation and Freedom*, 752–756.

131. Fanon, *Black Skin, White Masks*, 202 (emphasis in original).

132. On this point, see Jean-Paul Sartre, *Being and Nothingness* (New York: Washington Square, 1984).

133. Fanon, *Black Skin, White Masks*, 205; Fanon, *Oeuvres*, 250. Hortense Spillers offers a critical analysis of this passage and links it to Nietzschean thought in *Black, White, and in Color: Essays on American Literature and Culture* (Chicago: University of Chicago Press, 2003), 36.

134. Fanon, *Black Skin, White Masks*, 199, 200.

135. Fanon, *Black Skin, White Masks*, 201 (translation modified). For the original, see Fanon, *Oeuvres*, 247.

136. Césaire, as cited in Fanon, *Black Skin, White Masks*, 163 (my emphasis).

137. Fanon, *Black Skin, White Masks*, 204 (emphasis in original, translation modified). For the original, see Fanon, *Oeuvres*, 251.

138. Gary Wilder has similarly underscored how Fanon's conclusion attempts "to leap out of rather than work through colonial racism" in "Race, Reason, Impasse: Césaire, Fanon, and the Legacy of Emancipation," *Radical History Review*, no. 90 (Fall 2004): 56.

139. Fanon, *Black Skin, White Masks*, 206 (emphasis in original, translation modified). For the original, see Fanon, *Oeuvres*, 251.

140. "Man's misfortune, Nietzsche said, was that he was once a child." Fanon, *Black Skin, White Masks*, xiv. Gordon has recently argued that Fanon wrongly attributes this view to Nietzsche and that it was actually developed by Simone de Beauvoir. This is not an entirely unfounded attribution on Fanon's part, however, since Nietzsche was a thinker of childhood and its defects, most notably in *Human, All Too Human: A Book For Free Spirits*, trans. R. J. Hollingdale (Cambridge: Cambridge University Press, 1996). See Gordon, *What Fanon Said*, 29–30. In an earlier work, Gordon traces this view of childhood back to Jean-Jacques Rousseau. See *Fanon and the Crisis of European Man*, 80.

141. As Fanon puts it, "My book is, I hope, a mirror with a progressive infrastructure where the black man can find the path to disalienation." Fanon, *Black Skin, White Masks*, 161.

142. Fanon, *Black Skin, White Masks*, 206.

143. Fred Moten in Stefano Harney and Fred Moten, *The Undercommons: Fugitive Planning & Black Study* (New York: Minor Compositions, 2013), 108.

144. Stuart Hall, "The After-life of Frantz Fanon: Why Fanon? Why Now? Why *Black Skin, White Masks?*" in *The Fact of Blackness: Frantz Fanon and Visual Representation*, ed. Alan Read (Seattle: Bay Press, 1996), 34 (emphasis in original). Hall arrives at this conclusion via Benita Parry, "Signs of Our Times: A Discussion of Homi Bhabha's *The Location of Culture*," *Third Text* 8, nos. 28–29 (1994): 5–24.

3. WRITINGS ON THE ALGERIAN REVOLUTION

1. For the congress papers and these messages, see the volume *1er Congrès International des Écrivains et Artistes Noirs* (Paris: Présence Africaine, 1956).

2. *1er Congrès International*, 380–381. For an account of the congress and its significance in Fanon's life, see David Macey, *Frantz Fanon: A Biography* (London: Verso, 2012), 276–289. See also James Baldwin's first-hand account of the event in "Princes and Powers," in *The Price of the Ticket: Collective Nonfiction 1948–1985* (New York: St. Martin's, 1985), 41–63.

3. Frantz Fanon, "Letter to the Resident Minister (1956)," in *Toward the African Revolution: Political Essays*, trans. Haakon Chevalier (New York: Grove, 1967), 53.

4. Alice Cherki similarly argues that the paper given at this congress "marked a new phase in Fanon's intellectual evolution." See Alice Cherki, *Frantz Fanon: A Portrait*, trans. Nadia Benabid (Ithaca, NY: Cornell University Press, 2006), 87.

5. Frantz Fanon, "Racism and Culture," in *Toward the African Revolution*, 31 (translation modified). For the original, see Frantz Fanon, *Oeuvres* (Paris: La Découverte, 2011), 715.

6. See G. W. F. Hegel, *Phenomenology of Spirit*, trans. A. V. Miller (Oxford: Oxford University Press, 1977).

7. Fanon, "Racism and Culture," 38.

8. Fanon, "Racism and Culture," 32–33, 41.

9. Fanon, "Racism and Culture," 40.

10. Fanon, "Racism and Culture," 40.

11. Fanon, "Racism and Culture," 33–34.

12. Fanon, "Racism and Culture," 34.

13. Fanon, "Racism and Culture," 32.

14. Fanon, "Racism and Culture," 35.

15. Fanon, "Racism and Culture," 39.

16. Karl Marx and Friedrich Engels, "Manifesto of the Communist Party," in *Collected Works*, vol. 6, *Marx and Engels 1845–1848* (New York: International, 1976), 496.

17. Fanon, "Racism and Culture," 36, 41.

18. Fanon, "Racism and Culture," 42.

19. See Frantz Fanon, *Black Skin, White Masks*, trans. Richard Philcox (New York: Grove, 2008), 89–119.

20. Fanon, "Racism and Culture," 43.

21. See Fanon, *Black Skin, White Masks*, 111–119.

22. Fanon, "Racism and Culture," 43.

23. Fanon, "Racism and Culture," 43.

24. Fanon, "Racism and Culture," 44 (translation modified). For the original, see Fanon, *Oeuvres*, 726. The English translation of this text renders *"prise en charge"* as "recognize and accept," which fails to capture the medical undertones of a phrase that is often used to describe the act of nurturing or caring for someone in a hospital setting. In the journal of the Blida-Joinville Psychiatric Hospital, Fanon discusses his appreciation for this phrase insofar as it means not only keeping a patient from dying but "above all [giving] him or her the chance to live." See Frantz Fanon, *Alienation and Freedom*, ed. Jean Khalfa and Robert J. C. Young, trans. Steven Corcoran (London: Bloomsbury, 2018), 321.

25. Fanon, "Racism and Culture," 33.

26. Slavoj Žižek, "Class Struggle or Postmodernism? Yes, Please!," in Judith Butler, Ernesto Laclau, and Slavoj Žižek, *Contingency, Hegemony, Universality: Contemporary Dialogues on the Left* (London: Verso, 2000), 102.

27. Friedrich Nietzsche, as paraphrased in Alain Badiou, *The Century*, trans. Alberto Toscano (Cambridge: Polity, 2007), 31.

28. See Fanon, *Black Skin, White Masks*, 164.

29. Since the articles of *El Moudjahid* were published anonymously and were the product of collective discussions among the newspaper's team of writers, Fanon's publisher, François Maspero, sought to identify which were definitively written by Fanon, requesting aid from the paper's editor-in-chief, Rédha Malek, as well as from Fanon's spouse, Josie Fanon. Despite this consultation work, there has been some controversy concerning the true authorship of the articles included in *Toward the African Revolution*. This is in part because Malek's list of publications and the list

put together by Josie Fanon do not entirely coincide, and Maspero's selection diverges slightly from both as well. Maspero's selection also does not entirely coincide with a third list put together by his colleague Giovanni Pirelli, in consultation with Josie Fanon. Moreover, Alice Cherki, who worked alongside Fanon in Algeria and Tunisia, has argued that at least one of the articles included in Maspero's anthology is falsely attributed to Fanon. To my knowledge, such a charge has not been raised against any of the articles discussed in this chapter. But with the recent publication of *Alienation and Freedom*, which anthologizes further articles from *El Moudjahid*, this debate over authorship may begin again. The edited volume includes all the articles from *El Moudjahid* that appeared in the aforementioned lists but did not make it into Maspero's selection as well as certain articles from the newspaper that, in the judgement of the editors, "seemed to be at least broadly informed by Fanon's thinking." For a more detailed discussion of these articles and their publication history, see Jean Khalfa's introduction to the "Political Writings" section in Fanon, *Alienation and Freedom*, 533–537. See also Cherki, *Frantz Fanon*, 109, 190, 245n12.

30. Rédha Malek, as cited by Khalfa in Fanon, *Alienation and Freedom*, 535 (translation modified). For the original, see Frantz Fanon, *Écrits sur l'aliénation et la liberté*, ed. Jean Khalfa and Robert J. C. Young (Paris: La Découverte, 2015), 450.

31. On Fanon's "persistent instabilities," see Benita Parry, *Postcolonial Studies: A Materialist Critique* (London: Routledge, 2004), 48.

32. Frantz Fanon, "Algeria Face to Face with the French Torturers," in *Toward the African Revolution*, 65.

33. Fanon, "Algeria Face to Face," 65.

34. Fanon, "Algeria Face to Face," 64.

35. Fanon, "Algeria Face to Face," 72.

36. Fanon, "Algeria Face to Face," 72; Fanon, *Oeuvres*, 752.

37. Frantz Fanon, "A Democratic Revolution," in *Alienation and Freedom*, 570 (translation modified). For the original, see Frantz Fanon, *Écrits sur l'aliénation et la liberté*, 477.

38. Frantz Fanon, "French Intellectuals and Democrats and the Algerian Revolution," in *Toward the African Revolution*, 80–81.

39. I see a strong elective affinity between Mao and Fanon on this point, but I am not necessarily arguing that the former directly influenced the latter's thinking. It may be worth noting, however, that Fanon's library included a rather extensive collection of works by Mao. See Fanon, *Alienation and Freedom*, 762–764. One of the recently anthologized articles from *El Moudjahid* also favorably cites Mao and gestures toward establishing a formal relationship between Algeria and the People's Republic of China. See Frantz Fanon, "The Rising Anti-imperialist Movement and the Slow-wits of Pacification," in *Alienation and Freedom*, 625–631.

40. Mao Tse-Tung, "On Contradiction," in *On Practice and Contradiction* (London: Verso, 2007), 79. For more on the historically variable nature of the principal contradiction in a given society, see Mao's discussion of the dynamic relationship between the Chinese Communist Party and the nationalist Kuomintang, in "On Contradiction," 82–84. See also Slavoj Žižek's introduction, "Mao Tse-Tung, the Marxist Lord of Misrule," in *On Practice and Contradiction*, 1–28.

41. G. W. F. Hegel, *Hegel's Logic*, trans. William Wallace (Oxford: Oxford University Press, 1975), 133. For a discussion of how Hegel's Understanding (*Verstand*) points

to "non- or pre-dialectical, maybe even anti-dialectical thinking," see Fredric Jameson, *Valences of the Dialectic* (London: Verso, 2010), 87–88.

42. Fanon, "French Intellectuals," 82.

43. Fanon, "French Intellectuals," 82–83 (translation modified). For the original, see Fanon, *Oeuvres*, 762.

44. Fanon, "French Intellectuals," 83.

45. Frantz Fanon, "Decolonization and Independence," in *Toward the African Revolution*, 101.

46. G. W. F. Hegel, *The Philosophy of History*, trans. J. Sibree (Amherst, NY: Prometheus, 1991), 142.

47. Without mentioning "Decolonization and Independence," Ato Sekyi-Otu relatedly reads Fanon as anticipating the claim—developed by later thinkers—that the colonial experience was one of "interrupted history." See "Fanon and the Possibility of Postcolonial Critical Imagination," in *Living Fanon: Global Perspectives*, ed. Nigel Gibson (New York: Palgrave Macmillan, 2011), 55.

48. On this kind of dialectical movement, see Jameson, *Valences of the Dialectic*, 48–49.

49. Fanon, "Decolonization and Independence," 101.

50. Fanon, "Decolonization and Independence," 105 (translation modified). For the original, see Fanon, *Oeuvres*, 791.

51. Fanon, "Decolonization and Independence," 103; Fanon, *Oeuvres*, 789.

52. On this aspect of the Haitian revolution, see Toussaint L'Ouverture, *The Haitian Revolution*, ed. Nick Nesbitt (London: Verso, 2008); and Nick Nesbitt, *Universal Emancipation: The Haitian Revolution and the Radical Enlightenment* (Charlottesville, VA: University of Virginia Press, 2008). See also Fanon's discussion of the demand in Benin for immediate independence: Frantz Fanon, "The Lesson of Cotonou," in *Toward the African Revolution*, 127–131.

53. Such heterodox Marxist thinking can be traced back to Marx himself. See Kevin Anderson, *Marx at the Margins: On Nationalism, Ethnicity, and Non-Western Societies* (Chicago: Chicago University Press, 2010); and Massimiliano Tomba, *Marx's Temporalities* (Chicago: Haymarket, 2013).

54. Fanon, "Decolonization and Independence," 101.

55. Fanon, *Oeuvres*, 787.

56. Fanon, "Decolonization and Independence," 100 (translation modified). For the original, see Fanon, *Oeuvres*, 786.

57. Fanon, "Decolonization and Independence," 102–103.

58. Fanon, *Parallel Hands*, in *Alienation and Freedom*, 113–164.

59. Frantz Fanon, *A Dying Colonialism*, trans. Haakon Chevalier (New York: Grove, 1965), 69 (translation modified). For the original, see Fanon, *Oeuvres*, 305.

60. Fanon, *A Dying Colonialism*, 27–28.

61. Fanon, *A Dying Colonialism*, 30 (translation modified). For the original, see Fanon, *Oeuvres*, 267.

62. On this issue of translation, see Macey, *Frantz Fanon*, 399. The alternative translation further verifies Rey Chow's argument, made in her seminal essay on *Black Skin, White Masks*, that what is required when confronting Fanon's discussions of gender and sexuality "is not exactly an attempt to 'restore' the woman of color by giving her a voice, a self, a subjectivity; rather we need to examine *how* the woman of

color has *already* been given agency—by examining the form which this attributed agency assumes." Rey Chow, "The Politics of Admittance: Female Sexual Agency, Miscegenation, and the Formation of Community in Frantz Fanon," in *Frantz Fanon: Critical Perspectives*, ed. Anthony C. Alessandrini (London: Routledge, 1999), 43 (emphasis in original).

63. Fanon, *A Dying Colonialism*, 46–47 (translation modified). For the original, see Fanon, *Oeuvres*, 283–284.

64. On this point, see, for example, Friedrich Nietzsche, *On the Genealogy of Morality*, trans. Maudemarie Clark and Alan J. Swensen (Indianapolis, IN: Hackett, 1998).

65. Fanon, *A Dying Colonialism*, 42, 63.

66. Deleuze, as cited in Jameson, *Valences of the Dialectic*, 117. The English translation of this text renders the passage slightly differently. See Gilles Deleuze, *Difference and Repetition*, trans. Paul Patton (New York: Columbia University Press, 1995), 55.

67. Fanon, *A Dying Colonialism*, 49.

68. Diana Fuss, *Identification Papers: Readings on Psychoanalysis, Sexuality, and Culture* (New York: Routledge, 1995), 150. Fuss oddly presents this argument as missing in Fanon's account of the veil and attributes the idea to someone else.

69. Fanon, *A Dying Colonialism*, 63.

70. Fanon, *A Dying Colonialism*, 48. Fanon's account of women's participation in the Algerian Revolution has been contested as historically inaccurate. For an alternative narrative, see Djamila Amrane, *Les femmes algériennes dans la guerre* (Paris: Plon, 1991). See also Macey, *Frantz Fanon*, 399.

71. Fanon, *A Dying Colonialism*, 50 (my emphasis, translation modified). For the original, see Fanon, *Oeuvres*, 287.

72. As Nigel Gibson rightly observes, the notion of "an authentic birth without any previous instruction has resonance throughout Fanon's work." What is missing from this observation is how such a notion diverges from and is in tension with Fanon's conceptualization of dialectical mutations. See Nigel Gibson, *Fanon: The Postcolonial Imagination* (Cambridge: Polity, 2003), 143.

73. For readers interested in a more nuanced account of how Algerian women militants represented themselves, their motivations, and their involvement in the struggle, see, for example, Zohra Drif, *Mémoires d'une combattante de l'ALN: Zone Autonome d'Alger* (Algiers: Chihab Éditions, 2013). My thanks to Jill Jarvis for pointing me to this reference.

74. Friedrich Nietzsche, "The Birth of Tragedy," in *Basic Writings of Nietzsche*, trans. Walter Kaufmann (New York: Random House, 2000), 30–144. By drawing a comparison between Fanon and Nietzsche, I diverge from Lou Turner's intriguing but ultimately unconvincing suggestion that the previously cited passage alludes to Hegel's *Phenomenology of Spirit* and in particular to its discussion of Antigone. See Lou Turner, "Fanon and the FLN: Dialectics of Organization and the Algerian Revolution," in *Rethinking Fanon: The Continuing Dialogue*, ed. Nigel Gibson (New York: Humanity, 1999), 398–399. For another reading of this passage that combines Hegel and Nietzsche, see Zahid Chaudhary, "Subjects in Difference: Walter Benjamin, Frantz Fanon, and Postcolonial Theory," *differences* 23, no. 1 (May 2012): 166–171.

75. Keith Ansell-Pearson, *How to Read Nietzsche* (New York: W. W. Norton, 2005), 13. The coupling of contrary tendencies admittedly sounds dialectical, so much so that Nietzsche would later characterize *The Birth of Tragedy* as "smell[ing] offensively Hegelian." It would nonetheless be good to recall Deleuze's argument on Nietzsche's tragic thinking: "Not all relations between 'same' and 'other' are sufficient to form a dialectic, even essential ones: everything depends on the role of the negative in this relation." Gilles Deleuze, *Nietzsche and Philosophy*, trans. Hugh Tomlinson (New York: Columbia University Press, 2006), 8. For Nietzsche's reappraisal of *The Birth of Tragedy*, see Friedrich Nietzsche, "Ecce Homo," in *Basic Writings of Nietzsche*, 726.

76. This turn of phrase takes its inspiration from Gareth Williams's discussion of José Carlos Mariátegui and the latter's Nietzschean theorization of modernity as the birth of Peruvian tragedy. See Gareth Williams, *The Other Side of the Popular: Neoliberalism and Subalternity in Latin America* (Durham, NC: Duke University Press, 2002), 236–238.

77. Fanon, *A Dying Colonialism*, 61.

78. Fanon, *A Dying Colonialism*, 63.

79. See my discussion of these papers in chapter 1.

80. Fanon, *A Dying Colonialism*, 58.

81. Fanon, *A Dying Colonialism*, 59.

82. Fanon, *A Dying Colonialism*, 61.

83. Fanon, *A Dying Colonialism*, 63.

84. Fanon, *A Dying Colonialism*, 59.

85. Fanon, *A Dying Colonialism*, 60 (translation modified). For the original, see Fanon, *Oeuvres*, 295.

86. Fanon, *A Dying Colonialism*, 109 (emphasis in original, translation modified). For the original, see Fanon, *Oeuvres*, 342. Marie-Aimée Helie-Lucas takes Fanon to task for this optimistic account of the transformation of the family structure during the struggle for liberation, describing it as a myth that makes illegible the persistence of gender inequality during the revolution. See Marie-Aimée Helie-Lucas, "Women, Nationalism, and Religion in the Algerian Liberation Struggle," in Gibson, *Rethinking Fanon*, 271–282. See also T. Denean Sharpley-Whiting's rejoinder to this argument in "Fanon's Feminist Consciousness and Algerian Women's Liberation: Colonialism, Nationalism, and Fundamentalism," in Gibson, *Rethinking Fanon*, 348–350.

87. Fanon, *A Dying Colonialism*, 109–110 (translation modified). For the original, see Fanon, *Oeuvres*, 342.

88. Fanon, *A Dying Colonialism*, 63.

89. Fanon, *A Dying Colonialism*, 70.

90. On this point, see, for example, Angel Rama, *Writing Across Cultures: Narrative Transculturation in Latin America*, trans. David Frye (Durham, NC: Duke University Press, 2012).

91. Frantz Fanon and Jacques Azoulay, "Social Therapy in a Ward of Muslim Men: Methodological Difficulties," in Fanon, *Alienation and Freedom*, 353—371.

92. Fanon and Azoulay, "Social Therapy," 362–363, 371.

93. Fanon and Azoulay, "Social Therapy," 364.

94. Fanon, *A Dying Colonialism*, 70–71 (translation modified). For the original, see Fanon, *Oeuvres*, 306.
95. It should be noted that *L'An V de la révolution algérienne* was posthumously reprinted with a new title as *Sociologie d'une révolution*. This new title may have contributed to rendering illegible Fanon's critique of sociology within the text. Mention of such a critique is absent, for example, in the following canonical essay on the subject: Renée T. White, "Revolutionary Theory: Sociological Dimensions of Fanon's *Sociologie d'une révolution*," in *Fanon: A Critical Reader*, ed. Lewis R. Gordon, T. Denean Sharpley-Whiting, and Renée T. White (Cambridge: Blackwell, 1996), 100–109. For the revised title, see Frantz Fanon, *Sociologie d'une révolution (L'an V de la révolution algérienne)* (Paris: Maspero, 1966).
96. See Walter Benjamin, *The Work of Art in the Age of Its Technological Reproducibility and Other Writings on Media*, ed. Michael W. Jennings, Brigid Doherty, and Thomas Y. Levin (Cambridge, MA: Harvard University Press, 2008). See also Michael Jennings's introductory essay, "The Production, Reproduction, and Reception of the Work of Art," in *Work of Art*, 9–18.
97. Fanon, *A Dying Colonialism*, 72.
98. This is not meant to be read as a criticism of Benjamin, since his essay on art in the age of technological reproducibility elaborates its analysis precisely through the historicization of technology. See Benjamin, "The Work of Art in the Age of Its Technological Reproducibility: Second Version," in *Work of Art*, 19–55.
99. On Fanon's "phenomenology of reception," see Michael Allan, "Old Media / New Futures: Revolutionary Reverberations of Fanon's Radio," *PMLA* 134, no. 1 (January 2019): 188.
100. Fanon, *A Dying Colonialism*, 73.
101. Fanon, *A Dying Colonialism*, 89. As Fanon states in the chapter on Western medicine, which parallels his discussion of the French radio, "It is not possible for the colonized society and the colonizing society to agree to pay tribute, at the same time and in the same place, to a single value." Fanon, *A Dying Colonialism*, 126.
102. Fanon, *A Dying Colonialism*, 75 (translation modified). Note that the English translation of this text renders the French "*mutations*" as "development" while keeping more faithfully to the original French terminology at other moments. See Fanon, *Oeuvres*, 310.
103. Fanon, *A Dying Colonialism*, 82 (translation modified). The English translation once again obscures Fanon's repetition of the French word "*mutation*," this time rendering it as "shift." For the original, see Fanon, *Oeuvres*, 317.
104. Gibson makes a very similar argument when dealing with *A Dying Colonialism*'s account of Western medicine and its mutation. See Nigel Gibson, "Radical Mutations: Fanon's Untidy Dialectic of History," in Gibson, *Rethinking Fanon*, 420–421. See also Gibson, *Fanon: The Postcolonial Imagination*, 127–156.
105. Fanon, *A Dying Colonialism*, 89 (translation modified). For the original, see Fanon, *Oeuvres*, 323. On cultural anthropophagy, see Oswald de Andrade, "Cannibalist Manifesto," trans. Leslie Bary, *Latin American Literary Review* 19, no. 38 (1991): 38–47. It is possible that Fanon learned of this metaphor for transformative cultural incorporation from the Brazilian writer Mário de Andrade, who was present alongside Fanon at the International Congress of Black Writers and Artists

in 1954. An earlier influence might have been Suzanne Césaire, who wrote in the cultural journal *Tropiques* that "Martinican poetry will be cannibal or it will not be." See Suzanne Césaire, *The Great Camouflage: Writings of Dissent (1941—1945)*, ed. Daniel Maximin, trans. Keith Walker (Middletown, CT: Wesleyan University Press, 2012), 27.

106. Fanon, *A Dying Colonialism*, 84 (translation modified). For the original, see Fanon, *Oeuvres*, 318.

107. Fanon, *A Dying Colonialism*, 84.

108. Attending to this detail adds some much-needed nuance to the argument—advanced by numerous critics—that Fanon's commitment to categories like "the people" or "the nation" denies or papers over difference. See, for example, John Mowitt, "Algerian Nation: Fanon's Fetish," *Cultural Critique*, no. 22 (Autumn 1992): 165–186; and Homi Bhabha, "Foreword: Framing Fanon," in Frantz Fanon, *The Wretched of the Earth*, trans. Richard Philcox (New York: Grove, 2004), x. Fanon might be more helpfully read alongside recent attempts to theorize the internal difference or plurality of the category "people." See Bruno Bosteels, "Introduction: This People Which is Not One," in Alain Badiou et al., *What Is a People?* (New York: Columbia University Press, 2016), 1–20. See also Judith Butler, "'We, the People': Thoughts on Freedom of Assembly," in Badiou et al., *What is a People?*, 49–64.

109. Fanon, *A Dying Colonialism*, 84 (translation modified). For the original, see Fanon, *Oeuvres*, 319.

110. Fanon, *A Dying Colonialism*, 90n8 (translation modified). For the original, see Fanon, *Oeuvres*, 324n6.

111. Fanon, *A Dying Colonialism*, 91.

112. Fanon, *A Dying Colonialism*, 89–90.

113. Fanon, *A Dying Colonialism*, 91. Here I diverge from Brian T. Edwards, who reads Fanon's essay as promoting the creation of a non-French French, an Algerian French, that would contribute to the disappearance of Arabic within the Algerian nation. See "Fanon's al-Jaza'ir, or Algeria Translated," *Parallax* 8, no. 2 (2002): 99–115.

114. Fanon, *A Dying Colonialism*, 92. Although lost in translation, it is important to note that Fanon plays with the difference between "*langue*" and "*langage*" to distinguish the "new language [*langage*] of the nation" from the "three languages [*langues*]" or tongues that serve as the channels through which this new "*langage*" makes itself known. On this point, see Ronald A. T. Judy, "On the Politics of Global Language, or Unfungible Local Value," *boundary 2* 24, no. 2 (Summer 1997): 118–119. For the original French passages, see Fanon, *Oeuvres*, 323, 326.

115. Fanon, *A Dying Colonialism*, 85 (translation modified). For the original, see Fanon, *Oeuvres*, 320.

116. Fanon, *A Dying Colonialism*, 85–86 (translation modified). For the original, see Fanon, *Oeuvres*, 320.

117. Fanon, *A Dying Colonialism*, 87, 94 (translation modified). For the original, see Fanon, *Oeuvres*, 321, 328.

118. For more on the radio's decentering of revolutionary authority and its facilitation of participatory political organizing, see Gibson, "Radical Mutations," in *Rethinking Fanon*, 422–431. See also Ian Baucom, "Frantz Fanon's Radio: Solidarity, Diaspora,

and the Tactics of Listening," *Contemporary Literature* 42, no. 1 (Spring 2001): 15–49.

119. Fanon, *A Dying Colonialism*, 87. Here the reader might recall Jacques Lacan's theorization of the "fictional structure" of truth. See Jacques Lacan, "Psychoanalysis and Its Teaching," in *Écrits: The First Complete Edition in English*, trans. Bruce Fink (New York: W. W. Norton, 2007), 376. See also Lacan, "The Subversion of the Subject and the Dialectic of Desire in the Freudian Unconscious," in *Écrits*, 684. On the implications of truth's fictional structure for dream interpretation, see Slavoj Žižek, "Freud Lives!," *London Review of Books* 28, no. 10 (May 2006), https://lrb.co.uk/the-paper/v28/n10/slavoj-zizek/freud-lives. See also Gibson's analogy between the interpretation of dream fragments and the interpretation of the radio's static in *Fanon: The Postcolonial Imagination*, 151.

120. On these kinds of performative speech acts, see Butler, "'We, the People,'" 52–53.

121. Fanon, *A Dying Colonialism*, 96 (emphasis in original, translation modified). For the original, see Fanon, *Oeuvres*, 329.

122. Ato Sekyi-Otu, *Fanon's Dialectic of Experience* (Cambridge, MA: Harvard University Press, 1996), 201.

123. Fanon, *A Dying Colonialism*, 95 (translation modified). Note that the English version of this text translates *"se différencie"* as "became transformed," which obscures Fanon's interest in undifferentiated and differentiated approaches to cultural phenomena. For the original, see Fanon, *Oeuvres*, 328.

124. Fanon, *A Dying Colonialism*, 140.

125. Macey, *Frantz Fanon*, 385. Irene Gendzier helpfully contextualizes Fanon's argument in relation to the Soummam Declaration of 1956, which held that "the Algerian Revolution does not have as its goal to 'throw into the sea' Algerians of European origin, but to destroy the inhuman colonial yoke." See *Frantz Fanon: A Critical Study* (New York: Pantheon, 1973), 175.

126. Fanon, *A Dying Colonialism*, 152.

127. Fanon, *A Dying Colonialism*, 158 (translation modified). For the original, see Fanon, *Oeuvres*, 389.

128. Fanon, "French Intellectuals and Democrats," 81; Fanon, *Oeuvres*, 760.

129. Fanon, "French Intellectuals and Democrats," 82–83 (translation modified). For the original, see Fanon, *Oeuvres*, 762.

130. Fanon, *A Dying Colonialism*, 149.

131. I am borrowing this image of discrepant friction between different conceptual paradigms from Anne McClintock. See her discussion of Fanon's internal division with respect to agency in *Imperial Leather: Race, Gender, and Sexuality in the Colonial Contest* (New York: Routledge, 1995), 363.

4. THE WRETCHED OF THE EARTH (PART I)

1. Frantz Fanon, "De la violence," *Les Temps Modernes* 16, no. 181 (May 1961): 1453–1493. Frantz Fanon, *Les damnés de la terre* (Paris: Maspero, 1961). The main difference between these two texts is Fanon's addition of the section, "On Violence in the International Context," to the version of the essay printed in *The Wretched of the Earth*. Note that future citations of this text will refer to the following English

translation: Frantz Fanon, *The Wretched of the Earth*, trans. Richard Philcox (New York: Grove, 2004). Given my attention to Fanon's use of language, I will also frequently refer to the original French version anthologized here: Frantz Fanon, *Oeuvres* (Paris: La Découverte, 2011), 419–681.

2. Fanon, *Wretched*, 21 (translation modified). For the original, see Fanon, *Oeuvres*, 469.

3. Fanon, *Wretched*, 21 (translation modified). For the original, see Fanon, *Oeuvres*, 469.

4. On the centrality of decision for Fanon, see Lewis R. Gordon, *Fanon and the Crisis of European Man: An Essay on Philosophy and the Human Sciences* (New York: Routledge, 1995), 5–12. See also Peter Hallward, "Fanon and Political Will," *Cosmos and History* 7, no. 1 (2011): 104–127.

5. Fanon, *Wretched*, 1 (my emphasis, translation modified). For the original, see Fanon, *Oeuvres*, 451.

6. Even when Fanon recognizes in another text from roughly the same period that an individual country might achieve decolonization through nonviolence, he argues that such an achievement can only be understood within a broader, international context of violent struggle against the colonial world: "Raising the problem of a non-violent decolonization is less the postulation of a sudden humanity on the part of the colonialist than believing in the sufficient pressure of the new ratio of forces on an international scale. It is clear, for example, that France has initiated a process of decolonization in Africa south of the Sahara. This innovation without violence has been made possible by the successive setbacks to French colonialism in the other territories." Frantz Fanon, "Accra: Africa Affirms Its Unity and Defines Its Strategy," in *Toward the African Revolution: Political Essays*, trans. Haakon Chevalier (New York: Grove, 1967), 155.

7. Fanon, *Wretched*, 31. Here I diverge from Robert J. C. Young, who argues that Fanon's theorization of decolonization as a universally violent phenomenon is an "inaccurate generalization." Robert J. C. Young, *Postcolonialism: An Historical Introduction* (Cambridge: Blackwell, 2001), 281. My reading is also meant to caution against conflating formal independence with decolonization. For an example of this kind of conflation, see Neil Lazarus, *The Postcolonial Unconscious* (Cambridge: Cambridge University Press, 2011), 175.

8. See, for example, Hannah Arendt's infamous defamation of Fanon in *On Violence* (New York: Harcourt, 1970). For an excellent rejoinder, see Nick Nesbitt, *Caribbean Critique: Antillean Critical Theory from Toussaint to Glissant* (Liverpool: Liverpool University Press, 2013), 192–215.

9. Fanon, *Wretched*, 23.

10. Fanon, *Wretched*, 1 (my emphasis, translation modified). For the original, see Fanon, *Oeuvres*, 451.

11. Fanon, *Wretched*, 1 (my emphasis).

12. Friedrich Nietzsche, as paraphrased in Alain Badiou, *The Century*, trans. Alberto Toscano (Cambridge: Polity, 2007), 31. Fanon's commentators have also described decolonizing violence as a kind of "divine violence," in Walter Benjamin's sense of the term. For a Derridean discussion of Fanon and Benjamin on violence, see Samira Kawash, "Terrorists and Vampires: Fanon's Spectral Violence of Decolonization," in *Frantz Fanon: Critical Perspectives*, ed. Anthony C. Alessandrini (London: Routledge, 1999), 235–257. For what might be characterized as a more Jacobinist reading of Fanon and Benjamin on violence, see Nesbitt, *Caribbean Critique*, 199–200.

13. Fanon, *Wretched*, 15.
14. Fanon, *Wretched*, 2 (translation modified). For the original, see Fanon, *Oeuvres*, 451–452.
15. For a reading of Fanon on violence that emphasizes the process over the end goal, see Edward Said, *Culture and Imperialism* (New York: Vintage, 1994), 268–274.
16. Here I am bending a phrase from Homi Bhabha's foreword to *The Wretched of the Earth* so as to make it signify otherwise. Bhabha deploys the notion of "double temporality" to distinguish between a "universalizing, generalizing tendency in Fanon's writings" and a "critical, political stance" that is "less universalist in temper and more strategic, activist, and aspirational." As will become apparent in what follows, my argument diverges from Bhabha's insofar as I interpret both temporalities of decolonization as pointing toward universalist projects. See Homi Bhabha, "Foreword: Framing Fanon," in Fanon, *Wretched*, xvii.
17. Fanon, *Wretched*, 17–20.
18. Fanon, *Wretched*, 21, 29, 31.
19. Fanon, *Wretched*, 31.
20. Fanon, *Wretched*, 43, 51 (translation modified). The English translation by Philcox renders "*la phase insurrectionnelle*" as "the insurrectional stage" yet translates "*la deuxième phase*" as "the second phase," making Fanon's reference to a first phase difficult to locate for the anglophone reader. For the original, see Fanon, *Oeuvres*, 488, 495.
21. Fanon, *Wretched*, 2 (translation modified). For the original, see Fanon, *Oeuvres*, 452.
22. Fanon, *Wretched*, 2 (translation modified). For the original, see Fanon, *Oeuvres*, 452.
23. Fanon, *Wretched*, 2 (translation modified). For the original, see Fanon, *Oeuvres*, 452.
24. For a thorough overview of the contentious debate surrounding the relationship between Fanon's *The Wretched of the Earth* and Sartre's *Critique of Dialectical Reason*, as well as a balanced and convincing response to the most vocal critics on the matter, see Ben Etherington, "An Answer to the Question: What is Decolonization? Frantz Fanon's *The Wretched of the Earth* and Jean-Paul Sartre's *Critique of Dialectical Reason*," *Modern Intellectual History* 13, no. 1 (2016): 151–178. See, relatedly, Kathryn Batchelor, "Fanon's *Les damnés de la terre*: Translation, De-Philosophization and the Intensification of Violence," *Nottingham French Studies* 54, no. 1 (March 2015): 7–22.
25. Concerning the impact *Critique of Dialectical Reason* had on Fanon, see David Macey, *Frantz Fanon: A Biography* (London: Verso, 2012), 448–450.
26. Sartre's full definition of praxis can be found here: Jean-Paul Sartre, *Critique of Dialectical Reason*, vol. 1, trans. Alan Sheridan-Smith (London: Verso, 2004), 734.
27. See Sartre, *Critique*, 722–723. For a concise overview of the *Critique*'s theorization of colonialism, see Paige Arthur, *Unfinished Projects: Decolonization and the Philosophy of Jean-Paul Sartre* (London: Verso, 2010), 81–82.
28. On the practico-inert in Fanon and Sartre, see Nesbitt, *Caribbean Critique*, 198. See also Arthur, *Unfinished Projects*, 85.
29. Fanon, *Wretched*, 5.
30. See, on this point, Etherington, "An Answer," 168. See also Achille Mbembe, *On the Postcolony* (Berkeley: University of California Press, 2001), 173–211; and Achille Mbembe, *Critique of Black Reason*, trans. Laurent Dubois (Durham, NC: Duke University Press, 2017), 104–110, 162–170.
31. Sartre, *Critique*, 730. Robert Bernasconi notes how Sartre's concept of antagonistic reciprocity also resonates with what Fanon calls the "reciprocal homogeneity" of

colonialist violence and the counterviolence of the colonized. See Robert Bernasconi, "Fanon's *The Wretched of the Earth* as the Fulfillment of Sartre's *Critique of Dialectical Reason*," *Sartre Studies International* 16, no. 2 (2010): 39. On "reciprocal homogeneity," see Fanon, *Wretched*, 46.

32. Fanon, *Wretched*, 44. Fredric Jameson reads this point, through Sartre, back into Hegel on recognition: "I would want to argue that the culmination in contemporary thought of this Hegelian theme [of recognition] is to be found in Frantz Fanon's notion of 'redemptive violence' which, developing out of the Sartrean notion of otherness as conflict, posits a second moment of the Master/Slave struggle in which the Slave rises against the Master and compels recognition in the form of fear very much in the spirit and the letter of Hegel's initial text." Fredric Jameson, *The Hegel Variations: On the Phenomenology of Spirit* (London: Verso, 2010), 90.

33. Fanon, *Wretched*, 6, 43.

34. Sartre, *Critique*, 133 (emphasis in original).

35. For Sartre's account of evil, the non-human, violence, and Manichaeanism, see *Critique*, 132–150.

36. Fanon, *Wretched*, 50.

37. Frantz Fanon, *A Dying Colonialism*, trans. Haakon Chevalier (New York: Grove, 1965), 147–162.

38. Fanon, *Wretched*, 14; Fanon, *Oeuvres*, 463.

39. Nesbitt, *Caribbean Critique*, 193. See, relatedly, Ethan Kleinberg, "Kojève and Fanon: The Desire for Recognition and the Fact of Blackness," in *French Civilization and its Discontents: Nationalism, Colonialism, Race*, eds. Tyler Edward Stovall and Georges Van den Abbeele (Lanham, MD: Lexington, 2003), 115–128.

40. Alexandre Kojève, *Introduction to the Reading of Hegel: Lectures on the Phenomenology of Spirit*, trans. James H. Nichols, Jr. (Ithaca, NY: Cornell University Press, 1969), 29 (my emphasis). Hegel's famous account of the master-slave dialectic can be found here: G. W. F. Hegel, *Phenomenology of Spirit*, trans. A. V. Miller (Oxford: Oxford University Press, 1977), 111–119.

41. Kojève, *Introduction to the Reading of Hegel*, 225n22 (emphasis in original).

42. Jameson, *Hegel Variations*, 57.

43. Fanon, *Wretched*, 4 (translation modified). For the original, see Fanon, *Oeuvres*, 454.

44. Aristotle, as cited in Ato Sekyi-Otu, *Fanon's Dialectic of Experience* (Cambridge, MA: Harvard University Press, 1996), 55 (emphasis in original).

45. For the distinction between contradiction and antinomy, see Fredric Jameson, *The Seeds of Time* (New York: Columbia University Press, 1994), 1–5. On Hegel's conceptualization of contradictory opposition as a response to both Aristotelian and Kantian reasoning, see Jameson, *Hegel Variations*, 47–48.

46. This is a very popular position in the secondary literature on Fanon. See, for example, Robert Bernasconi, "Casting the Slough: Fanon's New Humanism for a New Humanity," in *Fanon: A Critical Reader*, ed. Lewis R. Gordon, T. Denean Sharpley-Whiting, and Renée T. White (Cambridge: Blackwell, 1996), 119; Nigel Gibson, "Radical Mutations: Fanon's Untidy Dialectic of History," in *Rethinking Fanon: The Continuing Dialogue*, ed. Nigel Gibson (New York: Humanity, 1999), 408–446; and Michael Azar, "In the Name of Algeria: Frantz Fanon and the Algerian Revolution," in *Critical Perspectives*, 25–28.

47. Fanon, *Wretched*, 43 (translation modified). For the original, see Fanon, *Oeuvres*, 488.

48. Fanon, *Wretched*, 43n5.

49. See Frantz Fanon, "Racism and Culture," in *Toward the African Revolution*, 29–44.

50. Fanon, *Wretched*, 10. While using similar vocabulary, my treatment of subtraction as tied to nondialectical destruction is not to be confused with Alain Badiou's efforts to distinguish and, in a certain sense, oppose these two terms. See Badiou, *Century*, 64–65. For a reading of Fanon through Badiou's notion of subtraction, see Nesbitt, *Caribbean Critique*, 208.

51. Fanon, *Wretched*, 9 (translation modified). For the original, see Fanon, *Oeuvres*, 458.

52. Fanon, *Wretched*, 9 (translation modified). For the original, see Fanon, *Oeuvres*, 458.

53. Here I have in mind how Judith Butler conceptualizes the articulation of competing universalities in "Competing Universalities," in Judith Butler, Ernesto Laclau, Slavoj Žižek, *Contingency, Hegemony, Universality: Contemporary Dialogues on the Left* (London: Verso, 2000), 136–181.

54. Fanon, *Wretched*, 6 (translation modified). For the original, see Fanon, *Oeuvres*, 455.

55. Fanon, *Wretched*, 9, 50.

56. Michael Hardt and Antonio Negri, *Empire* (Cambridge, MA: Harvard University Press, 2000), 132.

57. Fanon, *Wretched*, 6 (translation modified). For the original, see Fanon, *Oeuvres*, 455.

58. Fanon, *Wretched*, 42; Fanon, *Oeuvres*, 488.

59. Aimé Césaire, *Discourse on Colonialism*, trans. Joan Pinkham (New York: Monthly Review, 2000), 36. As Macey convincingly points out, Fanon implicitly alludes to Césaire's *Discourse* in his own analysis of the relationship between colonialism and fascism. See Macey, *Frantz Fanon*, 466. Conjuring Césaire, Sartre likewise refers to the moment of African decolonization as "the age of the boomerang" in his preface to *The Wretched of the Earth*. See Jean-Paul Sartre, preface to Fanon, *Wretched*, liv. Finally, for Marx and Engels on the notion of the bourgeoisie producing its own gravediggers, see Karl Marx and Friedrich Engels, "Manifesto of the Communist Party," in *Collected Works*, vol. 6, *Marx and Engels 1845–1848* (New York: International, 1976), 496.

60. Sartre, *Critique*, 733 (emphasis in original). Sartre returns to this idea in his preface to *The Wretched of the Earth*: "For it is not first of all *their* violence, it is ours, on the rebound, that grows and tears them apart." Sartre, preface to Fanon, *Wretched*, lii (emphasis in original).

61. Sartre, *Critique*, 733.

62. Fanon, *Wretched*, 50–51.

63. Hardt and Negri, *Empire*, 132.

64. Fanon, *Wretched*, 5 (translation modified). For the original, see Fanon, *Oeuvres*, 455.

65. On this point, see Slavoj Žižek, "Mao Tse-Tung, the Marxist Lord of Misrule," in Mao Tse-Tung, *On Practice and Contradiction* (London: Verso, 2007), 1–28.

66. Fanon, *Wretched*, 8.

67. Fanon, *Wretched*, 9, 11.

68. Fanon, *A Dying Colonialism*, 89.

69. Fanon, *Wretched*, 8 (my emphasis, translation modified). For the original, see Fanon, *Oeuvres*, 457.

70. Fanon, *Wretched*, 10–11.

71. Fanon, *Wretched*, 9.

72. Fanon, *Wretched*, 12.

73. Fanon, *Wretched*, 50. Neil Lazarus has argued that Fanon exaggerates the extent to which colonization destroys precolonial culture, looking instead to Amílcar Cabral's more optimistic assessment of the survival and future of African traditions in the face of colonial domination. See Neil Lazarus, "Disavowing Decolonization: Fanon, Nationalism, and the Question of Representation in Postcolonial Theory," in *Critical Perspectives*, 172. Reiland Rabaka intriguingly reads Cabral as supplementing Fanon on this same issue in *Forms of Fanonism: Frantz Fanon's Critical Theory and the Dialectics of Decolonization* (Lanham, MD: Lexington, 2010), 187–188.

74. Fanon, *Wretched*, 12.

75. Fanon, *Wretched*, 20. Lazarus recognizes this inconsistency regarding the future of traditional African cultures, describing it as an "imprecision on Fanon's part." See Lazarus, "Disavowing Decolonization," 171.

76. Fanon, *Wretched*, 56.

77. Sekyi-Otu, *Fanon's Dialectic of Experience*, 25.

78. Fredric Jameson, *Valences of the Dialectic* (London: Verso, 2010), 43. See also Jameson, *Seeds of Time*, 4.

79. On the notion of "missed encounter" or "*desencuentro*," see Álvaro García Linera, "Indianismo y marxismo: El desencuentro de dos razones revolucionarias," in *La potencia plebeya: Acción colectiva e identidades indígenas, obreras y populares en Bolivia*, ed. Pablo Stefanoni (Buenos Aires: Prometeo, 2008), 373–392. See, relatedly, Bruno Bosteels, *Marx and Freud in Latin America: Politics, Psychoanalysis, and Religion in Times of Terror* (London: Verso, 2012), 1–27; Patrick Dove, "The *Desencuentros* of History: Class and Ethnicity in Bolivia," *Culture, Theory and Critique* 56, no. 3 (September 2015): 313–332; and Jeffrey L. Gould, "Ignacio Ellacuría and the Salvadorean Revolution," *Journal of Latin American Studies* 47, no. 2 (May 2015): 285–315.

80. Fanon, *Wretched*, 63 (translation modified). For the original, see Fanon, *Oeuvres*, 509.

81. See, on this point, Lou Turner and John Alan, "Frantz Fanon, World Revolutionary," in *Rethinking Fanon*, 110.

82. Fanon, *Wretched*, 63 (translation modified). For the original, see Fanon, *Oeuvres*, 509.

83. Fanon, *Wretched*, 63–64 (translation modified). For the original, see Fanon, *Oeuvres*, 509.

84. Fanon, *Oeuvres*, 509. Louis Althusser and Étienne Balibar would go on to theorize the notion of *décalage*, commonly translated as "dislocation," in very similar terms. See *Reading Capital*, trans. Ben Brewster (London: Verso, 2006). See, relatedly, Massimiliano Tomba, *Marx's Temporalities* (Chicago: Haymarket, 2013); and Vittorio Morfino, *Plural Temporality: Transindividuality and the Aleatory Between Spinoza and Althusser* (Chicago: Haymarket, 2014).

85. Fanon, *Wretched*, 65.

86. Fanon, *Wretched*, 64. For Fanon's discussion of implementing European methods of psychiatric treatment in North Africa, see Frantz Fanon and Jacques Azoulay, "Social Therapy in a Ward of Muslim Men: Methodological Difficulties," in *Alienation and Freedom*, ed. Jean Khalfa and Robert J. C. Young, trans. Steven Corcoran (London: Bloomsbury, 2018), 353–371.

87. Fanon, *Wretched*, 64.

88. See Marx and Engels, "Manifesto of the Communist Party," 519.

89. See Fanon, "Racism and Culture," 39.

90. Marx and Engels, "Manifesto of the Communist Party," 494.

91. For this line of argument in other contexts, see Dipesh Chakrabarty, *Provincializing Europe: Postcolonial Thought and Historical Difference* (Princeton, NJ: Princeton University Press, 2000); and Walter D. Mignolo, *Local Histories / Global Designs: Coloniality, Subaltern Knowledges, and Border Thinking* (Princeton, NJ: Princeton University Press, 2012).

92. Fanon, *Wretched*, 23.

93. Dogmatists from around the world have criticized Fanon's heterodox understanding of Marxism. For the classic rejoinder to these criticisms, see Immanuel Wallerstein, "Fanon and the Revolutionary Class," in *The Essential Wallerstein* (New York: New Press, 2000), 14–32. On the dialectical relationship between negative and positive universality, see Étienne Balibar, *The Philosophy of Marx*, trans. Chris Turner (London: Verso, 2017), 39–40.

94. On deprovincialization, see Harry Harootunian, *Marx After Marx: History and Time in the Expansion of Capitalism* (New York: Columbia University Press, 2015), 1–20; and Gary Wilder, *Freedom Time: Negritude, Decolonization, and the Future of the World* (Durham, NC: Duke University Press, 2015), 9–10, 258. See, relatedly, Mbembe, *Critique of Black Reason*, 8.

95. Fanon, *Wretched*, 66.

96. Fanon, *Wretched*, 66. For Marx's discussion of the "conservative peasant," see Karl Marx, "The Eighteenth Brumaire of Louis Bonaparte," in *Collected Works*, vol. 11, *Marx and Engels 1851–1853* (New York: International, 1979), 188.

97. Fanon, *Wretched*, 66–67.

98. Fanon, Wretched, 67 (translation modified). For the original, see Fanon, Oeuvres, 513.

99. Fanon, *Wretched*, 67–68 (translation modified). For the original, see Fanon, *Oeuvres*, 513.

100. Fanon refers explicitly to the "torturing parachutists" of the French colonial forces in one of his articles for *El Moudjahid*. See Frantz Fanon, "Decolonization and Independence," in *Toward the African Revolution*, 103.

101. What I am calling "internal colonization" draws inspiration from Moira Fradinger's discussion of "binding violence" in *Binding Violence: Literary Visions of Political Origins* (Stanford, CA: Stanford University Press, 2010).

102. Fanon, *Wretched*, 65.

103. Fanon, *Wretched*, 69.

104. This complicates Françoise Vergès's claim that, for Fanon, "memories are shackles to progress and movement." See Françoise Vergès, "Chains of Madness, Chains of Colonialism: Fanon and Freedom," in *The Fact of Blackness: Frantz Fanon and Visual Representation*, ed. Alan Reed (Seattle: Bay Press, 1996), 63.

105. Fanon, *Wretched*, 70–71 (translation modified). For the original, see Fanon, *Oeuvres*, 516.

106. Fanon, *Wretched*, 76.

107. Fanon, *Wretched*, 77.

108. Fanon, *Wretched*, 77.

109. Fanon, *Wretched*, 78 (translation modified). For the original, see Fanon, *Oeuvres*, 522.

110. Fanon, *Wretched*, 78. Here I am evoking Althusser's theorization of aleatory materialism, which notably resonates with Fanon's analysis at this precise moment in

the argument. See Louis Althusser, "The Underground Current of the Materialism of the Encounter," in *Philosophy of the Encounter: Late Writings, 1978–1987*, trans. G. M. Goshgarian (London: Verso, 2006), 163–207.

111. Fanon, *Wretched*, 79 (translation modified). For the original, see Fanon, *Oeuvres*, 523–524.

112. Fanon, *Wretched*, 79 (emphasis in original, translation modified). For the original, see Fanon, *Oeuvres*, 523.

113. Fanon, *Wretched*, 81. For Marx's discussion of the lumpenproletariat's reactionary tendencies, see "The Eighteenth Brumaire," 99–197.

114. Fanon, *Wretched*, 83; Fanon, *Oeuvres*, 527.

115. Fanon, *Wretched*, 83 (translation modified). For the original, see Fanon, *Oeuvres*, 527.

116. On how forgetting contributes to action and life, see Friedrich Nietzsche, *Untimely Meditations*, ed. Daniel Breazeale (Cambridge: Cambridge University Press, 1997), 57–124.

117. John E. Drabinski, "Fanon's Two Memories," *South Atlantic Quarterly* 112, no. 1 (2013): 20. For a related argument, see Vergès, "Chains of Madness," 63.

118. Fanon, *Wretched*, 84.

119. See Frantz Fanon, *Parallel Hands*, in *Alienation and Freedom*, 113–164.

120. Fanon, *Wretched*, 88 (my emphasis, translation modified). For the original, see Fanon, *Oeuvres*, 532.

121. Fanon, *Wretched*, 85 (translation modified). For the original, see Fanon, *Oeuvres*, 529.

122. See, for example, Fanon, "Decolonization and Independence," 103; Fanon, *Oeuvres*, 789.

123. Frantz Fanon, *Black Skin, White Masks*, trans. Richard Philcox (New York: Grove, 2008), 113. I discuss *négritude*'s absolutity and its necessary contribution to dialectical movement in chapter 2.

124. Fanon, *Wretched*, 84.

125. Fanon, *Wretched*, 85.

126. Fanon, *Wretched*, 91.

127. Fanon, *Wretched*, 86 (translation modified). For the original, see Fanon, *Oeuvres*, 530.

128. Alain Badiou develops the idea of "politics without party" throughout his intellectual career. See, for example, his interview with Peter Hallward, included as an appendix in Alain Badiou, *Ethics: An Essay on the Understanding of Evil*, trans. Peter Hallward (London: Verso, 2001), 95–100. For a panoramic view of the idea and its various iterations, refer to Bruno Bosteels, *Badiou and Politics* (Durham, NC: Duke University Press, 2011).

129. The reader will detect a strong elective affinity between Fanon and Mao on this point. See, for example, Mao Tse-Tung, "Where Do Correct Ideas Come From?," in *On Practice and Contradiction*, 167–169.

130. Fanon, *Wretched*, 86, 90–91.

131. Fanon, *Wretched*, 90.

132. Fanon, *Wretched*, 92.

133. Fanon, *Wretched*, 91.

134. Fanon, *Wretched*, 92–93 (translation modified). For the original, see Fanon, *Oeuvres*, 535–536.

135. Nigel Gibson, *Fanon: The Postcolonial Imagination* (Cambridge: Polity, 2003), 166.

136. Fanon, *Wretched*, 88–89 (translation modified). For the original, see Fanon, *Oeuvres*, 532.
137. Jean-Paul Sartre, *Black Orpheus*, trans. S. W. Allen (Paris: Présence Africaine, 1976), 59. See also Fanon, *Black Skin, White Masks*, 111.
138. Sartre, *Black Orpheus*, 60.
139. Fanon, *Black Skin, White Masks*, 111–119.
140. Glen Sean Coulthard highlights the important role Nietzschean resentment plays in *The Wretched of the Earth*'s theorization of decolonization in *Red Skin, White Masks: Rejecting the Colonial Politics of Recognition* (Minneapolis: University of Minnesota Press, 2014), 113–115. See, relatedly, David Marriott, *Haunted Life: Visual Culture and Black Modernity* (New Brunswick, NJ: Rutgers University Press, 2007), 233–241.
141. Fanon, *Wretched*, 95; Fanon, *Oeuvres*, 537–538.
142. Most major works on Fanon positively cite *Fanon's Dialectic of Experience* at some point in the development of their argument. For two recent examples, see Peter Hudis, *Frantz Fanon: Philosopher of the Barricades* (London: Pluto, 2015); and Christopher J. Lee, *Frantz Fanon: Toward a Revolutionary Humanism* (Athens: Ohio University Press, 2015).
143. Sekyi-Otu, *Fanon's Dialectic of Experience*, 104, 117.
144. See, on this point, Macey, *Frantz Fanon*, 450.

5. THE WRETCHED OF THE EARTH (PART II)

1. I offer a detailed discussion of this tendency among critics in the introduction to this book.
2. On the notion of repression and its return, see Sigmund Freud, "Repression," in *The Standard Edition of the Complete Psychological Works of Sigmund Freud*, vol. 14, trans. James Strachey (London: Vintage, 2001), 141–158.
3. Frantz Fanon, *The Wretched of the Earth*, trans. Richard Philcox (New York: Grove, 2004), 101.
4. Karl Marx and Friedrich Engels, "Manifesto of the Communist Party," in *Collected Works*, vol. 6, *Marx and Engels 1845–1848* (New York: International, 1976), 487.
5. Fanon, *Wretched*, 101.
6. Fanon, *Wretched*, 98.
7. To cite the most obvious example, Fanon extracts a passage from *The Eighteenth Brumaire* to use as an epigraph in *Black Skin, White Masks*, trans. Richard Philcox (New York: Grove, 2008), 198.
8. Karl Marx, "The Eighteenth Brumaire of Louis Bonaparte," in *Collected Works*, vol. 11, *Marx and Engels 1851–1853* (New York: International, 1979), 103.
9. Fanon, *Wretched*, 98.
10. Fanon, *Wretched*, 119.
11. Fanon, *Wretched*, 105.
12. Fanon, *Wretched*, 103. Grant Farred very powerfully describes this historical transition in the following way: "The 'wretched' of the anticolonial struggle has, it seems, mutated into the 'wretchedness' of the decolonized state. Whereas the

'wretched' constituted a cadre of political radicals intent on overthrowing the colonial regime, Fanon's recalling of that term—that arresting transition from noun to adjective—iterates a profound political concern: 'wretchedness' is a regressive, reactionary tendency." Grant Farred, "Wretchedness," in *Living Fanon: Global Perspectives*, ed. Nigel Gibson (New York: Palgrave Macmillan, 2011), 170.

13. Fanon, *Wretched*, 109.
14. Fanon, *Wretched*, 110.
15. Fanon, *Wretched*, 113.
16. Fanon, *Wretched*, 115.
17. Frantz Fanon, *Oeuvres* (Paris: La Découverte, 2011), 558–559.
18. Fanon, *Wretched*, 119.
19. For a discussion of Marx's own trajectory beyond Eurocentrism and a unilinear conception of historical time, see Kevin Anderson, *Marx at the Margins: On Nationalism, Ethnicity, and Non-Western Societies* (Chicago: University of Chicago Press, 2010). See also Harry Harootunian, *Marx after Marx: History and Time in the Expansion of Capitalism* (New York: Columbia University Press, 2015); and Massimiliano Tomba, *Marx's Temporalities* (Chicago: Haymarket, 2013).
20. Fanon, *Wretched*, 119 (translation modified). For the original, see Fanon, *Oeuvres*, 563.
21. See Teodor Shanin, ed., *Late Marx and the Russian Road: Marx and 'the Peripheries of Capitalism'* (New York: Monthly Review Press, 1983). Peter Hudis likewise draws a parallel between Fanon and the late Marx in *Frantz Fanon: Philosopher of the Barricades* (London: Pluto Press, 2015), 124–125.
22. Marx and Engels, "Manifesto of the Communist Party," 477.
23. Fanon, *Wretched*, 121.
24. Fanon, *Wretched*, 120 (translation modified). For the original, see Fanon, *Oeuvres*, 564.
25. Fanon, *Wretched*, 56; Fanon, *Oeuvres*, 501.
26. Fanon, *Wretched*, 119.
27. Fanon, *Wretched*, 127.
28. Fanon, *Wretched*, 130; Fanon, *Oeuvres*, 572.
29. See Nigel Gibson, "A Wholly Other Time? Fanon, the Revolutionary, and the Question of Organization," *South Atlantic Quarterly* 112, no. 1 (Winter 2013): 43.
30. Fanon, *Wretched*, 128.
31. Reiland Rabaka, *Forms of Fanonism: Frantz Fanon's Critical Theory and the Dialectics of Decolonization* (Lanham, MD: Lexington, 2010), 156. Peter Hallward relatedly argues that Fanon "is most distant from Lenin or Mao" when he maintains that "the people rather than their leaders or party is the only adequate subject of political will." Peter Hallward, "Fanon and Political Will," *Cosmos and History* 7, no. 1 (2011): 113.
32. Nick Nesbitt, *Caribbean Critique: Antillean Critical Theory from Toussaint to Glissant* (Liverpool: Liverpool University Press, 2013), 206.
33. Fanon, *Wretched*, 124 (translation modified). For the original, see Fanon, *Oeuvres*, 568.
34. This is not to say that Fanon is no longer committed to a reciprocal relationship between the masses and the party leadership, but enlightening politicization, as Fanon conceives of it at this point in his argument, does not seem to move in both directions. Richard Philcox's translation is misleading on this point. Fanon writes: "La circulation du sommet à la base et de la base au sommet doit être un principe rigide." Philcox's translation reads: "The flow *of ideas* from the upper echelons to

the rank and file and vice versa must be an unwavering principle." But just a few sentences later, Fanon reveals that it is not ideas but rather "*forces* from the rank and file which rise up to energize the leadership and permit it dialectically to make a new leap forward." See Fanon, *Wretched*, 138 (my emphasis). Compare with Fanon, *Oeuvres*, 580.

35. Fanon, *Wretched*, 137.

36. Aijaz Ahmad similarly argues that the "extreme decentralization of authority and construction of organs of popular power" is "a classically Marxist solution" insofar as it contributes to "the withering away of the state." See "Frantz Fanon: The Philosophical Revolutionary," *Naked Punch*, November 26, 2012, http://nakedpunch.com /articles/156.

37. Fanon, *Wretched*, 134–135, 139–140.

38. Fanon, *Wretched*, 138 (translation modified). For the original, see Fanon, *Oeuvres*, 580.

39. Fanon, *Wretched*, 141 (translation modified). For the original, see Fanon, *Oeuvres*, 582.

40. Gibson likewise reads Fanon's example of bridge building as a metaphor for the relationship between the party's intellectual leaders and the masses. See Nigel Gibson, *Fanon: The Postcolonial Imagination* (Cambridge: Polity, 2003), 197.

41. Fanon, *Wretched*, 140–141 (translation modified). For the original, see Fanon, *Oeuvres*, 582.

42. Fanon, *Wretched*, 50 (translation modified). For the original, see Fanon, *Oeuvres*, 495.

43. Jean-Paul Sartre, *Critique of Dialectical Reason*, vol. 1, trans. Alan Sheridan-Smith (London: Verso, 2004), 46.

44. Fanon might be read here as elaborating upon Sartre's claim, during his own discussion of the Algerian War, that decolonizing violence forms "an initially negative unity whose content would be defined in struggle: the Algerian nation." Sartre, *Critique*, 733.

45. While focusing on Fanon's elective affinity with Jean-Jacques Rousseau, Jane Gordon reaches a similar conclusion: "The boundaries of the emergent nation . . . are not based on racial, ethnic, or religious membership but on a particular brand of committed, decisive, and divisive action in which anyone could in theory engage." Jane Gordon, *Creolizing Political Theory: Reading Rousseau through Fanon* (New York: Fordham University Press, 2014), 134. David Macey likewise asserts that Fanon's "nationalism is a nationalism of the political will, not of ethnicity. And this nationalism is what allows him to speak in *Sociologie d'une révolution* and *Les Damnés de la terre* of 'we Algerians.'" David Macey, *Frantz Fanon: A Biography* (London: Verso, 2012), 385. To offer a final example, for Peter Hallward, Fanon's argument hinges on a distinction between "*deliberate* engagement" and "shared cultural essence." See Peter Hallward, *Absolutely Postcolonial: Writing Between the Singular and the Specific* (Manchester: Manchester University Press, 2001), 128 (emphasis in original).

46. See Frantz Fanon, *A Dying Colonialism*, trans. Haakon Chevalier (New York: Grove, 1965), 84.

47. Natalie Melas, "Humanity / Humanities: Decolonization and the Poetics of Relation," *Topoi* 18 (1999): 17. Pheng Cheah similarly recasts Fanon's conceptualization of the nation as "not a preexisting entity but something persistently reformulated by the experience of the masses in their ongoing struggle." Pheng Cheah, *Spectral Nationality: Passages of Freedom from Kant to Postcolonial Literatures of Liberation* (New York: Columbia University Press, 2003), 218.

48. Fanon, *Wretched*, 144 (my emphasis, translation modified). For the original, see Fanon, *Oeuvres*, 585.
49. Fanon, *Wretched*, 142–143 (translation modified). For the original, see Fanon, *Oeuvres*, 584.
50. Fanon, *Wretched*, 133.
51. Sartre, *Critique*, 310.
52. Fanon, *Wretched*, 143–144 (translation modified). For the original, see Fanon, *Oeuvres*, 584–585.
53. For a helpful discussion of Fanon's use of this keyword in *Black Skin, White Masks*, see Jeremy Matthew Glick, *The Black Radical Tragic: Performance, Aesthetics, and the Unfinished Haitian Revolution* (New York: New York University Press, 2016), 38–39.
54. For more on these texts and when they were written, see Macey, *Frantz Fanon*, 371. I have slightly modified Philcox's English translation of the paper's title, replacing "mutual" with "reciprocal," since the latter is closer to the original French: "*Fondements réciproques de la culture nationale et des luttes de libération.*" For the English translation, see Fanon, *Wretched*, 170. For the original, see Fanon, *Oeuvres*, 613.
55. "If we decide to trace these various phases of development in the works of colonized writers, three stages [*temps*] emerge." Fanon, *Wretched*, 158; Fanon, *Oeuvres*, 601.
56. Fanon, *Wretched*, 159.
57. Fanon, *Wretched*, 170.
58. Frantz Fanon, "Racism and Culture," in *Toward the African Revolution: Political Essays*, trans. Haakon Chevalier (New York: Grove, 1967), 31, 34.
59. Fanon, *Wretched*, 171.
60. "Like adopted children who only stop investigating their new family environment once their psyche has formed a minimum core of reassurance, the colonized intellectual will endeavor to make European culture his own." Fanon, *Wretched*, 156.
61. Fanon, *Wretched*, 159.
62. Fanon, *Wretched*, 156. For Fanon's brief mention of the second phase of the colonized intellectual taking place after independence, see *Wretched*, 161.
63. Fanon, *Wretched*, 156.
64. Fanon, *Wretched*, 148, 157.
65. Fanon, *Wretched*, 159.
66. Fanon, *Wretched*, 148, 153, 155.
67. Fanon, *Wretched*, 152, 157 (translation modified). For the original, see Fanon, *Oeuvres*, 595, 600.
68. Fanon, *Wretched*, 172–173.
69. Fanon, *Wretched*, 159, 175.
70. Fanon, *Wretched*, 151.
71. Fanon, *Wretched*, 150.
72. Fanon, *Wretched*, 150.
73. Fanon, *Wretched*, 150; Fanon, *Oeuvres*, 594.
74. Fanon, *Wretched*, 154 (translation modified). For the original, see Fanon, *Oeuvres*, 597.
75. Fanon, *Wretched*, 149.
76. Fanon, *Wretched*, 148.
77. Fanon, *Wretched*, 157.

78. Fanon, *Wretched*, 148 (my emphasis, translation modified). For the original, see Fanon, *Oeuvres*, 592.

79. Fanon, *Wretched*, 156.

80. Fanon, *Wretched*, 155 (translation modified). For the original, see Fanon, *Oeuvres*, 598.

81. Fanon, *Wretched*, 155.

82. Fanon, *Wretched*, 148. Fanon makes this same point in his paper for the 1956 congress: "This rediscovery, this absolute valorization almost in defiance of reality, objectively indefensible, assumes an incomparable and subjective importance." See Fanon, "Racism and Culture," 43.

83. Fanon, *Wretched*, 160–161.

84. Fanon, *Wretched*, 160; Fanon, *Oeuvres*, 603.

85. Fanon, *Wretched*, 161 (translation modified). For the original, see Fanon, *Oeuvres*, 603.

86. Fanon, *Wretched*, 163 (my emphasis, translation modified). For the original, see Fanon, *Oeuvres*, 605.

87. Fanon, *Oeuvres*, 605.

88. Fanon, *Wretched*, 10–11.

89. Fanon, *Wretched*, 168 (translation modified). For the original, see Fanon, *Oeuvres*, 610.

90. Fanon, *Wretched*, 168 (translation modified). For the original, see Fanon, *Oeuvres*, 610.

91. Fanon, *Wretched*, 177.

92. Fanon, *Wretched*, 177.

93. Fanon, *Wretched*, 179 (translation modified). For the original, see Fanon, *Oeuvres*, 621.

94. Fanon, *Wretched*, 170 (translation modified). For the original, see Fanon, *Oeuvres*, 613.

95. Fanon, *Wretched*, 174 (translation modified). For the original, see Fanon, *Oeuvres*, 616.

96. Fanon, *Wretched*, 176 (translation modified). For the original, see Fanon, *Oeuvres*, 618.

97. Fanon, *Wretched*, 20.

98. Fanon, *Wretched*, 167.

99. Fanon, *Wretched*, 174–175 (translation modified). For the original, see Fanon, *Oeuvres*, 617.

100. Fanon, *Wretched*, 177 (translation modified). For the original, see Fanon, *Oeuvres*, 620.

101. Fanon, *Wretched*, 179 (translation modified). For the original, see Fanon, *Oeuvres*, 621.

102. See G. W. F. Hegel, *Phenomenology of Spirit*, trans. A. V. Miller (Oxford: Oxford University Press, 1977), 111–119. For a discussion of how Hegel may himself be translating from the colonial situation to arrive at this idea, see Susan Buck-Morss, *Hegel, Haiti, and Universal History* (Pittsburgh: Pittsburgh University Press, 2009).

103. Fanon, *Wretched*, 180. To appreciate how Fanon is polemically responding to a broader debate taking place at the time regarding the possibility of decolonization without national independence, refer to the following work: Gary Wilder, *Freedom Time: Negritude, Decolonization, and the Future of the World* (Durham, NC: Duke University Press, 2015).

104. Fanon, *Wretched*, 179.

105. Gibson helpfully notes how the three phases of the colonized intellectual pass through the movement of negation and negating the negation in *Postcolonial Imagination*, 169. See also Robert J. C. Young, *Empire, Colony, Postcolony* (Oxford: Wiley-Blackwell, 2015), 100.

106. Fanon, *Wretched*, 178 (translation modified). For the original, see Fanon, *Oeuvres*, 620.

107. David Scott, *Refashioning Futures: Criticism After Postcoloniality* (Princeton, NJ: Princeton University Press, 1999), 204.

108. Hallward, *Absolutely Postcolonial*, 50 (emphasis in original).

109. Judith Butler, "Violence, Nonviolence: Sartre on Fanon," in *Senses of the Subject* (New York: Fordham University Press, 2015), 196.

110. Fanon, *A Dying Colonialism*, 30.

111. Karl Marx and Friedrich Engels, "The German Ideology," in *Collected Works*, vol. 5, *Marx and Engels 1845–1847* (New York: International, 1976), 49 (emphasis in original).

112. Samira Kawash, "Terrorists and Vampires: Fanon's Spectral Violence of Decolonization," in *Frantz Fanon: Critical Perspectives*, ed. Anthony C. Alessandrini (London: Routledge, 1999), 256.

113. Here I am taking my interpretative cue from the argument Bruno Bosteels develops in *The Actuality of Communism* (London: Verso, 2011). See also Fredric Jameson, *The Hegel Variations: On the Phenomenology of Spirit* (London: Verso, 2010), 69–74.

114. Melas, "Humanity / Humanities," 16. I slightly diverge from Melas, however, in my reading of the actuality, rather than what Melas characterizes as the "necessary potentiality," of the new humanism. See Melas, "Humanity / Humanities," 17 (emphasis in original).

115. Fanon, *Wretched*, 180.

116. Fanon, *Wretched*, 181.

117. Fanon, *Wretched*, 233.

118. Fanon, *Wretched*, 181 (translation modified). For the original, see Fanon, *Oeuvres*, 625. My thinking about this passage and its significance for the broader argument of *The Wretched of the Earth* is inspired by and indebted to a paper Cate Reilly gave at the May 2016 Latin American Studies Association Congress titled, "Psychiatry's Vertigo: Fanon in the Clinic and the Case Histories of *Les damnés de la terre*."

119. Though not the most literal translation, Philcox's choice to render "*inopportun*" as "untimely" perceptively invites associations with the popular Nietzschean idea of untimeliness. See, on this point, Friedrich Nietzsche, *Untimely Meditations*, ed. Daniel Breazeale (Cambridge: Cambridge University Press, 1997).

120. Fanon, *Wretched*, 51.

121. Fanon, *Wretched*, 219 (my emphasis).

122. Fanon, *Wretched*, 182–183.

123. Comparing decolonizing violence to a *pharmakon* has its limits insofar as Fanon theorizes the former's valences dialectically whereas, for Jacques Derrida, *pharmakon*'s play between remedy and poison is "something quite different from . . . the dialectic of opposites." See Jacques Derrida, *Dissemination*, trans. Barbara Johnson (London: Athlone, 1981), 99. Fred Moten offers a related account of anticolonial resistance and/as pathology in his reading of Fanon. See "The Case of Blackness," *Criticism* 50, no. 2 (March 2008): 177–218.

124. Butler, "Violence, Nonviolence," 187.

125. Jean-Paul Sartre, preface to Fanon, *Wretched*, lv.

126. Sartre, "Preface," lxii. This passage is strikingly similar to the famous line from Richard Wagner's *Parsifal*: "The wound can be healed only by the spear which

smote it." On the political and philosophical implications of this statement, see Slavoj Žižek, "The Politics of Redemption, or, Why Richard Wagner is Worth Saving," in *Lacan: The Silent Partners*, ed. Slavoj Žižek (London: Verso, 2006), 231–269.

127. Fanon, *Wretched*, 50.

128. Fanon, *Wretched*, 220.

129. Fanon, *Wretched*, 181 (translation modified). For the original, see Fanon, *Oeuvres*, 625.

130. On this point, in addition to chapter 1 of this book, see Robert J. C. Young, "Fanon, Revolutionary Playwright," in Frantz Fanon, *Alienation and Freedom*, ed. Jean Khalfa and Robert J. C. Young, trans. Steven Corcoran (London: Bloomsbury, 2018), 72–74.

131. Sartre, "Preface," lv.

132. Here I diverge from Butler, who makes the following claim: "Of course, there is a question of whether violence as a pure instrument can remain as such or whether it comes to define, haunt, and afflict the polity that instates itself through violent means. Neither Sartre nor Fanon asks this question." In this section of the book, I will show how Fanon does indeed ask this question. See Butler, "Violence, Nonviolence," 191.

133. Fanon, *Wretched*, 181.

134. Fanon, *Wretched*, 184.

135. Gerard Aching highlights the untimely disjuncture between the fifth chapter and earlier statements made in *The Wretched of the Earth*, focusing in particular on how Fanon's case studies problematize the Manichaean politics of decolonization outlined in "On Violence." What is missing from this analysis is a discussion of how many ideas from the first chapter reappear in the fifth chapter, such that the tension Aching identifies is not only noticeable *between* chapters but also *within* each chapter. See Gerard Aching, "No Need for an Apology: Fanon's Untimely Critique of Political Consciousness," *South Atlantic Quarterly* 112, no. 1 (Winter 2013): 23–38.

136. Drucilla Cornell, afterword to *What Fanon Said: A Philosophical Introduction to His Life and Thought*, by Lewis R. Gordon (New York: Fordham University Press, 2015), 146–147.

137. Fanon, *Wretched*, 184–185.

138. Fanon, *Wretched*, 184n23.

139. See Frantz Fanon, *Parallel Hands*, in *Alienation and Freedom*, 113–164.

140. See Jean-Paul Sartre, *Being and Nothingness: A Phenomenological Essay on Ontology*, trans. Hazel E. Barnes (New York: Washington Square, 1984), 65–69. The English translation of Sartre's text makes it difficult to appreciate Fanon's engagement with it, since the French term that both thinkers use—"*angoisse*"—is rendered as "anguish" rather than "anxiety." For the original, see Jean-Paul Sartre, *L'être et le néant: Essai d'ontologie phénoménologique* (Paris: Gallimard, 1943), 65–67. Compare with Fanon, *Oeuvres*, 628.

141. Sartre, *Being and Nothingness*, 69.

142. Sartre, *Being and Nothingness*, 70 (emphasis in original).

143. Sartre, *Being and Nothingness*, 70.

144. Freud argues, for example, that unconscious processes are "indestructible" and that "in the unconscious nothing can be brought to an end, nothing is past or forgotten." See Sigmund Freud, *The Interpretation of Dreams*, trans. James Strachey

(New York: Basic, 2010), 576. On the return of the repressed, see also Freud, "Repression," 141–158.

145. Fanon, *Wretched*, 219 (translation modified). For the original, see Fanon, *Oeuvres*, 660.

146. Fanon, *Wretched*, 229 (translation modified). For the original, see Fanon, *Oeuvres*, 668–669.

147. Gibson, "A Wholly Other Time?," 51.

148. Gibson, "A Wholly Other Time?," 50. Gibson's preference for reading Fanon dialectically will lead him to resolve the tension almost as soon as he alludes to its existence. As I have argued throughout this book, however, it is often more illuminating to avoid the temptation of converting Fanon into a consistent thinker and instead consider how the tensions and discontinuities in his writings reveal surprising facets of (the subterranean) Fanon's thought.

149. Fanon, *Wretched*, 233 (translation modified). For the original, see Fanon, *Oeuvres*, 672.

150. Fanon, *Wretched*, 235 (translation modified). For the original, see Fanon, *Oeuvres*, 673. My analysis of this passage draws inspiration from Walter Benjamin's theorization of awakening in a collective and political key. See Walter Benjamin, *The Arcades Project*, trans. Howard Eiland and Kevin McLaughlin (Cambridge, MA: Harvard University Press, 2002). See, relatedly, Susan Buck-Morss, "The City as Dreamworld and Catastrophe," *October* 73 (Summer 1995): 3–26.

151. See Fanon, *Wretched*, 236–237.

152. Fanon, *Wretched*, 235.

153. For Hegel's argument that "it is the necessary fate of Asiatic Empires to be subjected to Europeans," see G. W. F. Hegel, *The Philosophy of History*, trans. J. Sibree (Amherst, NY: Prometheus, 1991), 142.

154. Fanon, *Wretched*, 237.

155. On the concept of provincialization, see Dipesh Chakrabarty, *Provincializing Europe: Postcolonial Thought and Historical Difference* (Princeton, NJ: Princeton University Press, 2000). Chakrabarty would likely go further than Fanon here and argue that the notion of historical development must itself be provincialized as a secular and Western understanding of time that does not neutrally encompass all life-worlds. See in the aforementioned book his chapter titled, "Translating Life-Worlds into Labor and History," 72–96.

156. Fanon, *Wretched*, 236.

157. On this point, see Wilder, *Freedom Time*, 9–12.

158. Fanon, *Wretched*, 236.

159. Fanon, *Wretched*, 236.

160. Fanon, *Wretched*, 236 (translation modified). For the original, see Fanon, *Oeuvres*, 674.

161. Fanon, *Wretched*, 236.

162. Fanon, *Wretched*, 238. On deprovincialization, see Harootunian, *Marx After Marx*, 1–20; and Wilder, *Freedom Time*, 9–10, 258. See, relatedly, Achille Mbembe, *Critique of Black Reason*, trans. Laurent Dubois (Durham, NC: Duke University Press, 2017), 8.

163. Fanon, *Wretched*, 237 (translation modified). For the original, see Fanon, *Oeuvres*, 675.

164. Fanon, *Wretched*, 237. Sartre's call to produce a "true and positive humanism" to replace bourgeois humanism may have been a source of inspiration as well as a target of critique in Fanon's account of the limits of European thought. See Sartre, *Critique*, 800.

165. For a helpful discussion of Fanon and his relationship with European humanism, see Anthony C. Alessandrini, *Frantz Fanon and the Future of Cultural Politics: Finding Something Different* (New York: Lexington, 2014), 53.

166. Fanon, *Wretched*, 238.

167. Fanon, *Wretched*, 239 (translation modified). For the original, see Fanon, *Oeuvres*, 676.

168. Alberto Toscano offers a brief but suggestive discussion of how Fanon and Kamau Brathwaite imagine the possibility of "a break, a salutary interruption in the (political, technological, metaphysical) dialectic of Europe." See "'European nihilism' and beyond: commentary by Alberto Toscano," in Alain Badiou, *The Century*, trans. Alberto Toscano (Cambridge: Polity, 2007), 199. See also Édouard Glissant's characterization of Fanon as a thinker who *"acted on his ideas"* and therefore "took full responsibility for *a complete break."* Édouard Glissant, *Caribbean Discourse: Selected Essays*, trans. J. Michael Dash (Charlottesville: The University Press of Virginia, 1989), 25 (emphasis in original).

169. On Fanon's "emphatically new" humanism, see Melas, "Humanity/Humanities," 16. See also Young's discussion of Fanon's humanism as a new humanism that strives to be distinguished from "a humanism which harks back critically, or uncritically, to the mainstream Enlightenment culture." Robert J. C. Young, *White Mythologies: Writing History and the West* (New York: Routledge, 2004), 165. It is worth noting that both of these texts diverge from Alessandrini's previously cited reading of Fanon on European humanism. This disagreement in the literature on Fanon, as in other cases, can be traced back to a disagreement *within* Fanon himself.

170. Philcox's English translation renders *"il faut faire peau neuve"* as "we must make a new start." For a discussion of this mistranslation, see Alessandrini, *Frantz Fanon*, 82.

CONCLUSION

1. Frantz Fanon, *Black Skin, White Masks*, trans. Richard Philcox (New York: Grove, 2008), 1 (translation modified). For the original, see Frantz Fanon, *Oeuvres* (Paris: La Découverte, 2011), 71.

2. Fanon, *Black Skin, White Masks*, 1.

3. Fanon, *Black Skin, White Masks*, 1 (translation modified). For the original, see Fanon, *Oeuvres*, 71.

4. Karl Marx, "Theses on Feuerbach," in *Collected Works*, vol. 5, *Marx and Engels, 1845–1847* (New York: International, 1975), 5 (emphasis in original).

5. Achille Mbembe, *Critique of Black Reason*, trans. Laurent Dubois (Durham, NC: Duke University Press, 2017), 162.

6. Gary Wilder, *Freedom Time: Negritude, Decolonization, and the Future of the World* (Durham, NC: Duke University Press, 2015), 258.

7. Audre Lorde, *Sister Outsider* (Berkeley, CA: Crossing Press, 2007), 112, 123.

8. Lorde, *Sister Outsider*, 112. For an excellent discussion of Lorde's aphorism and its implications, see Jack Halberstam, "Vertiginous Capital or, The Master's Toolkit," *Bully Bloggers*, July 2, 2018, https://bullybloggers.wordpress.com/2018/07/02/vertigi nous-capital-or-the-masters-toolkit-by-jack-halberstam/.

9. Robin D. G. Kelley, *Freedom Dreams: The Black Radical Imagination* (Boston: Beacon, 2002), 181.

10. Judith Butler, "Restaging the Universal: Hegemony and the Limits of Formalism," in Judith Butler, Ernesto Laclau, Slavoj Žižek, *Contingency, Hegemony, Universality: Contemporary Dialogues on the Left* (London: Verso, 2000), 15.

11. This line of reasoning is especially popular within certain circles of postcolonial and decolonial theory, but it is gaining traction in other Left discourses as well. On the universal denunciation of the universal in postcolonial studies, see Peter Hallward, *Absolutely Postcolonial: Writing Between the Singular and the Specific* (Manchester: Manchester University Press, 2001), 20–61, 176–187.

12. For some examples of this scholarship, see Kelley, *Freedom Dreams*, 172–181; Wilder, *Freedom Time*, 1–16; Gary Wilder, "Here / Hear Now Aimé Césaire!" *South Atlantic Quarterly* 115, no. 3 (July 2016): 585–604; Carole Boyce Davies, *Left of Karl Marx: The Political Life of Black Communist Claudia Jones* (Durham, NC: Duke University Press, 2008); Brent Hayes Edwards, "The Shadow of Shadows," *positions* 11, no. 1 (Spring 2003): 11–49; Natalie Melas, "Humanity / Humanities: Decolonization and the Poetics of Relation," *Topoi* 18 (1999): 13–28; Fred Moten, *The Universal Machine* (Durham, NC: Duke University Press, 2018); Nick Nesbitt, *Universal Emancipation: The Haitian Revolution and the Radical Enlightenment* (Charlottesville: University of Virginia Press, 2008); and Nick Nesbitt, *Caribbean Critique: Antillean Critical Theory from Toussaint to Glissant* (Liverpool: Liverpool University Press, 2013). Scholarship on the related issue of black internationalism could also be consulted here. See Keisha N. Blain, *Set the World on Fire: Black Nationalist Women and the Global Struggle for Freedom* (Philadelphia: University of Pennsylvania Press, 2018); Keisha N. Blain and Tiffany M. Gill, ed., *To Turn the Whole World Over: Black Women and Internationalism* (Urbana: University of Illinois Press, 2019); Brent Hayes Edwards, *The Practice of Diaspora: Literature, Translation, and the Rise of Black Internationalism* (Cambridge, MA: Harvard University Press, 2003); and Minkah Makalani, *In the Cause of Freedom: Radical Black Internationalism from Harlem to London* (Chapel Hill: University of North Carolina Press, 2011).

13. In addition to Fanon's entire body of work, see, for example, Aimé Césaire, *Discourse on Colonialism*, trans. Joan Pinkham (New York: Monthly Review, 2000); Aimé Césaire, "Letter to Maurice Thorez," trans. Chike Jeffers, *Social Text* 28, no. 2 (Summer 2010): 145–152; Suzanne Césaire, *The Great Camouflage: Writings of Dissent (1941–1945)*, ed. Daniel Maximin, trans. Keith Walker (Middletown, CT: Wesleyan University Press, 2012); C. L. R. James, *The Black Jacobins: Toussaint L'Ouverture and the San Domingo Revolution* (New York: Vintage, 1989); C. L. R. James, "Dialectical Materialism and the Fate of Humanity," in *The C. L. R. James Reader*, ed. Anna Grimshaw (Oxford: Blackwell, 1992), 153–181; and Claudia Jones, "A People's Art is the Genesis of their Freedom," in *Claudia Jones: Beyond Containment*, ed. Carole Boyce Davies (Oxford: Ayebia Clarke, 2011), 166–167.

14. These questions develop out of a reading of Fanon alongside the following essays: Étienne Balibar, "Ambiguous Universality," in *Politics and the Other Scene*, trans.

Christine Jones, James Swenson, Chris Turner (London: Verso, 2002), 146–176; and Judith Butler, "Competing Universalities," in Butler, Laclau, and Žižek, *Contingency, Hegemony, Universality*, 136–181.

15. On this point, see Gavin Arnall, "The Idea(s) of Occupy," *Theory & Event* 15, no. 2 (June 2012), https://muse.jhu.edu/article/478363.

16. Comité Clandestino Revolucionario Indígena, "Cuarta declaración de la selva lacandona," *Enlace Zapatista*, January 1, 1996, http://enlacezapatista.ezln.org.mx/1996/01/01/cuarta-declaracion-de-la-selva-lacandona/ (my translation).

BIBLIOGRAPHY

1er Congrès International des Écrivains et Artistes Noirs. Paris: Présence Africaine, 1956.

Aching, Gerard. "No Need for an Apology: Fanon's Untimely Critique of Political Consciousness." *South Atlantic Quarterly* 112, no. 1 (Winter 2013): 23–38.

Adkins, Amey Victoria. "Black / Feminist Futures: Reading Beauvoir in *Black Skin, White Masks.*" *South Atlantic Quarterly* 112, no. 4 (Fall 2013): 697–723.

Adorno, Theodor W., and Max Horkheimer. *Dialectic of Enlightenment: Philosophical Fragments.* Trans. Edmund Jephcott. Stanford: Stanford University Press, 2002.

Ahmad, Aijaz. "Frantz Fanon: The Philosophical Revolutionary." *Naked Punch*, November 26, 2012. http://nakedpunch.com/articles/156.

Alessandrini, Anthony C. *Frantz Fanon and the Future of Cultural Politics: Finding Something Different.* Lanham, MD: Lexington, 2014.

Alessandrini, Anthony C., ed. *Frantz Fanon: Critical Perspectives.* New York: Routledge, 1999.

Allan, Michael. "Old Media / New Futures: Revolutionary Reverberations of Fanon's Radio." *PMLA* 134, no. 1 (January 2019): 188–193.

Althusser, Louis. "From *Capital* to Marx's Philosophy." In *Reading Capital*, trans. Ben Brewster, 13–69. London: Verso, 2006.

Althusser, Louis. "The Underground Current of the Materialism of the Encounter." In *Philosophy of the Encounter: Later Writings, 1978–1987*, trans. G.M. Goshgarian, 163–207. London: Verso, 2006.

Althusser, Louis, and Étienne Balibar. *Reading Capital.* Trans. Ben Brewster. London: Verso, 2006.

Amrane, Djamila. *Les femmes algériennes dans la guerre.* Paris: Plon, 1991.

Anderson, Kevin. *Marx at the Margins: On Nationalism, Ethnicity, and Non-Western Societies.* Chicago: University of Chicago Press, 2010.

Ansell-Pearson, Keith. *An Introduction to Nietzsche as Political Thinker.* Cambridge: Cambridge University Press, 1994.

Arendt, Hannah. *On Violence*. New York: Harcourt, 1970.

Aristotle. *Poetics*. Trans. Malcolm Heath. New York: Penguin, 1997.

Arnall, Gavin. "Alejo Carpentier's *El siglo de las luces*: The Translation of Politics and the Politics of Translation." *Journal of Latin American Cultural Studies* 21, no. 1 (April 2012): 87–102.

Arnall, Gavin. "Hacia una teoría de la práctica teórica: Mariátegui, marxismo y traducción." *Escrituras americanas* 2, no. 2 (December 2017): 43–80.

Arnall, Gavin. "The Idea(s) of Occupy." *Theory & Event* 15, no. 2 (June 2012). https://muse.jhu.edu/article/478363.

Arnall, Gavin. "Remembering the Sixties: On Julio Cortázar's *Hopscotch* and Time." *MLN* 134, no. 2 (March 2019): 360–381.

Arnall, Gavin. "Repeating Translation, Left and Right (and Left Again): Roberto Bolaño's *Between Parentheses* and *Distant Star*." *CR: The New Centennial Review* 17, no. 3 (Winter 2017): 237–263.

Arnold, A. James. *Modernism & Negritude: The Poetry and Poetics of Aimé Césaire*. Cambridge, MA: Harvard University Press, 1998.

Arthur, Paige. *Unfinished Projects: Decolonization and the Philosophy of Jean-Paul Sartre*. London: Verso, 2010.

Azar, Michael. "In the Name of Algeria: Frantz Fanon and the Algerian Revolution." In Alessandrini, *Frantz Fanon*, 21–33.

Badiou, Alain. *The Century*. Trans. Alberto Toscano. Cambridge: Polity, 2007.

Badiou, Alain. *Deleuze: The Clamor of Being*. Trans. Louise Burchill. Minneapolis: University of Minnesota Press, 2000.

Badiou, Alain. *Ethics: An Essay on the Understanding of Evil*. Trans. Peter Hallward. London: Verso, 2001.

Badiou, Alain. *Metapolitics*. Trans. Jason Barker. London: Verso, 2005.

Badiou, Alain. "Who Is Nietzsche?" *Pli* 11 (2001): 1–11.

Badiou, Alain, Pierre Bourdieu, Judith Butler, Georges Didi-Huberman, Sadri Khiari, and Jacques Rancière. *What Is a People?* Trans. Jody Gladding. New York: Columbia University Press, 2016.

Baldwin, James. "Princes and Powers." In *The Price of the Ticket: Collective Nonfiction 1948–1985*, 41–63. New York: St. Martin's, 1985.

Balibar, Étienne, "Ambiguous Universality." In *Politics and the Other Scene*, trans. Christine Jones, James Swenson, and Chris Turner, 146–176. London: Verso, 2002.

Balibar, Étienne. *The Philosophy of Marx*. Trans. Chris Turner. London: Verso, 2017.

Ball, Jared, Todd Steven Burroughs, Hate, and Frank B. Wilderson III. "Irreconcilable Anti-Blackness and Police Violence." *iMWiL!*, October 2014. https://imixwhatilike.org/2014/10/01/frankwildersonandantiblackness-2/.

Batchelor, Kathryn. "Fanon's *Les damnés de la terre*: Translation, De-Philosophization and the Intensification of Violence." *Nottingham French Studies* 54, no. 1 (March 2015): 7–22.

Baucom, Ian. "Frantz Fanon's Radio: Solidarity, Diaspora, and the Tactics of Listening." *Contemporary Literature* 42, no. 1 (Spring 2001): 15–49.

Baugh, Bruce. *French Hegel: From Surrealism to Postmodernism*. New York: Routledge, 2003.

Benjamin, Walter. *The Arcades Project*. Trans. Howard Eiland and Kevin McLaughlin. Cambridge, MA: Harvard University Press, 2002.

Benjamin, Walter. "The Task of the Translator." In *Selected Writings*. Vol. 1, *1913–1926*, ed. Marcus Bullock and Michael W. Jennings, 253–263. Cambridge, MA: Harvard University Press, 1996.

Benjamin, Walter. "The Work of Art in the Age of Its Technological Reproducibility: Second Version." In *The Work of Art in the Age of Its Technological Reproducibility and Other Writings on Media*, ed. Michael W. Jennings, Brigid Doherty, and Thomas Y. Levin, 19–55. Cambridge, MA: Harvard University Press, 2008.

Bernasconi, Robert. "Casting the Slough: Fanon's New Humanism for a New Humanity." In *Fanon: A Critical Reader*, ed. Lewis Gordon, T. Denean Sharpley-Whiting, and Renée T. White, 113–121. Cambridge: Blackwell, 1996.

Bernasconi, Robert. "Fanon's *The Wretched of the Earth* as the Fulfillment of Sartre's *Critique of Dialectical Reason*." *Sartre Studies International* 16, no. 2 (2010): 36–47.

Bessone, Magali. "Introduction: Frantz Fanon, en équilibre sur la *color line*." In Frantz Fanon, *Oeuvres*, 37–43. Paris: La Découverte, 2011.

Bhabha, Homi K. "Foreword: Framing Fanon." In Frantz Fanon, *The Wretched of the Earth*, trans. Richard Philcox, vii–xli. New York: Grove, 2005.

Bhabha, Homi K. "Foreword: Remembering Fanon: Self, Psyche, and the Colonial Condition." In Frantz Fanon, *Black Skin, White Masks*, trans. Charles Lam Markmann, xxi–xxxvii. London: Pluto, 2008.

Bhabha, Homi K. *The Location of Culture*. New York: Routledge, 1994.

Blain, Keisha N. *Set the World on Fire: Black Nationalist Women and the Global Struggle for Freedom*. Philadelphia: University of Pennsylvania Press, 2018.

Blain, Keisha N. and Tiffany M. Gill, ed. *To Turn the Whole World Over: Black Women and Internationalism*. Urbana: University of Illinois Press, 2019.

Bogues, Anthony. *Empire of Liberty: Power, Desire, & Freedom*. Hanover, NH: Dartmouth College Press, 2010.

Bosteels, Bruno. *The Actuality of Communism*. London: Verso, 2011.

Bosteels, Bruno. *Badiou and Politics*. Durham, NC: Duke University Press, 2011.

Bosteels, Bruno. "Introduction: This People Which is Not One." In Badiou, Bourdieu, Butler, Didi-Huberman, Khiari, and Rancière, *What Is a People?*, 1–20.

Bosteels, Bruno. *Marx and Freud in Latin America: Politics, Psychoanalysis, and Religion in Times of Terror*. London: Verso, 2012.

Bosteels, Bruno. "Radical Antiphilosophy." *Filozofski Vestnik* 29, no. 2 (2008): 155–187.

Boyce Davies, Carole. *Left of Karl Marx: The Political Life of Black Communist Claudia Jones*. Durham, NC: Duke University Press, 2008.

Bray, Mark. *Translating Anarchy: The Anarchism of Occupy Wall Street*. Winchester: Zero, 2013.

Brecht, Bertolt. "A Short Organum for the Theatre." In *Brecht on Theatre: The Development of an Aesthetic*, 179–205. New York: Hill and Wang, 1964.

Brennan, Timothy. *Borrowed Light: Vico, Hegel, and the Colonies*. Stanford, CA: Stanford University Press, 2014.

Brown, Wendy. "Resisting Left Melancholia." In *Loss: The Politics of Mourning*, ed. David L. Eng and David Kazanjian, 458–466. Berkeley: University of California Press, 2003.

Buck-Morss, Susan. "The City as Dreamworld and Catastrophe." *October* 73 (Summer 1995): 3–26.

Buck-Morss, Susan. *Hegel, Haiti, and Universal History*. Pittsburgh, PA: Pittsburgh University Press, 2009.

Bulhan, Hussein Abdilahi. *Frantz Fanon and the Psychology of Oppression*. New York: Plenum, 1985.

Butler, Judith. "Competing Universalities." In Butler, Laclau, and Žižek, *Contingency, Hegemony, Universality*, 136–181.

Butler, Judith. "Restaging the Universal: Hegemony and the Limits of Formalism." In Butler, Laclau, and Žižek, *Contingency, Hegemony, Universality*, 11–43.

Butler, Judith. "Violence, Nonviolence: Sartre on Fanon." In *Senses of the Subject*, 171–198. New York: Fordham University Press, 2015.

Butler, Judith. "'We, the People': Thoughts on Freedom of Assembly." In Badiou, Bourdieu, Butler, Didi-Huberman, Khiari, and Rancière, *What Is a People?*, 49–64.

Butler, Judith, Ernesto Laclau, and Slavoj Žižek. *Contingency, Hegemony, Universality: Contemporary Dialogues on the Left*. London: Verso, 2000.

Cassin, Barbara, ed. *Dictionary of Untranslatables: A Philosophical Lexicon*. Trans. Steven Rendall, Christian Hubert, Jeffrey Mehlman, Nathanel Stein, and Michael Syrotinski. Princeton, NJ: Princeton University Press, 2014.

Césaire, Aimé. *Discourse on Colonialism*. Trans. Joan Pinkham. New York: Monthly Review, 2000.

Césaire, Aimé. "Discours sur le colonialisme." In *Poésie, Théâtre, Essais et Discours*, ed. Albert James Arnold, 1448–1476. Paris: Planète libre, 2013.

Césaire, Aimé. "Letter to Maurice Thorez." Trans. Chike Jeffers. *Social Text* 28, no. 2 (Summer 2010): 145–152.

Césaire, Aimé. "Notebook of a Return to the Native Land." In *The Collected Poetry*, trans. Clayton Eshleman and Annette Smith, 32–85. Berkeley: University of California Press, 1983.

Césaire, Aimé. *Toussaint Louverture: La Révolution française et le problème colonial*. Paris: Présence Africaine, 2000.

Césaire, Suzanne. *The Great Camouflage: Writings of Dissent (1941–1945)*. Ed. Daniel Maximin. Trans. Keith Walker. Middletown, CT: Wesleyan University Press, 2012.

Chakrabarty, Dipesh. *Provincializing Europe: Postcolonial Thought and Historical Difference*. Princeton, NJ: Princeton University Press, 2000.

Chaudhary, Zahid. "Subjects in Difference: Walter Benjamin, Frantz Fanon, and Postcolonial Theory." *differences: A Journal of Feminist Cultural Studies* 23, no. 1 (May 2012): 151–183.

Cheah, Pheng. *Spectral Nationality: Passages of Freedom from Kant to Postcolonial Literatures of Liberation*. New York: Columbia University Press, 2003.

Cherki, Alice. *Frantz Fanon: A Portrait*. Trans. Nadia Benabid. Ithaca, NY: Cornell University Press, 2006.

Chow, Rey. "The Politics of Admittance: Female Sexual Agency, Miscegenation, and the Formation of Community in Frantz Fanon." In Alessandrini, *Frantz Fanon*, 34–56.

Ciccariello-Maher, George. *Decolonizing Dialectics*. Durham, NC: Duke University Press, 2017.

Comay, Rebecca. *Mourning Sickness: Hegel and the French Revolution*. Stanford, CA: Stanford University Press, 2010.

Comité Clandestino Revolucionario Indígena. "Cuarta declaración de la selva lacandona." *Enlace Zapatista*, January 1, 1996. http://enlacezapatista.ezln.org.mx/1996/01/01/cuarta-declaracion-de-la-selva-lacandona/.

Cornell, Drucilla. Afterword to *What Fanon Said: A Philosophical Introduction to His Life and Thought*, by Lewis R. Gordon, 143–147. New York: Fordham University Press, 2015.

Coulthard, Glen Sean. *Red Skin, White Masks: Rejecting the Colonial Politics of Recognition*. Minneapolis: University of Minnesota Press, 2014.

De Andrade, Oswald. "Cannibalist Manifesto." Trans. Leslie Bary. *Latin American Literary Review* 19, no. 38 (1991): 38–47.

de Ípola, Emilio. *Althusser, The Infinite Farewell*. Trans. Gavin Arnall. Durham, NC: Duke University Press, 2018.

Deleuze, Gilles. *Difference and Repetition*. Trans. Paul Patton. New York: Columbia University Press, 1995.

Deleuze, Gilles. *Nietzsche and Philosophy*. Trans. Hugh Tomlinson. New York: Columbia University Press, 2006.

Deleuze, Gilles, and Félix Guattari. *Anti-Oedipus: Capitalism and Schizophrenia*. Trans. Robert Hurley, Mark Seem, and Helen Lane. Minneapolis: University of Minnesota Press, 2005.

Derrida, Jacques. *Dissemination*. Trans. Barbara Johnson. London: Athlone, 1981.

Derrida, Jacques. "Roundtable on Translation." In *The Ear of the Other*, trans. Peggy Kamuf, 93–162. Lincoln, NE: University of Nebraska Press, 1985.

Derrida, Jacques. *Specters of Marx: The State of the Debt, The Work of Mourning and the New International*. Trans. Peggy Kamuf. New York: Routledge, 1994.

Derrida, Jacques. "What is a 'Relevant' Translation?" Trans. Lawrence Venuti. *Critical Inquiry* 27, no. 2 (Winter 2001): 174–200.

Dove, Patrick. "The *Desencuentros* of History: Class and Ethnicity in Bolivia." *Culture, Theory and Critique* 56, no. 3 (September 2015): 313–332.

Drabinski, John E. "Fanon's Two Memories." *South Atlantic Quarterly* 112, no. 1 (2013): 5–22.

Drif, Zohra. *Mémoires d'une combattante de l'ALN: Zone Autonome d'Alger*. Algiers: Chihab Éditions, 2013.

Edwards, Brent Hayes. *The Practice of Diaspora: Literature, Translation, and the Rise of Black Internationalism*. Cambridge, MA: Harvard University Press, 2003.

Edwards, Brent Hayes. "The Shadow of Shadows." *positions: east asia cultures critique* 11, no. 1 (Spring 2003): 11–49.

Edwards, Brian T. "Fanon's al-Jaza'ir, or Algeria Translated." *Parallax* 8, no. 2 (2002): 99–115.

Etherington, Ben. "An Answer to the Question: What is Decolonization? Frantz Fanon's *The Wretched of the Earth* and Jean-Paul Sartre's *Critique of Dialectical Reason*." *Modern Intellectual History* 13, no. 1 (2016): 151–178.

Fanon, Frantz. "Accra: Africa Affirms Its Unity and Defines Its Strategy." In *Toward the African Revolution*, 153–157.

Fanon, Frantz. "Algeria Face to Face with the French Torturers." In *Toward the African Revolution*, 64–72.

Fanon, Frantz. *Alienation and Freedom*. Ed. Jean Khalfa and Robert J. C. Young. Trans. Steven Corcoran. London: Bloomsbury, 2018.

Fanon, Frantz. *Black Skin, White Masks*. Trans. Richard Philcox. New York: Grove, 2008.

Fanon, Frantz. *Black Skin, White Masks*. Trans. Charles Lam Markmann. London: Pluto, 2008.

Fanon, Frantz. "Conducts of Confession in North Africa (2)." In *Alienation and Freedom*, 413–416.

Fanon, Frantz. "Day Hospitalization in Psychiatry: Value and Limits." In *Alienation and Freedom*, 473–509.

Fanon, Frantz. "Decolonization and Independence." In *Toward the African Revolution*, 99–105.

Fanon, Frantz. "De la violence." *Les Temps Modernes* 16, no. 181 (May 1961): 1453–1493.

Fanon, Frantz. "A Democratic Revolution." In *Alienation and Freedom*, 569–573.

Fanon, Frantz. *A Dying Colonialism*. Trans. Haakon Chevalier. New York: Grove, 1965.

Fanon, Frantz. *Écrits sur l'aliénation et la liberté*. Ed. Jean Khalfa and Robert J. C. Young. Paris: La Découverte, 2015.

Fanon, Frantz. "Ethnopsychiatric Considerations." In *Alienation and Freedom*, 405–408.

Fanon, Frantz. "French Intellectuals and Democrats and the Algerian Revolution." In *Toward the African Revolution*, 76–90.

Fanon, Frantz. "Hier, aujourd'hui et demain." In *Écrits sur l'aliénation et la liberté*, 235–237.

Fanon, Frantz. *Les damnés de la terre*. Paris: Maspero, 1961.

Fanon, Frantz. *Les Mains parallèles*. In *Écrits sur l'aliénation et la liberté*, 91—133.

Fanon, Frantz. "The Lesson of Cotonou." In *Toward the African Revolution*, 127–131.

Fanon, Frantz. "Letter to Maurice Despinoy." In *Alienation and Freedom*, 349–352.

Fanon, Frantz. "Letter to the Resident Minister (1956)." In *Toward the African Revolution*, 52–54.

Fanon, Frantz. "L'hospitalisation de jour en psychiatrie, valeur et limites." In *Écrits sur l'aliénation et la liberté*, 397–416.

Fanon, Frantz. "Mental Alterations, Character Modifications, Psychic Disorders and Intellectual Deficit in Spinocerebellar Heredodegeneration: A Case of Friedreich's Ataxia with Delusions of Possession." In *Alienation and Freedom*, 203–275.

Fanon, Frantz. "The 'North African Syndrome.'" In *Toward the African Revolution*, 3–16.

Fanon, Frantz. *Oeuvres*. Paris: La Découverte, 2011.

Fanon, Frantz. *Parallel Hands*. In *Alienation and Freedom*, 113–164.

Fanon, Frantz. "Racism and Culture." In *Toward the African Revolution*, 31–44.

Fanon, Frantz. "The Rising Anti-imperialist Movement and the Slow-wits of Pacification." In *Alienation and Freedom*, 625–631.

Fanon, Frantz. *Sociologie d'une révolution (L'an V de la révolution algérienne)*. Paris: Maspero, 1966.

Fanon, Frantz. *Toward the African Revolution: Political Essays*. Trans. Haakon Chevalier. New York: Grove, 1967.

Fanon, Frantz. *The Wretched of the Earth*. Trans. Richard Philcox. New York: Grove, 2004.

Fanon, Frantz. "Yesterday, Today, and Tomorrow." In *Alienation and Freedom*, 282–283.

Fanon, Frantz, and Jacques Azoulay. "Daily Life in the Douars." In Fanon, *Alienation and Freedom*, 373–384.

Fanon, Frantz, and Jacques Azoulay. "Social Therapy in a Ward of Muslim Men: Methodological Difficulties." In Fanon, *Alienation and Freedom*, 353–371.

Fanon, Frantz, and Jacques Azoulay. "La socialthérapie dans un service d'hommes musulmans: difficultés méthodologiques." In Fanon, *Écrits sur l'aliénation et la liberté*, 297–313.

Fanon, Frantz, and Charles Geronimi. "Day Hospitalization in Psychiatry: Value and Limits. Part Two: Doctrinal Considerations." In Fanon, *Alienation and Freedom*, 495–509.

Fanon, Frantz, and Charles Geronimi. "L'hospitalisation de jour en psychiatrie, valeur et limites. Deuxième partie: considérations doctrinales." In Fanon, *Écrits sur l'aliénation et la liberté*, 417–429.

Fanon, Frantz, and Charles Geronimi. "TAT in Muslim Women: Sociology of Perception and Imagination." In Fanon, *Alienation and Freedom*, 427–432.

Fanon, Frantz, and Raymond Lacaton. "Conducts of Confession in North Africa (1)." In Fanon, *Alienation and Freedom*, 409–412.

Fanon, Frantz, and François Sanchez. "Maghrebi Muslims and Their Attitude to Madness." In Fanon, *Alienation and Freedom*, 421–425.

Fanon, Joby. *Frantz Fanon, My Brother: Doctor, Playwright, Revolutionary*. Trans. Daniel Nethery. Lanham, MD: Lexington, 2014.

Farred, Grant. "Imperative of the Now." *South Atlantic Quarterly* 112, no.1 (Winter 2013): 1–4.

Farred, Grant. "Wretchedness." In *Living Fanon: Global Perspectives*, ed. Nigel Gibson, 159–172. New York: Palgrave Macmillan, 2011.

Fradinger, Moira. *Binding Violence: Literary Visions of Political Origins*. Stanford, CA: Stanford University Press, 2010.

Freud, Sigmund. "Analysis Terminable and Interminable." In *Standard Edition of the Complete Psychological Works of Sigmund Freud*. Vol. 23, trans. James Strachey, 211–253. London: Vintage, 2001.

Freud, Sigmund. *The Interpretation of Dreams*. Trans. James Strachey. New York: Basic, 2010.

Freud, Sigmund. "Repression." In *Standard Edition of the Complete Psychological Works of Sigmund Freud*. Vol. 14, trans. James Strachey, 141–158. London: Vintage, 2001.

Fuss, Diana. *Identification Papers: Readings on Psychoanalysis, Sexuality, and Culture*. New York: Routledge, 1995.

García Linera, Álvaro. "Indianismo y marxismo: El desencuentro de dos razones revolucionarias." In *La potencia plebeya: Acción colectiva e identidades indígenas, obreras y populares en Bolivia*, ed. Pablo Stefanoni, 373–392. Buenos Aires: Prometeo, 2008.

Garza, Alicia. "A Herstory of the #BlackLivesMatter Movement." *The Feminist Wire*, October 7, 2014. https://thefeministwire.com/2014/10/blacklivesmatter-2/.

Gates, Jr., Henry Louis. "Critical Fanonism." In *Tradition and the Black Atlantic: Critical Theory in the African Diaspora*, 83–112. New York: BasicCivitas, 2010.

Gendzier, Irene. *Frantz Fanon: A Critical Study*. New York: Pantheon, 1973.

Gibson, Nigel. "Fanon and the Pitfalls of Cultural Studies." In Alessandrini, *Frantz Fanon*, 99–125.

Gibson, Nigel. *Fanon: The Postcolonial Imagination*. Cambridge: Polity, 2003.

Gibson, Nigel. Introduction to *Rethinking Fanon*, 9–46.

Gibson, Nigel. "Radical Mutations: Fanon's Untidy Dialectic of History." In Gibson, *Rethinking Fanon*, 408–446.

Gibson, Nigel, ed. *Rethinking Fanon: The Continuing Dialogue*. New York: Humanity, 1999.

Gibson, Nigel. "The Specter of Fanon: The Student Movements and the Rationality of Revolt in South Africa." *Social Identities: Journal for the Study of Race, Nation and Culture* 23, no. 5 (2017): 579–599.

Gibson, Nigel. "A Wholly Other Time? Fanon, the Revolutionary, and the Question of Organization." *South Atlantic Quarterly* 112, no. 1 (Winter 2013): 39–55.

Gibson, Nigel. "Why Frantz Fanon Still Matters: Failure and Reciprocity." *The Critique*, June 14, 2016. http://thecritique.com/articles/why-frantz-fanon-still-matters/.

Gibson, Nigel, and Roberto Beneduce. *Frantz Fanon, Psychiatry and Politics*. London: Rowman & Littlefield, 2017.

Glick, Jeremy Matthew. *The Black Radical Tragic: Performance, Aesthetics, and the Unfinished Haitian Revolution*. New York: New York University Press, 2016.

Glissant, Édouard. *Caribbean Discourse: Selected Essays*. Trans. J. Michael Dash. Charlottesville: The University Press of Virginia, 1989.

Gordon, Jane. *Creolizing Political Theory: Reading Rousseau Through Fanon*. New York: Fordham University Press, 2014.

Gordon, Lewis R. *Existentia Africana: Understanding Africana Existential Thought*. New York: Routledge, 2000.

Gordon, Lewis R. *Fanon and the Crisis of European Man: An Essay on Philosophy and the Human Sciences*. New York: Routledge, 1995.

Gordon, Lewis R. *What Fanon Said: A Philosophical Introduction to His Life and Thought*. New York: Fordham University Press, 2015.

Gordon, Lewis R., George Ciccariello-Maher, and Nelson Maldonado-Torres. "Frantz Fanon, Fifty Years On: A Memorial Roundtable." *Radical Philosophy Review* 16, no. 1 (2013): 307–324.

Gordon, Lewis R., T. Denean Sharpley-Whiting, and Renée T. White. "Introduction: Five Stages of Fanon Studies." In *Fanon: A Critical Reader*, ed. Lewis R. Gordon, T. Denean Sharpley-Whiting, and Renée T. White, 1–8. Cambridge: Blackwell, 1996.

Gould, Jeffrey L. "Ignacio Ellacuría and the Salvadorean Revolution." *Journal of Latin American Studies* 47, no. 2 (May 2015): 285–315.

Gramsci, Antonio. *Further Selections from the Prison Notebooks*. Ed. Derek Boothman. London: Lawrence & Wishart, 1995.

Gramsci, Antonio. "The Revolution Against *Capital*." In *Pre-Prison Writings*, 39–42. Ed. Richard Bellamy. Trans. Virginia Cox. Cambridge: Cambridge University Press, 1994.

Gramsci, Antonio. *Selections from the Prison Notebook*. Ed. Quintin Hoare and Geoffrey Nowell Smith. New York: International, 1971.

Halberstam, Jack. "Vertiginous Capital or, The Master's Toolkit." *Bully Bloggers*, July 2, 2018. https://bullybloggers.wordpress.com/2018/07/02/vertiginous-capital-or-the -masters-toolkit-by-jack-halberstam/.

Hall, Stuart. "The After-life of Frantz Fanon: Why Fanon? Why Now? Why *Black Skin, White Masks*?" In *The Fact of Blackness: Frantz Fanon and Visual Representation*, ed. Alan Read, 12–37. Seattle: Bay Press, 1996.

Hallward, Peter. *Absolutely Postcolonial: Writing Between the Singular and the Specific.* Manchester: Manchester University Press, 2001.

Hallward, Peter. "Fanon and Political Will." *Cosmos and History: The Journal of Natural and Social Philosophy* 7, no. 1 (2011): 104–127.

Hardt, Michael, and Antonio Negri. *Empire.* Cambridge, MA: Harvard University Press, 2000.

Harney, Stefano, and Fred Moten. *The Undercommons: Fugitive Planning & Black Study.* New York: Minor Compositions, 2013.

Harootunian, Harry. *Marx after Marx: History and Time in the Expansion of Capitalism.* New York: Columbia University Press, 2015.

Hegel, G. W. F. *Hegel's Logic.* Trans. William Wallace. Oxford: Oxford University Press, 1975.

Hegel, G. W. F. *Hegel's Philosophy of Right.* Trans. T. M. Knox. Oxford: Oxford University Press, 1967.

Hegel, G. W. F. *Phenomenology of Spirit.* Trans. A. V. Miller. Oxford: Oxford University Press, 1977.

Hegel, G. W. F. *The Philosophy of History.* Trans. J. Sibree. Amherst, NY: Prometheus, 1991.

Hegel, G. W. F. *Science of Logic.* Trans. A. V. Miller. New York: Routledge, 2010.

Helie-Lucas, Marie-Aimée. "Women, Nationalism, and Religion in the Algerian Liberation Struggle." In Gibson, *Rethinking Fanon*, 271–282.

Heller, Erich. *The Importance of Nietzsche: Ten Essays.* Chicago: University of Chicago Press, 1988.

Henry, Paget. "Africana Phenomenology: Its Philosophical Implications." *CLR James Journal* 11, no. 1 (Summer 2005): 79–112.

Hudis, Peter. *Frantz Fanon: Philosopher of the Barricades.* London: Pluto, 2015.

James, C. L. R. *The Black Jacobins: Toussaint L'Ouverture and the San Domingo Revolution.* New York: Vintage Books, 1989.

James, C. L. R. "Dialectical Materialism and the Fate of Humanity." In *The C. L. R. James Reader*, ed. Anna Grimshaw, 153–181. Oxford: Blackwell, 1992.

James, C. L. R. *Notes on Dialectics: Hegel, Marx, Lenin.* Westport, CT: Lawrence Hill, 1981.

Jameson, Fredric. *Brecht and Method.* London: Verso, 1998.

Jameson, Fredric. *The Hegel Variations: On the Phenomenology of Spirit.* London: Verso, 2010.

Jameson, Fredric. "Persistencies of the Dialectic: Three Sites." In *Valences of the Dialectic*, 279–290.

Jameson, Fredric. *The Seeds of Time.* New York: Columbia University Press, 1994.

Jameson, Fredric. "The Three Names of The Dialectic." In *Valences of the Dialectic*, 3–70.

Jameson, Fredric. *Valences of the Dialectic.* London: Verso, 2010.

Jennings, Michael. "The Production, Reproduction, and Reception of the Work of Art." In Benjamin, Walter. *The Work of Art in the Age of Its Technological Reproducibility and Other Writings on Media*, ed., Michael W. Jennings, Brigid Doherty, and Thomas Y. Levin, 9–18. Cambridge, MA: Harvard University Press, 2008.

Jones, Claudia. "A People's Art is the Genesis of their Freedom." In *Claudia Jones: Beyond Containment*, ed. Carole Boyce Davies, 166–167. Oxford: Ayebia Clarke, 2011.

Judy, Ronald A. T. "On the Politics of Global Language, or Unfungible Local Value." *boundary 2* 24, no. 2 (Summer 1997): 101–143.

Kawash, Samira. "Terrorists and Vampires: Fanon's Spectral Violence of Decolonization." In Alessandrini, *Frantz Fanon*, 235–257.

Keeling, Kara. "'In the Interval': Frantz Fanon and the 'Problems' of Visual Representation." *Qui Parle* 13, no. 2 (2003): 103–110.

Keeling, Kara. *Queer Times, Black Futures*. New York: New York University Press, 2019.

Kelley, Robin D. G. *Freedom Dreams: The Black Radical Imagination*. Boston: Beacon, 2002.

Kelley, Robin D. G., Fred Moten, and Maisha Quint. "Do Black Lives Matter? Robin DG Kelley and Fred Moten in Conversation." Critical Resistance Event, Oakland, California, December 13, 2014. http://criticalresistance.org/do-black-lives-matter -robin-dg-kelley-and-fred-moten-in-conversation/.

Khalfa, Jean. "Fanon, Revolutionary Psychiatrist." In Fanon, *Alienation and Freedom*, 167–202.

Khalfa, Jean. *Poetics of the Antilles: Poetry, History and Philosophy in the Writings of Perse, Césaire, Fanon and Glissant*. Oxford: Peter Lang, 2016.

Kleinberg, Ethan. "Kojève and Fanon: The Desire for Recognition and the Fact of Blackness." In *French Civilization and its Discontents: Nationalism, Colonialism, Race*, ed. Tyler Edward Stovall and Georges Van den Abbeele, 115–128. Lanham, MD: Lexington, 2003.

Kojève, Alexandre. *Introduction à la lecture de Hegel*. Paris: Gallimard, 1980.

Kojève, Alexandre. *Introduction to the Reading of Hegel: Lectures on the Phenomenology of Spirit*. Trans. James H. Nichols Jr. Ithaca, NY: Cornell University Press, 1969.

Lacan, Jacques. "Psychoanalysis and Its Teaching." In *Écrits: The First Complete Edition in English*, trans. Bruce Fink, 364–383. New York: W. W. Norton, 2007.

Lacan, Jacques. "The Subversion of the Subject and the Dialectic of Desire in the Freudian Unconscious." In *Écrits: The First Complete Edition in English*, trans. Bruce Fink, 671–702. New York: W. W. Norton, 2007.

Lazarus, Neil. "Disavowing Decolonization: Fanon, Nationalism, and the Question of Representation in Postcolonial Theory." In Alessandrini, *Frantz Fanon*, 161–194.

Lazarus, Neil. *The Postcolonial Unconscious*. Cambridge: Cambridge University Press, 2011.

Lee, Christopher. *Frantz Fanon: Toward a Revolutionary Humanism*. Athens: Ohio University Press, 2015.

Lenin, V. I. "Conspectus of Hegel's book *The Science of Logic*." In *Collected Works*, Vol. 38, 85–237. Moscow: Progress Publishers, 1976.

Lenin, V. I. *Revolution at the Gates: A Selection of Writings from February to October 1917*. London: Verso, 2004.

Loomba, Ania. *Colonialism/Postcolonialism*. New York: Routledge, 2015.

Lorde, Audre. *Sister Outsider*. Berkeley, CA: Crossing, 2007.

L'Ouverture, Toussaint. *The Haitian Revolution*. Ed. Nick Nesbitt. London: Verso, 2008.

Luescher, Thierry M. "Frantz Fanon and the #MustFall Movements in South Africa." *International Higher Education*, no. 85 (March 2016): 22–24.

Macey, David. *Frantz Fanon: A Biography*. London: Verso, 2012.

Makalani, Minkah. *In the Cause of Freedom: Radical Black Internationalism from Harlem to London*. Chapel Hill: University of North Carolina Press, 2011.

Maldonado-Torres, Nelson. *Against War: Views from the Underside of Modernity*. Durham, NC: Duke University Press, 2008.

Maldonado-Torres, Nelson. "Fanon and Decolonial Thought." In *Encyclopedia of Educational Philosophy and Theory*, ed. Michael A. Peters, 799–803. Singapore: Springer, 2017.

Mariátegui, José Carlos. "Anniversary and Balance Sheet." In *José Carlos Mariátegui: An Anthology*, ed. Harry E. Vanden and Marc Becker, 127–131. New York: Monthly Review, 2011.

Marriott, David. *Haunted Life: Visual Culture and Black Modernity*. New Brunswick, NJ: Rutgers University Press, 2007.

Marriott, David. "Whither Fanon?" *Textual Practice* 25, no. 1 (2011): 33–69.

Marriott, David. *Whither Fanon? Studies in the Blackness of Being*. Stanford, CA: Stanford University Press, 2018.

Marx, Karl. "Capital: A Critique of Political Economy, Volume I." In *Collected Works*. Vol. 35, *Marx*, 7–807. New York: International, 1996.

Marx, Karl. "The Eighteenth Brumaire of Louis Bonaparte." In *Collected Works*. Vol. 11, *Marx and Engels 1851–1853*, 99–197. New York: International, 1979.

Marx, Karl. *Grundrisse: Foundations of the Critique of Political Economy (Rough Draft)*. Trans. Martin Nicolaus. New York: Penguin, 1993.

Marx, Karl. "Theses on Feuerbach." In *Collected Works*. Vol. 5, *Marx and Engels 1845–1847*, 3–5. New York: International, 1975.

Marx, Karl, and Friedrich Engels. "The German Ideology." In *Collected Works*. Vol. 5, *Marx and Engels 1845–1847*, 19–539. New York: International, 1976.

Marx, Karl, and Friedrich Engels. "Manifesto of the Communist Party." In *Collected Works*. Vol. 6, *Marx and Engels 1845–1848*, 477–519. New York: International, 1976.

Mbembe, Achille. *Critique of Black Reason*. Trans. Laurent Dubois. Durham, NC: Duke University Press, 2017.

Mbembe, Achille. *On the Postcolony*. Berkeley: University of California Press, 2001.

Mbembe, Achille. "The State of South African Political Life." *Africa Is a Country*, September 19, 2015. https://africasacountry.com/2015/09/achille-mbembe-on-the-state -of-south-african-politics.

McClintock, Anne. *Imperial Leather: Race, Gender, and Sexuality in the Colonial Contest*. New York: Routledge, 1995.

McCulloch, Jock. *Black Soul, White Artifact: Fanon's Clinical Psychology and Social Theory*. Cambridge: Cambridge University Press, 1983.

Melas, Natalie. "Humanity / Humanities: Decolonization and the Poetics of Relation." *Topoi* 18 (1999): 13–28.

Mezzadra, Sandro, and Brett Neilson. *Border as Method, or, the Multiplication of Labor*. Durham, NC: Duke University Press, 2013.

Mignolo, Walter D. *Local Histories / Global Designs: Coloniality, Subaltern Knowledges, and Border Thinking*. Princeton, NJ: Princeton University Press, 2012.

Mignolo, Walter D. "Yes, We Can: Non-European Thinkers and Philosophers." *Al Jazeera*, February 19, 2013. https://aljazeera.com/indepth/opinion/2013/02/20132 672747320891.html.

Mignolo, Walter D., and Catherine E. Walsh. *On Decoloniality: Concepts, Analytics, Praxis*. Durham, NC: Duke University Press, 2018.

Mirzoeff, Nicholas. "Mindful Occupation." *Occupy 2012: A Daily Observation on Occupy*, May 5, 2012. https://nicholasmirzoeff.com/O2012/2012/05/05/mindful-occupation/.

Morfino, Vittorio. *Plural Temporality: Transindividuality and the Aleatory Between Spinoza and Althusser*. Chicago: Haymarket, 2014.

Moten, Fred. "Black Op." *PMLA* 123, no. 5 (2008): 1743–1747.

Moten, Fred. "The Case of Blackness." *Criticism* 50, no. 2 (March 2008): 177–218.

Moten, Fred. *The Universal Machine*. Durham, NC: Duke University Press, 2018.

Mowitt, John. "Algerian Nation: Fanon's Fetish." *Cultural Critique*, no. 22 (Autumn 1992): 165–186.

Munif, Yasser. "Frantz Fanon and the Arab Uprisings: An Interview with Nigel Gibson." *Jadaliyya*, August 17, 2012. https://jadaliyya.com/Details/26906.

Nergaard, Siri, and Robert J. C. Young. "Interview with Robert J. C. Young." *translation: a transdisciplinary journal*. Accessed January 30, 2018. http://translation.fusp.it/interviews/interview-with-robert-j.c.-young.

Nesbitt, Nick. *Caribbean Critique: Antillean Critical Theory from Toussaint to Glissant*. Liverpool: Liverpool University Press, 2013.

Nesbitt, Nick. *Universal Emancipation: The Haitian Revolution and the Radical Enlightenment*. Charlottesville: University of Virginia Press, 2008.

Nesbitt, Nick. *Voicing Memory: History and Subjectivity in French Caribbean Literature*. Charlottesville: University of Virginia Press, 2003.

Nietzsche, Friedrich. *Ainsi parlait Zarathoustra: Un livre pour tout le monde et personne*. Trans. Henri Albert. Paris: Société du 'Mercure de France,' 1898.

Nietzsche, Friedrich. *Also sprach Zarathustra: ein Buch für Alle und Keinen*. Leipzig: C. G. Naumann, 1893.

Nietzsche, Friedrich. "The Birth of Tragedy." In *Basic Writings of Nietzsche*, trans. Walter Kaufmann, 29–144. New York: Random House, 2000.

Nietzsche, Friedrich. "Ecce Homo." In *Basic Writings of Nietzsche*, trans. Walter Kaufmann, 655–800. New York: Random House, 2000.

Nietzsche, Friedrich. *Human, All Too Human: A Book for Free Spirits*. Trans. R. J. Hollingdale. Cambridge: Cambridge University Press, 1996.

Nietzsche, Friedrich. *La Volonté de puissance: essai d'une transmutation de toutes les valeurs: études et fragments*. Trans. Henri Albert. Paris: Librairie Générale Française, 1991.

Nietzsche, Friedrich. "Letter to Strindberg, 8 December 1888." In *Selected Letters of Friedrich Nietzsche*, ed. Christopher Middleton, 328–330. Indianapolis, IN: Hackett, 1996.

Nietzsche, Friedrich. *On the Genealogy of Morality*. Trans. Maudemarie Clark and Alan J. Swensen. Indianapolis, IN: Hackett, 1998.

Nietzsche, Friedrich. "On the Uses and Disadvantages of History for Life." In *Untimely Meditations*, ed. Daniel Breazeale, 57–124. Cambridge: Cambridge University Press, 1997.

Nietzsche, Friedrich. *Thus Spoke Zarathustra: A Book for All and None*. Ed. Adrian del Caro and Robert B. Pippin. Cambridge: Cambridge University Press, 2006.

Nietzsche, Friedrich. *Untimely Meditations*. Ed. Daniel Breazeale. Cambridge: Cambridge University Press, 1997

Nietzsche, Friedrich. *The Will to Power*. Ed. Walter Kaufmann. New York: Vintage, 1968.

Olaloku-Teriba, Annie. "Afro-Pessimism and the (Un)Logic of Anti-Blackness." *Historical Materialism* 26, no. 2 (2018). http://historicalmaterialism.org/index.php /articles/afro-pessimism-and-unlogic-anti-blackness.

Parry, Benita. *Postcolonial Studies: A Materialist Critique.* London: Routledge, 2004.

Parry, Benita. "Problems in Current Theories of Colonial Discourse." *Oxford Literary Review* 9, nos. 1/2 (1987): 27–58.

Parry, Benita. "Signs of Our Times: A Discussion of Homi Bhabha's *The Location of Culture*." *Third Text* 8, nos. 28–29 (1994): 5–24.

Rabaka, Reiland. *Forms of Fanonism: Frantz Fanon's Critical Theory and the Dialectics of Decolonization.* Lanham, MD: Lexington, 2010.

Rabaka, Reiland. *The Negritude Movement: W. E. B. Du Bois, Leon Damas, Aimé Césaire, Léopold Senghor, Frantz Fanon, and the Evolution of an Insurgent Idea.* Lanham, MD: Lexington, 2015.

Rama, Angel. *Writing Across Cultures: Narrative Transculturation in Latin America.* Trans. David Frye. Durham, NC: Duke University Press, 2012.

Ransby, Barbara. *Making All Black Lives Matter: Reimagining Freedom in the 21st Century.* Oakland: University of California Press, 2018.

Read, Alan, ed. *The Fact of Blackness: Frantz Fanon and Visual Representation.* Seattle: Bay Press, 1996.

Reilly, Cate. "Psychiatry's Vertigo: Fanon in the Clinic and the Case Histories of *Les damnés de la terre*." Paper presented at the Congress of the Latin American Studies Association, New York, NY, May 2016.

Robcis, Camille. "François Tosquelles and the Psychiatric Revolution in Postwar France." *Constellations: An International Journal of Critical and Democratic Theory* 23, no. 2 (June 2016): 212–222.

Robinson, Cedric. "The Appropriation of Frantz Fanon." *Race & Class* 35, no. 1 (1993): 75–91.

Roisman, Hanna M., ed. *The Encyclopedia of Greek Tragedy.* Oxford: Wiley-Blackwell, 2012.

Roth, Michael S. *Knowing & History: Appropriations of Hegel in Twentieth-Century France.* Ithaca, NY: Cornell University Press, 1988.

Said, Edward. *Culture and Imperialism.* New York: Vintage, 1994.

Said, Edward. "Traveling Theory Reconsidered." In Gibson, *Rethinking Fanon*, 197–214.

Said, Edward. *The World, the Text, and the Critic.* Cambridge, MA: Harvard University Press, 1983.

Salem, Sara. "A Revolutionary Lifeline: Teaching Fanon in a Postcolonial World." *Historical Materialism* blog, August 16, 2017. http://historicalmaterialism.org/blog /revolutionary-lifeline-teaching-fanon-postcolonial-world.

Sartre, Jean-Paul. *Being and Nothingness: A Phenomenological Essay on Ontology.* Trans. Hazel E. Barnes. New York: Washington Square, 1984.

Sartre, Jean-Paul. *Black Orpheus.* Trans. S. W. Allen. Paris: Présence Africaine, 1976.

Sartre, Jean-Paul. *Critique of Dialectical Reason.* Vol. 1. Trans. Alan Sheridan-Smith. London: Verso, 2004.

Sartre, Jean-Paul. *L'être et le néant: Essai d'ontologie phénoménologique.* Paris: Gallimard, 1943.

Sartre, Jean-Paul. "A Plea for Intellectuals." In *Between Existentialism and Marxism*, trans. John Matthews, 228–285. London: Verso, 2008.

Sartre, Jean-Paul. Preface to *The Wretched of the Earth*, by Frantz Fanon, xliii–lxii. Trans. Richard Philcox. New York: Grove, 2004.

Scott, David. *Refashioning Futures: Criticism and Postcoloniality*. Princeton, NJ: Princeton University Press, 1999.

Sekyi-Otu, Ato. "Fanon and the Possibility of Postcolonial Critical Imagination." In *Living Fanon: Global Perspectives*, ed. Nigel Gibson, 45–60. New York: Palgrave Macmillan, 2011.

Sekyi-Otu, Ato. *Fanon's Dialectic of Experience*. Cambridge, MA: Harvard University Press, 1996.

Sexton, Jared. "Afro-Pessimism: The Unclear Word," *Rhizomes: Cultural Studies in Emerging Knowledge*, no. 29 (2016). http://rhizomes.net/issue29/sexton.html.

Sexton, Jared. "Ante-Anti-Blackness: Afterthoughts." *Lateral: Journal of the Cultural Studies Association*, no. 1 (2012). https://doi.org/10.25158/L1.1.16.

Sexton, Jared. "The Social Life of Social Death: On Afro-Pessimism and Black Optimism." *InTensions Journal*, no. 5 (2011): 1–47.

Sexton, Jared. "Unbearable Blackness." *Cultural Critique* 90 (Spring 2015): 159–178.

Sexton, Jared, and Daniel Colucciello Barber. "On Black Negativity, or the Affirmation of Nothing." *Society & Space*, September 18, 2017. http://societyandspace.org/2017/09/18/on-black-negativity-or-the-affirmation-of-nothing/.

Sexton, Jared, and Huey Copeland. "Raw Life: An Introduction." *Qui Parle* 13, no. 2 (Spring/Summer 2003): 53–62.

Shanin, Teodor, ed. *Late Marx and the Russian Road: Marx and 'the Peripheries of Capitalism'*. New York: Monthly Review, 1983.

Sharpley-Whiting, T. Denean. "Fanon and Capécia." In Alessandrini, *Frantz Fanon*, 57–74.

Sharpley-Whiting, T. Denean. "Fanon's Feminist Consciousness and Algerian Women's Liberation: Colonialism, Nationalism, and Fundamentalism." In Gibson, *Rethinking Fanon*, 329–353.

Singh, Julietta. *Unthinking Mastery: Dehumanism and Decolonial Entanglements*. Durham, NC: Duke University Press, 2018.

Sitrin, Marina. *Everyday Revolutions: Horizontalism and Autonomy in Argentina*. New York: Zed, 2012.

Sitrin, Marina, and Dario Azzelini. *They Can't Represent Us! Reinventing Democracy from Greece to Occupy*. London: Verso, 2014.

Spillers, Hortense. *Black, White, and in Color: Essays on American Literature and Culture*. Chicago: University of Chicago Press, 2003.

Strauss, Leo. *Persecution and the Art of Writing*. Chicago: University of Chicago Press, 1980.

Taylor, Keeanga-Yamahtta. *From #BlackLivesMatter to Black Liberation*. Chicago. Haymarket, 2016.

Tomba, Massimiliano. *Marx's Temporalities*. Chicago: Haymarket, 2013.

Toscano, Alberto. "'European nihilism' and beyond: commentary by Alberto Toscano." In Alain Badiou, *The Century*, 179–201.

Tosquelles, François, and Frantz Fanon. "Indications de la thérapeutique de Bini dans le cadre des thérapeutiques institutionnelles." In Fanon, *Écrits sur l'aliénation et la liberté*, 243–249.

Tosquelles, François, and Frantz Fanon. "Indications of Electroconvulsive Therapy Within Institutional Therapies." In Fanon, *Alienation and Freedom*, 291–298.

Tosquelles, François, and Frantz Fanon. "On an Attempt to Rehabilitate a Patient Suffering from Morpheic Epilepsy and Serious Character Disorders." In Fanon, *Alienation and Freedom*, 299–305.

Tosquelles, François, and Frantz Fanon. "On Some Cases Treated with the Bini Method." In Fanon, *Alienation and Freedom*, 285–290.

Tosquelles, François, and Frantz Fanon. "Sur quelques cas traités par la méthode de Bini." In Fanon, *Écrits sur l'aliénation et la liberté*, 238–242.

Traverso, Enzo. *Left-Wing Melancholia: Marxism, History, and Memory*. New York: Columbia University Press, 2017.

Tremblay, Jean-Thomas. "Being Black and Breathing: On 'Blackpentecostal Breath.'" *Los Angeles Review of Books*, October 19, 2016. https://lareviewofbooks.org/article /being-black-and-breathing-on-blackpentecostal-breath/.

Tse-Tung, Mao. "On Contradiction." In *On Practice and Contradiction*, 67–102. London: Verso, 2007.

Tse-Tung, Mao. "Where Do Correct Ideas Come From?" In *On Practice and Contradiction*, 167–169. London: Verso, 2007.

Turner, Lou. "Fanon and the FLN: Dialectics of Organization and the Algerian Revolution." In Gibson, *Rethinking Fanon*, 369–407.

Turner, Lou, and John Alan. "Frantz Fanon, World Revolutionary." In Gibson, *Rethinking Fanon*, 103–118. New York: Prometheus, 1999.

Vergès, Françoise. "Chains of Madness, Chains of Colonialism: Fanon and Freedom." In *The Fact of Blackness: Frantz Fanon and Visual Representation*, ed. Alan Read, 46–75. Seattle: Bay Press, 1996.

Vergès, Françoise. "To Cure and to Free: The Fanonian Project of 'Decolonized Psychiatry.'" In *Fanon: A Critical Reader*, ed. Lewis Gordon, T. Denean Sharpley-Whiting, and Renée T. White, 85–99. Cambridge: Blackwell Publishers, 1996.

Villalobos-Ruminott, Sergio. *Heterografías de la violencia. Historia, Nihilismo, Destrucción*. Buenos Aires: La Cebra, 2016.

Wallerstein, Immanuel. "Fanon and the Revolutionary Class." In *The Essential Wallerstein*, 250–268. New York: New Press, 2000.

Warren, Calvin L. *Ontological Terror: Blackness, Nihilism, and Emancipation*. Durham, NC: Duke University Press, 2018.

Watson, Jini Kim, and Gary Wilder. "Introduction: Thinking the Postcolonial Contemporary." In *The Postcolonial Contemporary: Political Imaginaries for the Global Present*, ed., Jini Kim Watson and Gary Wilder, 1–29. New York: Fordham University Press, 2018.

White, Renée T. "Revolutionary Theory: Sociological Dimensions of Fanon's *Sociologie d'une révolution*." In *Fanon: A Critical Reader*, ed. Lewis Gordon, T. Denean Sharpley-Whiting, and Renée T. White, 100–109. Cambridge: Blackwell, 1996.

Wilder, Gary. *Freedom Time: Negritude, Decolonization, and the Future of the World*. Durham, NC: Duke University Press, 2015.

Wilder, Gary. *The French Imperial Nation-State: Negritude and Colonial Humanism Between the Two World Wars*. Chicago: University of Chicago Press, 2005.

Wilder, Gary. "Here / Hear Now Aimé Césaire!" *South Atlantic Quarterly* 115, no. 3 (July 2016): 585–604.

Wilder, Gary. "Race, Reason, Impasse: Césaire, Fanon, and the Legacy of Emancipation." *Radical History Review*, no. 90 (Fall 2004): 31–61.

Wilderson, III, Frank B. *Red, White & Black: Cinema and the Structure of U.S. Antagonisms.* Durham, NC: Duke University Press, 2010.

Williams, Gareth. *The Other Side of the Popular: Neoliberalism and Subalternity in Latin America.* Durham, NC: Duke University Press, 2002.

Williams, Raymond. *Modern Tragedy.* Stanford: Stanford University Press, 1966.

Wright, Richard. *12 Million Black Voices.* New York: Basic, 2002.

Wynter, Sylvia. "Towards the Sociogenic Principle: Fanon, Identity, the Puzzle of Conscious Experience, and What It Is Like to Be 'Black.'" In *National Identities and Sociopolitical Changes in Latin America,* ed. Mercedes F. Durán-Cogan and Antonio Gómez-Moriana, 30–66. New York: Routledge, 2001.

Yancy, George, and Judith Butler. "What's Wrong with 'All Lives Matter'?" *New York Times,* January 12, 2015. https://opinionator.blogs.nytimes.com/2015/01/12/whats-wrong-with-all-lives-matter/.

Young, Robert J. C. *Empire, Colony, Postcolony.* Oxford: Wiley-Blackwell, 2015.

Young, Robert J. C. "Fanon, Revolutionary Playwright." In Fanon, *Alienation and Freedom,* 47–48.

Young, Robert J. C. "Frantz Fanon and the Enigma of Cultural Translation." *translation: a transdisciplinary journal* (Summer 2012): 1–10.

Young, Robert J. C. *Postcolonialism: An Historical Introduction.* Cambridge: Blackwell, 2001.

Young, Robert J. C. *Postcolonialism: A Very Short Introduction.* Oxford: Oxford University Press, 2003.

Young, Robert J. C. *White Mythologies: Writing History and the West.* New York: Routledge, 2004.

Zalloua, Zahi. "Decolonial Particularity or Abstract Universalism? No, Thanks! The Case of the Palestinian Question." *International Journal of Žižek Studies* 13, no. 1 (2019): 83–120.

Zibechi, Raúl. *Dispersing Power: Social Movements as Anti-State Forces.* Trans. Ramor Ryan. Oakland, CA: AK Press, 2010.

Žižek, Slavoj. "Class Struggle or Postmodernism? Yes, Please!" In Butler, Laclau, and Žižek, *Contingency, Hegemony, Universality,* 90–135.

Žižek, Slavoj. "*Da Capo Senza Fine.*" In Butler, Laclau, and Žižek, *Contingency, Hegemony, Universality,* 213–262.

Žižek, Slavoj. "Freud Lives!" *London Review of Books* 28, no. 10 (May 2006). https://lrb.co.uk/the-paper/v28/n10/slavoj-zizek/freud-lives.

Žižek, Slavoj. "Holding the Place." In Butler, Laclau, and Žižek, *Contingency, Hegemony, Universality,* 308–329.

Žižek, Slavoj. *In Defense of Lost Causes.* London: Verso, 2009.

Žižek, Slavoj. *Less Than Nothing: Hegel and the Shadow of Dialectical Materialism.* London: Verso, 2012.

Žižek, Slavoj. "Mao Tse-Tung, the Marxist Lord of Misrule." In Mao, *On Practice and Contradiction,* 1–28.

Žižek, Slavoj. "The Politics of Redemption, or, Why Richard Wagner is Worth Saving." In *Lacan: The Silent Partners*, ed. Slavoj Žižek, 231–269. London: Verso, 2006.

Žižek, Slavoj. *Tarrying with the Negative: Kant, Hegel, and the Critique of Ideology*. Durham, NC: Duke University Press, 1993.

Žižek, Slavoj. *The Ticklish Subject: The Absent Centre of Political Ontology*. London: Verso, 2000.

Žižek, Slavoj. *Welcome to the Desert of the Real: Five Essays on September 11 and Related Dates*. London: Verso, 2002.

Zupančič, Alenka. *The Shortest Shadow: Nietzsche's Philosophy of the Two*. Cambridge, MA: MIT Press, 2003.

INDEX